S0-AZU-688

# The Crisis of the Roman Republic

Views and Controversies about Classical Antiquity
*General Editor: M. I. Finley*

*Also published:*

Slavery in Classical Antiquity
*Edited by M. I. Finley*

The Language and Background of Homer
*Edited by G. S. Kirk*

Alexander the Great: the Main Problems
*Edited by G. T. Griffith*

Plato, Popper and Politics
*Edited by Renford Bambrough*

*In preparation:*

Philip of Macedon and Athens
*Edited by S. Perlman*

# The Crisis of the Roman Republic

*Studies in Political and Social History*

*Selected and introduced by*

ROBIN SEAGER

*Lecturer in Ancient History*
*in the University of Liverpool*

HEFFER / *Cambridge*
BARNES & NOBLE / *New York*

*This volume first published in 1969*
*by W. Heffer & Sons Limited*
*Cambridge, England*

SBN 85270 024 5

*Photographically reprinted in Great Britain*
*by Lowe & Brydone (Printers) Limited*
*London, NW10*

# Contents



*The pagination of the present volume is given in square brackets*

## Contributors

E. Badian, *Professor of Ancient History, University of Leeds*

J. P. V. D. Balsdon, *Fellow of Exeter College, Oxford*

Henry C. Boren, *Professor of History, University of North Carolina*

T. Robert S. Broughton, *Paddison Professor of Classics, University of North Carolina*

P. A. Brunt, *Fellow of Gonville and Caius College, Cambridge, formerly Fellow of Oriel College, Oxford*

†M. I. Henderson, *Fellow of Somerville College, Oxford*

A. N. Sherwin-White, *Fellow of St John's College and Reader in Ancient History in the University of Oxford*

Ch. Wirszubski, *Shalom Horowitz Professor of Classics, Hebrew University of Jerusalem*

Z. Yavetz, *Associate Professor of Ancient History, Tel-Aviv University*

## Acknowledgements

Acknowledgements for permission to use material reproduced in this volume are due to:

The Authors
Franz Steiner Verlag
The Society for the Promotion of Roman Studies
Editions Mouton & Co.
Ecole Pratique des Hautes Etudes
The British School at Rome
The Editors, *Latomus*
The Cambridge Philological Society

# Introduction

The deserved success of earlier volumes in this series should by now have made it unnecessary to defend its existence or explain its general nature. The present book, however, differs somewhat from its predecessors, each of which dealt with a relatively limited and precisely defined theme or set of themes, for in this volume papers are assembled on several subjects related at first sight only in period. Also lacking is the neat presentation of opposing points of view on a single issue. For this there are two main reasons. The number and diversity of the topics to be covered meant that the sheer weight of available material was immense—one could for instance easily fill a book this size with articles on *otium cum dignitate* alone—and that no single theme could claim what might be thought its fair share of space. Secondly, a problem arose with which previous editors have also been confronted : the issues dealt with are often of such magnitude that, where divergent views have been put forward in print, one side of the argument may exist in article form, whilst the other occupies a book. Thus the various questions connected with the *equites* have called forth not only the papers reproduced here and many others, but also books both moderate in compass, like H. Hill's *The Roman Middle Class* (Oxford, 1952), and very weighty, as the recent work of C. Nicolet, *L'ordre équestre à l'époque républicaine* (Paris, 1966). A brief sketch of the principles involved in my selection of material may go some way towards clarifying the purpose of the book and perhaps towards justifying its apparent incoherence.

The most important negative criterion was the decision to exclude all papers concerned only with specific problems of factual detail. This policy was not dictated by any belief that detailed questions of fact are not worth bothering about or that the vast amount of literature devoted to them is not of sufficient merit to deserve reproduction. Much of the finest work which has been done on the late republic has in fact been directed towards the answering of such questions. But to present a fair selection of such work in a volume of this scope would have been quite impossible, and so it seemed preferable to exclude all articles of this type in favour of those which treated of more general matters. I have also omitted everything which dealt with any aspect of the career of Julius Caesar, on the assumption that a separate volume in the series might one day be dedicated to his achievements. The absence of two major general issues may arouse more complaint and be less easy to defend, namely the agrarian problem and the enfranchisement of Italy. The reason is a practical one. The English language (to which I have deliberately confined myself) lacks good general treatments of these subjects in article form. Important advances in both fields have recently been made, in the main by Italian scholars. Therefore it seemed best to refer the reader to the survey given by Badian in the *Forschungsbericht* with which this volume opens. The value of this work for all the fields which it covers will at once become clear to those who now meet it for the first time; it is to be hoped that Badian will soon undertake its continuation, a task for which he is uniquely qualified. In the meantime mention should be made of two valuable papers by P. A. Brunt, *The Army and the Land in the Roman Revolution* (*JRS* 52, 1962, 69 ff.) and *Italian Aims at the Time of the Social War* (*JRS* 55, 1965, 90 ff.).

Despite certain portents in the course of the second century (cf. A. E. Astin, *Scipio Aemilianus*, Oxford, 1967), the tribunate of Ti. Gracchus is the first great historical turning-point in the period. The agrarian side of the crisis which provoked his reform has, as remarked above, given rise to little work in English suitable for inclusion. But Boren's article on the urban aspect of the crisis focuses attention on factors which are often neglected in supposedly comprehensive assessments of the Gracchi. There is also a purely practical reason for reprinting it here : it first appeared in a journal which, at least in libraries where ancient history is still treated as a branch of classics rather than of history, is housed in a different room or on a different floor from journals devoted to the history of Greece and Rome, and as every teacher knows, few students will take the trouble to walk up an extra flight of stairs or round one more corner.

The next three articles deal with the *equites*. The first question which must be faced, and which has just begun to attract renewed attention, is simply : who were the *equites* ? Received opinion assumes for Cicero's day a distinction between on the one hand the *equites equo publico*, the members, that is, of the equestrian centuries, still limited to 1,800 *iuniores*, and on the other hand the *equites* of the Gracchan juries, the *publicani*, holders of the equestrian census. This assumption is challenged by Mrs Henderson in favour of the view that all those who are called *equites* belonged to the equestrian centuries, which had ceased to be restricted to 1,800 members, and held the public horse. A more protracted defence of this thesis may be found in Nicolet's book. The problem is a difficult one, but to my mind the passages cited to show that the title *eques Romanus* indicates 'some rank or standing over and above the mere census' do not in fact prove that the census was not a sufficient, as well as a necessary condition of equestrian status. The grant of the gold ring, e.g. by Verres or by Sulla to the actor Roscius, need not be assumed technically to validate a claim to equestrian rank; it might merely give it colour and respectability and serve as a kind of testimonial to future censors. The text which most strongly supports Mrs Henderson's view is undoubtedly that from the sixth *Philippic*, where the centuries of *equites equo publico* are described as an *ordo* which should have adopted Cicero as its patron. But it is perhaps not impossible that once, in a very polemical passage, the orator should have put himself forward as the most plausible patron of the 1,800 *iuniores*. At all events the nature of equestrian interests and the part played by the *equites* in politics are subjects fundamental to our understanding of the late republic, in which, although progress is now being made, some deep-rooted misconceptions are proving hard to dislodge. Brunt's article covers the most important question of all: to what extent, if at all, were the *equites* a coherent unit with common political aims? Despite the widespread view that C. Gracchus created the equestrian order as a political force, the problem first appears earlier, as Brunt says; it is true that C. Gracchus exploited an existing grievance. Nevertheless, the institution of equestrian courts is still the natural starting-point for discussion of the struggle between the *equites* and the senate, for the issue of the courts was the major unifying factor among those whose first collective name, according to the elder Pliny, was *iudices*. The infiltration of *equites* into the senate is a relatively minor matter, and it would in any case be dangerous to equate a desire to secure entry into the senate with a yearning to lead an active political life. The vast majority of senators, of whom we never hear, were probably not very political.

Like a large part of Mrs Henderson's article, Broughton's *Comment* on Brunt's paper deals chiefly with the early principate, and so its relevance to this book might be called into question. It is however problems of social development, like the growth of the equestrian order, which are most gravely distorted by the imposition on their own organic structure of schemata dictated by the practical necessities of teaching. The dates which mark the beginnings and ends of periods of academic study are inevitably drawn from the superficies of politics, and it may do the student (and perhaps not only the student) no harm to be reminded that, whatever his syllabus may say, history does not consult examiners' convenience by falling of its own accord into self-sufficient sections each a hundred years long, and that its processes do not grind to a halt in mid-career just because some politician has bribed his way into office, started a war, or died a violent death.

The theme of the *equites* leads naturally to that of the courts, which provided the chief cause of dissent between the orders. Here again my choice has been determined by the desire to present a general treatment of the subject: an article on the *repetundae* court, rather than articles, whatever their worth, on individual *repetundae* laws. Balsdon's discussion has never been superseded, in English or any other language. But other problems remain, in particular the question of what other courts there were and who controlled them. Brunt says something of this in an appendix, and a summary of other recent work on the subject, indicating the difficulties that still exist, will be found in Badian's report. By far the most important subsequent study of the subject is W. Kunkel's *Untersuchungen zur Entwicklung des römischen Kriminalverfahrens in vorsullanischer Zeit* (München, 1962: a long review by P. A. Brunt in *Tijdschrift voor Rechtsgeschiedenis* 32, 1964, 440 ff.).

The murder of Ti. Gracchus was said to have introduced violence into the domestic politics of Rome, and the violence of everyday political life in Cicero's day is notorious. Sherwin-White's article deals with one aspect of the problem, the use of the army, or more precisely of soldiers, in politics. In so doing he highlights the fact that Sulla's march on Rome in 88 marked a new stage in the decline of the republic. But although Marius never used his legions to threaten the state and the weapon he forged was left for another to wield, the part played by the Marian veterans in politics had profound, though brief, significance. Saturninus, treading in the steps of the Gracchi, was aware of the principal danger he had to face: murder by the defenders of the established order. His predecessors had lacked forces adequate for their protection, but for Saturninus the Marian veterans were a potential means of supplying this deficiency. Hindsight makes the result seem inevitable: a clash of interests and consequent rupture between the revolutionary or reforming tribune and the general who saw his men employed for purposes of which he had no reason to approve. The lesson of Saturninus' clash with Marius was plain. No tribune could maintain himself in power without appeal to physical force, but a tribune could acquire no army of his own. If he tried, as Saturninus tried, to use borrowed strength, a conflict of interests and loyalties was bound to come sooner or later. Saturninus' failure marks the end of an era; after him no one tried again. The bogy of 'tribunician government', which some historians still see as the threatened alternative to senatorial control in the last century of the republic, was quite unreal. To threaten the republic a man must have at his disposal not borrowed veterans, but an army under his own command, which would follow when he ordered it to march on Rome. Sulla ushered in the age of the contumacious general, beside whom the popular tribunes of the previous era had been nothing but a minor nuisance.

Sherwin-White also raises questions of method, but at least for such matters as are treated in this book the observable facts are encouraging. Where such a phenomenon as the rise of Marius is concerned, methods which on the surface may seem sharply opposed have led, as Badian remarks, to very similar results.

The other chief aspect of violence in the late republic concerns the *plebs*: that use of mobs which is associated above all with the names of Clodius and Milo. Not only the composition and motivation of the groups which adhered to such leaders, but also other problems connected with the *plebs*, form a branch of history which has been much neglected. The dictum that history is the history of the ruling class seems to have been too shortsightedly applied. Even if the *plebs* is of interest only because it was sometimes exploited by its betters, that fact alone should be enough to earn it some attention. Such attention is at last beginning to be vouchsafed. The mob has recently been studied by P. A. Brunt ('The Roman Mob', *Past and Present* 35, 1966, 3 ff.), but the most striking contribution to our knowledge of the *plebs* has been a series of studies by Yavetz, one of which is reproduced here. This article and those on *Levitas popularis* (*Atene e Roma* 10, 1965, 97 ff.) and *Plebs sordida* (*Athenaeum* 43, 1965, 295 ff.) will, it is to be hoped, be followed by others, whilst his forthcoming book, *Plebs and Caesar*, should mark a considerable advance.

To understand the forces which shaped political events and the elaborate structure of Roman society, it is necessary to study in detail the social, moral and political concepts which the Romans used in justifying and explaining their actions. Questions of method are relevant here. Much of the earlier work on the subject, most of it undertaken in Germany, adopted a purely philological standpoint. Such studies are not of course useless to the historian, but their value is naturally greatly increased if account is taken of the political context in which an idea or slogan makes its appearance. The first work in English devoted to a single concept which kept historical factors in the foreground was Ch. Wirszubski's book *Libertas as a Political Idea at Rome during the Late Republic and Early Principate* (Cambridge, 1960), and his article on *cum dignitate otium* displays the same emphasis on the historical setting. One of the fundamental principles for the investigation of the conceptual background of Roman politics cannot be better expressed than in his own words: 'the explanation of the meaning and purpose of *cum dignitate otium* is to be sought in the first place in Roman politics and not in Greek philosophy'. The application of this dictum extends far beyond its immediate context; it may serve as a guide and a warning for all who seek to throw light on Roman political slogans, a field in which much still remains to be done.

But at the same time it must nevertheless be remembered that many of the concepts most important in political history, such as *fides*, *clientela* and *amicitia*, were by no means limited in their operation to the political sphere. Concentration on politics to the exclusion of all else may lead to oversimplification and excessive rigidity of interpretation. The foundation on which all study of social and political concepts must be based is of course M. Gelzer's *Die Nobilität der römischen Republik* (Leipzig/Berlin, 1912; reprinted in *Kleine Schriften* I, Wiesbaden, 1962 : English translation forthcoming), perhaps the greatest work on Roman history ever written. That book appeared at a time when the pernicious notion of Roman political parties still required to be banished from history; in it the political functions of such ideas as *clientela* and *amicitia* took pride of place. But it is only in defiance of Gelzer's warnings that some historians have used his methods to build up patterns of groups and 'factions' which are almost as precisely defined and inflexible as the political parties of nineteenth-century scholarship—and in consequence almost as baneful for a proper understanding of the period. This failure to do justice to the complexity and fluidity of the relationships which influenced politics at Rome can only be aggravated by neglect of the non-political aspects of 'political' concepts. Against this tendency Brunt's treatment of *amicitia* should serve as a valuable corrective, for it takes a term, the political significance of which is undisputed, and does justice, without losing sight of that significance, to other important factors which governed its usage. Because men who co-operated in politics were sometimes called *amici*, we must not fall into the trap of supposing that only common political interests could create *amicitia*, or that friendship could not survive a difference of political opinion. Again the principle of method involved is valid beyond the immediate scope of this paper.

Such then is this book. I can only hope that the merits of its parts will win compassion for its formal deficiencies as a whole. In conclusion I should like to express my personal thanks to all the authors and publishers concerned for their ready co-operation, and to the publisher and the general editor of the series for their promptitude and courtesy in advice and assistance to one inexperienced in such tasks.

ROBIN SEAGER

# Errata

(Minor typographical errors unlikely to cause confusion have been omitted)

HENDERSON
p. 61 n. 4 : read : p. 71, n. 64
p. 62 l. 47 : read : Cic.

BRUNT
p. 119 n. 5 l. 7 : insert : of
p. 120 n. 4 : read : *Athen.* XXXII
p. 128 n. 2 : read : Qu.
p. 145 l. 25 : read : Calpurnian

BROUGHTON
p. 154 l. 33 : read : δημαγωγοί
p. 154 n. 3 : read : χρήμασιν, ἐπ', ἐνίους, πολλοὺς
p. 157 l. 13 : read : *timidos*

BALSDON
p. 105 l. 21 : read : L.

SHERWIN-WHITE
p. 7 l. 39 : read : *adulescentulus*

YAVETZ
p. 505 l. 14 : delete comma after *hercle*
p. 505 l. 28 : read : Subura
p. 505 n. 2 : read : Madvig : in
p. 505 n. 3 : read : *erecta*
p. 505 n. 4 : read : IX
p. 507 l. 1 : read : *convallibus, coenaculis sublatam*
p. 510 l. 10 : read : Chrysippus
p. 511 l. 12 : read : of
p. 511 n. 2 : read : XXXV

B

# I

*E. Badian*

From the Gracchi to Sulla (1940–1959)

# *FORSCHUNGSBERICHT*

## FROM THE GRACCHI TO SULLA

## (1940–59)

*Note*: During the last twenty years there has been an immense amount of work on this as on other periods of antiquity. No survey can hope to be complete, particularly since wartime conditions during the first few years and publishing delays during the last few have made it impossible for anyone to see all the work published. I have given as full a bibliography as possible at the end of this survey and have confined discussion to a few fields in which important progress appears to have been made or at least important questions asked.

### (i) General

Syme's *The Roman Revolution* appeared in 1939, and although Syme only glanced at the period here considered, it is not too much to say that a great deal of the progress since made in the study of it has been inspired by that great work. The older accounts – e. g. that of Last in the *Cambridge Ancient History* – on the whole show a distribution of interest not unlike that of Appian and Livy: interest is concentrated on war and sedition, on crises rather than on processes, on outstanding figures rather than on the social and political background. As a result, a series of incidents takes the place of a history, and the patchwork is held together by generalisations based on no evidence. Where, however, this temptation was overcome – as, e. g., by Carcopino and Lanzani –, the processes were seen in the light of modern ones, without much regard for the known facts of Roman politics and society[1]. Recent historians – largely under the influence of Gelzer, Münzer and Syme – have at last attempted to pave the way for a coherent history of the period, yet one that should not impose an anachronistic pattern[2].

[1] Note, e. g., the instructive sub-title of Lanzani's useful study *Mario e Silla* (1915): 'Storia della democrazia romana negli anni 87–82 a. Cr.' In Carcopino's work in the *Histoire romaine*, note such headings as 'La réaction modérée et P. Licinius Crassus', or 'L'Asie, la Gaule et le redressement démocratique'. It is interesting that even Gabba, in his earlier work, uses such terms as 'Marian democrats', which his own work was helping to put out of court. This anachronistic approach vitiates much Marxist historiography (e. g. Mashkin). See the useful discussion by Vittinghoff in *Saeculum* 1960, 89f.

[2] Much new work, of course, still uses the old categories and generalisations (e. g. Andreotti and Hill (1)). It must be realised that a true history of this or any other period of antiquity will, in a sense, never be possible, owing to the scarcity of evidence even for the relatively best-documented periods. (See Heuss, p. 27, for a useful warning).

It is fortunate that prosopographical research – the chief instrument of this new approach – has better tools at its disposal than ever before. The *Real-Encyclopädie* is at last nearing completion (all the names of importance for this period have been treated), and Broughton's *Magistrates of the Roman Republic*[3] has been the foundation of much of the work of the last few years. Thus Astin and Chantraine have been able, independently of each other, to investigate the *cursus honorum* before Sulla and to dispose once and for all of an old problem by showing that the praetorship, followed by a clear *biennium*, was a prerequisite for the consulate before Sulla as after, but that the quaestorship (which could be held at a very early age) was not[4].

The most important work, as far as sources are concerned, is Gabba's edition of Appian *b. c.* i, with his companion volume on Appian's sources[5]. The former – the first proper historical commentary on the book – has at once become a classic and is quite indispensable. The latter, while containing much material of great interest, has not found much approval with its main thesis that most of Appian's *Civil Wars* is based on Asinius Pollio. This revival of an old heresy cannot be supported by what little we know about Pollio (at least as far as book i is concerned), and reviewers have not been slow to point this out. Another important edition is the second edition of Malcovati's *Oratorum Romanorum Fragmenta* – a great improvement on the first, both in the quantity and in the quality of the fragments and in arrangement and typography. A large number of the authors concerned were important public figures during this period, and their *disiecta membra* can now be conveniently inspected[6]. There is also much of value in Valgiglio's editions of some important *Lives* of Plutarch (Valgiglio (1), (3), (4)).

Few books specially treat the period as a whole. Perhaps the most interesting is Smith (1), ascribing the collapse of the Roman Republic to a moral failure, for which he holds the Gracchi responsible. For reasons set out in detail by various reviewers[7], it is impossible to accept the author's main

[3] Broughton (1). The important *Supplement* to this, embodying comments by many scholars on the original edition, as well as all new work in this vast field, has just appeared (New York, 1960). I should like to repeat (what I have written elsewhere) that most of my own work would have been impossible without Broughton.

[4] Gabba, previously committed (in (9)) to the view of Afzelius (3), has unfortunately refused to acknowledge this ((13), 138). He does not, however, contest their arguments, especially those of Astin, which seem decisive.

[5] Gabba (1) and (2).

[6] There are still some unfortunate omissions, especially of popular orators. (See Badian (13) for some comments.) The new edition, by E. W. Gray, of Greenidge-Clay, *Sources for Roman history*, 133–70 *B. C.* (Oxford, 1960), must be mentioned as a valuable tool, though it cannot be discussed in detail.

[7] Note especially Cuff – a careful analysis, correcting both the author's exaggeration of the contrast between pre-Gracchan and post-Gracchan society and the anti-liberal view of society implicit in the book – and Deman (from a Marxist point of view and with frequent citations of Mashkin, but better informed).

heses – that Rome was an 'integrated society' until the Gracchi intervened, and that they initiated a period of moral decline, which was not arrested until Augustus restored the integrated society on a new level: he ignores too much of the evidence for political life before the Gracchi and cannot answer the obvious question of why the integrated society should have crumbled so easily; nor will he persuade most readers to share his preference for the 'integrated' society of Augustan Rome (not to mention that of the early second century B. C.) over that of the late Republic. It is fatally easy to succumb to 'golden age' theories, and Smith echoes the views of optimates of Cicero's day and, to some extent, those of Augustan court circles. But it is salutary to remember that in the 'integrated' society of the early Empire the age of Cicero and of *libertas* could count as a golden age. This whole question has been treated with refreshing clarity and good sense by Hampl.

A brief, but important, general survey of the period is given by Heuss, in an attempt to define the concept of the 'Roman Revolution'. He makes the point – worth stressing against some Marxist theories – that the social system was never attacked as such during the whole period of the 'Revolution' (least of all, perhaps, in the slave wars, which have engaged so much of the attention of some scholars), and he comes to conclusions very similar to my own[8] on the importance of the Social War in injecting organised force into the political conflict, and of Sulla in recognising the possibilities of the 'client army' created (but not exploited) by Marius.

Of general histories treating the period, Pareti and Scullard deserve special mention. Pareti's volume, like the rest of his great work, is beautifully produced and gives constant references to the sources (but no modern bibliography). Unfortunately, it cannot be recommended with real confidence, since it mingles orthodoxy and heresy, the sound and the eccentric, often with very inadequate discussion and no reference to other modern treatments. It is chiefly the expert in the period who can safely appreciate its individual brilliance. Scullard's short book contains the best account at present available. Clear and readable, it incorporates (in the text or at least in the notes) the results of nearly all recent work, and the lucid and concise discussion in the notes gives plentiful references. It is a sane and a scholarly book. The specialist will at times feel impatient at the author's caution about admitting new ideas or abandoning exploded traditions; but it is undoubtedly the right approach for a work of this kind[9].

[8] In Badian (1). On the political unimportance of the problem of slavery, see Tibiletti (5) 258, 270f.

[9] A large part of my own book (see last note) deals with this period, from a special point of view.

## (ii) The Gracchi

Apart from the *leges repetundarum* and agrarian problems (for both of which, see below), remarkably little of any real importance has been done. Gelzer's rather pessimistic view of work on the period as a whole[10] is more applicable to this portion of it than to most others. The most interesting new contribution is Boren's demonstration[11] that there was an urban as well as an agrarian economic crisis for Tiberius to overcome: the influx of booty and tribute due to victorious wars led to considerable building activity, which, by attracting people to Rome, helped to depopulate the countryside; building seems to have stopped by 138, and the plight of those affected was aggravated by the rise in grain prices caused by the slave war in Sicily. Public spending on a large scale was only resumed by C. Gracchus and seems to go on after his fall, thus to some extent restoring urban prosperity. Though Boren at times overstates his case and falls into the old error of supposing himself to have found the key to Ti. Gracchus' programme (an error which, when writing carefully, he avoids), it seems clear that this aspect of the crisis must henceforth be borne in mind along with others more often cited. There is less to be said for his attempt[12] to correlate the coinage of *c.* 145–110 with political events. In this case – as in the rest of the large amount of numismatic work done on the period – the numismatists will have to reach some firm conclusions on the dating of the various emissions and of the (crucial) retariffing of the denarius, before they can claim that their work has begun to be really illuminating to historians. One need only compare the dates proposed by Sydenham with those of Mattingly[13] and those of Boren himself, and all these with the tables in Pink's monumental work, to see that significant agreement is as remote as ever. Moreover, it is clear (i. a.) from Boren's article that many dates can be gained only by arguing from known events – which lands those who wish to show a correlation between the coins and the events in the position of begging the question in order to assert a tautology.

There is probably not much more to be said on that favourite subject, the theoretical background of the Gracchan reforms. Nothing much, at all events, *has* been said recently. The figure of Blossius of Cumae has been rescued from indiscriminate identification with Greek philosophy and reclaimed for Italy and in fact Capua. It would be interesting if more could be found out about

[10] *Gnomon* 1959, 181: '... daß bei dem emsigen Umwälzen der alten Kontroversen ... kaum durchschlagende neue Ergebnisse herausgekommen sind'. This judgment, surely unfair to Gelzer's own work, is about as applicable to the age of Marius as to that of Augustus. [11] Boren (2). [12] Boren (3).

[13] See Sydenham (1) 221 f. (with Mattingly's notes at the end of the volume). Not many of the historical conclusions drawn by these great scholars will seem acceptable to historians.

the ideas and character of that important man[14]. I have tried to show how, whatever the influence of advisers and philosophers, the minds of both Ti. and C. Gracchus largely moved within traditional Roman aristocratic categories: *fides, pietas, dolor, dignitas*[15]. This is not, of course, to deny (or, for that matter, to assert) the genuineness of their reforming zeal or of their opponents' fear at their temporary success. It is interesting that, in Tiberius' case, it was the visit of Eudemus of Pergamum to the hereditary patron of his country that raised Tiberius' *inuidia* to a dangerous level.

The intricate political situation in the decade between the Gracchi cannot easily be studied from what sources we have. Even so, more can probably be done than has been done so far. I have devoted some attention to the origin of the 'Italian problem' during that time[16]. That Tiberius confined his land grants to citizens[17] ('perseuerauit in ciuibus', as Cicero says) is doubted (not denied) by Gabba, but accepted by most others. There is no good reason to believe that he took much thought for the allies: Velleius' rhetorical flight (ii 2,3) is surely not to be taken seriously, any more than his statement (ii 6,2) that Gaius tried to extend the citizenship 'paene usque Alpis'[18]. What reference to his care for the allies there is in the sources is apparently due to later importation, probably ultimately based on Gracchan propaganda. We happen to know from Plutarch that the purple patch about Tiberius' shocked realisation of the state of the countryside on a journey through Etruria comes from a βιβλίον by his brother Gaius[19]. The enigmatic personality and pro-

[14] See Dudley, as improved by Brown, who recognises that there is a possibility (no more) of our being able, by careful work, to trace the connection between the Greek and Italic influences, or to show the absence of one. This suggestion has not yet been followed up.

[15] Badian (1) 169f., 180f. Brown has made the interesting suggestion that Tiberius may have envisaged a military career for himself. Gabba (12) has rightly insisted that these must not be regarded as the *only* motives for the Gracchan reforms. There is no one explanation for such complex actions, and much time has been wasted, by historians ancient and modern, in trying to find one single and sufficient motive for such men as the Gracchi, Marius, Sulla, or M. Drusus. My own point, in this case, was not so much to establish motives, as to discover some categories of thought within which various motives operated. Reflection on the case of Cicero (who, incidentally, never had any doubts about seeing the Gracchi in this light) will be helpful. Tibiletti (5) 252f. and 270 (citing Kovalev) has stressed the (in the strict sense) reactionary nature of Tiberius' agrarian programme, revolutionary though the actual proposals were.

[16] Op. cit. 174f. In my main conclusion I agree with Bernardi (1), to whom, in spite of differences in detailed interpretation (e. g. on the law of Pennus), I am much indebted.

[17] As I have again tried to argue (op. cit. 169f.).

[18] The latter is misinterpreted by Fraccaro (2) 86, who thinks that it may mean 'settlement of citizens' as far as the Alps. But as the immediate context shows ('dabat ciuitatem omnibus Italicis, extendebat eam paene usque Alpis'), Velleius is thinking of grants of citizenship.

[19] I cannot understand how Gabba (12) 194 can reject as 'hypothetical' my citation of Plutarch's reference to C. Gracchus' βιβλίον about his brother (for which, see, e. g.,

gramme of M. Fulvius Flaccus – a great general and (surprisingly) a scholar, and clearly the leader of the 'Gracchan' faction in the middle twenties and perhaps even in 123, but played down by both the Optimate tradition (which hated him) and the later 'Popular' mythology centred in the persons of the Gracchi themselves – has received some welcome light from Fraccaro, who showed[20] his importance in the conquest of Gallia Transalpina and his leading role (quite unattested in the literary sources) in the colonisation of the district west of Dertona. I have tried to establish the connection between Flaccus' plans for enfranchisement coupled with land reform and the alien act of Pennus, which C. Gracchus opposed. It is clear that Flaccus did not at any time desert the cause of reform or (as is often alleged in modern accounts) trade his principles for an easy triumph; and his success in securing election, as well as the loyalty of the People to him and to C. Gracchus, should be sufficient to dispose of the belief that the People were spontaneously and blindly opposed to any extension of the franchise[21]. This opposition was aroused and carefully fostered by the enemies of C. Gracchus. More enquiry is needed into the play of faction round Scipio Aemilianus; in spite of the paucity of evidence, it should not be beyond modern scholarship to rescue some of the political history of the years between the Gracchi and – necessarily connected with it – of the years preceding the tribunate of Tiberius[22]. It is clear, at any rate, that the 'allied problem' arose as a by-product of Roman party politics and disappears from view with the end of the movement for land reform[23].

I have tried to establish a rough chronology for C. Gracchus' tribunates; this differs somewhat from Fraccaro's chronology – the only detailed previous attempt that I have seen – and has consequently been vigorously attacked by Gabba[24]. There is no point in repeating the argument. Gabba (following Fraccaro) seems to have too much confidence in the clarity and excellence of Appian's account.[25] In any case he has read my argument rather hastily (e. g. the misquotation and misrepresentation p. 195, n. 1). More attention by other

Misch, *Gesch. d. Autobiographie*, 247f.), in order to accept as *fact* (to judge by his wording) the fantastic chain of hypotheses by which Fraccaro sought to show that the speeches assigned to Tiberius in Appian and Plutarch are fragments of genuine ones preserved by Nepos. (On Vettius I agree with Gabba (l. c.), though he claims to disagree with me.)

[20] Fraccaro (2). On Fulvius see Cic. *Br.* 108 (often neglected). [21] Badian (1) 176f.

[22] The only specialised recent enquiry (van den Bruwaene (2)) is quite unreliable. (Thus, e. g., he claims – without mentioning the famous acephalous inscription – that Popillius had a 'programme nettement déclaré d'opposition à la réforme agraire', and that Ap. Claudius tried to enter into a family of superior rank by marrying a daughter to Ti. Gracchus!) On Schur's fantastic treatment of the 'Scipionic circle', see Syme (3), 105f. See now Scullart, *JRS* 1960, 59f.

[23] Thus Bernardi (1). The disappearance, of course, was illusory.

[24] Badian (1) 299f.; Gabba (12) 194f.

[25] Similarly even in the case of Tiberius, where Appian is admittedly much better. (Cf. Badian (1) 172, 296f.)

scholars to this crucial point (which is by no means settled) would be welcome. The trouble has been that, although every account of C. Gracchus necessarily implies a chronological scheme, this has rarely been made explicit by scholars, and the reader usually finds it very difficult to relate modern accounts to a satisfactory (or indeed even a merely consistent) chronology.

### (iii) Leges Repetundarum

This is one field in which there appears to have been an important piece of new evidence: the Tarentine fragment published by Bartoccini and frequently discussed since. We are now in the embarrassing position of having fragments of various laws of this kind – from the great law connected with the name of Bembo to tiny fragments stowed away in *CIL* i² 2, 595 f. –, which we have not yet succeeded in matching with the few laws reported by the literary tradition. Several important discussions of this whole question have appeared. Tibiletti (4) and Serrao (2) deserve special mention: the latter, unfortunately, is not likely to be easily accessible to ancient historians outside Italy and, consequently, has not had all the attention it undoubtedly deserves[26]. Tibiletti surveys all our information on the whole subject, with new observations on a great many points – too many to be even summarily listed here. He tries, tentatively (as he admits), to match literary and epigraphical evidence (80 f.), and he proposes (pp 23 f.) a significant alteration in the commonly accepted arrangement and restoration of the Bembo fragments. This latter, sound though it seems at first sight, will not be finally acceptable until Tibiletti (or someone else) has correspondingly reconstructed the *Lex Agraria* on the reverse. It is surprising that this has not yet been attempted in the years since his survey appeared[27]. Serrao's work, in subtlety of argument and brilliance of exposition, is one of the finest pieces of constructive historical scholarship that has appeared on this period in recent years. Starting from the simple question of whether or not, under each law, citizen *patroni* were legally required as prosecutors on behalf of the allies, he attempts to answer this question by careful scrutiny of each case and to reconstruct the series of laws in the light of their attitude on this matter and against the background of the rest of the evidence. He believes that *patroni* were required before 123,

[26] The publication of Fraccaro's old and inaccessible paper on this question in Fraccaro (1) ii 255 f. is worth recording as an event of importance for the study of the subject. As F. recognises, the original article seems to have remained unknown to most scholars outside Italy, though they usually accepted his view at second hand.

[27] I list his arrangement and identification of the laws down to 91: (1) *lex Sempronia* (about July 123); this is the law of the *tabula Bembina*; (2) *lex Acilia* (perhaps around 111; unknown to what purpose or effect); (3) *lex Seruilia Caepionis* (early 106; this is perhaps the law of the Tarentine fragment); (4) *lex Seruilia Glauciae* (101 or 100, according to whether in his tribunate or in his praetorship; this is probably the Latin law of Bantia).

since *legis actio sacramento* (*Lex Rep.* 13) was impossible for foreigners. The Law of the Bembo tablets (which he identifies with the *lex Sempronia*) introduced the great change of allowing provincials to prosecute (the *patronum dari* of 9f. being optional, the patroni are mere 'assistenti giudiziari' and there is no *diuinatio*): in this way C. Gracchus genuinely tried to strengthen the confidence of the *socii* in Roman justice. The Tarentine fragment shows the Gracchan spirit in its rewards to successful foreign prosecutors; but by the time of Cicero *nominis delatio* is the prerogative of a single Roman patron and *diuinatio* is established. The change is more likely to be due to the 'Optimate' law of Caepio than to the 'Popular' law of Glaucia. Caepio may have limited the right to prosecute to citizens and Glaucia then extended it to Latins (which would explain the famous *pro Balbo* 54); and *diuinationes* are attested both under the law of Caepio and under that of Glaucia, since of the three in Cic. *div. in Caec.* 63 at least that of Flaccus must come in 91 and that of Albucius in 104, i. e. before the passing of Glaucia's law. The Tarentine fragment must therefore be anterior to both the *leges Seruiliae*, and Serrao consequently identifies it with the *lex Acilia* mentioned by Cicero. (Serrao also discusses the development of the private process *repetundarum*, which he traces back to the cases brought after Sept. 1st under *Lex Rep.* 7f., and the later development of the *repetundae* courts down to Augustus. On this, cf. also Serrao (1) 13f. (with comments by Tibiletti (7)).

Serrao has acutely noticed a most important aspect of this legislation, which seems to have escaped the attention of previous scholars. He must surely be right, in view of the explicit testimony of *div. in Caec.*, in stressing the restriction of *nominis delatio* under Sulla's law: all that the Sicilians can do is *in fidem* (of a Roman patron) *confugere*; and even of would-be patrons, only one is permitted to *nomen deferre.* This obviously contrasts with the implications in the two epigraphical laws, that *nominis delatio* is open to non-citizens, and that it is open to more than one person (though only the chief agent can gain citizenship). However, his account must be corrected in one detail: there is no evidence for *diuinatio* under Glaucia's law, since the case of Flaccus (*div. in Caec.* 63) fairly obviously refers to the *cos.* 100 (before his consulship), who can therefore hardly have been tried under that law[28]. In the light of this, we may wonder why Cicero had to go back over thirty years, and beyond Glaucia's law, for his cases: it is possible that *diuinatio* was not required under Glaucia's law, though it had been previously and was restored by Sulla. This does not affect – in fact, it tends to strengthen – the author's main conclusion that it was Caepio who introduced the restriction to a single prosecutor.

The fact that in these cases cited by Cicero it was Roman ex-quaestors who competed for *nominis delatio* – and were refused permission – does not, however,

[28] See Badian (9) 10 (with notes); *MRR Suppl.* (n. 3, above) 65.

imply that *socii* were at the time not allowed to prosecute: of the three cases, Cicero specifies only one as precisely parallel to his own, i. e. one in which an ex-quaestor was defeated in the *diuinatio* by a Roman patron chosen by the provincials concerned. This shows that the other two cases were *not* of this nature – we have no reason for asserting that the sucessful opponents of those ex-quaestors were necessarily Roman citizens. The passage tells us nothing about Caepio's provisions on eligibility for *nominis delatio*. Something can, however, be gathered in another way: I have tried to show by detailed consideration of Cic. *Balb.* 54 that it was Caepio who restricted eligibility to citizens and Latins[29], and I have seen no good argument against this interpretation, which fits in very well with the Optimate policy (successful in the event) of detaching the Latins from the other allies. Glaucia does not seem – as far as we can tell from Cic., l. c. – to have repeated the restriction on eligibility: in the political situation of 100 (when Glaucia's law appears to have been passed – see Piganiol (1)) this was impossible. He may, however, as we have seen, have repealed the need for *diuinatio*, which must have greatly lessened an ally's chance of being chosen prosecutor and thus becoming eligible for citizenship. We know, of course, that at least two Latins did gain citizenship by successful prosecutions, quite possibly under this law (Cic., l. c.).

Next, C. Gracchus and the *lex Acilia*. I have tried to show[30] that 123 or 122 would be a very suitable date for the tribunate of an Acilius Glabrio. Against those who insist that C. Gracchus' law must have been a *lex Sempronia*, it is worth repeating (a) that there may well have been more than one law; (b) that, in any case, no source speaks in so many words of a *lex Sempronia* (Tac. *ann.* xii 60 can hardly be taken technically). The *lex Rubria*, of course, provides a perfect example of C. Gracchus' use of a colleague to pass an important law; yet some sources (e. g. Livy *per.* lx; Vell. ii 7) appear to ascribe the foundation of Junonia to C. Gracchus himself. Had it not been for the accident of Plutarch's casual mention of Rubrius, there would have been subtle speculation among scholars about the 'mysterious' *lex Rubria* mentioned in the *Lex Agraria*. The drafting of such laws was (as we can see) such a complicated task that a legislator with a programme as extensive as that of C. Gracchus could not always attend to its details himself. On the other hand, the hypothesis that the *lex Acilia* was quietly passed, without fuss or bother, around 111 – as Tibiletti and Serrao have to assert – is not only *a priori* unlikely (in view of the fierce contests attending all the laws of this kind of which we hear during this period), but disproved by the wording of Cicero's reference to Acilius and his achievement. The case for identifying the *lex Acilia* with part of C. Gracchus' legislation seems to me to stand, as does that for

[29] Badian (3). In this I was anticipated by Luzzatto (3), then inaccessible to me. His *auctoritas* is welcome support.

[30] Badian (2). On this whole question, see Gabba's judicious discussion in (2) 338f.

identifying it with the great *Lex Repetundarum*. There remain the conflicting traditions about C. Gracchus' law(s) on the subject. Here no real progress has been made. I have propounded what appears to me the best explanation that can be constructed from the evidence; but the problem is far from solved. As in so many cases, this is no reason for thinking it insoluble. On the oddly named *lex ne quis iudicio circumueniatur*, Miner's suggestion that it should be dissociated from the extortion laws is being developed by Miss Ewins in an important article forthcoming in *JRS* 1960, which goes far towards removing this from the list of unsolved puzzles[31].

No solution seems in sight for the problem of matching the 'literary' and the 'epigraphical' (as we may call them) extortion laws. Apart from the great *Lex Repetundarum*, there is simply not enough left of the inscriptions to make discussion profitable. It is not surprising that all the various attempts can be fairly plausibly supported: it all threatens to become a parlour game. The *iusiurandum in legem*, common to the Tarentine fragment and the Latin law of Bantia, places these two laws *prima facie* in the last years of the century; but, of course, it does nothing to show what kind of law each of them is. It certainly seems most plausible, with Luzzatto (5) (though it is hard to see a political connection with the 'SC ultimum'), to regard the oath as 'Popularis', and the identification of either of these laws with the Optimate one of Caepio is therefore most improbable[32]. But whether either of them is Glaucia's law (and, if so, which), or Saturninus' *maiestas* law, or some other law of this period (for, after all, nothing in the literary sources led us to expect the 'Pirate Law') – that, at present, is anybody's guess.

So far we have not had to consider the question of whether, during this period, there is any difference between what the sources call *leges iudiciariae* and what may be called *leges repetundarum*. Fraccaro[33] showed that the former term does not always appear to be used with a precise technical meaning, and

[31] Cicero praises Acilius' 'uim et acrimoniam ad resistendum hominibus audacissimis' (a passage I discussed op. cit.). Tibiletti has convincingly shown that Acilius need not have been (in fact, probably was not) a colleague of Rubrius. I myself (op. cit), accepting this, was rash in continuing to identify the Rubrius of *IGRR* iv 1028 (of the 'lex Rubria et Acilia' (?)) with the founder of Junonia-Carthage. There is no more support for this than for the whole traditional interpretation of the inscription. He may equally well have been an earlier member of his *gens* (a Rubrius is attested as *tr. pl.* 133: *MRR* i 493), and so, for that matter, may the Acilius. We had better agree to ignore the inscription in future discussions of C. Gracchus. On the *lex ne quis iudicio circumueniatur*, see also Gabba (11).

[32] Tibiletti (4) 57 f. has shown that there was nothing unconstitutional about demanding such an oath and has traced its origins. But no such oath is in fact known to have been exacted before the period of Saturninus and Glaucia, and we know that they did use the oath and aroused much opposition by doing so, at least on one occasion (App. *b. c.* i 29). Thus (despite Gabba *ad loc.*) we should, in the present state of the evidence, assign the other laws that include such an oath to the same period, where there is plenty of room for them.

[33] Op. cit. (n. 26, above).

his view – that there are, during this period, no *leges iudiciariae* in Mommsen's sense – has been accepted (at first, second or third hand) by most historians. Oddly enough, there survives, parallel to and unaffected by this, a school of jurists who continue to distinguish between *leges iudiciariae* and *leges repetundarum* as dealing, respectively, with jurors (or jury courts) in general and the extortion court in particular[34]. It is interesting that Schönbauer[35], who knows the work of both schools with a thoroughness probably unequalled today, has revived the opinion that Glaucia's *lex repetundarum* could not derogate from Caepio's *lex iudiciaria*, but could only provide an exception to it for the case of the extortion courts[36]. It is a strong argument in favour of such a view – now advanced with such distinguished *auctoritas* – that the terms (expressed or implied) do not overlap in our sources[37].

It is a pity that we do not know when the various permanent courts (other than *repetundarum*) were created: Mommsen refused to guess, and there is very little unambiguous evidence. However, it is certain that the *quaestio de ueneficiis* existed before Sulla, and almost certain that those for *ambitus* and *maiestas* did; and the *quaestio peculatus* must have existed by 86 B. C., when Pompey had to defend himself for his father's misuse of public funds, if not by 101 B. C.[38]. It is therefore perfectly possible that *leges iudiciariae* – laws dealing with *iudicia* in general – should have been known by the end of the 2nd century, and that they were distinct from laws dealing with any one *quaestio* (e. g. *repetundarum*). Fraccaro's thesis that in the time of the Gracchi (for which we have no evidence of the existence of any permanent *quaestio* other than *repetundarum*) there were no such general laws, and his demonstration that private *iudices* are altogether irrelevant to this series of laws, do not affect this question at all. We cannot be absolutely certain of the composition of the juries in each of these special courts; but it is very likely that each, as it was

[34] Thus recently Pontenay de Fontette, quite unaware of the view held by practically all historians. [35] (3) 37f.

[36] But is not precisely this, properly speaking, *derogatio*?

[37] *Lex iudiciaria*: of C. Gracchus (Plut. *C. Gr.* 5, and, by implication, some of the Latin sources); of Q. Caepio (Cic. *inv.* i 92); of M. Drusus (Livy *per.* lxxi); and, by implication, of M. Plautius (Cic. *ap.* Asc. 79 Cl.) and of Sulla (see below). *Lex repetundarum* is a convenient modern term. For laws which this description seems to fit, see below. Thomsen (1) illustrates the confusion on this matter that Schönbauer rightly castigates in much modern writing: while following Mommsen in this distinction, he refuses to follow the sources in their terminology and distributes the laws between the two categories to suit his own theories.

[38] *Veneficia*: *Insc. It.* xiii 3, 70b. *Ambitus*: strongly suggested by the trial of Marius (Plut. *Mar.* 5; Val. Max. vi 9, 14) and other cases about this time (Cic. *Br.* 113; *de or.* ii 280). *Maiestas*: it would be eccentric to deny that Saturninus set up a permanent court for his new crime. *Peculatus*: Plut. *Pomp.* 4 (cf. Cic. *Br.* 230). See *RE* Suppl.-Bd. vii 826f. and cf. Last in *CAH* ix 893. There is no reason to think that the *quaestio* in which L. Hostilius Tubulus disgraced himself in 142 (Broughton (1) i 475) was a permanent court.

created, received the same kind of constitution as the *quaestio repetundarum*, which was the first of them. We happen to know that the *lex Mamilia*, establishing a special *quaestio*, used *Gracchani iudices*[39]; and we may safely assume this of other courts of the period, special (e. g. the trial of the Vestals) or permanent (e. g. the *ambitus* court that acquitted Marius)[40]. Thus, when the law of Caepio is reported to have dealt with *iudicia*, it is surely arbitrary and unjustified to confine this to one *iudicium* that happens to interest us: Schönbauer (3) is surely right in reaffirming that it dealt with *iudicia* in general[41]. When Cicero makes M. Antonius say[42] that he renewed the hatred of the *equites Romani, apud quos tum iudices causa agebatur* (i. e., the trial of C. Norbanus for *maiestas*!), for Q. Caepio, *a quo erant ipsi propter iudicia abalienati*, it is almost impossible to assume for this the artificially limited meaning of '*iudicia repetundarum*'.

The law of Glaucia, however, was undoubtedly a *lex repetundarum*: we know that it introduced *comperendinatio*[43]. Having seen that Caepio's law was not, we may now notice that Cicero tells us, in a well-known passage, that there was no other *lex repetundarum* after Glaucia's until Sulla's[44]. This confirms the view advanced above, that the *lex Plautia* was a *lex iudiciaria*, dealing with *iudicia* in general; and this is also clearly suggested by Cicero's reference to it[45]. Sulla, who reorganised the whole system of criminal law, seems to have done so (in the most economical way) by passing both a general *lex iudiciaria* and *leges* establishing each individual court: i. e., he passed both a *lex iudiciaria* and (i. a.) a *lex repetundarum*, as indeed the sources imply.

The history of the *quaestiones* during this period may therefore be reconstructed as follows: C. Gracchus (probably through the agency of Acilius, and by means of the law that survives) established the class that was called *iudices Gracchani* as jurors in the *quaestio repetundarum*, then the only permanent court. This was almost certainly the first time that persons other than

[39] Cic. *Br.* 128. [40] Cf. Badian (6) 94.

[41] But not merely with *iudices*, as some jurists have arbitrarily assumed: there is no evidence for such a narrow meaning, and the word itself does not make it probable. We have seen that the law of Caepio appears to have regulated the *praemia* of successful prosecutors (n. 29, above, and text) and perhaps introduced *diuinatio* (n. 28 and text): these, like the composition of the juries and (no doubt) other provisions of a general nature, will have been taken over from the *quaestio repetundarum* by each permanent court, as it was established. As we have seen, the provision on *praemia* of Caepio's *lex iudiciaria* was not changed by Glaucia's *lex repetundarum*. [42] Cic. *de or.* ii 199.

[43] See Balsdon's irrefutable treatment in *PBSR* 1938, 108f.

[44] Cic. *Rab. Post.* 9: 'sin hoc totidem uerbis translatum caput est quod (?) fuit non modo in Cornelia, sed etiam ante in lege Seruilia ....'.

[45] *ap.* Asc. 79 Cl.: 'memoria teneo, cum primum senatores cum equitibus Romanis lege Plotia iudicarent [i. e., the first case *of any sort* tried by the new juries], ... Cn. Pompeium causam lege Varia de maiestate dixisse' [i. e., a particular application of the *lex iudiciaria* to the *quaestio maiestatis*].

senators had sat on juries in criminal trials. These *iudices Gracchani* were also used for other *quaestiones* that were gradually established on the model of the extortion court, as well as for special juries. Q. Caepio introduced mixed juries throughout the system as it then stood[46] and also reorganised the courts in other respects (we happen to know about one or two; but Caepio's law, supported by the *boni*, may well have amounted to a proper reorganisation of the system that had sprung up rather haphazardly). Glaucia reorganised the extortion court, taking the opportunity of capturing the support of the class of *iudices Gracchani* (Cic. *Brut.* 224) by restoring 'Equestrian' juries to that court, in which that class had the greatest interest: there is no reason whatever to think that he dealt with the other courts. What juries Saturninus put in charge of his *quaestio maiestatis* could in any case be conjectured and is, in fact, shown by the trial of Norbanus. M. Livius Drusus tried to restore Caepio's system, but failed; but M. Plautius finally arrived at a compromise that seems to have stood until Sulla's legislation, which entrusted all the criminal courts to the Senate[47].

## (iv) Ager Publicus

A great deal has been written about the agrarian background to the crisis that the Gracchi tried to solve. By far the best and most important work has been done by Tibiletti[48]. The depopulation of Italy and, in particular, the shrinking number of *assidui* – not fully compensated by a gradual lowering of the minimum census –, with the serious social and military consequences that led to several attempts at reform (culminating in that of Ti. Gracchus), can now be clearly followed, chiefly owing to the work of distinguished Italian scholars, and so can the development of *latifundia* and the legal and political precedents of Ti. Gracchus' reform[49]. We must here confine ourselves to problems strictly within the period[50].

[46] On this point the discussion of Balsdon (op. cit. (n. 43, above)) is not likely to be superseded. Piotrowicz' attempt to revive the view that the law of Caepio was not passed rests purely on invalid general considerations and shows that there is no evidence for such a view.

[47] On the trial of Norbanus, see n. 42 (above) with text. – It will be seen that I cannot agree with the view of Henderson, according to which (as far as I can understand it) the *quaestio repetundarum* was originally a kind of omnibus criminal court, especially after C. Gracchus extended liability to all senators and protection to citizens as well as foreigners; and it was only Sulla who established separate *quaestiones*. All the evidence shows that in this field as in most others (see below) Sulla merely reorganised and extended what had already grown up. Sherwin White (2), replying to Henderson in a masterly survey of the *crimen repetundarum*, incidentally demolished many of her hypotheses on other *crimina*. For another equestrian *maiestas* (?) jury, see Cic. *Rab. perd.* 24.

[48] Tibiletti (1), (2), (5) – this last with numerous references to modern work, including work done in Eastern Europe.

[49] See, in addition to the above, especially Bernardi (1) and (2), Burdese, Gabba (1) and (2). This immense subject, not strictly within the period (though of crucial importance

The precise content of the *lex de modo agri publici*, as it (theoretically) stood before 133, is clearly set out by Gabba[51]. Tibiletti's conclusion that the law was much more generous than has often been believed – that the pasture was *additional* to the 500 *iugera* of 'occupied' land, and that the 500 small beasts were *additional* to the 100 large ones – has not been shaken by the few scholars who have objected to it. Tiberius' law, though formally related to this tradition, was in fact entirely different in spirit. Dealing only (it seems) with the occupied land, it granted full security of possession for the lawful 500 iugera and, in addition to enforcing the new *modus*, at once set about redistributing the land thus reclaimed by the State[52]. The constitution of the agrarian commission has not yet been clarified. Carcopino's view of an annually rotating chairmanship, doubted by some scholars even when first propounded, has unfortunately tended to creep into the standard works as a fact, although it is pure guesswork persuasively propounded. Scullard has now tentatively rejected it, and the whole matter needs new investigation[53]. The view that the *tresuiri* had to submit to annual reelection deserves serious consideration, especially in view of the fact that in *Lex Rep.* 22 the office is inserted between *III uir cap.* and *tr. mil.* (it is put last in 13 and 16). Even if, as far as we know (which is not very far), only death seems to have actually led to changes in

to it), cannot be treated here. A detail worth mentioning is the importance of Numidicus' speech (see Berger) *de prole augenda* of 131. (See Bernardi's discussion of this.)

[50] Gabba (1) and particularly (2) should be consulted throughout this section. These problems can never again be discussed without reference to his clear exposition and judicious comments. Tibiletti (5) gives a general survey of agrarian problems during the period.

[51] (2) 21 (based chiefly on Tibiletti's work).

[52] The statement – almost universal in modern works – that 250 *iugera* were allowed for each son up to two is purely a modern attempt to combine the 500 *iugera* of the main tradition with the 1000 of Livy *per.* lviii and *vir. ill.* 64. Many of those who repeat the statement do not seem to be aware of this, and it is hardly ever explicitly admitted. Yet the *ad hoc* device is methodologically dubious, and since there are other alternatives (e. g., two different measures, as – almost certainly – in the tradition on C. Gracchus' jury law), it must not be stated as a fact. The limitation to sons is quite unconvincing and must surely be wrong (cf. Appian's παισὶν ἐμπροίκιον δεδομένην). But in any case, it is difficult to see (in view of the demographic problem – for which, see above – and in view of Tiberius' general intentions, which (see Tibiletti (5) 254f.) were far from hostile to the class of large landowners) what conceivable motive Tiberius could have had for discouraging fertility among large *possessores* to a point below replacement rate. The *lex Julia*, sometimes cited as parallel, in fact shows a significant contrast (see App. *b. c.* ii 10): there is no special addition for children (only a minimum of three children required for eligibility in the first place); almost certainly, in view of later Imperial parallels, we should translate 'children' and not 'sons'; and above all, the number of children is fixed at three (i. e. *above* replacement rate) and not two. This is reasonable demographic policy, while that which modern scholars unanimously attribute to Ti. Gracchus is illogical to the point of wrong-headedness.

[53] See Gabba (2) 26f. (accepting Carcopino, but mentioning other views). Gabba now ((13) 137) seems to be ready to change his mind, and it is to be hoped that the question will be carefully re-examined.

personnel, this is clearly no obstacle to such a view, nor is the fact that the office could be held together with ordinary annual magistracies. It is not impossible that in 121, at the time of his death, M. Fulvius Flaccus was no longer a colleague of C. Gracchus in the latter's commission (whether or not this is the commission – continued or revived – of Ti. Gracchus: a matter that needs further investigation): Sallust certainly implies this (*Jug.* 42,1 'nobilitas .... Gaium (Gracchum) ..... triumuirum coloniis deducundis cum M. Fuluio Flacco ferro necauerat'); but he may be inaccurate or misinformed. Chantraine's attempt to deduce the end of the agrarian commission in 119 from the supposed immunity from prosecution of its members is not convincing; but this latter point deserves consideration, dissociated from the purpose for which the author tries to use it[54]. The phrase ἐπὶ δίκαις ἐν ἀργίᾳ γεγονότες (App. *b. c.* i 27) is as inexplicable as ever. Gabba ((2), *ad loc.*) thinks that some statement about the commissioners has dropped out of our text before the phrase, and this seems reasonable; but it is hard to reconstruct one that is both acceptable Greek and acceptable sense. Nor is there any agreement yet on the approximately 15 years during which, according to Appian, the work of the Gracchi was undone by three laws. I believe, with Gabba[55], that the period is to be taken from 123 B. C.; but Chantraine has recently advanced new arguments, based on a close study of Appian's usage, for the view that Appian means 133.

The three agrarian laws themselves are as much debated as ever. Broughton unfortunately followed D'Arms[56] in his discussion, in retaining the reading Βόριος for the second of the legislators; but that of three agrarian laws during this period one should have been passed by Sp. Thorius (as Cicero tells us) and one by a 'Borius' – a *nomen* quite unknown otherwise – surely strains credulity. The emendation 'Thorius' is inevitable[57]. There still remain the further questions of whether Appian was *right* in assigning his second law to Thorius (in view of what Cicero tells us about Thorius' law), and whether the extant *Lex Agraria* should be identified with the second or the third of Appian's laws[58]. There seems, at any rate, to be no good reason for accusing Appian of a mistake: Cicero's two brief references to the *lex Thoria* (*Brut.* 136; *de or* ii 284) are respectively so ambiguous and so vague that it is methodologically unsound

[54] See Gabba (13), l. c. If the commissioners had to submit to annual re-election, immunity while they were in office becomes much more likely (unlike the rest of Chantraine's thesis). The cumulation of this magistracy with others is, of course, no obstacle.

[55] Gabba, l. c. (reaffirming earlier views).

[56] AJPh 1935, 232f.

[57] Douglas (1) 389 has shown that the name is likely to be 'Thōrius'. But since Appian, who transliterated it from a Latin source, would hardly know the quantity of the -o-, it is not really relevant.

[58] D'Arms's attempt (see n. 56, above) to use the 'chronology' of the period in Cicero's *Brutus* in order to move Thorius' law down to a much later date is pointless. Douglas, while demonstrating this, tries to cling to the belief that Cicero treats the period chronologically and that some more or less precise information of this sort can be extracted.

to use them as evidence against Appian[59]. The second problem cannot be properly discussed at a length in keeping with this survey, and there is no certain or easy answer[60]. But a few points should be briefly made. First, if Appian's 15 years (see above) are indeed to be counted from 123, it seems pretty clear that the evolution he summarises cannot have come to an end in 111. Why, indeed, should Appian say 'fifteen' years, if 'thirteen' would be both more accurate and rhetorically more effective? It seems to me inescapable, if we believe that the period from C. Gracchus' agrarian law to the third law of Appian is 15 years, that the *Lex Agraria* of 111 can only be the second of those laws and there must have been a third one *c.* 109–8[61]. This was one of the starting-points of Carcopino's attempt to identify that third law with the *Lex Mamilia* (etc.) put by Ernst Fabricius in 109 – an attempt worth making at the time, but now generally abandoned[62]; the original conclusion will stand quite independently of Fabricius' further elaboration. If, on the other hand, we count the 15 years from 133, then we may assume (with, most recently, Chantraine) that the second law came *c.* 119/8 (the *Lex Agraria* of 111 being the third) and that Appian regards *it* as completing the main process of undoing the work of the Gracchi, with the third law a mere appendix. But – as Gabba has shown – even a cursory reading of Appian makes it clear that this is not what Appian in fact thought[63]: in particular, the People were deprived of διανομαί (according to Appian's statement) only by the *third* of the laws. From all of which it follows that this view is untenable. Those who believe that Appian counts the 15 years from 133 can thus hardly avoid the view that *all three* of Appian's laws were passed by 119/8 and that he then loses interest in agrarian matters and does not mention our *Lex Agraria* of 111 at all[64]. This view cannot be

But his involved manoeuvres make it quite clear that the attempt is not worth making: whatever Cicero's intention, it was anything but a straightforward chronology, and we should *first* have to be sure of the chronology, in order to disengage his guiding principles. D'Arms's attempt to show that there were more laws than Appian reports, based on his vicious premiss, is quite unsuccessful: it seems that we must make the best of our old evidence.

59 The more so since Appian's text must first be emended with the help of these two passages! (See above and cf. Douglas, l. c.)

60 Of recent writers, Burdese, Gabba and Kaser identify the *Lex Agraria* with Appian's third law; and Douglas identifies it with the *lex Thoria*, which he thinks is the third law. The view that it is the second law has not had recent advocates. (See Gabba (2) *ad loc.*)

61 Gabba (2) 64f. (cf. (13) 137) recognises the strength of this argument, which makes his views on the matter *prima facie* self-contradictory. His attempt to overcome the contradiction, in spite of subtle linguistic argument, seems to me unsuccessful.

62 See recently Herrmann.

63 Gabba, ll. cc. Incidentally, Gabba can hardly be right in retaining the reading ἐσπάνιζον ἔτι μᾶλλον ... καὶ διανομῶν καὶ νόμων, in spite of his note *ad loc.*: ἐσπάνιζον νόμων does not make good sense, as indeed Gabba's translation shows ('rimasero ancor piú di prima privi ... di leggi').

64 The hopeless ἐπὶ δίκαις ... (see above) is no help to any thesis.

proved wrong, but seems to me artificial and implausible, and I therefore prefer the view outlined above: that Appian's second law (the *lex Thoria*, almost certainly) is the *Lex Agraria* of 111, and there was another law *c.* 109–8. In spite of all that has been written about it, this problem can do with further – really careful – attention, guided solely by the sources.

The *Lex Agraria* itself has been studied with painstaking care, against the background of Roman agrarian institutions, and many results of value for the study of these latter, and of Roman law as a whole, have been gained[65]. These cannot be set out in detail here. Unfortunately Kaser, on whose work many other scholars in this field have built, used highly conjectural methods, on *a priori* foundations, in deciding what was new and what tralatician in the *Lex Agraria*. Thus, regarding (without much evidential basis) the freedom from rent conferred by lines 1—20 on land made private as the greatest innovation[66], he concluded that it must be Appian's third law and that *ager priuatus uectigalisque* existed before and was, in fact, the type of the Gracchan assignations, retained until (or reintroduced by) the third law. De Martino has shown that there were many intermediate categories between 'public' and 'private' land – a distinction soon as hazy legally as it was usually unimportant in practice – and it is doubtful whether rigid legal classification (usually from the point of view of Classical law) does justice to the conditions in which the agrarian laws concerned were actually passed and applied and the social and political problems which it was their principal purpose to solve[67]. The conclusion that the exemption from *uectigal* in ll. 1—20 was the principal novelty is accepted by Gabba (2) (*ad* App. *b. c.* i 27) and becomes the mainstay of his own theory of the agrarian laws[68]. In fact, line 25 mentions a *uectigal* on *ager publicus ultra modum* and this makes it difficult to see how this could be Appian's third law abolishing *uectigalia*[69]. (How the money thus collected was to be used we cannot tell; but, of course, the law may well have provided for this.) Considering what we know of the tralatician character of much Roman legislation, which could take whole sections over *verbatim* from previous laws[70], it is surely quite unjustifiable to seize, *a priori*, on a particular section of the *Lex Agraria*

[65] Chiefly by Italian scholars: Tibiletti, Burdese, Serrao, de Martino, and, of course, Gabba. But one of the basic studies is Kaser's. I have not seen Pérez Leñero's work.

[66] Op. cit. 15f.

[67] This is not to deny that there is a great deal of value in much of this legal study. But for a balanced view of the whole problem in its background we must turn to a historian: Tibiletti. Burdese's clarification of Tiberius' aims (that he did not intend to convert the free pasture into allotments for cultivation and indeed did not deal with it at all) has been accepted by Tibiletti (5) – perhaps rightly. For a convenient summary of Serrao's subtle and scholarly work (Serrao (2)), see Tibiletti (7).

[68] Which is not entirely self-consistent or satisfactory (see above).

[69] Gabba rightly points out the inconsistency of Burdese's argument on this point.

[70] See, e. g., Cic. *Rab. Post.* 9 (quoted n. 44, above).

as an innovation, and to use this personal preference as a key to the history of agrarian legislation in this period[71].

Finally, a protest must be made against the continuing habit of assigning to the consuls of 112 some legislation giving the allies privileges on *ager publicus*[72]. Surely their names in *Lex Agr.* 29 merely provide a consular date (the rights of both citizens and allies are to be maintained as they stood in 112, the year previous to the passing of the law); if anyone chooses to ascribe a special law to them, he will have to ascribe a long list of laws to P. Mucius Scaevola and L. Calpurnius Piso (*coss.* 133), who are so often mentioned!

## (v) The Rise of Marius

Little new light has been thrown on Roman politics during nearly two decades following the death of C. Gracchus. It is a crucial and ill-documented period[73]: crucial, because it sees a whole series of attempts to break the power of the *nobiles*, and a hardening of social distinctions[74] which both reacts against and in turn increases the pressure of ambitious new men, skilful at stirring up the mob and arousing the new class of the *Gracchani iudices* in defence of its interests. Careful work on these two decades is needed and would probably be as revealing as work on the nineties has been.

The first problem is that of the immediate consequences of the death of C. Gracchus. Modern accounts have tended to glide over it by vague phrases about 'compromise' and 'moderation'. But this is taking Opimius' *concordia* too seriously and ignoring his reign of terror. Wise statesmanship had not been conspicuously demonstrated by the Senate during the years 123—121; nor was it in later years, whenever the *boni* disposed of sufficient power to make it unnecessary. I have tried to trace some of the events that compelled the murderers of the *Gracchani* to acknowledge, if not defeat, at least the limitations of their victory[75]. With the acquittal of L. Opimius and the recall of P. Popillius Laenas, the year 120 set the seal of legal approval on the victory of the *boni* and marks the height of their triumph. But then the victors' vin-

[71] It is worth repeating here that the work of Tibiletti (4) on the *Lex Repetundarum* (see n. 27, above, with text) has made a reconsideration of the received text of the *Lex Agraria* an urgent necessity.

[72] Rightly ignored by Broughton (1), this has turned up again in Boren (1) and – surprisingly – in Scullard.

[73] Greenidge-Clay[2] devotes only about 19 pages to the internal history of the years 120–104, compared with 15 for the years 123–1.

[74] Afzelius (2) has persuasively argued that this was the time when the word 'nobilis' came to have the clear-cut and almost technical meaning that Gelzer has demonstrated for the age of Cicero.

[75] See Badian (6), where the evidence for the interpretation here summarised is set out in detail. P. Decius was *aemulus M. Fului* [Flacci], therefore a middle-aged man when he sought the tribunate.

dictiveness overreached itself. The turning-point seems to have been reached when P. Decius, the man who had failed to get his *inimicus* L. Opimius convicted, was himself put on trial *repetundarum*: the *Gracchani iudices* refused to convict a man who, until recently, had been of their order. In the same year (119) C. Carbo, the turncoat ex-Gracchan who had defended Opimius, was prosecuted by young L. Crassus and forced to commit suicide, and a young *nouus homo* from Arpinum, who owed his tribunate to the Metelli, used it to democratise voting procedure in the Assembly: C. Marius had entered upon the political scene.

It is not too much to say that it is the year 119, rather than the tribunates of the Gracchi, that marks the beginning of the long Revolution. Individuals had played at being 'populares' before, and measures had been passed against the Senate's will. But a man's year of office – even *all* his years of office – passed quickly, and *optimi cuiusque auctoritas* remained. By 120 it must have looked as if the Gracchi, though a most regrettable incident, would soon be forgotten: the voters had returned to their natural allegiance. It was only the following year that revealed the alarming truth. The law courts were now controlled by a new class, becoming conscious of its power, and even the rulers' control of the Assembly (which had been reaffirmed in the victories of 120) was fatally weakened. There could be no return. 118 saw the establishment of the colony of Narbo Martius – a *causa popularis*, disliked by the *factio* (Cic. *Brut.* 160 et al).

The life and career of Marius, with its background, has been studied to better effect than most parts of this period. Born of a good municipal family (as Madvig showed long ago), and sufficiently well-connected to gain the protection of Scipio Aemilianus, he had nevertheless at first decided upon an 'Equestrian' career (as we may now call it), amassing wealth as a *publicanus*[76]. That much must be believed, in view of his later wealth and his connection with that class; and it is confirmed by his early attempt to gain municipal office (Val. Max. vi 9,14). Passerini long ago[77] destroyed the legend of Marius as the simple soldier not at home in politics and investigated the tendentious accounts in the sources that helped to create this odd picture of the man who was seven times consul. Equally pernicious is the picture of Marius as a 'democratic' leader, asserting the rights of the People against the Senate. Neither of these conventional portraits has quite disappeared from textbooks and lecture rooms. But recent research has stressed the fact (obvious to the Romans and clear in the sources) that Marius, at first a *nouus homo* trying to build up a *factio* to make up for his *nouitas*, becomes (once successful) a *nouus homo* trying to be accepted as *princeps ciuitatis*: when unsuccessful in this, he is forced – entirely against his intention and inclination – to make common cause with

[76] For his financial and commercial interests and his wealth, see Carney (7) 80f.; though his career as a *publicanus* must surely precede his official *cursus*.

[77] *Athenaeum* 1934, 10f., 109f., 257f., 348f.

rebels and exiles in order to avenge himself on the shrewd politicians who had cheated him of *auctoritas*[78].

We still know little about his early career. Presumably his quaestorship and certainly his tribunate were due to his patrons, the Metelli. Seizing his chance in his tribunate, he did not hesitate to turn against them in order to become *popularis*: though, by opposing a corn bill, he kept the door open. The result of this first clumsy political effort was far from satisfactory: the Metelli remained implacable and the People apparently were not won over. Only lavish use of his money seems to have secured Marius a praetorship in 115 and he barely escaped conviction for bribery – a verdict that was ignored by the censors (one of them Metellus Diadematus, which shows that the feud continued). Quiet and inconspicuous in his praetorship (unlike his colleague P. Decius, who got into further trouble), he was allowed to proceed to a proconsulate in Spain, where he gained moderate distinction. He appears to have realised that further progress was impossible, unless he made up his quarrel with his old patrons, and – as far as we know – to have kept out of the political agitations (still too little investigated) of the next few years. We next meet him as legate of Q. Metellus in Numidia (109), which shows that he had been forgiven, perhaps because he had thus kept in the background. His intrigues in Numidia and the fortunate chance (as it appears to have been) that made the popular leaders in Rome ready to hail the *nouus homo*, finally gave him the consulship, at the cost of a more serious quarrel with the Metelli.

The wars in Africa, Gaul and Italy have been much discussed. Particular attention has, of course, been paid to Sallust, both to his moral and political ideas and to the details of the *bellum Jugurthinum*[79]. But this is not the time for a summary, since the publication of Syme's Sather Lectures on Sallust is pending.

[78] On this and what follows, see Badian (1) 194f., (6) 94f., and especially (7), where my view of Marius is developed in detail. Sherwin-White (3), arguing from different premisses and rejecting the methods of 'the Münzer school', has come to conclusions very similar to those of Gabba, Carney and myself, who clearly belong to the school he attacks. I myself find little to disagree with in Sherwin-White's lucid discussion, except for his description of the methods that I have presumably been using. (That 'no one ever changed his opinions or his side' is surely not implied either by Münzer or by any competent user of prosopographical method. Cf., e. g., Badian (7) for an attempt to use prosopographical method for a detailed investigation of such changes in the nineties.) This agreement on the main outlines of the portrait of Marius shows that the time is now ripe for a proper modern biography of Marius. It is to be hoped that either Gabba (who has done more than anyone else to revolutionise our approach to this period) or Carney (who has particularly devoted himself to the study of Marius, with many important results – see, e. g., his new article in *WS* 1960, f., which unfortunately appeared too late to be fully considered in this survey) will give us this biography. It would help to consolidate what has been gained and to spread awareness of it.

[79] Leeman (1) has collected works up to 1950. I have included the most important relevant work in the bibliography.

On the German Wars, we have now probably got over the pre-War German attempts (notably Miltner), perhaps inspired by political as much as by purely historical considerations, to depict the invasion of Italy as based on a brilliant strategic plan for a three-pronged invasion, carried out (particularly by the Cimbri) with true Germanic heroism.[79a] It is most unlikely that the barbarians had any far-sighted plans and, on the contrary, very likely indeed that they followed wherever booty seemed in prospect and would have been pleased, almost at any stage, to be allowed to settle unmolested. The Romans – and especially Marius – were unwilling to consider such a compromise, and Marius' actual handling of the war is a paradigm of professional strategy, tactics and discipline, deployed against unthinking barbarian bravery[80]. The campaign of Vercellae has been notably clarified by Zennari's scholarly investigation into the meaning of the word (a Celtic word, denoting a spot where metal could be mined, and therefore a common place name – 'Campi Raudii' apparently has a similar meaning) and localisation of the Vercellae of the battle on the lower Po near Rovigo: the statue of Marius at Ravenna (Plut. *Mar.* 2,1) is probably connected with this. This study makes all earlier discussions of the battle – or later ones written in ignorance of it – obsolete.

Events in Rome immediately before Saturninus' first tribunate, as well as those between the two tribunates, need further investigation. It would help if we could securely identify the epigraphical laws we have (see s. (iii) above), since the literary tradition is clearly incomplete and unsatisfactory, being chiefly interested in riots and in the fate of Q. Metellus Numidicus. Since we cannot, any attempt to fit the 'Pirate Law' (*FIRA* 9) into a coherent pattern of policy is bound to be unsuccessful. But it is clear that the programme of Saturninus is the direct outcome of that much-discussed measure of Marius' first consulate, the creation of the proletarian army. Gabba ((3) and (5)) has shown that it was only the last step of a series forced upon the Romans by increasing manpower shortage in the 2nd century, and that the revolutionary importance that this final step nevertheless turned out to possess was not apparent at the time[81]. This, indeed, appears to be one of the most solid and most important achievements of modern research on Marius[82].

[79a] (Added in proof:) This theory has now unfortunately turned up again in Heuss's *Römische Geschichte*, though shorn of its racialist implications.

[80] See, e. g., Andreotti 71 f.; Donnadieu; and (with reservations) Sadée.

[81] There is no good reason to doubt that the Italian allies, who had long had similar difficulties, followed the Roman lead. Gabba, in his reaction against the traditional view, originally tended to underestimate the effect of the reform on the Plebs and on Italy. (See Badian (1) 197 f.)

[82] On the census figures, skilfully interpreted by Gabba, see his defence of his views: Gabba (6). Though I doubt whether, in view of the corruption of figures in manuscripts, much stress should be laid on any one figure (e. g. the excessively debated one for 131), no one can doubt the importance of a correct assessment of the series as a whole.

The first effect of the mass enrolment of proletarians was that, with the war over, these men had to be provided for: *exercitum deducere* (except in the technical sense required for a triumph) was impossible, and it seems that for the German War Marius preferred to use, in the main, the new recruits trained by P. Rutilius Rufus, while a large part of his African veterans, apparently unwilling to embark on another war, were left in Africa, no doubt with a promise that their commander would look after their interests. This, whether or not Marius had foreseen it, was agreeable enough to him: it would give him, the *nouus homo*, the far-flung *clientelae* that were the birthright of the nobles whom he wanted to equal. In view of his quarrel with the Metelli (who would like nothing better than to discredit him), solid opposition could be expected, and his necessary absence would make it difficult for him to overcome it. It was in these circumstances that he allied himself with a young man of praetorian family, L. Appuleius Saturninus, who had a personal grievance against the *factio*. The first tribunate of Saturninus (as we may surely now agree) saw the passing of the great laws providing for the settlement of Marius' veterans in Africa, and additional evidence has recently been found for the fact that prosperous towns in Imperial Africa remembered their Marian origins[83]. It is unlikely that Saturninus intended to use violence for political ends: he was merely following in the footsteps of a whole generation of 'Popular' tribunes. But the Optimates used force against his corn law, hoping that they could deal with him as they had with the Gracchi. Saturninus learnt the lesson and used the Marian veterans to full effect. Moreover, by passing his *lex de maiestate*, he forged a powerful weapon against the *factio*'s addiction to violence against popular leaders.

During the next two years unrest continued. Marius, meanwhile, was away from Rome, and although he allowed Saturninus to carry legislation on his behalf, he was trying to appear to be above political differences. It is unlikely that the Optimates opposed his series of consulships[84], and he himself used his marriage relationship to the Julii Caesares in order to prepare his return to the fold and acceptance as saviour and *princeps ciuitatis* – much to the delight of unlucky nobles ready enough to seize the support he offered[85]. Yet when elected to a sixth consulship for 100 by a grateful People, with a noble Valerius Flaccus as his obedient colleague, he did not drop his useful Popular ally, but helped to secure Saturninus' election to another tribunate and – no doubt, though this is not explicitly attested – Glaucia's to a praetorship[86].

[83] See Quoniam.

[84] See Sherwin White (3). Arausio had shown the need for continuity in supreme command.

[85] See Badian (7) 322 f.: Marius' kindness to Q. Catulus, brother of one of the Caesares, and the marriage of C. Caesar (father of the Dictator) to an Aurelia.

[86] See especially Livy *per.* lxix, making it clear that the force used was, at least to a

There can be no doubt that co-operation between Marius and the two demagogues continued for the greater part of the year. We know that the votes and the fists of Marius' veterans provided a large part of their strength, and it is clear that colonies in Transalpine Gaul and in Corsica were intended to satisfy the veterans of the German Wars, as those in Africa had satisfied the veterans of the Numidian War. Marius had no intention of using veteran garrisons (as Sulla was later to do) as a basis for personal domination in Rome, but he still hoped to use them to increase his *auctoritas* by extending his *clientelae*. The year 100 marks the climax and the turning-point of Marius' career. At the head of a faction that comprised nobles (especially those hoping to profit by his help), the *ordo equester* (to which he was linked by bonds of birth and interests), important Italian elements, and for a time perhaps (through Saturninus and Glaucia) also a considerable section of the Roman Plebs, and supported by his veterans, he had all the prerequisites for establishing personal rule; but he still thought of the game of politics in terms of the old rules and hankered after recognition and respectability. When Saturninus and Glaucia went too far, threatening to acquire power and influence independent of his own, Marius needed little persuasion to let himself be used to save the state for his enemies[87].

large extent, that of Marius' veterans hoping for more allotments. On the offices held by Saturninus and Glaucia, Gabba (9) has at last clearly sorted out the confused evidence. It should now be regarded as certain that Saturninus was *tr. pl.* 103 and 100 and Glaucia *tr. pl.* 101 and *pr.* 100.

[87] The chronology of the riots has been discussed, with important results (i. a.) for our knowledge of the magistrates of those years, by Gabba (2) 105f., 110f. (regrettably disregarded in the *Supplement* to *MRR* (see n. 3, above)). Gabba (12) 196[1] has reaffirmed his earlier view that the whole of Saturninus' legislation of 100 was annulled by the Senate. Unfortunately he presents no new arguments for this view, and his old ones were demolished in advance by Passerini. Not only does Cic. *leg.* ii 14 say that M. Drusus' laws, *unlike* the others mentioned (including those of Saturninus), were thus annulled (see Passerini, op. cit. 348f., with fine sensibility for Ciceronian Latin), but Cic. *Balb.* 48 makes it quite clear that, when Matrinius was prosecuted, the prosecutor could not deny the validity of the law concerned and therefore had to urge that, since part of it had not in fact been carried out (a very different matter!), the rest had also lapsed. Gabba (4) 17[2], trying to meet this obvious point, involves himself in a peculiar contradiction: he appears to say that, although the law *was* annulled, it would have been 'too difficult' to invalidate the citizenship of those who had received it under the law; yet this is precisely what was attempted (by means of a prosecution in the courts), simply because the law as a whole was still valid. No conceivable motive could have prevented the prosecutor of Matrinius from citing the Senate's invalidation of the law concerned, if this invalidation had in fact taken place. His roundabout methods, as Passerini saw, make it clear that there was no such thing for him to cite.

## (vi) The Decline of Marius

The nineties are an important and difficult period – important because they led to the eruption of the Social War, difficult because Cicero was too young to have accurate personal recollections of it[88], Sallust did not choose to write on it, while Livy, not interested in politics and not skilled at disengaging its vicissitudes, left hardly any account of the period to serve as a basis for later chroniclers. Yet there is a great deal of evidence scattered in our sources, and patient fitting together by several workers in this field has shed a welcome amount of light upon what was once one of the 'dark ages' of Roman history[89]. Unfortunately this period – like all periods for which the evidence is difficult to assemble – has had its share of the reckless and the paradox-mongers, who tend to obscure the genuine progress that has been made[90]. We still, from time to time, come across the statement that M. Scaurus and P. Rutilius Rufus must have been enemies in 92, because they opposed each other in 116 (though the opposite can be, and has been, demonstrated); or that M. Scaurus and C. Marius must have been firm friends, because Scaurus handed Marius a sword and exhorted him to save the state in 100. This kind of thing regrettably justifies Sherwin – White's strictures[91]. (On Scaurus, see Cic. *prov. cons.* 19.)

That the decade is one of tension and intrigue is obvious from the series of political trials (some of them, unfortunately, not datable) that culminates in the trial of P. Rutilius Rufus and the attempted prosecution of M. Scaurus, and from the *lex Licinia Mucia* (following immediately upon the censorship of 97/6), pointing straight towards the Social War. Nor should we forget the tension in Asia Minor, which was to erupt in the Mithridatic War. Gabba has analysed the social background of this period in some brilliant studies: in particular, the influence of new men (in some cases, it seems, new citizens) from the country districts – Etruria, Campania, perhaps Picenum – should be noted.

[88] This appears very clearly from Carney's excellent study of Cicero's picture of Marius (see n. 78, above): Cicero's references to the years around and just after the turn of the century, when compared with other good sources, show not only bias (which might be discounted), but simple ignorance.

[89] See, e. g., the odd misconception about the 'felicity' of the period in *CAH* ix 173.

[90] It is chiefly they who merit the denunciations of Sherwin-White (n. 78, above). But it is the task of the historian to weigh and evaluate modern no less than ancient writing.

[91] See n. 78 (above). On 100, see Val. Max. iii 2, 8; *vir. ill.* 72, 9: the point is that Scaurus, as *princeps senatus*, had to give the first – and, in view of the unanimity of respectable opinion, the only – *sententia* when Marius consulted the House (Cic. *Rab. perd.* 20; *vir. ill.* 73, 10; *et al.*). As we have seen, Marius, who hoped for a strong mandate, was ready enough to obey. Pliny's notorious 'Mariani sodalicii rapinarum prouinciarum sinus' (*n. h.* xxxvi 116: of Scaurus) is quite useless as evidence. (For an attempt to interpret the difficult phrase, see *Athenaeum* 1956, 120[3] – admittedly not conclusive.) It is odd that those who wish Scaurus and Rutilius to be enemies in the nineties have never, apparently, thought of using Tac. *ann.* iii 66. (Not that it would help them much: see Badian (8).)

Throughout this time, probably, the ruling circles of the Latins were receiving Roman citizenship and, at least in some cases, becoming politically active in Rome[92]. Some of our evidence is difficult to interpret. It is tempting to believe that the closing of the schools of the *rhetores Latini* by the censors of 92 (Suet. *gramm.* 25; Cic. *de or.* 93) must have some political significance; but we have just been again warned not to overestimate the topicality of their exercises[93]. The red herring that should at last be removed is the 'literary circle of Q. Catulus', with all its supposed 'progressive' implications, which would have been so abhorrent to that self-satisfied aristocrat. A literary historian (Bardon) has brilliantly exposed the myth, which does no honour to the critical ability of scholars[94].

Some phases of the political struggle of this decade are mirrored in the coinage: Carney (7) has collected some striking examples, many of them not recognised before. Particularly interesting is the coin propaganda round the Cimbric victory. Marius, aiming at a distinguished *clientela*, after raising Catulus to an unhoped-for consulship, had shared his Cimbric triumph with him; but Catulus would not acknowledge indebtedness to the *nouus homo*. He claimed the principal share in the victory, and he soon found eager supporters in the Metelli (now irreconcilably estranged from Marius) and their circle – especially, we may believe, P. Rutilius Rufus, the solid merits of whose consulship had also been eclipsed by that more flamboyant leader, and whose enmity towards him, later immortalised in his memoirs, colours much of our tradition. Whatever the merits of the case, Marius' attempted *rapprochement* with the *nobiles* foundered on it. Fiercely hated by the surviving supporters of Saturninus and Glaucia, he failed to find the gratitude and loyalty he had expected among the *nobiles*, who naturally preferred to rally round the family of the Metelli and secure the recall of Numidicus. Chastened and affronted, Marius left for the East, in order not to watch the return of his enemy. His hopes that, after six consulships, his career would be crowned – like Cato's before him – by a censorship (no doubt with L. Valerius Flaccus as his colleague) had to be abandoned. But Marius still had friends and even in absence was far from powerless: two of his attested allies (L. Flaccus and the orator M. Antonius) secured the censorship, and Marius himself was given the outstanding honour of an augurate conferred in absence. He could now return without flagrant humiliation.

Anyone attempting to interpret the events of the next few years must first establish a precise chronology: failure to do this – failure, indeed, to realise

[92] See Gabba (5), (7), (8). For *ciuitas per magistratum*, see Tibiletti (3). I am not convinced by Bradeen's attack on this. [93] Douglas, *CQ* 1960, 76f.

[94] The 'circle of Catulus' has just been revived by Alfonsi in *Hommages Herrmann* (1960), 61f., with all the old arguments, including even the identification of the noble poet Porcius Licinus with an ex-slave of C. Gracchus! It is to be hoped that this will meet with the fate it deserves. There is more to be said for the identification of Valerius Aedituus with Valerius Soranus (see Alfonsi (1) and (2); Gabba (7)), though even this is far from certain.

the importance of doing it – has been one important factor in keeping the nineties a 'dark age'. As in the whole of the history of the Roman Republic, Broughton's *Magistrates* has laid a solid foundation. Inevitably, it enshrines some traditional errors; but since it carefully collects the evidence, they can now be corrected[95]. Chief among them is the date assigned to the praetorship of L. Sulla, for which there is not a shred of evidence in the passages cited in support of it, and which must be replaced in 97, where the sources appear to put it and where it fits in with what we know of the history of Asia in this decade. A more difficult problem is the date of Q. Mucius Scaevola's government of Asia. It has been held, on the strength of Asconius 14 (Cl.), that Scaevola refused to take up a province after his consulship and that his Asian proconsulship must therefore follow his praetorship[96]. But there is no good reason for drawing this conclusion from Asconius' statement, and nowhere in our sources is there any hint of a long interval (which would be difficult to account for) between the proconsulate and the revenge of the Equites on the unfortunate P. Rutilius Rufus. There has been little support for the attempt to upset the natural (post-consular) date, and even Broughton, who rejected it, now seems to incline towards acceptance[97]. With these questions settled, it becomes possible to follow the events in Asia Minor during this decade, which were to lead to the Mithridatic War. Scaevola's proconsulate appears to have been a special mission to settle a disturbed and resentful province; having completed his reorganisation in nine months, he had no reason to stay longer and could, with a clear conscience, leave his equally upright and equally learned legate P. Rufus in charge. Rufus, however, necessarily offended the *publicani* and, on his return, was attacked by them; and Marius, with interests of his own in Asia, but above all seizing his chance of striking at the hated circle of P. Rufus and of again appearing as the champion of the Equites, helped to ensure Rufus' conviction and to press for attacks on M. Scaurus and other hostile leaders.

I have tried to trace the political struggles and intrigues of this decade, placing the great political trials in their context and analysing the composition of the factions that opposed and supported Marius[98]. The former, as may be expected, centres in the Metelli, whose ramifications (chiefly thanks to the fertility of Macedonicus) penetrated widely among the *nobilitas*. Marius' friends, numerous and far from powerless (as we have seen) in 98, tended to drift

[95] On what follows, see my attempts to establish the chronology and bring out its implications in Badian (5) and (11). The results, of course, can by no means be claimed as final. [96] Thus (chiefly) Balsdon, *CR* 1937, 8f.

[97] *Supplement* (see n. 3, above) 42. The obvious later date is accepted, i. a., by Magie (*Roman Rule in Asia Minor*), Hill (1), Pareti, Smith (2).

[98] Badian (7). The analysis there given is far from exhaustive; its chief purpose was to throw some light on the great trials and, in doing so, to sketch the revolution in political alignments between 100 and 91.

away from him, until even M. Antonius is found among his enemies. Fortunately, the composition of the staffs of the two consuls at the outbreak of the Social War throws some unexpected light on Marius' friends and enemies at the time: it can be shown that all those on P. Lupus' staff of whom anything positive is known were Marius' friends, all those on L. Caesar's staff of whom anything positive is known his enemies, and we have sufficient further indications to recognise that it was in this way that *concordia* was established in the emergency. It can also be shown that the circle that supported the tribunate of M. Drusus (i.e., as Cicero repeatedly tells us, the *factio* then all-powerful in the Senate) was that of Marius' enemies. This is far from unexpected, for it was Drusus' aim to steal Marius' support away from him and to lead Equites, plebs and Italians back to their traditional allegiance to the *nobilitas*.

## (vii) The Allies

The origin and general background of the Social War has been illuminated by Gabba's fine study[99]. Although, as his reviewers have pointed out, some of his principal theses are overstated – particularly his conclusion that the leaders of the Allied revolt were in the main successful *negotiatores*, who wanted the citizenship in order to further their economic interests by controlling policy –, there is no doubt that Gabba has made one of the most important and consistent attempts to answer the puzzling question of why the Allies, who were not very interested in the citizenship in the time of the Gracchi, rose in desperate rebellion when they were disappointed of obtaining it in 91. The terms of the problem are given and cannot be denied (even though it is true that *some* of the Allies – e. g. Heraclea and Naples, mentioned by Cicero – were not too eager for the gift in 90), and Gabba rightly stresses the absurdity of Cicero's naive *obiter dictum* (*off*. ii 75) that the Social War was, *via* Drusus' tribunate, caused by the nobles' wish to regain control of the law-courts. The problem is not always so clearly seen. Thus Bernardi's study, acute and admirable in many details, gives the impression that the Italian problem, raised by the Gracchan agrarian programme, was solved by the winding up of that programme, and that it was not raised again until Drusus, renewing the programme, had to face the same difficulties as the Gracchans. It is Gabba's chief merit (both in this work and in his other studies on this period) to have shown that this will not do and that the question of the Allies did not simply disappear until 91: there was a building up of tension, which culminated in the eruption of 91. The economic motivation suggested is less acceptable. As the reviewers have pointed out, the backwoodsmen who formed the core of the revolt cannot easily be connected with the great families of *negotiatores* – of whom (as Sherwin-White remarks) more than we often think will, in any case,

[99] Gabba (8). See the reviews by Balsdon and Sherwin-White.

have been Roman citizens. Above all, Gabba exaggerates the extent to which the *ordo equester* had a consistent foreign (or, indeed, any other) policy. In this he is far from alone: the 'expansionism' of the Equites appears in the pages of many great scholars. More important still: Roman leaders like C. Gracchus, Glaucia and Saturninus, and Marius himself (to mention only a few in our period), hoped to gain the support of the *ordo* for a policy. But, as Cicero knew (though he himself forgot it when his hopes deluded him), the Equites were essentially unpolitical, seeking *otium* and their profits. On particular issues that affected them – e. g. control of the law-courts – they could be rallied to defend their interests; but which the particular issue settled, they felt no loyalty towards their benefactors or (as far as we can see) even hatred towards their opponents and were perfectly content to let those whose business it was get on with governing the state. Had it not been so, the year 119 might have seen the beginning of the final overthrow of the oligarchy. As it was, the mirage of an 'Equestrian party' proved the undoing of many Popular politicians, and the oligarchy, though severely shaken and never again secure, continued to run the state until it disintegrated under the impact of quite different forces. The Equites could impose or block a particular measure and thus prevent a policy from being pursued; but they were never capable of pursuing a policy.

The fundamental reasons why the Allies wanted the citizenship are probably as simple and direct as Sherwin-White (in *The Roman Citizenship*) has stated them: a desire for equality and protection against arbitrary ill-treatment. But Gabba has at last documented the obvious (yet sometimes questioned) corollary that the Italian upper classes wanted a share in Roman political life, by careful analysis of the part that Italians in fact played in it during the first generation or so after the War. On the other hand, he did not succeed in explaining why the Italians fought when they did, nor why some of them continued fighting when all they had to do in order to become citizens was to accept the *lex Julia*. The Italians, in fact, were tired of being used as pawns in the game of domestic Roman politics[100]. Marius, in particular, by widespread personal grants (demonstrable especially in Umbria), had raised hopes among them, and Saturninus, no doubt inspired by Marius, had evolved a complicated scheme that came near to the later Imperial conception of citizenship as a reward for military service. It was Marius' friends who, as censors in 97/6, must have allowed the citizen rolls to become inflated with Italians; the very next year, however, brought the *lex Licinia Mucia* and consequent *quaestiones*. Though Marius saved his client T. Matrinius, and – through this precedent – many others he had illegally enfranchised, it is clear that the rolls were to be thoroughly purged in the censorship of 92/1, especially when L. Crassus – one

[100] I have devoted some attention to this question in Badian (1) and (7).

of the authors of the law – was made censor. When Marius made his personal – though, as it turned out, not very lasting – peace with the consuls of 95 and, after indecisive skirmishes in the courts, *concordia* was patched up again, many of the Italians began to see that no one at Rome had their interests genuinely at heart: Asconius (p. 67 Cl.) is not far wrong in making the *lex Licinia Mucia* one of the chief causes of the War.

It was at this stage that the mounting tension became obvious to some of the leaders of the *factio*: it was becoming clear that enfranchisement could not be indefinitely delayed and that (as Gabba has shown) new citizens tended to be *Mariani*. When, in 92, Marius rallied the *ordo equester* against his old enemy P. Rutilius Rufus, and his new friend Q. Caepio threatened to continue the attack against other prominent members of the *factio*, M. Scaurus and L. Crassus (both of them known, previously, for anti-Italian sentiments), and with them the great majority of the *boni* and (therefore) of the Senate, came round to the revolutionary view that the only policy that held out long-term profit to them was to bring about enfranchisement in such a way as to attach the new citizens to themselves, and to use this support to maintain their control of the law-courts, which they hoped to be able to seize by using the plebs against the Equites. The result was the 'package deal' of M. Drusus in 91[101], which, whatever its details (and some of them are far from clear), was certainly to satisfy the poor with land and cheap corn, the Italians with the franchise, and the ruling oligarchy with control of the courts and a vast new citizen *clientela*, which would make its rule more stable than it had been for a generation.

The vexed question of the opposition to M. Drusus, and especially that of the 'Etruscans and Umbrians' of App. *b. c.* i 36, continues to be discussed[102]. Gabba has made it clear that the incident of their arrival must be put towards the end of Drusus' life, i. e. in the autumn. The view that they came to oppose

[101] Fully discussed, e. g., by Bernardi (1). Cf. Gabba (2) *ad* App. *b. c.* i 35; Syme (3) 106. On the sources, see Haug 103f. The 'package deal' was so carefully balanced, and so advantageous to the oligarchy, that there is no reason to doubt that men like Crassus and Scaurus (known as M. Drusus' supporters) had helped to think it all out from the start. On Drusus' plans for the law-courts and the question of whether he intended to raise equites to the Senate, see Gabba, l. c.; Haug, l. c. (with references): that he did is explicitly asserted *vir. ill.* 66, 4 and seems to be meant App. *b. c.* i 35. It seems very likely that this is true, since he must have planned some benefit for the Equites in his scheme. If so, it would also help to explain the hostility of some nobles, notably the consul L. Philippus (on whom see Thomsen (1): he was no friend of the Equites, at least originally). Drusus' noble supporters no doubt thought that the addition to the Senate of even 300 *homines noui paruique senatores* would not seriously challenge their rule by *auctoritas*. Their view was apparently later shared by Sulla and, on the whole, confirmed by events. But at the time there could legitimately be two opinions on this.

[102] Most recently by Gabba (12) 196f., with important chronological arguments, defending his view as outlined in the text.

Italian (i. e. their own) enfranchisement, which they later cheerfully accepted after (in fact) fighting hard for it,[103] is so difficult and improbable that something would seem to be wrong with this reconstruction. This improbability is heightened by the further one that the 'package deal' of Drusus should have been split up in such a way as to leave the *rogatio de sociis* (logically an integral part of it, as indeed most accounts recognise) until several months after the other laws. To meet this difficult reconstruction, I have suggested that the law had indeed been passed long before, but that the δοκιμασία for which all these preparations were made was the scrutiny of Drusus' law by the Senate, which (as we know from Cicero) did in fact take place some time before his death and did lead to the annulment of the laws[104]. On this view, which still seems to me the only tenable one, the course of events becomes plausible and indeed simple. It was not the *enfranchisement* law, but the *agrarian* (or colonial) law (νόμος τῆς ἀποικίας, as Appian explicitly – and inaccurately – says), which they noisily opposed. And since no one has ever suggested that *this* law had not yet been passed by October, Appian can hardly mean anything but the scrutiny in which (the Italians hoped) the law would be annulled by the Senate[105]. Etruscans and Umbrians no doubt hoped to gain citizenship without paying the extortionate price demanded by Drusus' agrarian and colonial plans. It is significant that it was these nations that felt this hope most strongly: they are the ones where Marius' enfranchisements, and later support for

[103] This, in outline, is Gabba's view. He has to get over the unpalatable, but well-established, facts (l. c.) by claiming that the rising in Etruria and Umbria was 'di poco momento, breve e localizzato'. But cf. Oros. v 18, 17: 'Porcius Cato praetor Etruscos, Plotius legatus Umbros [the *whole* of these nations, as is confirmed for the Livian tradition by *per.* lxvi] plurimo sanguine impenso et difficillimo labore uicerunt' – surely sufficient comment.

[104] Badian (1) 218f. Whether Appian intended this by δοκιμασία (a word which elsewhere he uses for a vote in the Assembly, but which, as a mere matter of Greek, is perfectly capable of such a meaning – a meaning, indeed, much closer to its original one), or whether – here as elsewhere in his much compressed account ('molto sunteggiato', as Gabba rightly remarks) – he has distorted and misunderstood a complicated notice in his source – this is a very minor matter, on which we can hardly express an opinion. But that δοκιμασία nowhere actually has this meaning (thus rightly Gabba, repeating my own remarks) is quite irrelevant: neither this nor any other word that I know of is ever used by any Greek author in this meaning, for the simple reason that the procedure does not happen to be named in our Greek sources (as I had pointed out, l. c.). It is anybody's guess how it *would* have been named, if it *had* been; and the word δοκιμασία is a better candidate than most.

[105] The reference is as clear in Gabba's careful and accurate translation as in Appian's text: 'Gli alleati Italici ... erano in ansia anch'essi, *per la legge coloniaria*, temendo che ... [they would lose some land]. Etruschi ed Umbri, che avevano gli stessi timori degli altri alleati Italici. ... apertamente protestavano *contro la legge* ed attendevano il giorno della votazione' (Gabba (2) 375; my italics). I do not see how Gabba's Italian readers can take the protest as referring to something quite different from the colonial law.

Marius, are amply attested. It is clear that, when Marius saw his programme stolen by his enemies, he roused his own clients to defeat the plan[106].

The details of the Social War[107] have been considerably clarified by Haug's examination of the sources and by Salmon's careful analysis of the Italian armies and their leaders. Voirol, in a paper unfortunately rather inaccessible, has neatly illustrated the increasing bitterness among the Italians as the war progressed, by a selective analysis of their coinage, which (he claims) begins with bilingual issues modelled on Roman coins and went on to increasingly nationalist and anti-Roman ones. Meyer has shown how little truth there is in the conventional modern account of the advanced 'federal' organisation of the Italians, who, in fact, progressed little further than their enemies beyond the idea of city-state organisation[108]. Gabba's careful discussion (in (2)) of Appian's account of the war (with a folding map at the end of the book) is one of the most useful parts of that exemplary edition.

There has been much discussion about the laws by which the Italians were enfranchised. The *lex Julia, lex Calpurnia* and *lex Plautia Papiria* are known. Niccolini thought that the *lex Calpurnia* (which he put early in 89) restricted the freedom of *imperatores* to enfranchise for merit, as provided by the *lex Julia*; but, as Gabba (l.c.) has pointed out, Calpurnius must be dated in 90[109], and there is no noticeable difference between the provisions of the two laws on this subject. But Niccolini's point that the *lex Julia* was probably passed *early* in 90 appears sound, and it is difficult (with Gabba) to fit in the *lex Calpurnia* before it. Biscardi is probably right in thinking the *lex Julia* a law hastily passed to deal with a desperate situation: it is unlikely that it went into all the necessary legal detail, and the *lex Plautia Papiria* makes it all but certain that it did not. The *lex Calpurnia* is probably merely one of several consequential decrees, putting the provisions of the *lex Julia* into effect in particular cases. The haphazard and accidental manner in which we hear of it (as contrasted with the ample transmission of the *lex Julia*) makes it very likely that it is far from being the only such law: any theory so economical that it does not allow for other laws (unknown to us) is a little suspect. As for the *lex Plautia Papiria*, I have tried to point out that what little we know about it –

[106] Gabba (12) 197[2] rejects this obvious conclusion without discussion – I do not see on what grounds, since it is independent of the views that he attacks in the rest of that note. He is right in rejecting my earlier view that the masses of free Etruscans (peasants and shepherds) who later supported Marius were necessarily small landowners: many of them will have been the Etruscan equivalent of *coloni*. For a warning against the common tendency to overestimate the extent and importance of *latifundia*, see Kuzishchin.

[107] On the ancient names for the War, see Haug, 234f. The name we use is Livy's. For the Latins in the War, see Tibiletti (3). The Italian coinage is catalogued (without much historical discussion) by Pagani.

[108] The conventional account is unfortunately still in Scullard, though he was able to add a reference to Meyer.

[109] See also Syme (1) 58.

and this does not include its date – does not justify us in speaking of it as a major enfranchising law: it is merely cited as dealing with the small technical point of *ciues adscripti*, a class into which Cicero's client Archias happened to fall[110]. There is no reference in any ancient source to any major enfranchising law other than the *lex Julia*; though its provisions, as we have seen, probably had to be adapted, and perhaps extended, to individual cases from time to time[111].

## (viii) Sulla

Not much has been written on the events of 88–82[112]. The importance of the Social War in accustoming the new 'client army'[113] to fighting in Italy against old comrades, for ideals far from clear, and in fact most often simply at a leader's command – this is now generally recognised. Cn. Pompeius Strabo and L. Sulla were the first to see the possibilities of the instrument that Marius had created, but (as his total lack of preparations to meet Sulla's march on Rome shows) had never dreamt of using in this way. At Sulla's first attempt the officers refused to follow him; such scruples are never found again in later civil wars. It is worth noting (see Gabba, and Suolahti, *Junior Officers*) that henceforth the social gulf between officers and men tended to narrow.

Sulla's character and his aims have been much discussed. Balsdon (1) has tried to prune the common picture of Sulla the mystic (thus recently again Berve: 'the tool of a higher will', his protecting 'Venus' being in fact a goddess

[110] Badian (9).

[111] One such case (that of Tuder) happens to be recorded (Sisenna fr. 119 P), although the supplementary law is not named and its arrangements are not given in detail. For the general effect of the *lex Julia*, see especially Cic. *Balb*. 21. Velleius' 'qui arma aut non ceperant aut deposuerant maturius' (ii 16), often represented to be a legal restriction inherent in the *lex Julia*, is merely a common-sense statement of its *de facto* immediate application: had it been a quotation, we should have expected subjunctives. Velleius would have been most surprised that he could be thus misunderstood. But between this misunderstanding of his Latin and the arbitrary misinterpretation of the *lex Plautia Papiria* (it sometimes seems unfortunate that the *pro Archia* is one of the surviving and not one of the lost speeches), the whole history of the enfranchising laws, as it appears in our standard works, is pure modern fiction. On the matter of the tribes into which the new citizens were divided, not much progress has been made. Salmon 179f. gives an interesting summary of what can be gathered of Roman methods. Biscardi (2) is ingenious, but fails to find an acceptable meaning for the crucial δεκατεύοντες in Appian: his discussion of the relation of tribes and centuries in the *comitia centuriata* arrives (as it seems any such discussion must arrive) at purely arbitrary figures. For the *lex Pompeia*, commonly said to have enfranchised the Cispadanes and given Latin status to the Transpadanes, see Ewins (2): its guiding principle was much simpler, its effect more complex and less clear-cut.

[112] For a very summary account, see Badian (1) 230f.

[113] On this, see Gabba (5) and (8) – mostly, of course, dealing with a slighly later period, as far as this phenomenon is concerned. See also Heuss 10f.

from Asia Minor) back to what the evidence actually supports. There is very little evidence for any association of Sulla with Venus in Italy. If Sulla built the temple of Venus Felix (not, apparently, a very important building), it is indeed remarkable that neither Plutarch nor any other source gives him credit for it; and in any case, he did at least as much for various other gods. Nor (as Balsdon shows) is even the association of the colonial name 'Veneria' with Sulla really certain. His *felicitas* (see Erkell, 72f.), on closer investigation, appears to be the traditional quality of the Roman *imperator*. The name Ἐπαφρόδιτος has baffled modern research, as it apparently baffled Plutarch. That Sulla must have picked it up in Greece (Balsdon) is surely obvious. There is, however, no evidence – and there has been no really convincing conjecture – on how and precisely why he did so. But we know that Roman nobles could acquire names in the most extraordinary ways: witness that Scipio (RE s. v. 'Cornelius', 354) who was called 'Serapio' because he resembled a slave by that name and who seems to have been satisfied to keep the name thus acquired. Ἐπαφρόδιτος (= Latin 'Venustus' (see Erkell 82)) strikes one as a slave's name, and it may well have been transferred to Sulla as a nickname, which Sulla – realising its etymological possibilities, and perhaps genuinely impressed with its auspicious sound – decided to keep and use[114]. It is, however, remarkable that we have no certain evidence for its use before 81, while there is plentiful evidence after. Sulla's personal mysticism (not, apparently, linked with any particular deity) is attested well before – certainly in the dream during the march on Rome. Though some of the aura with which he surrounded himself was undoubtedly policy (as in the case, also, of Sertorius), we can hardly doubt his genuine mysticism and superstition, which he shared with other great leaders and generals, and of which we have concrete evidence in the names he gave his twin children and in his notorious testamentary advice to L. Lucullus. Far from being a sign of modesty, the belief in his luck was part of his pride, in which, however, we need seek nothing Oriental and nothing Greek. (His attitude to the Greek gods, finding expression in the compulsory loans he took from them, is well known). Though the extravagant theses of Carcopino and Lanzani will not find much support today (even Valgiglio (2) is more cautious), the last word on the 'enigma of Sulla' has by no means been spoken. In view of the nature of our evidence, it is doubtful whether much further progress can be expected[115]; but it has been shown, for this period as for few others, that it would be rash to deny the possibility and that new methods may some day bring a significant advance. Thus Cesano, by a detailed analysis of Sulla's coinage (particularly his rather unsuccessful attempt to introduce a gold coinage), has been able to throw some light on his *Reichsgedanke* and, above all, has decisively disproved Carcopino's

[114] This is based on Balsdon's explanation. [115] See Gabba (14) 140f.

thesis that he aimed at introducing a kind of Hellenistic kingship. Indeed, his coins are far less 'monarchical' than those of the great *imperatores* of the succeeding generation.

It is clear that, like a greater revolutionary adventurer half a century later, Sulla paid as much attention to constitutional forms as the realities of power permitted. The farce of his election to the dictatorship as the result of a law passed by an *interrex* has been shown by Castello to be within the elastic framework of *mos maiorum*, and in the case of Sulla, as in that of Augustus, studies of this (*prima facie*) excessively scholastic kind are in fact of great value in the characterisation of the régime. Even the lawlessness of the initial period seems to have received the 'legal' cover of an act of indemnity, and there is no evidence for acts of violence after that initial period[116]. We should like to know more about the consuls for 81 and the reasons for their election – but we probably never shall. It is surely remarkable that Cicero gives us no information on his namesake Decula, except that he failed to get an aedileship. The contrast with 80 – the consulate of L. Sulla himself and of Q. Metellus Pius, his most distinguished aide – that contrast is remarkable and instructive. It is not certain whether Sulla retained the dictatorship; though Appian, influenced (as he confesses) by the practice of Imperial consulates, thought that he did (*b. c.* i 103, *init.*). There is no indication that Livy thought so, and we have yet to find a document that calls him both consul and dictator. (Cf., most recently, Dunant-Pouilloux, *Thasos* ii 37f.). In the light of what evidence we have, it is very probable that he did not: that he abdicated in stages, being dictator to the end of 81, consul (with a colleague) in 80, and finally *priuatus* in 79. Since the bulk of his legislation must have been passed in 81, it looks as if 80 was to be the inauguration of *res publica restituta*. This would appear far more in keeping with the evidence, and with the spirit of what we know of his legislation, than the picture commonly found in the textbooks, which is still to some extent under the influence of Carcopino's brilliant fantasy. It also helps us to understand the background to the defence of the *mulier Arretina* and of Sex. Roscius. Chrysogonus, behaving – naturally enough – like the slave of a Hellenistic king, was out of place in Sulla's Republic, and Sulla could be made to realise this as easily as any other Roman aristocrat[117].

[116] Gabba (2) 276f., not recognising this, is led into impossible difficulties by trying to shift the date of the execution of Q. Lucretius Ofella, who sought the consulship when he had not held any other office, from its attested place in late 82. There is no reason to reject the sources: the *cursus honorum* to which Ofella would not submit was (whether or not Appian was aware of this – a question, as so often, difficult to answer) the pre-Sullan one, as recently clarified by Astin. This makes the incident far more instructive. On the *leges Valeriae*, see Gabba (2) 341f. On the traditionalism behind Sulla's dictatorship, see also Wilcken.

[117] On the *pro Roscio Amerino*, see Krawczuk; Badian (1) 249f.; and cf. Afzelius (1). On the difference between 81 and 80, see especially Krawczuk, who, however, still thinks

The details of his reforms need a great deal more study, before a valid general judgment can be attempted. It should no longer be said that he was a mere reactionary, blindly trying to restore dead forms[118]. He seems, on the other hand, to have attempted no great reforms, to have had no great political vision. As far as any general conclusions can be drawn from our present inadequate knowledge of his legislation, it looks as though he attempted a compromise, recognising and (to some extent) codifying recent developments where they seemed to him healthy, and trying to excise them from the constitution where they seemed dangerous. We have seen that the system of *quaestiones* seems to have been well developed by his day; he recognised and extended it, although it had certainly not proved wholly satisfactory. It seems to have been the usual practice, as it had developed during this period, for senior magistrates to stay in Rome during their year of office and go to a province after; Sulla so arranged things that this would – through pressure of business – be necessary for praetors, while he may have laid it down as the rule for consuls[119]. On the other hand, the disturbed conditions of the great wars of the age of Marius, and particularly of the Social and Civil Wars, had established a habit of long provincial tenures – as many as seven years at times – and Sulla had seen the use to which, in the age of the 'client army', such long commands might be put by unscrupulous men[120]. He therefore tried to ensure that there should be enough senior administrators available *ex magistratu* each year to make long tenures unnecessary, and he circumscribed the powers of proconsuls during their tenure. He seems to have hoped that the whole system would become self-adjusting; but in this, as is known, he was mistaken, and the precedents from recent times of crisis prevailed as soon as new crises appeared.

him dicator in 80. I have unfortunately, owing to language difficulties, not been able to profit fully from Krawczuk's most interesting article (despite kind assistance from Mr. Sealey): a translation into a Western language (e. g. in *BCO*) would be welcome. The 10000 slaves liberated to pack the hostile Plebs (see Češka) help to show Sulla's concern for legal forms: there is no need to pack an assembly, unless one proposes to give it something to do. Naturally, this concern was always kept strictly within the bounds of political realism. The tension thus created has in part landed us with the 'enigma of Sulla'. On *r. p. restituta* in 80, see Cic. *Rosc. Am.* 139 – surely not spoken under the dictatorship!

[118] This view is effectively castigated by Gabba (14) – a discussion that is essential reading on Sulla.

[119] It is generally recognised that there were exceptions to this after Sulla (see Last, *CAH* ix 294f.; Balsdon, *JRS* 1939, 58f.) and we cannot say whether it was custom or law. The Senate had (or assumed) wide powers of dispensation in such constitutional matters (cf. its powers on the rearrangement of *prouinciae* in an emergency). But the rule, such as it was, seems to have existed even before Sulla.

[120] On these long commands see Badian (9), developed and traced further back by Carney (6). Whatever the political interpretation, the facts, now that they have been recognised, are indisputable.

In the case of armies and provinces, Sulla seems also to have consecrated custom. Smith (2), in an important study, has shown that 'standing armies' had begun to appear in key provinces. Sulla recognised the practice[121]. Nor does it seem likely that he created any new provinces. Cilicia had been a recognised *prouincia* before: it seems to have meant a watch on the pirates of the eastern Mediterranean. There is no evidence that Sulla made it a province in the territorial sense,[122] any more than there is for his establishment of a province of Gallia Cisalpina. Though Ewins (2) has not succeeded in finding any real arguments for her thesis that it was established by the *lex Pompeia* of 89 – the connection with Italy seems to have been strong during the following years –, there is, on the other hand, good reason for doubting whether it had a recognised separate existence even after Sulla: M. Lepidus (*cos.* 78) certainly seems to have received the whole of Gallia as his province[123]. Provincial administration even after Sulla, as certainly before, was far less cut and dried than we – under the spell of the Empire and of Mommsen – are apt to believe.

The only other point on which considerable progress has been made is Sulla's attitude to the Equites and his recruitment of that Senate to which he proceeded to entrust supreme authority. As so often in this survey, it is Gabba whom we must salute as the author of this progress[124]. He has investigated the recruitment of the Senate, showing that about half the new Senate will have consisted of Equites as we usually understand this term, and many of them were in fact of Italian origin. Nor is there any truth in the common statement that Sulla banished the *publicani* from Asia[125]. The myth of Sulla's championship of the nobility at the expense of the Equites is one invented and propagated by interested ancient cources (Cicero bears a large

121 Smith, against the trend of his own evidence, ascribes the creation of such 'standing armies' to Sulla. But the provinces he actually lists divide into those (e. g. the Spains) where he has shown that the system existed before, and those (e. g. Syria) where Sulla can have had nothing to do with it. The history of the 'standing army' in disturbed provinces seems to be, quite simply, that the Senate had for decades been trying to establish such a sensible system (e. g. in Spain, for which Livy gives us some evidence), but did not fully succeed until Marius' army reform at last dealt with the chronic manpower shortage.

122 See discussion in Badian (11).

123 Sulla himself seems to have considered taking the Cisalpina as a province in 79, no doubt in order to have an army on the borders of Italy (see Gabba (2) 283). But by the end of 80 he probably judged this unnecessary and was eager to divest himself of political responsibility. It should be recognised that almost anything could be a *prouincia*, and that a *prouincia Cisalpina* does not imply an intention of setting up a self-contained administrative unit under regular administration (which is what we ought to mean by a 'province'), any more than the frequent *prouincia Italia* implies this for Italy.

124 Gabba (2) 343f. conveniently summarises the conclusions reached in his earlier work. Cf. also Gabba (11), stressing that Sulla, unlike M. Drusus, did not make equites liable to charges of judicial corruption. This is a decisive argument against the traditional view of Sulla's 'hatred' of that class.

125 Shown by Brunt.

part of the blame), and it is reassuring that we can now penetrate behind it. It is tempting to believe (with Gabba) that Sulla's recruitment of the Senate followed M. Drusus' abortive attempt: as we have seen, Drusus had been supported by the *factio* (notably by M. Scaurus, the distinguished protagonist of the Metelli), and Sulla, who married Scaurus' widow, Metella, owed his rise and, in particular, his consulate to the favour of that *factio*. As we have also seen, he was not remarkable for original political ideas[126].

## (ix) Conclusion

It has been the aim of this survey to indicate in what fields, within this crucial period, progress has been made and what points particularly need further investigation. On the whole, what is needed is continued detailed enquiry, putting our scattered evidence to the best possible use and thickening the texture of the weave: in fact, the sort of work that Gabba has so brilliantly done for so many problems. In this period as in few others in Roman history, there has been a tendency to repeat a few tralatician 'facts' without scrutiny of the sources and to base general judgments on prejudice rather than on evidence. Recent work has provided some of the evidence on which a proper history of the period may be based[127]. We must find much more.

Durham (England) and Seattle (Wash., U.S.A.) E. Badian

[126] It should perhaps be specially mentioned that the traditional view that he abolished the censorship has also been shown to be without foundation: it is far more likely that the reason for the failure to appoint censors between 80 and 70 is connected with the enrolment of the Italians (see Gabba (10) 135f.).

[127] It will be interesting, as a measure of our progress, to compare the volume on this period in the *Storia di Roma* series (when it appears) with the treatment (as we have seen, now in many respects out of date) in the *Cambridge Ancient History*. – I should like to record my thanks to the Durham Colleges Research Fund for their generosity, and to Sir Ronald Syme, Miss U. Ewins and Professor T. F. Carney for advice and assistance. They are not, of course, responsible for any of the views I have expressed. I should also like to thank Professor M. H. Chambers for reading the proofs and eliminating some errors.

## BIBLIOGRAPHY

*Note*: This list is intended to be complete as far as articles are concerned; it has had to be selective as regards books. I shall be very grateful for notification (or, if possible, offprints) of works omitted, as also of future work on this period. Summaries of articles are given where this was thought useful and could not be done in the text of the survey. The presence or absence of a summary does not constitute a judgment on the importance or quality of the work concerned. Only very few book reviews are mentioned, and the choice has necessarily been rather arbitrary. Those omitted (which include nearly all my own) are not necessarily unimportant; but those included have been judged essential. Difficulties of language and accessibility have prevented inclusion and full utilisation of some work in Slavonic languages; this again is not meant as a judgment of value. A useful bibliography of Soviet work on Roman history will be found in VDI 1957, 3, 42f. (by Kovalev).

Abbreviations, throughout, are those of L'Année Philologique. Works not accessible to me are marked †.

Afzelius, A.

(1) 'Zwei Episoden aus dem Leben Ciceros', C & M 1942, 209f. [The *pro S. Roscio* brought no real danger to Cicero, but the *pro muliere Arretina* (*Caec.* 96f.) showed courage.]

(2) 'Zur Definition der römischen Nobilität vor der Zeit Ciceros', C & M 1945, 150f. [Time of Gracchi sees formation of 'Optimate' party and change in meaning of *nobilis* from descendant of curule magistrate to descendant of consul.]

(3) 'Lex annalis', C & M 1946, 263f.

Alföldi, A. Review of Pink.

Alfonsi, L.

(1) 'L'importanza politico-religiosa della "enunciazione" di Valerio Sorano', Epigraphica 1948, 81f.
[Soranus (= Aedituus) committed this sacrilege in 82, to help cause of Marians and Italians.]

(2) 'Nota all'articolo: L'importanza ...', Epigraphica 1949, 47f.
[Only pontifices, for ritual purposes, might utter this sacred name.]

Amelotti, M. 'L'epigrafe di Pergamo sugli ἀστύνομοι, SDHI 1958, 80f.
[Law in OGIS ii 483 taken over by Romans from Attalus III; such reception is normal Roman practice.]

Andreotti, R. Cajo Mario. Gubbio, 1940.

Arangio-Ruiz, V. 'Diritto romano e papirologia giuridica (1940–47)', Doxa 1949, 193f. (especially 227f.).

Astin, A. E. 'The lex annalis before Sulla', Latomus 1957, 588f.; 1958, 49f. Also as a booklet in the Collection Latomus, Bruxelles, 1958.

Avenarius, W. 'Die griechischen Vorbilder des Sallust', SO 1957, 48f.
[Usually well-known passages, learnt in his school-days.]

Badian, E.

(1) Foreign Clientelae. Oxford, 1958.
[Rev. Gabba, RFIC 1959, 189f.]

(2) '*Lex Acilia repetundarum*', AJPh 1954, 374f.

(3) '*Lex Servilia*', CR 1954, 101f.

(4) 'The date of Pompey's first triumph', Hermes 1955, 107f.
[Probably March 12th, 81 B. C.]

(5) 'Quintus Mucius Scaevola and the province of Asia', Athenaeum 1956, 104f.

(6) 'P. Decius P. f. Subulo', JRS 1956, 91f.

(7) 'Caepio and Norbanus', Historia 1957, 318f.

(8) 'Mam. Scaurus cites precedent', CR 1958, 216f.

(9) 'Notes on provincial governors from the social war down to Sulla's victory', PACA 1958, 1f.
[An attempt to establish the provincial *fasti* for this period of prolonged and irregular commands.]

(10) 'The early career of A. Gabinius (consul 58 B. C.)', Philologus 1959, 87f.
[The *tr. mil.* 86 identical with the *cos.* 58. Observations on Gabinii of this period.]

(11) 'Sulla's Cilician command', Athenaeum 1959, 279f.

(12) 'Caesar's *cursus* and the intervals between offices', JRS 1959, 81f.
[Our evidence suggests a privileged 'patrician' *cursus* in the late Republic, perhaps introduced by Sulla.]
(13) Review of Malcovati (1).

Balsdon, J. P. V. D.
(1) 'Sulla Felix', JRS 1951, 1f.
(2) Review of Gabba (8).

Bardon, H. 'Q. Lutatius Catulus et son "cercle littéraire"', LEC 1950, 145f.

Bartoccini, R. 'Frammento di legge romana rinvenuto a Taranto', Epigraphica 1947, 3f.

Benedict, C. H. 'The Romans in southern Gaul', AJPh 1942, 38f.

Berger, A. 'A note on Gellius, *n. A.* I 6', AJPh 1946, 320f.
[Speech 'de uxoribus ducendis' by Macedonicus.]

Bernardi, A.
(1) 'La guerra sociale e le lotte dei partiti in Roma', NRS 1944–5, 60f.
(2) 'Incremento demografico di Roma e colonizzazione latina dal 338 a. C. all'età dei Gracchi', NRS 1946, 272f.
[Gradual depopulation of Italy in the second century and efforts to deal with this.]

Berve, H. 'Sulla', Gestaltende Kräfte der Antike (München, 1949), 130f.

Bickel, E. 'C. Caesar L. f.', RhM 1957, 1f.
[Name and works of this man (killed 87), often confused with the Dictator in the sources.]

Bilinski, B. Accio ed i Gracchi. Roma, 1958.

Biscardi, A.
† (1) 'Auctoritas patrum': a series of articles in BIDR.
(2) 'La questione italica e le tribù sopprannumerarie', PP 1951, 241f.

Boren, H. C.
(1) 'Livius Drusus, *t. p.* 122, and his anti-Gracchan program', CJ 1956–7, 27f.
[Programme meant seriously. His sympathy for Italians shown by consular law of 112.]
(2) 'The urban side of the Gracchan economic crisis', AHR 1957–8, 890f.
(3) 'Numismatic light on the Gracchan crisis', AJPh 1958, 140f.

Bourne, F. C.
(1) 'The origins of Roman experiments in social welfare', CW 1950, 33f.
[Romans disliked state welfare schemes. 'New *clientela*', in second century, took place of such a scheme: private financial generosity due to Greek influence.]
(2) 'The Roman Republican census and census statistics', CW 1951–2, 129f.
[Zumpt's theory that all persons *sui iuris* normally included alone makes sense. Army figures based on supplementary list.]
(3) 'The Gracchan land law and the census', CW 1951–2, 180f.
[Rise in figures between 131 and 126 mainly due to large-scale emancipation of sons so that they could profit by allotments.]

Bracco, V. 'L'*elogium* di Polla', RAAN 1954, 5f.
[Acephalous *elogium* CIL i² 638 must be of T. Annius Luscus (*cos.* 153), since first to act in Lucania. He probably converted *ager scripturarius* to *a. uectigalis*. Topographical and historical considerations in support.]

Bradeen, D. W. 'Roman citizenship *per magistratum*', CJ 1958–9, 221f.
[Not known before 89, perhaps not before Empire.]

Broughton, T. R. S.
(1) The magistrates of the Roman Republic. 2 vols. New York, 1951–2.
(2) 'Notes on Roman magistrates', TAPhA 1946, 35f.
[First note deals with M. Antonius in Cilicia: probably praetor 102 and *pro cos.* 101–100.]

(3) 'The *elogia* of Julius Caesar's father', AJA 1948, 323f.
[Careers of Caesares in the nineties.]

(4) 'Notes on Roman magistrates', Historia 1953–4, 209f.
[M. Antonius the orator attested as augur. C. Marius' connection with Mother of the Gods.]

Brown, T. S. 'Greek influence on Tiberius Gracchus', CJ 1946–7, 471f.

Brunt, P. A. 'Sulla and the Asian publicans', Latomus 1956, 17f.
[Sulla restored the Gracchan system of tax collection in Asia, interrupted by the Mithridatic war.]

Bruwaene, M. van den

(1) 'Quelques éclaircissements sur le "*de haruspicum responsis*"', AC 1948, 81f.
[Document quoted refers to events of 90–88.]

(2) 'L'opposition à Scipion Émilien après la mort de Tiberius Gracchus', Phoibos 1950–51, 229f.

Büchner, K. Der Aufbau von Sallusts Bellum Jugurthinum. Hermes, Einzelschr. 9, Wiesbaden, 1953.

Burdese, A. Studi sull'ager publicus. Torino, 1952.

Burn, A. R. 'A Metellus in two passages of Dio', CR 1949, 52f.
[The importance of Q. Metellus Pius.]

Capozza, M. 'Le rivolte servili di Sicilia nel quadro della politica agraria romana', AIV 1956–7, 79f.
[Sources indicate use of numerous slaves for agriculture as well as pasture in Sicily: *latifundia* especially in eastern part. Chronology of campaigns. Settlement of M'Aquillius.]

Carcopino, J. 'Sur un passage de la chronique de Saint Jérome', Mél. Fr. Martroye (Paris, 1940), 73f.
['Census figure' for 86–5 cannot be real census figure, as no census completed; probably size of population of city of Rome itself. Similarly for figure for 147–6.]

Carney, T. F.

(1) 'Notes on Plutarch's life of Marius', CQ 1955, 201f.
[On 11, 9; 23, 4; 25, 3; 25, 7.]

(2) 'The death of Marius', AClass 1958, 117f.
[Cause pneumonia; Plutarch follows usual technique for such descriptions. Marius had been healthy before.]

(3) 'Marius' choice of battlefield in the campaign of 100', Athenaeum 1958, 229f.
[Choice of Vercellae determined by gold-mines in area. Political considerations behind this.]

(4) 'Was Rutilius' exile voluntary or compulsory?', Acta Iuridica 1958, 243f.
[Voluntary: exile not a legal penalty in Republic.]

(5) 'Once again Marius' speech after election in 108 B. C.', SO 1959, 63f.
[Speech in *b. J.* 85 parody of *elogium*; probably based on Marius' actual speech: similar in Plutarch.]

(6) 'The promagistracy at Rome, 121–81 B. C.', AClass 1959, 72f.

(7) 'Coins bearing on the age and career of Marius', NC 1959, 79f.

(8) 'Two notes on Republican Roman law', Acta Iuridica 1959, 229f. [232f.: Marius' trial for *ambitus* (116).]

(9) Review of Valgiglio (3).

Castello, C. 'Intorno alla legittimità della lex Valeria de Sulla dictatore', Studi De Francisci (Milano, 1956) iii 37f.

Cesano, S. L. 'Silla e la sua moneta', RPAA 1945–6, 187f.

Češka, J. 'Deset tisíc Corneliu', LF 1955, 177f., with Latin summary 181. See also BCO 1958, 15f.

Chantraine, H. Untersuchungen zur römischen Geschichte am Ende des 2. Jahrhunderts v. Chr. Kallmünz, 1959. [Rev. Gabba, Gnomon 1960, 136f.]

Charlier, R. 'La Numidie vue par Salluste. Cirta Regia: Constantine ou Le Kef?', AC 1950, 289f. [Le Kef, not Constantine.]

Cuff, P. J. Review of Smith (1).

Degrassi, A.

(1) 'Il monumento riminese di Q. Ovius Fregellanus', Athenaeum 1941, 133f. [He fled to Ariminum after destruction of Fregellae.]

(2) 'Epigrafia romana (1937–46)', Doxa 1949, 47f.

(3) 'Un nuovo miliario calabro della Via Popillia', Philologus 1955, 259f. [New milestone of praetor T. Annius T. f. probably put up by T. Annius Rufus (*cos.* 128) in his praetorship (probably 131): successor of P. Popillius Laenas in charge of new road begun by latter. Similarly Via Annia from Aquileia to (northern) Via Popillia. Via Annia in Etruria also his work. All this activity connected with Gracchan land distributions.]

Deman, A. Review of Smith (1).

De Martino, F. 'Ager privatus vectigalisque', Studi De Francisci (Milano, 1956) i 555f. [Details of this category unknown, but must be private (therefore not = *ager quaestorius*). One of several intermediate categories between fully public and fully private land. Must have persisted in Empire; remote precedent for *emphyteusis*.]

De Visscher, F. 'La dualité des droits de cité et la "mutatio civitatis"', Studi De Francisci (Milano, 1956) i 37f.; also BARB 1954, 49f. [In late Republic dual citizenship possible for enfranchised peregrini, as long as they did not come to Rome. Not contradicted by Cic. *Balb.* 11f.]

Donnadieu, A. 'La campagne de Marius dans la Gaule Narbonnaise (104–102 av. J. C.)', REA 1954, 281f.

D'Ors, A.

(1) 'Epigrafía jurídica griega y romana (1950–53)', SDHI 1954, 403f., especially 457f. (*leges repetundarum*).

(2) 'Epigrafía jurídica griega y romana (1954–56)', SDHI 1957, 475f., especially 518f. (*ager publicus* and *leges repetundarum*).

Douglas, A. E.

(1) 'The legislation of Spurius Thorius', AJPh 1956, 376f.

(2) 'Corrigenda', AJPh 1957, 89 (correcting some prosopographical errors in (1)).

Dow, S. 'Corinthiaca', HSCPh 1951, 81f. [Detailed discussion of CIL i² (Add.) 2662. Doubtfully accepts reference to M. Antonius (*cos.* 99), on grounds of orthography of inscription; but *names* would fit in with what we know of his grandson the Triumvir.]

Drexler, H. 'Zur Frage der „Schuld" des Tiberius Gracchus', Emerita 1951, 51f. [Diffuse philosophical disquisition, claiming that formal legal standards inapplicable to Ti. Gracchus and that morally he was right and his failure ultimately disastrous for the victors.]

Dudley, D. R. 'Blossius of Cumae', JRS 1941, 94f.

Duval, P.-M. 'A propos d'un milliaire de *Cneus Domitius Ahenobarbus Imperator* découvert dans l'Aude en 1949', CRAI 1951, 161f. [Stone must be dated 118.]

Ehrenberg, V. '*Imperium maius* in the Roman Republic', AJPh 1953, 113f.

Erkell, H. Augustus, Felicitas, Fortuna. Göteborg, 1952.

Ewins, U.
(1) 'The early colonisation of Cisalpine Gaul', PBSR 1952, 54f.
[Foundation dates of various colonies. In particular, Eporedia founded as counterblast to Saturninus' legislation in 100.]
(2) 'The enfranchisement of Cisalpine Gaul', PBSR 1955, 73f.

Fraccaro, P.
(1) Opuscula ii. Pavia, 1957.
(2) 'Un episodio delle agitazioni agrarie dei Gracchi', Robinson Studies (St Louis, Missouri, 1953) ii 884f. Reprinted (1) 77f.

Frank, E. 'Marius and the Roman nobility', CJ 1954–5, 149f.
[Marius on friendly terms with nobility (especially Scaurus) until 88. Sulla's relative failure in nineties due to Marius' hostility. Younger Marius' marriage to Licinia to be dated 92–1: meant to secure Marius' favour for Drusus; but Marius remained neutral 91.]

Fritz, K. von. 'Sallust and the attitude of the Roman nobility at the time of the wars against Jugurtha (112–105 B. C.)', TAPhA 1943, 134f.
[Sallust, unlike Posidonius, not trying to give objective account, but under pretence of objectivity to justify Popular against Senatorial party.]

Gabba, E.
(1) Appiano e la storia delle guerre civili. Firenze, 1956. [Rev. Gelzer, Gnomon 1958, 216f.]
(2) Appiani bellorum civilium liber I. Firenze, 1958.
(3) 'Le origini dell'esercito professionale in Roma: i proletari e la riforma di Mario', Athenaeum 1949, 173f.
(4) 'Ricerche su alcuni punti di storia Mariana', Athenaeum 1951, 12f.
[Saturninus' laws of 100 abrogated, but not those of 103.]
(5) 'Ricerche sull'esercito professionale romano da Mario ad Augusto', Athenaeum 1951, 171f.
(6) 'Ancora sulle cifre dei censimenti', Athenaeum 1952, 161f.
[Against Bourne (2), they include only *assidui*.]
(7) 'Politica e cultura in Roma agli inizî del I secolo a. C.', Athenaeum 1953, 259f.
(8) 'Le origini della guerra sociale e la vita politica romana dopo l'89 a. C.', Athenaeum 1954, 41f., 293f. [Rev. Balsdon, Gnomon 1954, 343f. Sherwin-White, JRS 1955, 168f.]
(9) 'Note Appianee', Athenaeum 1955, 218f.
[On *b. c.* i 28, 127; 29, 130; 100, 466.]
(10) 'Il ceto equestre e il Senato di Silla', Athenaeum 1956, 124f.
(11) 'Osservazioni sulla legge giudiziaria di M. Livio Druso (91 a. C.)', PP 1956, 363f.
(12) Review of Badian (1).
(13) Review of Chantraine.
(14) Review of Valgiglio (2).

Gagé, J. 'Les clientèles triomphales de la République romaine', RH 1956–57, 1f.
[Studies *clientela* of *ciues seruati* restored from captivity, etc., with other remarks on triumphs. Marius first to wear triumphal toga after triumph; this common later].

Garzetti, A.
(1) 'M. Licinio Crasso', I: Athenaeum 1941, 3f.
[Excellent study of his early years.]
(2) 'Plutarco e le sue "vite parallele" (Rassegna di studi 1934–52)', RSI 1953, 76f.
[Indispensable for recent work on the *Lives*.]

Gelzer, M.

(1) 'Cn. Pompeius Strabo und der Aufstieg seines Sohnes Magnus', AAWB 1942, no. 14. [First to analyse crucial importance of Strabo.]

(2) Review of Göhler, Rom und Italien (Breslau, 1939), Gnomon 1941, 145f. [Rejects Göhler's view that *socii* included in Tiberius Gracchus' distributions of land. Follows Zancan in identifying *Lex Agr.* with *lex Thoria* and Appian's third law.]

(3) Review of Hill (1).

(4) Review of Gabba (1).

Hampl, F. 'Römische Politik in republikanischer Zeit und das Problem des "Sittenverfalls"', HZ clviii, 1959, 497f.

Hands, A. R. 'Sallust and *dissimulatio*', JRS 1959, 56f. [Chief reason for Sallust's dislike of Scaurus (as of Cicero) is Scaurus' political adaptability and lack of firm principles, which are what Sallust admires.]

Haug, I. 'Der römische Bundesgenossenkrieg 91–88 v. Chr. bei Titus Livius', WJA 1947, 100f., 201f.

Henderson, M. I. 'The process "de repetundis"', JRS 1951, 71f.

Herrmann, L. 'La date de la lex Mamilia', RIDA 1948, 113f. [Rejects Fabricius' date 109. Probably 55.]

Heurgon, J.

(1) 'Note sur "l'âme vaste" de Catilina', BAGB 1949, 79f. [Catiline's 'uastus animus' (similarly Jugurtha's 'ingens animus' (*b. J.* 96, 3)) contrasts with virtue of 'magnitudo animi' (e. g. of Cato and Caesar).]

(2) 'The date of Vegoia's prophecy', JRS 1959, 41f. [This document (*Grom. vet.* i 350), discussed in detail, belongs to *c.* 91, in context of Drusus' reforms.]

Heuss, A. 'Der Untergang der römischen Republik und das Problem der Revolution', HZ clxxxii, 1956, 1f.

Hill, H.

(1) The Roman middle class in the Republican period. Oxford, 1952. [Rev. Gelzer, Gnomon 1953, 319f.]

(2) 'Roman revenues from Greece after 146 B. C.', CPh 1946, 35f. [Only rents and portoria.]

(3) 'The so-called lex Aufeia', CR 1948, 112f. [Really the *lex Aquillia* settling status of Asia.]

Instinsky, U. 'Sallust und der Ligurer (b. J. 93–4)', Hermes 1958, 502f. [Ligurian who led Marius' assault party depicted by Sallust as typical of his race.]

Kaser, M. 'Die Typen der römischen Bodenrechte in der späteren Republik', ZSS 1942, 1f.

Katz, S. 'The Gracchi: an essay in interpretation', CJ 1942–3, 65f. [Survey of numerous views on their aims and motives.]

Krawczuk, A. 'Date of delivery and political background of Cicero's speech "pro Sex. Roscio Amerino"' [in Polish], Eos 1954–5,2, 121f.

Kurfess, A. 'Zu Sallust, Jug. 16, 3', WJA 1947, 371. [Defends MS reading 'in amicis': Opimius cannot have been Jugurtha's enemy.]

Kuzishchin, V. 'The extension of *latifundia* in Italy at the end of the Republic' [in Russian], VDI 1957, 1, 64f. See Historia 1958, 504. [A very useful discussion, with full consideration of the sources, leading to a sensible rejection of over-emphasis on large-scale agricultural production at this period.]

Last, H. M. '*Cinnae quater consulis*', CR 1944, 15f. [Phrase (Suet. *Jul.* 1) not a date, but means 'of the Cinna who was four times consul'.]

Leeman, A.D.

(1) A systematical bibliography of Sallust (1879–1950). Mnemosyne Supplement 4, Leiden, 1952.

(2) 'Sallusts Prologe und seine Auffassung von der Historiographie. II. Das Jugurtha-Proömium'. Mnemosyne 1955, 38f.

Le Gall, J. 'La mort de Jugurtha', RPh 1944, 94f.

[Jugurtha strangled *in carcere*. Plutarch's account romance, perhaps meant to correspond to death of Marius.]

Lindsay, R. J. M. 'Defamation and the law under Sulla', CPh 1949, 240f.

[Cic. fam. iii 11, 2 not evidence that Sulla used *maiestas* law against defamation.]

Luzzatto, G. I.

(1) 'Appunti sul testamento di Tolemeo Apione a favore di Roma', SDHI 1941, 259f.

[Background to Apion's will of 96: prolonged diplomatic conflict between Rome and Egypt over control of Cyrenaica. Survey of known wills of this sort: they, as accepted by Rome, are legal basis of *libertas* of Greek cities in provinces concerned.]

(2) 'Sul nuovo frammento di legge romana rinvenuto a Taranto', ASP 1951, 28f.

[It is Glaucia's law; Bantia law is Saturninus' *maiestas* law.]

† (3) 'A proposito della lex Tarentina recentemente pubblicata', Munera Pringsheim (Athinai, 1953), 86f.

(4) 'Sul iusiurandum in legem dei magistrati e senatori romani', Scritti Borsi (Bologna, 1955).

[Defends identifications in (2). Oath anti-Senatorial: probably reply of Populares to *SC ultimum*.]

Malcovati, E.

(1) Oratorum Romanorum fragmenta². Torino, 1955. [Rev. Badian, JRS 1956, 218f.]

(2) 'Ad Cic. fam. ix 21, 3', Studi Funaioli (Roma, 1955), 216f.

['Sutorio atramento absolutus' refers to suicide.]

Marsh, F. B. A history of the Roman world from 146–30 B. C.² Ed. H. H. Scullard. London, 1953.

Mashkin, N. A. 'Roman political parties at the end of the second and beginning of the first centuries B. C.' [in Russian], VDI 1947, 3, 126f.

[A long critique of 'bourgeois' methods.]

Mattingly, H.

(1) 'Nomentanus', Proceedings of the Cambridge Philological Society 1950–1, 12f.

[Retariffing of *denarius* to be dated to time of C. Gracchus. NOM on coins of L. Atilius to be read 'Nomentani' – name for *ciues sine suffragio*, to which status C. Gracchus proposed to raise Latins.]

(2) 'Some new studies of the Roman Republican coinage. Roman denarii of the third period: the age of C. Gracchus', PBA 1953, 239f.

[Can be precisely dated *c.* 125–118. 'Nomentani' (see (1)).]

(3) 'The coinage of the age of Marius, *c.* 118–91 B. C.', PBA 1957, 196f.

[Analysis and attempt at dating.]

(4) 'A coinage of the revolt of Fregellae', ANSMusN 1958, 451f.

Mattingly, H. B. 'The denarius of Sufenas and the *ludi Victoriae*', NC 1956, 189f.

[Coin (probably 63–2) commemorates first celebration, by Sex. Nonius as quaestor, of Sulla's victory games at Praeneste, where they continued to be celebrated by urban quaestor.]

Meyer, H. D. 'Die Organisation der Italiker im Bundesgenossenkrieg', Historia 1958, 74f.

Miltner, F. 'Der Germanenangriff auf Italien in den Jahren 102–1 v. Chr.', Klio 1940, 289f.

Miners, N. J. 'The *lex Sempronia ne quis iudicio circumueniatur*', CQ 1958, 241f.

Niccolini, G. 'Le leggi *de civitate Romana* durante la guerra sociale', RAL 1946, 110f.

Onorato, G. O.

(1) 'La partecipazione di Cicerone alla guerra sociale in Campania', RAAN 1949–50, 415f.

(2) 'Pompei municipium e colonia romana', RAAN 1951, 115f.

[Social War in Campania, especially Nola and Pompei. Analysis of epigraphical evidence: *municipium* of Pompei alongside Sullan colony at least till 60 B. C. History of colony.]

Oost, S. I. 'The fetial law and the outbreak of the Jugurthine war', AJPh 1954, 147f.

[Stages of second-century pseudo-fetial procedure (as demonstrated by Walbank) seen in Sallust's account.]

Pagani, A. 'Le monete della guerra sociale', RIN 1944–7.

Pareti, L. Storia di Roma e del mondo romano iii. Torino, 1953.

Perrochat, P.

(1) 'Salluste et Thucydide', REL 1947, 90f.

[Detailed investigation of Thucydidean influence on Sallust; some reference to *b. J.*]

(2) 'Les digressions de Salluste', REL 1950, 168f.

[Digressions deliberately inserted for dramatic and compositional reasons.]

Piganiol, A.

(1) 'Sur la nouvelle table de bronze de Tarente', CRAI 1951, 58f.

[Perhaps Glaucia's law, of 100 (praetorship). Similarities to 'pirate law' and Latin law of Bantia.]

(2) 'Histoire romaine (1941–50)', RH ccix, 1953, 271f.; ccx, 1953, 64f.

(3) 'Histoire romaine (1951–1955)', RH ccxviii, 1957, 310f.; ccxix, 1958, 97f.

Pink, K. The triumviri monetales and the structure of the coinage of the Roman Republic. New York, 1952. [Rev. Alföldi, Gnomon 1954, 381f.]

[The most important attempt at establishing a firm chronology for the coinage of the period.]

Piotrowicz, L. 'La loi judiciaire de Q. Servilius Caepio de l'an 106', Sbornik Kazarow (Sofia, 1950), 191f.

[Cannot have been passed, since Caepio not strong enough to overcome opposition of *Equites* and Plebs. C. Memmius probably one of leaders of opposition to it.]

Plassart, A. 'Décrets de Thespies', RA 1949 (= Mélanges Picard), ii 825f.

[Decree honouring Q. Braetius (Sura), legate (of C. Sentius), 87.]

Quoniam, P. 'A propos d'une inscription de *Thuburnica* (Tunisie)', CRAI 1950, 332f.

Rambaud, M. 'Les prologues de Salluste et la démonstration morale dans son oeuvre', REL 1946, 115f.

[S.'s aim to show influence of certain human qualities on historical events.]

Raubitschek, A. E. 'Sylleia', Studies ... A. C. Johnson (Princeton, N. J., 1951), 49f.

[Earliest possible date for archonship of Apollodorus (IG ii² 1039) 80-79; thus *Sylleia* at Athens may be copied from Roman victory games, if they are victory games at all. Perhaps temporary renaming of traditional festival (this common Athenian practice): if so, probably Theseia.]

† Rimscha, H. von. Die Gracchen. München, 1949.

Sadée, E. 'Die strategischen Zusammenhänge des Kimbernkriegs 101 v. Chr.', Klio 1940, 225f.

St Martin, D. 'Il foedus romano con Callatis', Epigraphica 1948, 104f.

[Proposes date around 140. After 113, Roman activity in Black Sea area made Greek cities there welcome Mithridates.]

Salmon, E. T. 'Notes on the Social War', TAPhA 1958, 159f.

Savio, E. 'Intorno alle leggi suntuarie romane', Aevum 1940, 174f.

[Lists laws and censorial edicts dealing with subject.]

Schönbauer, E.
(1) 'Die Inschrift von Heraklea – ein Rätsel?', RIDA 1954, 373f.
[Not general *lex municipalis*; not Caesarian. Perhaps passed under Cinna.]
(2) 'Das Problem der beiden Inschriften von Bantia', RIDA 1955, 311f.
[Time before 100 too early for Latin law. Oscan side shows aristocratic order, probably as reintroduced by Sulla. Latin side will belong to time of Cinna; then annulled and tablet reused after Sulla's victory.]
(3) 'Die römische Repetundengesetzgebung und das neue Gesetzes-Fragment aus Tarent', AAWW 1956, 13f.
(4) 'Das Gesetzes-Fragment aus Tarent in neuer Schau', Jura 1956, 92f.
[Rejects identifications with *lex Sempronia, lex Acilia* or *lex Servilia Caepionis*. Not extortion law; perhaps treason law of 103.]

Schur, W.
† Das Zeitalter des Marius und Sulla. Klio, Beiheft 46, 1942. [Rev. Syme, JRS 1944, 103f.]

Scullard, H. H. From the Gracchi to Nero. London, 1959. And see Marsh.

Seletchki, 'When did the Romans lose Cirta in the Jugurthine war?' [in Russian], VDI 1957, 3, 167f. See Historia 1958, 508.

Sergeienko, M. E.
(1) 'Three versions in Plutarch's biography of Tiberius Gracchus' [in Russian], VDI 1956, 1, 47f. See Historia 1957, 381.
(2) 'The agrarian reform of Tiberius Gracchus and Appian's account' [in Russian], VDI 1958, 2, 150f. See Historia 1959, 504.

Serrao, F.
(1) La 'iurisdictio' del pretore peregrino. Milano, 1954. [Rev. Tibiletti, Athenaeum 1955, 387f.]
(2) 'Appunti sui "patroni" e sulla legittimazione all'accusa nei processi "repetundarum", Studi De Francisci (Milano, 1956) ii 471f.

Sevastianova, O. I. 'Appian and his Roman history' [in Russian], VDI 1950, 2, 253f. See Historia 1953–4, 119.

Sherwin-White, A. N.
(1) 'Poena legis repetundarum', PBSR 1949, 5f.
[During this period *infamia*, but no capital penalty; Sulla merely increased penalty financially.]
(2) 'The extortion procedure again', JRS 1952, 43f.
[Reply to Henderson.]
(3) 'Violence in Roman politics', JRS 1956, 1f.
(4) Review of Gabba (8).

Siber, H. 'Provocatio', ZSS 1942, 376f.
[Before C. Gracchus Senate could entrust magistrates having *imperium* with extraordinary *cognitio* exempt from *prouocatio*. Scaevola wanted this 133, but Nasica thought it insufficient. C. Gracchus abolished this and Senate substituted *SC ultimum*, which Populares never recognised.]

Skard, E. 'Marius speech in Sallust, Jug. chapter 85', SO 1941, 98f.
[Influenced by Cynicism.]

Smirin, V. M. 'Cicero's political position during the years of the Sullan dictatorship' [in Russian], VDI 1958, 4, 88f.
[Discussion in the light of Cic. *Quinct.* and *Rosc. Am.* See now Historia 1960, 512.]

Smith, R. E.
(1) The failure of the Roman Republic. Cambridge, 1955. [Rev. Cuff, Athenaeum 1956, 154f.; Deman, Latomus 1956, 272f.]

(2) Service in the post-Marian Roman army. Manchester, 1958.
(3) 'Roman literature after the Gracchi', G & R 1951, 123f.
[Sketches some of the views developed in (1).]

Steidle, W. Sallusts historische Monographien. Historia, Einzelschrift 3, Wiesbaden, 1958.

Sydenham, E. A.
(1) The Roman Republican coinage. London, 1952. With additional notes, important for this period, by H. Mattingly, pp. 221f.
(2) 'The date of Piso-Caepio', NC 1940, 164f.
[These *denarii*, on indications of finds, *c.* 96–5: to commemorate opponents of Saturninus.]

Syme, (Sir) R.
(1) 'Missing senators', Historia 1955, 52f.
[Names missed in Broughton (1). Now incorporated in Broughton's Supplement to MRR (New York, 1960).]
(2) 'Missing persons', Historia 1956, 204f.
[Names missed in RE viii A; some important ones for this period.]
(3) Review of Schur.

Taylor, L..R.
(1) 'Caesar's early career', CPh 1941, 113f.
[113f.: his nomination for the flaminate.]
(2) 'The rise of Julius Caesar', G & R 1957, 10f.
[A clear summary account for non-specialists.]

Thomsen, R.
(1) 'Das Jahr 91 v. Chr. und seine Voraussetzungen', C & M 1942-3, 13f.
(2) 'Erließ Tiberius Gracchus ein iustitium?', C & M 1944, 60f.
[Contrary to 'spirit of Roman public law' for *tr. pl.* to do this. Done by consul Scaevola.]

Tibiletti, G.
(1) 'Il possesso dell'*ager publicus* e le norme *de modo agrorum* sino ai Gracchi', Athenaeum 1948, 173f.; 1949, 3f.
(2) 'Ricerche di storia agraria romana', Athenaeum 1950, 183f.
(3) 'La politica delle colonie e città latine nella guerra sociale', RIL 1953, 45f.
(4) 'Le leggi *de iudiciis repetundarum* fino alla guerra sociale', Athenaeum 1953, 5f. and 396.
(5) 'Lo sviluppo del latifondo in Italia dall'epoca graccana al principio dell'Impero', Relazioni del X Congresso Internazionale di Scienze Storiche (Roma, 1955), ii 235f.
(6) 'Rome and the *ager Pergamenus*: the *acta* of 129 B. C.', JRS 1957, 136f.
[Discussion of 'SC on Adramyttium' and related texts.]
(7) Review of Serrao (1).

Valgiglio, E.
(1) Edition of Plutarch's Life of Sulla. Torino, 1954.
(2) Silla e la crisi repubblicana. Firenze, 1956.
[Rev. Gabba, Athenaeum 1957, 138f.]
(3) Edition of Plutarch's Life of Marius. Firenze, 1956. [Rev. Carney, JHS 1959, 172f.]
(4) Edition of Plutarch's Lives of the Gracchi. Roma, 1957.

Villers, R. 'Le dernier siècle de la République romaine: réflexions sur la dualité des pouvoirs', Mélanges H. Lévy-Bruhl (Paris, 1959), 307f.
[Survey of attempts to upset traditional political equilibrium. Tribunes failed because they had no homogeneous and organised support.]

Vitucci, G. 'Storia romana (1938–47)', Doxa 1949, 132f.

Völkl, K.

(1) 'Wie stark waren die Kimbern bei Vercellae (101 v. Chr.)?', AAHG 1953, 253f. [33 units; paper strength of 1000 each.]

(2) 'Zur zahlenmäßigen Stärke der Germanen bei Aquae Sextiae', AAHG 1954, 125f. [7000 to 10000 on the first day, over 20000 on the second, against Marius' (initial) 30000 to 35000.]

(3) 'Zum taktischen Verlauf der Schlacht bei Vercellae (101 v. Chr.)', RhM 1954, 89f.

Vogt, J.

(1) Struktur der antiken Sklavenkriege. Akad. d. Wissenschaften u. d. Literatur in Mainz, Abh. d. geistes- u. sozialwissenschaftlichen Klasse, 1957, 1. Wiesbaden, 1957.

(2) 'Pergamon und Aristonikos', Atti del III Congresso Internazionale di Epigrafia Greca e Latina (Roma, 1957), 45f.

[Detailed investigation of Roman war with Aristonicus and its background in Rome and Asia. Discussion of OGIS 435.]

Voirol, A. 'Die Münzen des Bellum sociale und ihre Symbolik', GNS 1953–4, 64f.

Volkmann, H. Sullas Marsch auf Rom. München 1958.

Vretska, K. Studien zu Sallusts Bellum Jugurthinum. SAWW ccxxix, 4. Wien, 1955.

Weiss, E. 'Ein Beitrag zur Frage nach dem Doppelbürgerrecht bei Griechen und Römern vor der Constitutio Antoniniana', JJP 1953–4, 71f.

[Rome did not permit retention of old citizenship, but only of selected rights and duties that had been part of it.]

Wilcken, U. 'Zur Entwicklung der römischen Diktatur', AAWB 1940, 1.

[Sulla revived traditional title and tried to retain old form of office as far as possible.]

Yarnold, E. J. 'The Latin law of Bantia', AJPh 1957, 163f.

[It is C. Gracchus' law against condemning a citizen to death *iniussu populi*: idea of oath later taken up by Saturninus.]

Zancan, P. 'Prolegomeni alla Giugurtina', ARIV 1942–3, 637f.; 1943–4, 143f.

Zennari, J. I Vercelli dei Celti nella valle Padana e l'invasione cimbrica della Venezia. Cremona, 1956.

Ziegler, K. 'L. Caecilius Metellus Diadematus', Gymnasium 1956, 483f.

[Nickname probably given by someone who remembered story of Ti. Gracchus and 'diadem'.]

## APPENDIX

Brink, A.

† 'De motieven van Tiberius Gracchus', TG 1941, 341f.

Gutiérrez Alviz, F.

† 'Los Gracos', Boletin de la Universidad de Granada 1945, 91f.

Mishulin, A. V.

† 'The slave revolts and the agrarian movement of the Gracchi' (in Russian). Moskva, 1940.

Nicolet, C.

'Confusio suffragorum', MEFR 1959, 145f.

[Accepts supposed law on this by C. Gracchus (Sall. ep. ad Caes. ii 8, 1) as important democratic reform, passed 123 to secure C. Gracchus' re-election and election of Fannius. Presupposes throughout that tribunes elected by centuries. Many interesting points of detail, but marred by extraordinary gaps in knowledge of historical background and modern work and by misuse of sources. Not likely to find much acceptance.]

'Note sur Appien, b. c. i 100, 467', MEFR 1959, 211f.

[Sulla's reforms as they affected legislative and electoral power of People. Comments as on previous entry.]

Passerini, A.

† Caio Mario. Roma, 1941.

Pérez Leñero, J.

† 'El "ager publicus" en el derecho romano', Revista de la Facultad de Derecho, Universidad de Madrid, 1948, 151f.

Smuts, F.

'Stoic influences on Tiberius Gracchus' (Afrikaans and English), A Class 1958, 106f.

[Orthodox treatment from philosophical point of view, divorced from historical background.]

Vavřínek, V.

'La révolte d'Aristonicos', Rozpravy Česk. Akad. Věd, Řada Společenských Věd, 1957, 2.

[Interesting Marxist interpretation of revolt and its consequences against social and economic background of Pergamum and of slave revolts of the period; hampered by ignorance – not the author's fault – of post-War Western work on Hellenistic and Roman history. – M' Aquillius' organisation established tax-farming (with *censoria locatio* in Rome) for countryside of Asia, exempting temples and cities. C. Gracchus, 'champion of the Equites', extended power of tax-farmers to cities and, by jury law, abolished governor's control over their activities.]

Zennari, J.

'La battaglia dei Vercelli o dei Campi Raudii', Annali della Biblioteca Governativa, Cremona, 1958, fasc. 2.

## II

*H. C. Boren*

# The Urban Side of the Gracchan Economic Crisis

# The Urban Side of the Gracchan Economic Crisis*

Henry C. Boren

THE critical period for the Roman Republic, it is often recognized, began in 133 B.C., the year of the tribuneship of Tiberius Gracchus. The measures which he and after him his brother Gaius (tribune in 123 and 122 B.C.) forced, over the opposition of most of the reluctant senatorial aristocracy, exposed the weaknesses of the Roman constitution with its dual development and divided responsibility and created new, irreconcilable factions whose strife eventually overthrew the Republic. The modern, who is likely to think of the English example of progress toward democracy through a series of concessions by the ruling classes, will perhaps conclude that the Gracchi only checked what might have been a similar evolution in Roman government. On the other hand, it is quite possible that Gaius Gracchus intended to foster development toward democracy, but along Greek lines, that is, by setting himself up as a tyrant, a popular champion, who would ally himself with the merchant class to destroy the power of the aristocratic families. Uncompromising nobles like Scipio Nasica and Lucius Opimius, who did not hesitate to use violence against the Gracchi and their followers, must certainly be held chiefly accountable for the vicious nature of the subsequent factional strife which racked the state until Augustus. In any case, the Gracchan period was the beginning of the end for the Republic and is consequently worth careful study.

It is the thesis of this paper that the most pressing problems, those which precipitated the disastrous political tug of war, were economic and that they were of a peculiarly urban nature not before fully recognized by historians of Rome. These conclusions are based partly on new evidence but depend primarily upon heretofore overlooked negative evidence and a fresh look at the traditional sources.

In their discussions of the economic crisis of this period, the historians, following Appian, Plutarch, and Tiberius Gracchus himself, have emphasized the rise of the slave-operated *latifundia,* the decline of the small farmer, and

* This study was made possible, in part, through a research grant from Southern Illinois University.

the failure to enforce the centuries-old Licinian-Sextian laws limiting individual holdings of public land. This is quite proper, up to a point, for there is no doubt that there was a serious agrarian social and economic crisis from which stemmed many serious problems. But it will be seen that for Rome the most troublesome problems were urban, though these were related, certainly, to agrarian conditions; further, the urban economic situation was the most important factor in the immediate crisis.

Evidence is presented in this paper to show that the city of Rome was generally prosperous during the middle of the second century, that spending on construction and luxuries was especially heavy in the years before the Gracchi, that there was a sharp decline in building and government spending generally just before 133, and that this decline, along with other economic factors, precipitated an especially acute crisis affecting particularly the city itself in 135–134, just as Tiberius Gracchus stood for office. It is inferred that the economy of the city had become geared closely to state expenditure, though, of course, it was also dependent upon heavy private spending in the area. The tremendous income and expenditure in the 140's and the sharp curtailment in succeeding years therefore reacted directly in every phase of the city's economy.

A survey of some widely used general works will show the extent to which this study modifies the customary views of the period. A. H. J. Greenidge, after giving some attention to the economic life of the city of Rome, says: "Italian agriculture was still the basis of the brilliant life of Rome. Had it not been so, the epoch of revolution could not have been ushered in by an agrarian law."[1] But the agrarian law did not "usher in" the epoch; Tiberius' measures were not seriously opposed as revolutionary until constitutional issues were injected into the struggle, when he challenged senatorial control of the provinces and of the public purse and threatened to make the tribuneship completely independent of senatorial authority by "recall" of unpopular tribunes and successive reelection of popular ones.[2]

Hugh Last writes of a general economic crisis in this period but refers primarily to the agricultural situation. He mentions the influx of large quantities of booty but notes the results only as they affected the rapid growth of the *latifundia*. He says: "Since there was no longer a livelihood to be got in

[1] *A History of Rome from the Tribunate of Tiberius Gracchus to the End of the Jugurthine War,* B.C. *133–104* (London, 1904), p. 59.

[2] It is worth noting that in its initial stages Tiberius' program was little more than an episode in the struggle between the Claudian and Scipionic factions. See Ronald Syme, *Journal of Roman Studies,* XXIV (1934), 104; K. Bilz, "Die Politik des P. Cornelius Scipio Aemilianus," *Würzburger Studien zur Altertumswissenschaft,* VII (1936), 66; also my article, "Livius Drusus, t. p. 122, and His Anti-Gracchan Program," *Classical Journal,* LII (1956), 27 f.

the countryside, there was a movement to the towns. . . . An export trade was the only hope of employment for the fresh arrivals." Though undeniable in part, each of these views requires reexamination. Last recognizes that Tiberius' main problem was to reduce the number of "paupers" in Rome.[3]

William E. Heitland discusses the subject in a conventional manner, remarking that "Gracchus . . . was right in recognizing the land-question as the fundamental problem of the state."[4] Tenney Frank also treats the period in the usual fashion,[5] and so, too, does H. H. Scullard, in his recent revision of Frank B. Marsh's survey of the later republic.[6] A few writers recognize to some degree that the city of Rome had its own problems, that the influx of booty in the middle of the century had its effect on the economy, and even that the wars of the 130's seriously drained the treasury.[7] The present writer, however, knows of no one who has sufficiently emphasized the impact of the influx of wealth on the economy of the city of Rome nor anyone who has closely considered the specifically urban side of the crisis with which Tiberius Gracchus tried to deal. Tiberius, of course, did make an agrarian law the core of his program, but the immediate crisis was less agrarian than urban, less concerned with land than with people. The land distribution law was merely his answer to the really pressing problem of what to do with the growing masses of the underprivileged in Rome.

Why had so many Latin and Italian small-holders streamed into the capital? It is not necessary to accept wholly the reasoning of Tiberius, who regarded the slave-operated *latifundia* as the chief factor in the migration. It would be equally logical to insist that the chief reason for the growing urban population in the United States today is the extensive adoption of modern farm machinery. The new and more profitable and efficient capitalistic farm operation in each instance certainly accounts for the dispossession of some farmers, but there are many reasons for such a migration. Early in the second century large numbers of men from the cities of the Italian allies already were flocking to Rome,[8] and there is no real evidence that the movement was not for the most part voluntary. The average Roman or Italian peasant living on his tiny hereditary acreage scrabbled desperately for a bare existence.

[3] In the *Cambridge Ancient History*, IX, 2–10.
[4] *The Roman Republic* (3 vols., Cambridge, Eng., 1923), II, 268.
[5] *An Economic History of Rome* (2d ed., Baltimore, Md., 1927), pp. 127 ff.
[6] *A History of the Roman World from 146 to 30* B.C. (2d ed., London, 1953), pp. 32 ff.
[7] See, for example, Guglielmo Ferrero, *The Greatness and Decline of Rome*, tr. Alfred E. Zimmern (5 vols., New York, 1907–1909), I, 50 ff.
[8] Livy 41.8. For a carefully written account of agricultural change in this period, see Tenney Frank, *Aspects of Social Behavior in Ancient Rome* (Cambridge, Mass., 1932), pp. 64 ff. Frank points out the possibility of overemphasizing the role of the *latifundia* in this period.

Surely he longed for something better. The ex-centurion who about 171 B.C. helped put down opposition to the military levy for the war against Perseus illustrates the bleak prospect the veterans faced.[9] This man, after twenty-two years of service in the army, had been willing to return to his inheritance—a single *iugerum* of land (about three fifths of a acre) and a small hut—but how many such veterans could endure the old family farm after service in Greece or Asia? Soldiers who became acquainted with city life often preferred its numerous opportunities and varied activities to the farm. Moreover, those who held no land were exempt from military service.

During most of the first two thirds of the second century Rome was a busy place, requiring large numbers of laborers and artisans. There was much construction, financed by indemnities, booty, tribute, and the income from mines. The armies were supplied, and ships were built; numerous shops supplied the needs of the city's growing population.[10] The extensive colonization programs of the 180's and 170's may indicate that during this period not all emigrating peasants could be assimilated into the urban population. Conversely, the cessation of colonization at mid-century (no Latin colonies were established after 181 and no Roman colonies between 157 and 122[11]) indicates that for many years before the Gracchi the migrating Romans and Italians were readily absorbed into the swelling, bustling metropolis.

A survey of economic activity affecting Rome in the first half of the second century and a more detailed study of the decade prior to 133 B.C. will both suggest what opportunities were available to immigrants in this period and help to show, as the result of an obvious interconnection between income and spending and economic well-being, what were the fluctuations in the city's economy in these years.

The first third of the century saw an influx of money to the city from indemnities (chiefly from Carthage, Macedonia, and Syria) and bullion from the Spanish mines that amounted to an estimated 300,000,000 *denarii*.[12] Much of the metal was quickly coined. It has been estimated that during a forty-three-year period 250,000,000 silver *denarii* were struck.[13] There was even an issue of gold coinage in 167 due to the "enormous quantities of gold staters . . . imported to Rome, partly as spoils of war and partly as payments of tribute."[14] Sale of slaves was a source of additional income. Individual sol-

[9] Livy 42.34.

[10] Greenidge speaks of the growth of the various trades in his *History*, p. 56.

[11] Velleius 1.15; Livy 11.34.

[12] Frank, *An Economic Survey of Ancient Rome*, Vol. I, *Rome and Italy of the Republic* (Baltimore, Md., 1933), p. 146.

[13] *Ibid.*

[14] Edward A. Sydenham, *The Coinage of the Roman Republic* (London, 1952), p. xxvi.

diers brought back booty. Macedonian mines were reopened in 158[15] and yielded some precious metals. By 157, a considerable surplus was reported in the treasury.[16] Despite a possible short deflationary period in the late 180's and 170's, the period generally was one of inflation—"inflation of a better kind, the issue of ever-increasing amounts of good money."[17] This new wealth of silver brought a change in the proportionate value of silver and copper, resulting in a gradual reduction of the weight of the bronze *as* from one ounce in 200 B.C. to half that amount at the end of the century (this may show merely that the *as* had become fiduciary coinage).

Money flowed rather freely in Rome in the decade of the 140's. Although the treasury was reported "in straits" from about 150 to about 146,[18] booty from Carthage, Corinth, and Macedonia soon bolstered public and private purses. Unfortunately, the available information is not very exact. According to Pliny, Carthage yielded 4,370 pounds of silver and "much" gold.[19] Frank estimates that Rome gained at least 45,000,000 *denarii* from both Carthage and Corinth.[20] Officers and soldiers brought back large amounts of private loot, especially from Corinth, and there were large numbers of slaves whose sale brought considerable sums. Rome, of course, had other sources of income. The productive mines in Spain, for example, increased in yield in this period.[21] Newly acquired gold mines in the Piedmont operated by Roman companies about this time produced so much metal that there was a considerable although short-lived drop in the value of gold.[22]

The extraordinary quantity of money moving into public and private coffers was not permitted to gather dust in the vaults. The years following 146 B.C. saw unusual spending in the city. Several important public buildings were put up in these years. Q. Caecilius Metellus, the conqueror of Macedonia, after his triumph built temples to Jupiter Stator and to Juno Regina, apparently within a magnificent portico erected shortly before.[23] Greek architects and sculptors were called in to design these buildings, which were

[15] Frank, *Economic Survey,* I, 256.

[16] Pliny *Natural History* 33.3.55. See the estimated balance sheet for the period 200–157 in Frank, *Economic Survey,* I, 145.

[17] Harold Mattingly, *Roman Coins from the Earliest Times to the Fall of the Western Empire* (London, 1928), p. 94.

[18] Frank, *Economic Survey,* I, 266.

[19] *Natural History* 33.141.

[20] *Economic Survey,* I, 230.

[21] Francis J. Wiseman, *Roman Spain* (London, 1956), p. 17; Frank, *Economic Survey,* I, 138.

[22] Strabo 4.6.12.

[23] See Samuel B. Platner and Thomas Ashby, *A Topographical Dictionary of Ancient Rome* (London, 1929), pp. 424, 304 f.; also Marian Elizabeth Blake, *Ancient Roman Construction in Italy from the Prehistoric Period to Augustine* (Washington, D. C., 1947), p. 131, with the references there cited, especially Velleius 1.11.3–5 and 2.1.1; Ferrero, I, 44, with references; Gaetano de Sanctis, *Storia dei Romani,* IV, 2 (Florence, 1953), pp. 76 ff., with his excellent notes.

reported to be the first temples in Rome of all-marble construction. "Liberated" Greek art works graced their interiors; in the central area before the temples were set Lysippus' famous statues of Alexander's generals. L. Mummius, the spoiler of Corinth, vowed a temple to Hercules Victor, which seems to have been dedicated by himself as censor in 142.[24] Pliny says Mummius filled Rome with statuary.[25] He furnished works of art, including statues by Praxiteles, for the embellishment of a temple dedicated to Felicitas, which was erected soon after 146 by L. Licinius Lucullus from booty taken in a Spanish campaign of 150–151.[26]

A major expenditure during the 140's was the construction of the Marcian aqueduct by Q. Marcius Rex at a cost of 180,000,000 *sesterces*.[27] At the same time (144–140 B.C.) Marcius repaired the Aqua Appia and the Aqua Anio Vetus. These additions to the water supply system testify to the almost explosive population growth of the city. Other major construction projects of the 140's included the rebuilding of the Pons Aemilius and the fortification of the Janiculum in 142.[28] Typical of the lavish expenditure of the times was the decision to gild the ceiling of the Capitoline temple, the first such ceiling in Rome.[29] Another large temple was undertaken in 138 B.C. by D. Junius Brutus Callaicus. Placed in the Circus Flaminius and dedicated to Mars, it contained statuary by Scopas.[30]

Significantly corroborative of heavy government spending in this period is the present author's statistical study of coin hoards of the time, which shows a relatively heavy volume of coinage for the 140's.[31] Since the Roman *tresviri monetales* ordinarily struck coins only as they were needed to meet expenses of state, coinage volume is a reliable reflection of public expenditure. Issues of *denarii* (to which the study was confined) during these years were consistently large—as one would expect on the basis of evidence presented in the paragraphs above.

It can be surmised that the years which saw such an extensive public building program also witnessed heavy spending by private persons. Much booty from the profitable wars of the 140's fell into private purses. Pliny associates the fall and looting of Corinth and Carthage with the introduction of new standards of luxury into the state.[32] In addition, contractors, artisans,

[24] Platner and Ashby, p. 256 (based on *Corpus Inscriptionum Latinarum*, I².626).

[25] *Natural History* 34.36.

[26] Platner and Ashby, p. 207.

[27] Frank, *Economic Survey*, I, 227.

[28] Platner and Ashby, pp. 397 f.

[29] Pliny *Natural History* 33.57.

[30] See references in Platner and Ashby, p. 328.

[31] "Numismatic Light on the Gracchan Crisis," *American Journal of Philology*, LXXIX (Apr., 1958), 140–155.

[32] *Natural History* 33.148–50.

and merchants would have prospered as a result of the heavy disbursements in and near Rome by the government. It must again be emphasized, however, that despite large private outlays which affected the prosperity level, it was inevitable that the general economy of the city should become intricately linked with the level of state expenditure and that any curtailment of that spending should immediately and disastrously react upon the economic fortunes of the masses of laborers and artisans at Rome.

In contrast with the prosperous 140's, the evidence—mostly negative—indicates a sharp reduction of public spending in the years after 138 B.C. Following construction of the temple to Mars in that year, there is no trace of further important public construction for thirteen years, until 125 B.C., when there was built the Tepulan aqueduct, less than a fifth as long as the Marcian, delivering less than a tenth the volume of water.[33] This sudden drop in the scale of public spending is corroborated by the statistical coin study mentioned above. Although the issues of coins cannot be dated with sufficient accuracy to permit a year-by-year analysis, the statistics show with high probability that the pattern of consistently large issues of *denarii* in the 140's was not repeated in the 130's. The total volume of coins struck in these years was decidedly lower.[34]

Additional evidence for the changed economic pattern of the 130's may be deduced from the nature of the wars Rome waged in this decade. These military operations, relatively minor, included wars against the Numantines in Spain, against the Scordisci in Macedonia, and against a slave revolt in Sicily. None of these conflicts could have produced much booty and no doubt, in fact, represented a net loss—which means that there was proportionally less available money to use for outlays in Rome. In the later stages of the Numantine War, Scipio Aemilianus used about sixty thousand troops;[35] the city provided little spoil, and in his triumph Scipio distributed only seven *denarii* each to his soldiers[36]—hardly enough for an extended spending spree in the big city! Probably the normal tribute from Spain was reduced by the disturbed conditions, and the flow of bullion from the mines may also have been lowered,[37] although the most productive mines, near New Carthage, probably were not affected. The repulsion of the Scordisci in Macedonia in 135 was no doubt a small task,[38] but for a time the tribute may

[33] Platner and Ashby, pp. 27 f.

[34] "Numismatic Light," pp. 144 f., 149 f.

[35] Wiseman, p. 25; cf. Frank, *Economic Survey,* I, 222 f.

[36] Florus 1.39; Pliny *Natural History* 33.141.

[37] Oliver Davies, *Roman Mines in Europe* (Oxford, 1935), p. 94.

[38] M. I. Rostovtzeff in *Social and Economic History of the Hellenistic World* (3 vols., Oxford, 1941), II, 758 f.

have been lessened and income from the mines reduced.[39] The most significant of these three military operations was the Sicilian Slave War, which worsened about 135 when Eunus organized the revolt into a war of serious proportions. Wide areas were devastated.[40] The grain tithe, on which Rome had come to depend not only for income but also for food, was in large part uncollectible. This cut in grain imports did much to precipitate the immediate crisis in Rome—which must now be scrutinized more closely.

The multitude of immigrants into Rome during the years before the Gracchi could not have relished their existence in the city, even though they came, for the most part, with a wave of prosperity. Housing was inadequate, and the newcomers were crowded into large, many-storied apartment houses called *insulae.* The long, gradual inflation which characterized most decades of the century brought with it gradually rising prices and no doubt tended to benefit the commercial classes. But in an age when there were no labor unions or cost-of-living wage increases to compensate, the economic condition of the lowest classes could not have been satisfactory even during the prosperity of the 140's. "The rise in prices was more automatic and inevitable than the rise in pay."[41] Moreover, the wars which brought huge booty to Rome had brought also large numbers of slaves. While many of these were used in farm operations, no doubt there was also a tendency in the city to replace free labor with slave labor, which during the 140's and for some years following was in such excellent supply. M. I. Rostovtzeff, noting that in Gracchan times there was unrest generally throughout the Mediterranean (and suggesting that this unrest was more important than the meager evidence indicates), attributes it in part to the abundance of cheap slave labor, which displaced free workers.[42] Fritz M. Heichelheim attributes these uprisings to a general drastic rise in grain prices, which reduced many of the proletarians to starvation levels.[43] The reported remarks to the Roman mob of Scipio Aemilianus, who called its members "step-children" of Italy and declared that he had brought most of them to Rome in chains,[44] indicate that there were numerous freedmen or others of foreign birth in the jeering crowd. If the lower-class wage earner lagged behind financially in times of

[39] These mines were almost worked out, however, and did not yield much ore. See Frank, *Economic Survey,* I, 256.

[40] Diodorus 36.1; Florus 2.7.

[41] Mattingly, *Roman Coins,* p. 94.

[42] *Op. cit.,* II, 756 f., 807 f. See also Greenidge, *History,* pp. 57 f., 203.

[43] See "On Ancient Price Trends from the Early First Millennium B.C. to Heraclius I," *Finanzarchiv,* XV (1954/55), 507.

[44] Valerius Maximus 6.2.3; Velleius 2.4.4.

relative prosperity, the years of depression in the 130's must have brought widespread unemployment and unrelieved misery.

The factor in the situation which was most critical, which aroused the leaderless mob, which cried out for action, which led to the election of Tiberius Gracchus, and which influenced the direction his reform program would take was a shortage of grain and the consequent high price for bread, both chiefly the result of the Sicilian Slave War. This seems certain, even in the absence of literary evidence. Grain prices were already extremely high.[45] The city of Rome had long depended on Sicily for grain. Cicero quotes old Cato as saying that Sicily was "the nation's storehouse, the nurse at whose breast the Roman people is fed."[46] Rome was accustomed not only to receive the grain tithe in tribute from Sicily but also to purchase additional quantities of Sicilian grain on the open market. Perhaps as much as 25 or 30 per cent of the Sicilian crop thus furnished bread for Rome's thousands.[47] Frank says that Rome, even before this period, was dependent for about half of all her grain on overseas imports, most, no doubt, from Sicily.[48] The substantial diminution of the Sicilian tenth and of regular, additional imports from Sicily therefore meant a shortage of tremendous proportions in Rome. Speculation surely followed, as was usual at Rome.[49] It appears also that grain prices in the Mediterranean area, already abnormally high, were further inflated by unusual pirate activity in this period.[50] The result was that at a time of economic distress for many wage earners, the price of bread, the staple of their diet, shot up to prohibitive levels. In Rome there must have been danger of actual starvation. Perhaps it was at this time that Lucilius wrote

> Deficit alma ceres,
> Nec plebes pane potitur.[51]

[45] Fritz M. Heichelheim, in the *Finanzarchiv* article, also "Römische Sozial- und Wirtschaftsgeschichte," in *Historia Mundi* (Bern, 1956), IV, 412, estimates a rise of grain prices in the Mediterranean area of 500 per cent between 140 and 138 B.C. and 1200 per cent between 140 and 127 B.C. (A personal letter from Heichelheim informs me the date 124 B.C. in *Historia Mundi* is a misprint.) These rather precise figures are based on a study of recent papyrus finds bearing on wheat prices, especially in Egypt. The same author, in *Wirtschaftliche Schwankungen der Zeit von Alexander bis Augustus* (Jena, 1930), p. 77, has noted the possible effect of the Sicilian Slave War on western Mediterranean markets.

[46] *In Verrem* 2.2.5.

[47] Vincent M. Scramuzza, *Roman Sicily* (Vol. III of *Economic Survey*), pp. 240–63.

[48] *Economic History,* p. 92.

[49] Theodor Mommsen, *The History of Rome,* tr. W. P. Dickson (4 vols., New York, 1887), IV, 597.

[50] See Heichelheim, *Wirtschaftliche Schwankungen,* p. 77; also Henry A. Ormerod, *Piracy in the Ancient World* (London, 1924), pp. 184 f.

[51] 5.fr.214; collected by W. H. Warmington for the Loeb Classical Library, *Remains of Old Latin* (Cambridge, Mass., 1938), III, 66.

To Tiberius Gracchus, it seemed that in one stroke all the social and economic changes of recent decades showed their direful consequences: the new *latifundia,* using slave labor, had drastically lowered the numbers of the old peasant stock; the immigration to Rome had given the city a numerous, noisy, and economically stricken human substratum; the new agriculture had concentrated on crops such as the olive and the grape, so that the agricultural area no longer could supply the city with grain and Rome was forced to depend on importation. Whatever proportion of this latter development was caused by the inability of Roman grain to compete with state and other imports was probably overlooked by Tiberius. Faced with the starveling proletariat and convinced that the problems were all of a piece, Tiberius saw an easy solution. He would relieve the overcrowded city and the unemployed by putting the latter on small farms. This would partially eliminate the extreme dependence on imports of overseas grain and at the same time inhibit the further development of the *latifundia,* or even reduce their numbers.

From a broader view, with longer perspective, it can now be seen that Tiberius oversimplified the problem, that the agricultural approach could not possibly have been extensive enough or popular enough with the lower-class Romans to solve the crisis, even if enough land had been available for distribution. Tiberius was not, in short, attempting to solve the most immediate, emphatically urban, problem. He was trying to turn back the clock. It must be admitted that Tiberius was actuated by other motives, of course. Appian reports, for example, his concern for the declining numbers of citizens eligible for army duty.[52]

The economic program begun by Gaius Gracchus ten years after the death of his brother is itself eloquent testimony that the problems with which he tried to deal were essentially urban. This has been rather generally recognized, though there has been a tendency to believe that these urban problems existed primarily as the result of the failure to solve the agrarian crisis. The material already presented will sufficiently modify this view. A reinterpretation of the literary evidence, with consideration of the negative evidence and with assistance from some new numismatic information, will serve to bring into clearer focus the conditions which the younger Gracchus faced.

The end of the Numantine War (133 B.C.) and the Sicilian Slave War (shortly after) ended the drain on the treasury from these unprofitable conflicts, and it may be assumed that normal income was restored from mines and tribute. The rich kingdom of Pergamum came to Rome by the will of

[52] Appian *Civil Wars* I.II.

Attalus III in 133 B.C., and although some years of military operations were required to establish firm Roman control, the full treasury appears immediately to have come to Rome; when in 132 the royal personal property was sold at public auction there, frenzied bidding was reported.[53] Regardless of the depressed situation of the wage earners, there were those whose purses permitted them to buy these evidences of having arrived in society. If the Attalid treasury was actually used, as Tiberius Gracchus proposed,[54] to stock the new small farms, this outlay may have had some effect on the city's economy. The numismatic study indicates at least some rise in public spending,[55] but there is exceptional difficulty in establishing chronology of coin issues in these years.

The continued absence of public construction, which was not resumed until Gaius Gracchus' program demanded it, does not indicate a very complete recovery of an economy so dependent on state spending in the area. It has already been pointed out that the only major item of public building in the 120's before the tribunate of Gaius Gracchus was a relatively small aqueduct built in 125. The need for another aqueduct so soon after the construction of the huge Aqua Marcia in the 140's implies that neither Tiberius Gracchus' land distribution scheme nor the depression did much to reduce the population of the city.

A reform of the coinage, which probably took place in the late 120's, appears to have been a deliberately inflationary measure and was perhaps designed to relieve the load of the debtor class. Outstanding numismatists of this period have assigned this reform—revaluation of the *denarius* from ten to sixteen *asses*—to the interval between 133 and 122 and have usually connected it with the programs of one of the Gracchi.[56] The present writer has shown conclusively that the early issues of the revalued *denarii* were quite small and consequently not connected with any large spending program.[57] Since the *as* was the money of account or of reckoning, the measure was certainly inflationary.[58] Later issues of the revalued *denarius* were much larger and are perhaps those which reflect the heavy spending of Gaius Gracchus. The implication, then, is that sometime during the 120's, most likely just before the election of Gaius, this revaluation was carried through because of

53 Pliny *Natural History* 33.149.

54 Plutarch *Tiberius Gracchus* 14.

55 "Numismatic Light," table A, p. 144, pp. 149 ff.

56 Sydenham, pp. xxviii f.; also Mattingly, in Appendix H of Sydenham, and in "Some New Studies of the Roman Republican Coinage," *Proceedings of the British Academy,* XVIII (London, 1933), 3–58.

57 "Numismatic Light," pp. 152 ff.

58 *Ibid.,* p. 153. For an opposing view, see Theodore V. Buttrey, Jr., "On the Retariffing of the Roman Denarius," American Numismatic Society *Museum Notes,* VII (1957), 57–65.

the deflated state of the monetary system, with the intention of giving relief to debtor groups. This move may have aided the poorer citizens somewhat, but it would have helped most the aristocrats who had been trying to keep up with the "Joneses"—the moneyed equestrians—and had run their estates into debt. This was probably the answer of the senatorial aristocrats to the continued economic difficulties of the 120's. But it was not enough.

Perhaps, as in the year when Tiberius Gracchus was elected to office, there was a particularly acute crisis in 123, again involving the grain supply and hence the price of bread, still abnormally high.[59] If Orosius may be trusted, a locust plague devoured the grain crops of Africa in 125 B.C.[60] This would naturally have affected grain prices all over the Mediterranean. A little later, a Roman commander, Fabius, confiscated grain in Spain and sent it to Rome.[61] Since it was normally unprofitable as well as unnecessary to ship grain that distance to Rome, there must have been great need for it. On the motion of Gaius Gracchus, Fabius was censured by the Senate—presumably for mistreating allies—and payment was ordered.[62] Certain of Gaius' own measures to ensure a stable grain supply through the building of granaries and to supply grain to the Roman poor at reduced prices certainly reflect ruinous fluctuations both in supplies and prices of grain and may also bear testimony to a particularly acute crisis, which brought about his election to office.

The heavy government outlays of 123 and 122 B.C. may have "pump primed" the economy of the city of Rome back to a semblance of prosperity. Besides the building of granaries and the subsidization of a grain supply for the poor, Gracchus also furnished clothing free to citizens in the army, constructed many miles of graded, expensive roads, and established colonies. Plutarch describes him as continually surrounded by numerous contractors and builders.[63] Gracchus' opponent in the tribunate in 122 B.C., Livius Drusus, with the backing of the Senate, also carried out a program to establish colonies, and some money would have been required for those which were actually established.[64] Ordinary public construction resumed in Rome in 121 B.C. when the consul, Opimius, built a basilica and refurbished the temple of Concord, and Q. Fabius Allobrogicus constructed the first of the great arches so typical of the Roman *fora* in later times.[65]

[59] Heichelheim estimates that grain prices in 127 were twelve times those of 140. See fn. 45. His research shows a lowering of prices after 127 but indicates a continuing high level for many years. See *Finanzarchiv*, XV, 508.

[60] 5.11.2.

[61] Plutarch *Gaius Gracchus* 6.

[62] *Ibid.*

[63] *Ibid.*, 6, 7.

[64] See my article "Livius Drusus," p. 31.

[65] Platner and Ashby, p. 590.

This enormous increase in spending in and about the city of Rome after 122 B.C.—corroborated in the author's numismatic statistical study[66]—no doubt put an end, at least temporarily, to the long-drawn economic depression. The supply of grain may, for a time, have been sufficient to prevent a continuation of the especially onerous hardship of high-priced bread in a time of deflation and unemployment. Prices seem to have declined, but not to the level of mid-century.[67] The problem of an adequate grain supply was not permanently solved and continued to plague the Roman authorities for centuries. Shortages of grain seem always to have given rise to an outcry of indignation demanding immediate action, as in the days of the Gracchi.

The conclusions reached in this paper can be summarized as follows. It appears that both of the Gracchi were faced with approximately the same problems: an overcrowded city, unemployment, unrest, and economic depression, plus an acute crisis due to grain shortage and consequent high prices of bread. Tiberius tried to solve the dilemma by reestablishing a class of "sturdy yeomen" (to use a term Englishmen have applied to about the same sort of program); Gaius, recognizing the failure of his brother's agrarian law, adopted other methods. The depression, which was tied in closely with the reduced level of state spending in the immediate vicinity of Rome, seems to have endured almost continuously for about fifteen years. The measures of the younger Gracchus, plus other stabilizing factors, appear to have e[illegible] the worst of the depression by 122 B.C.

*Southern Illinois University*

[66] "Numismatic Light," pp. 150 f.; cf. table A, p. 144.
[67] See fn. 59.

# III

*M. I. Henderson*

# The Establishment of the *Equester Ordo*

# THE ESTABLISHMENT OF THE *EQUESTER ORDO* *

By M. I. HENDERSON

A new moneyed class, thrusting rapidly to public estate in an ancient society, needed the enhancement of symbols and titles. Most Roman titles were military in origin, and it was natural to borrow the name of the old Roman cavalry, with its associations of high rank and property-census, antique tradition, and decorative imagery. Not less naturally, the military metaphors of the new civil *equites* concealed change and misled some secondary authors into anachronism. Modern historians too have been apt to assume the perpetuity of forms or conditions appropriate to the Servian Army, and long afterwards retailed in antiquarian descriptions of the 'exercitus urbanus'.[1] In general outline, indeed, the *comitia centuriata* may have retained its archaic structure; nevertheless, both Dionysius and Livy warn us plainly enough that changes had taken place. However modern hypotheses may attempt to reconcile the difference, the stark fact remains that two discrepant versions of the Servian system were current in the first century B.C.[2] Such institutions were perhaps not as static as the terminology which attached to them.

Still less static was the rising *ordo* which at some point usurped the title of *eques*. Notoriously, this title itself was applied to more than one category of persons within the political society (as opposed to the serving cavalry), not only at different times but at the same time. No uniform or simple definition of the so-called *equites* will serve; above all, data referring to the army of the past must not be unwarily imported into the political structure of a later age or the writer's own. This paper attempts to trace the connotations of the equestrian title in different periods examined separately; so far as possible from primary sources in each. It is convenient to begin with the last stage of the free Republic, where primary sources are not too scarce, although they may illustrate rather than resolve the ambiguities of the material.

## I. The Republic from 70 B.C.

It is agreed that the eighteen *centuriae equitum equo publico* were by this time obsolete as a military formation, and existed only in the voting *comitia centuriata*. It is also agreed that Cicero uses the term *equester ordo* of a body not confined to the 1,800 young men who traditionally formed these centuries.[3] But here the questions begin.

1. Were the voting *centuriae equitum* still numerically limited to 1,800 men?

No contemporary source warrants the assumption that they were. A fragment of the elder Cato implies some such limit in his own day, but it refers only to the old military establishment.[4] In the voting *comitia* the other centuries, at least, had been greatly enlarged by the admission of new citizens. There could be no purpose in limiting the number of constituents within any voting unit, nor in trimming a particular group of units to the requirements of an obsolete army. The *equitum centuriae* were certainly not immune from reform: on the contrary, their composition had been changed later than 129 B.C.[5]

2. Who, at this time, were the *equites equo publico*?

Sons of senators voted in the eighteen centuries with some undefined body of non-senatorial *equites*. The whole centuriate group is designated in *Phil.* VI, 13, where Cicero accuses L. Antonius of setting up a statue to himself with a fake inscription: 'ab equitibus Romanis equo publico . . . patrono.'[6] Cicero goes on: 'Quem umquam iste ordo adoptavit patronum? Si quemquam, debuit me.' Of what *ordo* could Cicero expect to be *patronus* (εἴ τις καὶ ἄλλος)? Of 1,800 young men, whom he nowhere mentions in all his lists of his friends and admirers? Only a preconceived theory could support that interpretation.

* Members of the Oxford Philological Society, to which an earlier version of this paper was read, are collectively thanked for useful criticisms. To P. A. Brunt, who read the present version in proof, I owe many apt suggestions.

[1] e.g., A. Stein, *Röm. Ritterstand*, ch. I (on the Republic). No full bibliography of the subject is attempted in this or the following notes.

[2] See Additional Note (below, p. 71).

[3] Strachan-Davidson, *Problems of Roman Criminal Law* II, 85 ff.; Hill, *Roman Middle Class*, 26.

[4] Cato, *ORF*², fr. 85 (see below, p. 110 f., n. 64).

[5] Cic. *De r.p.* IV, 2 (see below, pp. 70 ff.).

[6] Cf. *Phil.* VII, 16. The truth of the accusation is of course irrelevant.

*Iste ordo* should naturally and primarily refer to what Cicero elsewhere calls the *ordo equester*—the *publicani* (*flos equitum Romanorum*) or their peers, whose interests he had always defended as a *patronus* might have done.

3. Who were ' equitatus ille quem ego in clivo Capitolino te signifero ac principe collocaram ' (Cic. *Ad Att.* II 1 § VII) ?

Primarily, again, the *publicani* or their peers, whose *concordia* with the Senate was being advertised on the Nones of December, 63. But *adulescentes nobiles* were aligned with them in that formal demonstration, and the military metaphors of the *equitatus* are also applied to these. As Atticus was ' signifer ac princeps ' of the *publicani*, so the young L. Torquatus was, on the same occasion, ' princeps auctor signifer iuventutis '.[7] These young *senatorii* were certainly *equites equo publico*, members of the eighteen centuries ; [8] they certainly shared the XIV Rows of the Lex Roscia of 67 with the wider *equester ordo* which included the *publicani*.[9] Were not the *publicani* now arrayed with them as the non-senatorial members of this same body of *equites equo publico* ?

Not so, if the contemporary *equites equo publico* were subject (as scholars have surmised) to the general age-limit of military service in the Polybian army—forty-six exclusive. Atticus was turned forty-six before 63 B.C.[10] An age-limit, indeed, could serve no purpose after the military functions of the eighteen centuries were obsolete, and Mommsen believed that it had by now lapsed ; but its survival is inferred from *Comm. Pet.* 33, which represents the *equitum centuriae* as a small body of *adulescentes*. The question of this document's origin cannot be re-opened here,[11] but the particular item may be compared with data from other sources. Plutarch, too, represents Cicero's *equitatus* of 63 B.C. as νεανίσκοι.[12] We know that Plutarch conceived the *equites* of 70 B.C. *sub specie antiquitatis*, as a *transvectio* in which Pompeius apocryphally parades a quadruped before the censors.[13] The 1,800 young men may continue to ride on the authority of Plutarch and the *Commentariolum Petitionis*. But in Cicero's works, it should be noted, only the senatorial *equites* are ever described as *adulescentes* or *iuvenes* [14]—young, because they would normally enter the Senate at about thirty. This equestrian *iuventus* is associated with the *equitatus* of the senior Atticus and the *equester ordo* of the XIV Rows. It does not seem improbable that the eighteen centuries, like the rest of the *comitia*, now contained both *iuniores* and *seniores*, and that the *equites equo publico*, who were to exceed 5,000 in Augustan times, already numbered more than the old 1,800 cavalry. Traditionally, the eighteen centuries of *equites equo publico* were identified with the *equester ordo*.[15] Those who still limit them to 1,800 *iuniores* must suppose that the traditional connotation was broken when Cicero applied the term *equester ordo* to a wider body ; but if the eighteen centuries themselves were now a wider body, they could still be identified with the *equester ordo*, as they appear to be in *Phil.* VI, 13.

4. On this hypothesis, did the eighteen centuries now include the whole class of free-born *cives equestri censu* ?

Strachan-Davidson perceived the distinction implicit in Cicero's phrase: . . . ' Quem tu si *ex censu* spectas, *eques Romanus* est.' [16] To be an *eques* by census was good, but not yet an *eques* in some fuller sense, which can only be referred to the eighteen centuries. If these centuries now contained more than 1,800, the distinction is still implied ; and it has left further traces in this period. The Lex Roscia reserved special seats outside the XIV Rows for bankrupt *equites*—a concession to rank or standing over and above the mere census qualification (which Augustus later waived for former or hereditary *equites*).[17] Hereditary rank is recognized by the biographer of Atticus : ' a maioribus acceptam obtinuit equestrem dignitatem ' (Nepos, *Att.* 1 ; cf. id. *Pro Planc.* 32).

' Si ex censu spectas, eques Romanus est ' is still tantamount to a basic definition. The

[7] Cic. *Pro. Sull.* 34.

[8] Cic. *Pro Mur.* 73.

[9] Cic. *Phil.* II, 44.

[10] Born late in 110 (Nepos, *Att.* 21–22).

[11] *Epp. ad Quintum fratrem*, etc., ed. W. S. Watt (Oxford, 1958), 179 ff.; R. G. M. Nisbet, *JRS* 1961, 84 ff. Both refer correctly to the textual transmission with the spurious *epistula ad Octavianum*, which I missed by error in *JRS* 1950, 8 ff. J. P. V. D. Balsdon has kindly shown me his article (forthcoming in *CQ*) concluding that no proof is established for or against authenticity.

[12] *Caes.* 8.

[13] *Pomp.* 22. Pompeius had been consul and a senator for eight months.

[14] Cic. *Pro Mur.* 73 ; *Pro Sull.* 34 ; *Phil.* II, 16 and 44 ; Mommsen, *Sr.* III, 483 ff.

[15] Mommsen, *Sr.* III, 488 ff. ; see also below, p. 67.

[16] o.c. (n. 3), II, 86, quoting Cic. *Pro Rosc. com.* 42 and *Ad Q.F.* I, 2 VI.

[17] Cic. *Phil.* II, 44 ; Suet. *DA* 40.

civil title of *eques* nowhere appears dissociated from equestrian census, whatever its additional connotations. The term *equester ordo*, like the term *eques*, may have a double reference—either to the whole census class or to a more exclusive status. A rich *scriba* could call himself a member of the *equester ordo*. Yet it was deemed improper in a magistrate to give the equestrian gold ring to his *scriba* for wealth without virtue or merit besides.[18] Individual grants of the gold ring by magistrates or emperors were never controlled by forms of law, and we do not know whether it was expressly assigned to any class in Republican times; but the example of Verres' *scriba* shows, at least, that not every mark of equestrian rank or privilege was shared by the whole class of equestrian census.

The *tribuni aerarii* of the Lex Aurelia are sometimes comprised with the *decuria equitum* in the general description 'equites Romani',[19] from which it might be presumed that they were *equites* by census. This has been questioned on the strength of an inference from Schol. Bob., *In Clod. et Cur.* fr. 31. Cicero had made some joke to the effect that the *iudices* of Clodius would have fallen below the prescribed census without the bribes they had taken, and the scholiast specifies: 'amissis trecenis vel quadragenis millibus.' From these words it is conjectured that $\overline{\text{HS}}$ 300,000 was a census of *tribuni aerarii* between the *presumed* $\overline{\text{HS}}$ 400,000 of *equites* and the *later* (Augustan) *ducenarii*.[20] The scholiast does not deserve a combination so far-fetched. Perhaps he was not sure how much the Republican *census equester* was. At any rate, his elder and better colleague Asconius gives no support to the theory of two distinct census qualifications. After naming the three Aurelian *decuriae*, he continues: 'Rursus deinde Pompeius . . . promulgavit ut amplissimo ex censu, ex centuriis, aliter atque antea lecti iudices, aeque tamen ex iis tribus ordinibus, res iudicarent.'[21] Editors put in no commas before *aliter*, which they explain by the preceding words: the Lex Pompeia of 55 B.C. is supposed to have stepped up the census qualification for each *decuria*. But if so, Asconius should have written '*ampliori* ex censu'. And what is to be made of the next provision, 'ex centuriis'? A judiciary law could not alter the basic *classes* of the *comitia centuriata* without a *census populi*, which had not taken place since 70 B.C. The only innovation of 55 attested by Cic. *In Pis.* 94 (on which Asconius is commenting) concerned the selection and compulsion of individual *iudices*. 'Amplissimo ex censu ex centuriis' must surely refer to provisions of the Lex Aurelia which Pompeius reaffirmed and enforced: the rich and reluctant were compelled to serve, so that *iudices* should no longer (as in the Clodian trial) fall below the *amplissimus census*.[22] Only one census is here in question—the highest, which was the *census equester*. The inference is that it was prescribed for all *iudices*, including the *tribuni aerarii*.[23]

Asconius relates the *decuriae* both to the *centuriae* and to the *ordines*. *Ordo* is a word of general application, and Cicero uses it of the whole census class when he includes the *tribuni aerarii* among 'principes [equestris] ordinis' (*Pro Flacc.* 4). But in strict constitutional law the *comitia centuriata* was divided by *ordines* as well as by age and census. In *Pro Planc.* 21 Cicero distinguishes the two non-senatorial *decuriae* as *ordines* stratified above the *plebs* in the *comitia*: 'hi tot *equites Romani*, tot *tribuni aerarii*—nam *plebem* a iudicio dimisimus, quae cuncta comitiis adfuit.' In the *comitia* all these three *ordines* were present and voting for Plancius; in the *iudicium* only the first two remain. This connection of the *decuriae* with the *ordines* of the centuriate assembly was discerned by Hugh Last. As he noted, the censorship of 70 B.C. was restored for the express purpose of reconstituting the non-senatorial *iudices*;[24] accordingly, he based the Aurelian *decuria equitum* on the censorial *recognitio* of the *equitum centuriae*, and the *tribuni aerarii* on another

[18] Cic. II *Verr.* III, 181–187. A. Stein (o.c., n. 1, 36, 47 ff.) misinterprets Republican data by disregarding the impropriety of certain *viritim* grants. The mere fact that the gold ring was granted by Verres shows that it did not automatically ensue from equestrian census.

[19] Cic. *Pro Flacc.* 4; *Pro Rab. Post.* 14–15.

[20] Lange, *Röm. Alt.* I, 435; Zumpt, *Criminalr.* II *ii*, 194 (inferring the unattested Republican *census equester* from the Principate—a possible bet, but unsafe, since Augustus was given to reviewing census levels).

[21] Asc. 15.

[22] Compare Cic. *Ad Att.* I, 16 iii with *In Clod. et Cur.* fr. 31. Cicero, a rich and great man, did not want to serve (*In Pis.* 94). For the low social level of the Aurelian *iudices* generally, see *Pro Cluent.* 97 ff. (their names); together with all Cicero's polite expositions of law to the ignorant, and below, p. 66.

[23] Perhaps not *prescribed* for senatorial *iudices*, but *assumed* for senators before Augustus, since they began as *equites* (Cic. *Pro Sest.* 97; *Phil.* II, 44; Gelzer, *Nobilität*, = *Kl. Schr.* I, 20, 2), and could be demoted for bankruptcy (Asc. 74). In *Pro Sest.* 137, *industria* and *virtus* connote wealth and officer's rank.

[24] Cic. *In Caec.* 8; *CAH* IX, 336 ff.

recognized *ordo* of the *comitia centuriata*. His argument is not weakened but only simplified if, instead of defining the judicial *equites* as *equites equo publico* present or past, we can suppose them to be present members of the eighteen centuries, no longer limited to 1,800 young men.

Last conceded that the *tribuni aerarii* might have held some shadowy elective office and some distinct census; these conjectures are superfluous, based on no contemporary evidence, but merely on the assumption that the later political assembly exactly reproduced forms belonging to the military conditions of the past. In the archaic army each *ordo* was correlated with a peculiar census and equipment; but the military basis of the *classes* had disappeared since Marius or before, and the modern *equestris militia* was dissociated from the *equester census*.[25] In the civil constitution an *equester census* was attached to the corresponding *ordo*, but the *ordo senatorius* had no census of its own; nor is it likely that a specific assessment was imposed on every *ordo* of the *comitia* by some motiveless malignity, without military or fiscal purpose. No *census populi* was carried out from 70 B.C. until Augustus found new uses for it. The *classes* must have lost their ancient military precision,[26] and therefore much of their former practical importance. Their static *minima* could no longer reflect the real gradations of a society expanding in size and wealth. Judicial census was prescribed, but was hard to check or enforce except in cases of flagrant *egestas*. Bankrupts or other delinquents might be demoted from the Senate, or from the XIV Rows, or from their *tribus*, but we never hear of demotion or promotion from a *classis*. In the higher social strata the *classis* is overlaid by a structure of *ordines* subsisting on hereditary *dignitas* without censorial revision; lower down, the terms *classicus* and *infra classem*, used of the *prima classis* only, may suggest that inferior grades of census were by now confused or ignored. Property no longer sufficed to distinguish rank, as it had once distinguished the ranks of the army.

If it may be postulated that the Gracchan *iudices* were qualified, in the main, by a census,[27] the number so qualified must have risen rapidly through enrichment and enfranchisement. Within two generations, the descendants of the original class might be expected to assert their inherited dignity above the influx of *novi cives* and *nouveaux riches*, whom no census qualification could exclude. But social self-assertion required a basis in public law, and the censors of 70 B.C. were appointed to supply it. They will have picked their political allies, men of the social *milieu* of the pre-Sullan *iudices*, to form the eighteen centuries (with sons of senators), and the Aurelian *decuria equitum* could then be defined by reference to these centuries, with the judicial age-limits and non-senatorial birth. The *tribuni aerarii*, lifting one more title from the obsolete army ranks, formed another *decuria* and another centuriate *ordo*, lower in status but not in *census*. The class of *equester census* seems by this time to be wider still, for Cicero distinguishes the *tribuni aerarii* as a group above the *scribae*,[28] who were often wealthy; nor is it to be supposed that every other citizen of equestrian census was a scribe.

## II. Caesar's Dictatorship

'Quid? lege quae promulgata est de tertia decuria, nonne omnes iudiciariae leges Caesaris dissolvuntur? . . . At quae est ista tertia decuria? "Centurionum", inquit. Quid? isti ordini iudicatus lege Iulia, etiam ante Pompeia, Aurelia non patebat? "Census praefiniebatur", inquit. Non centurioni quidem solum, sed equiti etiam Romano; itaque viri fortissimi atque honestissimi, qui ordines duxerunt, res et iudicant et iudicaverunt' (Cic. *Phil.* I, 19–20).

The usual inference that Caesar retained only two *decuriae* is confirmed by Phil. V, 15: [M. Antonius] 'hanc tertiam decuriam *excogitavit*.' Suet. *DJ* 41 adds that Caesar's *decuriae* were of senators and *equites*: 'tribunos aerarios, quod erat tertium, sustulit.'[29]

[25] Cic. *Phil.* I, 20 (cf. Denniston, p. 179).

[26] Whether or not this is (as I believe) the meaning of *Dion. Hal.* IV 21: τῆς κλήσεως [τῶν λόχων] οὐκέτι τὴν ἀρχαίαν ἀκρίβειαν φυλαττούσης. κλῆσις should mean *classis*, as in IV, 20: see P. A. Brunt, *JRS* 1961, 82 (with Additional Note below, p. 71).

[27] See below, pp. 70 f.

[28] *In Cat.* IV, 15.

[29] cf. Dio XLIII, 26 (inaccurately formulated, but referring to the abolition of the third *decuria*). I cannot here agree with Brunt, *JRS* 1961, 76, n. 29.

'Non centurioni quidem solum' etc., does not imply a distinction of decurial census, for there was no census of centurions, and under the Lex Julia only one decurial census was involved. The distinction implied is of rank. Under all three laws (the argument runs) both centurions and *equites Romani* were subject to the prescribed census, and so—*itaque*—centurions too could be *iudices* (*sc.*, if they had this census). Under the Lex Julia, then, centurions could still be *iudices*. Therefore Caesar's one *decuria equitum* did not exclude any lower rank of persons who had previously been public *iudices*—nor indeed could he have wanted to reduce the numbers qualified for service. He abolished the *tribuni aerarii* as a *category*, but he introduced its *members* into his own *decuria equitum*, classifying all public *iudices* as *equites* and exploding the distinction of rank between them.

The policy was characteristic. If petty Italian *faeneratores* liked Caesar, the higher *equester ordo* was hostile [30]—and not only for the material loss of eastern tributary contracts. The episode of Laberius was remembered as a social insult for over 400 years. Laberius might pretend to be a blameless *eques Romanus* forced on to the stage, but the truth of it is known from Pollio: [31] the young Balbus, when he promoted a *histrio* to the gold ring and the XIV Rows at Gades, was deliberately imitating what Caesar had done in Rome. Already in 59 B.C. Caesar had threatened to repeal the Lex Roscia.[32] There is no direct proof that the Lex Roscia confined the XIV Rows to the higher Aurelian *equites*, nor that the new Lex Julia *theatralis* was Caesarian; the Dictator's acts were unfinished and ill recorded; but the affair of Laberius and the levelling of the Aurelian *decuriae* are enough evidence of his attitude to equestrian privilege. It was from this point that Augustus started to restore the prestige of the upper equestrian ranks.

## III. The Early Principate

For a preliminary classification of imperial *equites*, *ILS* provides a sufficient and convenient sample.[33] *Laticlavii* and others who moved into the Senate are excluded; the rest may be divided into four groups:—

(i) Seventy-eight men are *equo publico* but not *iudices*.
(ii) Twenty-one men are both *equo publico* and *iudices*.
(iii) Seventeen men are *iudices* but not *equo publico*.
(iv) Seventy-two men are *equites Romani* without the title *equo publico*.

In the Tabula Hebana (and by inference in the Lex Valeria Cornelia) the public *iudices* are expressly called *equites*; but this description is almost unique in imperial epigraphy. In one Tiberian inscription, *ILS* 6747, the word *equiti* is spilt into the judicial formula by some ignorant mistake: 'iudici de IIII decuriis *equiti* selectorum publicis privatisque.' In *ILS* 7122 (from Pannonia, third century A.D.) a *iudex* of the five *decuriae* is also described as *eques Romanus*. Otherwise, *iudices* may be additionally and separately entitled *equo publico*, as in (ii) above, or they may not, as in (iii). Some of these *iudices* at least must have had equestrian census, yet they leave the name of *eques Romanus* to (iv). Group (iv) is a mixed bunch, including colonial and municipal worthies from Italy and the provinces, some careers of the *equestris militia* and some of the centurion rank, some procurators, *scribae* and *viatores*. They must be distinguished from the group (i), in which the social level of careers is consistently higher, and the title is almost invariably abbreviated to *equo publico*. Group (iv) can scarcely have had anything in common beyond the equestrian census implied in their name. It seems that the plain title *eques Romanus*, as sometimes in the late Republic, now regularly denoted the general class of *cives equestri censu* without the status conferred by the *equus publicus* or by the office of *iudex*.

Groups (i) and (iii) overlap in (ii). Was there any necessary correlation between them? For instance, were the *iudices* regularly drawn from former (*equites*) *equo publico*? If so, it would be superfluous to record both titles, as is done in group (ii). Since, under Augustus,

[30] Cic. *Phil.* II, 94. *Faeneratores*: *Ad. fam.* VIII, 17 *ii*. On social classes of business men P. A. Brunt has kindly shown me a forthcoming paper.

[31] *Ad fam.* X, 32 *iii* (cf. ib. XII 18 *ii*; Gell. XVII, 14; Macrob. *Sat.* II, 7).

[32] Cic. *Ad Att.* II, 19 *iii*. It is *probable* that the Lex Roscia referred to *equites* in the stricter sense of the day. Imperial references (*e.g.* Hor. *Epod.* IV 16) do not necessarily retain the earlier historical connotation.

[33] See Appendix (below, p. 72). Since few inscriptions can safely be dated to the early Principate, chronological limits are here impracticable.

there were over 5,000 *equites equo publico* to barely 3,000 *iudices*,[34] no regular transition can be postulated; and in the inscriptions here classified nearly four-fifths of *equites equo publico* did not in fact become *iudices*. The evidence suggests two independent groups (i) and (iii), overlapping in (ii) but not necessarily correlated.

The *iudices* were a hard-worked class; Augustus, faced by a shortage of volunteers, had to lower the initial age and cut down *vacationes*.[35] By contrast, the *equites equo publico* have no functions attested in this period beyond funeral parades and the annual *transvectio*, revived by Augustus from far antiquity.[36] In our sample of inscriptions only a fifth of them served as *iudices*; out of ninety-nine verifiable careers only thirty-three record any military or administrative service, and of these only seven (all procurators) were among the emperor's equestrian *Beamten*. Most of group (i) are *boni et locupletes* of the Italian cities—men who could have entered the Senate, if they chose, without judicial or military drudgery—men like Ovid, ' usque a proavis vetus ordinis heres, non modo militiae turbine factus eques '.[37]

It was argued above that the *equites equo publico* of the late Republic were already exempt from the limits of number and age appropriate to active military service. Under Augustus, certainly, their number was unrestricted, and it must be inferred from Suet. *DA* 38 that no age limit was enforced. At first Augustus let them parade on foot if they were too old to ride; then—according as the text is read—[38] they could *either* give up the *equus publicus* if they did not want to keep it after thirty-five, *or* keep it if they did not want to give it up. The public horse was a fiction, and on either reading the age-limit did not operate in practice.[39] It was acknowledged in theory or ceremony, as a part of the military pretence and pageantry which Augustus staged in his *transvectio*, with the new uniform of the *trabea*, the olive wreath, and the embodied horse.

But the Republican *equites equo publico* had retained their place both in the topmost centuries of the *comitia* and (as interpreted above) in the higher *decuria equitum*, until Caesar knocked the two *decuriae* into one. Under Augustus their judicial function drops away, and it is not they, but the equestrian *iudices*, who stand with the senators in the topmost ten centuries of A.D. 5. The Lex Valeria Cornelia gave fresh constitutional recognition to these *iudices*, but the novelty need not be exaggerated. Their presence in the new ten centuries will seem the less surprising if it be admitted that a class of equestrian *iudices* had been incorporated in the topmost centuries since 70 B.C. Augustus was recomposing traditional elements—the *iudices*, still entitled *equites* in this comitial context, and the senators, who had belonged to the eighteen centuries till after 129 B.C.

The *iudices* perhaps appreciated this reward for toil, but it may not have been envied by the *equites equo publico*. By 63 B.C. attendance at the eighteen centuries' ballot was casual.[40] Who, in A.D. 5, would have exchanged the spectacular *transvectio* for precedence in the dull and desultory *comitia*? The *centuriae equitum*, wherever they voted, were now manifest in the *turmae*.[41] As for judicial work, it had long been shirked by the *élite* of both *ordines*. Catulus and his noble friends left it, till the Verrine crisis, to despised new senators; after 70, men of the better sort had to be compelled to it by the Lex Pompeia.[42] Augustus, while he restored his Senate's jurisdiction, released his senators from duty in the *iudicia publica*.[43]

[34] Dion. Hal. VI, 13; Plin. *NH* XXXIII, 30–31 (four *decuriae* with barely 1,000 in each, but the fourth was composed of members of the other three).

[35] Suet. *DA* 32.

[36] Suet. *DA* 38.

[37] *Am.* III, 15, 5–6. Cf. Suet. *DA* 40 (heredity). *ILS* 6640, though later, is typical. The idea that *equites equo publico* valued posts in the early Imperial service (Duff, *Freedmen*, 218) is illusory: for their class it was an *ambitio praepostera*.

[38] ' Mox reddendi equi gratiam fecit eis qui maiores annorum quinque et triginta retinere eum *nollent* ' (*mallent* em.: Mommsen, taking *gratiam fecit* to mean ' excused ').

[39] A *lower* age-limit presumably did operate to divide the adult *equites* from the *turmae* of the *iuventus*. But why did Augustus create these *equites iuniores* if their seniors were also a *iuventus* under 35? Neither body had any practical purpose to account for it.

[40] Cic. *Pro Mur.* 73: Natta makes an *acte de présence* on the special occasion of a relative's election. The centuriate group-vote made non-attendance easy, and July was hot. By A.D. 14 even the *plebs* cared little for elections (Tac. *A.* I, 15).

[41] Dion. Hal. VI, 13; *ILS* I, 314. Whether the eighteen centuries still survived in the *comitia* we do not know. The *turmae*, with their *VI viri centuriarum equitum*, seem to correspond to the *sex suffragia*, whose relation to the total of eighteen is also uncertain.

[42] Cic. I *Verr.* 49; contrast the *consilium* of the *iudicium Iunianum* (named in *Pro Cluentio, passim*). On the social level of *iudices* after 70, see above, p. 63, n. 22.

[43] *E silentio*, but the silence is too long and portentous to be negative. Augustus made amends for C. Gracchus by restoring the crucial *quaestio de repetundis* for the Senate to judge its peers; it was logical to leave common crimes to equestrian *iudices*.

He also needed an equestrian aristocracy to renew and sustain the *discrimina ordinum dignitatumque* : but he could not force it back to the judicial benches. He uplifted the caste humiliated by Caesar, and reconstituted the *equites equo publico* outside the *decuriae*, in his new organization of the centuriate *turmae*. This was to be his personal honours list and Order of Chivalry, emancipated from public and political services in the Republican sense, but reflecting the *Res Publica Reddita* in its antiquarian display, local munificence, and liege loyalty.

In the Tabula Hebana the *equites equo publico* figure only in the funeral parade ; and here a lacuna seems to leave room for only two of the three ranks of Dio's Augustan *cortèges* [44] :—(1) senators (2) οἱ ἱππεῖς οἱ ἐκ τοῦ τέλους, (3) οἱ ἄλλοι (ἱππεῖς). Since senators cannot be excluded, nor cited after the *equites*, the lacuna more probably contained a reference to senators than to a second group of *equites*. Nevertheless, we may ask which group is meant by ' the *equites* of the *ordo* ' (τέλος). Suetonius also distinguishes them. In *DA* 32 he deals comprehensively with the Augustan *iudices* ; in cc. 33–34 he turns to the Emperor's activities ; then, in cc. 35–40, he sets out the three *ordines* in their sequence—*Senatus*, *Equites*, *Populus*. Now these *Equites* are the *equites equo publico* ; it is they who stand between Senate and People as the *equester ordo* proper. The *iudices* are treated separately and apart, in another context. The term *equester ordo* (in the strict sense) consistently denoted the *equites equo publico*—first as the ancient cavalry, then as the Aurelian *decuria equitum* ; now it reverted from the *iudices* to the antiquarian horse-parade of the Augustan *turmae*.

So much, indeed, might be inferred from Pliny, if Pliny were believed. In *NH* XXXIII, 29–30 he states that the Augustan *iudices* were not called *equites* but *iudices*, and the title of *eques* subsisted in the *turmae equorum publicorum*. We all know better since the Tabula Hebana was revealed to us. Yet is it so certain that Pliny knew less ? He knew well enough that the *iudices* were called *equites* in Cicero's day, and again in his own.[45] In A.D. 23 (he relates) ' in unitatem venit equester ordo ' (c. 32). The *ordo* had somehow been split, and its two parts were reunited under Tiberius ; meanwhile the title of *eques* ' subsistebat '—remained valid—in the *turmae*. That the title was in fact used by others too was surely known to Pliny, and his readers needed no telling. What concerned him was its strict application at a particular date. For this strict application Pliny's criterion is not the Lex Valeria Cornelia ; there, in the context of the *comitia centuriata*, the *iudices* were indeed called *equites*, but elsewhere (as we have seen) they preferred the name of *iudex*. Pliny connotes the rank of *eques* strictly with its most coveted appurtenance, the *anuli aurei*. In cc. 29–33 his main theme is clear : Who had, and who came to have, the equestrian gold ring ? [46] But in his development of this theme there are problems to be faced.

c.30 : The four Augustan *decuriae* contained barely 1,000 *iudices* in each ; [47] most of the *iudices* had the iron ring, and were not called *equites* ; this title was proper to the *equites* of the *turmae* (who had the gold ring).

c. 32 : In A.D. 23 the *equester ordo* ' came to unity '. Since baser persons were usurping the gold ring, the qualifications for it were now defined as follows : (*a*) three generations of free birth and equestrian census, (*b*) the right of the XIV Rows *lege Iulia theatrali*. After this, people flocked (*gregatim*) to acquire the gold ring (*insigne id*).

c. 33 : Consequently Gaius added a fifth *decuria* ; the *decuriae* which under Augustus could not be filled no longer had room for the *iudices* ; in this promiscuous rush even *liberti* (illegally) got the gold ring (*ornamenta ea*).

So far the story is at least coherent. Under Augustus, when *iudices* mostly had the iron ring, they were hard to recruit (cf. Suet. *DA* 32) ; but after the right of the gold ring was defined as stated (c. 32), the Augustan *decuriae* were overflowed with aspirants to it. If these are the facts, it follows that the definition of A.D. 23 (while excluding baser persons) had

[44] Dio, LVI, 42 (cf. LV, 2). Tab. Heb. ll. 55–7, restored to include *equites* without the *equus publicus* by Ehrenberg and Jones (*Documents*, no. 94*a*) and more convincingly to include the senators by Oliver and Palmer (*AJP* 1954, 225 ff.).

[45] *NH* XXXIII, 34 (see also below, p. 70), and 29 (' quod antea ', etc.).

[46] i.e. through the regular and corporate channels : Pliny ignores *viritim* grants, which were capricious. (above, p. 63 and n. 18).

[47] i.e. 3,000 in all (p. 66, n. 34).

extended the gold ring of the *equites* to some or all of the *iudices* who had not possessed it before, so that it could now be acquired by judicial service.[48]

By the definition of A.D. 23 (probably quoted from a dated *SC*) the gold ring was not conferred for free birth and equestrian census alone: the right of the XIV Rows was an additional qualification. We should infer that by the Lex Julia *theatralis* the XIV Rows included (besides *equites equo publico*) those *iudices* who first acquired the gold ring in A.D. 23. The iron ring was still worn by some senators in the late Republic; and in Augustan times, since senators could wear it in mourning, it cannot have been a badge of servile birth or sub-equestrian census.[49]

But here follows the greatest difficulty of the whole excursus. In c. 33, concerning the inrush of *liberti* under Gaius, our text reads:— ' ut . . . passimque ad ornamenta ea etiam servitute liberati transiliant, quod antea numquam erat factum, *q̄m* * *in ferreo anulo et equites iudicesque intellegebantur*. adeoque id promiscuum esse coepit ut apud Claudium Caesarem . . . Flavius Proculus quadringentos ex ea causa reos postularet.'

* quoniam] in *del. Mayhoff*.

The *quoniam* clause is a double *non-sequitur*. (*a*) *Equites* had the gold ring by Augustan times, *iudices* acquired it under Tiberius—yet we are now told that previously to Gaius both *equites* and *iudices* had the iron ring (not the gold). (*b*) This statement is offered as the reason (*quoniam*) why the gold ring had never before been acquired by *liberti*—but it is no reason for that, and the true reason has already been given: *liberti* were disqualified by the definition of A.D. 23 (c. 32). Mere factual error cannot account for this: it is a mental or logical breakdown. No wonder that historians have despaired of Pliny's wits.[50]

Yet a question occurs: how is the clause to be construed? With deletion of *in*, it is supposed to mean: ' since both *equites* and *iudices* were known (i.e. diagnosed) by the iron ring.' Pliny's Latin may be eccentric, but this use of *intellegi* with ablative need not be fathered on him by an editor. The original text gives a well-warranted construction, which can only mean: ' since by the term *ferreus anulus* both *equites* and *iudices* were denoted ' (cf. Cic. *De off.* I, 142: ' εὐταξία, in qua intelligitur ordinis conservatio '). But why did not Pliny write ' in ferreo anulo *erant* ' (cf. c. 30)? ' In ferreo anulo *intellegebantur* ' is the construction of a note or gloss on words. A bewildered scholiast, failing to grasp the disqualification of *liberti*, seems to be guessing why they had never got the gold ring, somewhat as follows:— ' Assuming that the term *ferreus anulus* previously denoted both *equites* and *iudices*, then *liberti* who became *equites* or *iudices* would previously have got only the iron ring.' The clause irrelevantly breaks a clear sequence from the illegal intrusion of *liberti* to their later prosecution for it. A gloss may at least be suspected; and the rest of Pliny's account should be examined without prejudice.

It has already been noted that the iron ring did not under Augustus imply sub-equestrian census or standing. If Pliny is consistent with his theme, he should be speaking only of *iudices* who were in these respects equestrian. The fifth *decuria* of Gaius qualified for the gold ring by the definition of A.D. 23. But were Pliny's four Augustan *decuriae* all equestrian? Suet. *DA* 32 reckons only three, to which Augustus added a fourth of sub-equestrian census for cases ' de levioribus summis '—*iudicia privata*. Further, the Tiberian inscription *ILS* 6747, though otherwise garbled, is not necessarily wrong in its total of IIII *decuriae publicae privataeque* (quoted above, p. 65). Hence it is usually inferred that of Pliny's four *decuriae* one was sub-equestrian. Indeed, E. S. Staveley and A. H. M. Jones have suggested that of his eventual five *decuriae* only three were of equestrian census, and only these were among the ' iudices selecti ' who served in the *iudicia publica*. Their theory is based on two inscriptions, reading ' iudex selectus decuriis tribus ', and ' ex V decuriis

[48] Pliny implies that some *iudices* (not *maior pars*) had it before—presumably because they were also *equo publico*, as in group (ii) of the inscriptions classified above (p. 65). On the question of sub-equestrian *decuriae* see below, pp. 68 f.

[49] *Equites equo publico* certainly sat in the XIV Rows (Suet. *DA* 40). On the iron ring, ibid. 100; Pliny *NH* XXXIII, 21 (Republican senators). In Pliny's own day (ibid. 23; Petron. *Sat.* 32; younger Pliny *Epp.* VIII 6 iv) it was worn by rich *liberti*—but perhaps not before A.D. 23.

[50] ' Garbled information ' (A. H. M. Jones, *JRS* 1955, 16) would be too mild in this particular instance. I do not follow E. S. Staveley's attempt to defend it (*Rhein. Mus.* 1953, 203); and he interprets the clause as if it read ' . . . *esse* intellegebantur'.

decuriarum III '.[51] But the case is not compelling, for the term *iudex selectus* is elsewhere collocated with four or five *decuriae*; nor, if in two inscriptions *tres decuriae* are specially mentioned, does it follow that only these three were equestrian. In two other inscriptions, for that matter, one *prima decuria* is specially mentioned.[52] If either one or three could be accorded priority, the distinction can hardly be of census. The first three *decuriae* were certainly older than the fourth or fifth,[53] and nothing more is needed to account for these minor and infrequent boasts.

Pliny states (c. 31) that the *decuria* of *nongenti* was drawn from the other three Augustan *decuriae* (' ex *omnibus* electi ') as *custodes* of the urns ' in comitiis '. In the Tabula Hebana the comitial procedure begins with ' senatores itemque equites *omnium* decuriarum quae iudiciorum *publicorum* gratia constitutae sunt erunt '; from these, afterwards, the *nongenti* are drawn by lot.[54] The *nongenti* therefore included no sub-equestrian or private *iudices*. ' *Omnes* decuriae ' implies more than two—excluding the *nongenti*, who were not yet drawn. Theoretically, ' omnes ' might be made to include either (*a*) a senatorial *decuria*, or (*b*) some future *decuria* not yet created: but neither hypothesis is plausible.[55] The natural interpretation is that the *nongenti* were drawn from more than two equestrian *decuriae*, which would correspond to the three pre-existing *decuriae* specified by Pliny.

The conclusion might have been questionable if the difference between Pliny and Suetonius were substantial. But we now know that the *nongenti* were a creation of the Lex Valeria Cornelia of A.D. 5, existing only in the *comitia*, having no independent judicial function or membership. Suetonius was not obliged to mention them in his judicial context; and he correctly records the situation before A.D. 5, when in any context there were only three equestrian *decuriae* with a sub-equestrian fourth. This older reckoning survives in the garbled *ILS* 6747, either through ignorance or because the dedicatee was a *iudex* before A.D. 5. Pliny too, though he counts the *nongenti* as the fourth *decuria*, separates them from the first three: ' praeter hos etiamnum nongenti ' . . . whom he then defines by the peculiar electoral function which the Tabula Hebana has confirmed. It is his reckoning that differs from Suetonius, not the facts behind it; and it was Pliny's reckoning that became customary.

The titles of the Augustan *decuriae* are recorded by Pliny as if they were obsolete, and never more than ornamental. The decurial names of *iudices* and *selecti* can hardly have been statutory, for both denoted a wider body than one *decuria*. Even in a legal document, the fourth *decuria* is named by reference to informal usage: ' nongenti, sive ii custodes adpellantur.'[56] It was argued above that the *tribuni aerarii* had no distinct census, and that Caesar abolished the distinction of rank. The Augustan revival of the courtesy title is not significant. Before the Lex Aurelia, different judicial *decuriae* had been equal in rank and status. On the evidence of the Tabula Hebana it appears that Augustus reverted to the former condition of equality between *iudices* of the *iudicia publica*, with three—or, from A.D. 5, four—equestrian *decuriae*.

Equestrian, that is, by census and by comitial and judicial rank—not yet by the gold ring. If Pliny has been rightly interpreted, his evidence elucidates the groups exhibited by inscriptions (above, p. 65).

(i) The *equites equo publico*, transferred from the (former) Aurelian *decuria equitum* to the new Augustan *turmae*, are the *equester ordo* proper, having the gold ring and the XIV Rows without judicial service.

(ii) Some public *iudices* have the gold ring as being (also) *equites equo publico*.

(iii) Public *iudices* as such, though incorporated as *equites* in the *comitia centuriata* of A.D. 5, first acquire the gold ring in A.D. 23, thereby entering the *equester ordo* and bringing it ' in unitatem '. But (except in the *comitia*) they avoid the title of *equites*, for they are distinguished as public *iudices* (like the Aurelian *tribuni aerarii*) from the class of *equites Romani* by mere census and free birth.

[51] *ILS* 5016, 6862; see *opp. citt.* above (n. 50). I fully accept their view that ' iudex selectus ' = *iudex* of the *iudicia publica* (which implies equestrian census at least), but I would apply the term to all the V *decuriae*.

[52] *CIL* II, 4275, IX 5567.

[53] *Equestris hereditas* too had unofficial snob-value (Sen. *De ben.* III, 7 VII). The fifth *decuria* was polluted by newcomers, the fourth was drawn by lot: the first three were (by these standards) socially pure.

[54] Tab. Heb. ll. 11–14 (referring back to Lex Valeria Cornelia).

[55] (*a*) See above, (p. 66, n. 43); (*b*) Augustus could barely fill the present *decuriae* (above pp. 66 f.).

[56] Tab. Heb. ll. 13–15.

(iv) The general census class of *equites Romani*, not being public *iudices*, did not qualify for the new centuries of A.D. 5. From A.D. 23, again, it was through judicial service that the gold ring was acquired by *iudices* not being *equites equo publico*. The terms of the official definition are clear : the gold ring was not granted for birth and census without the XIV Rows *lege Iulia* ; and this right must have belonged to public *iudices* as such, since they were henceforth qualified for the gold ring.

The Emperor, of course, obeyed no rules ; he could bestow the gold ring at pleasure, with the money if it was needed, on any mime-actor or any *tribunus militum* scarred with the rope of slavery.[57] But it is over-simple to say that ' the gold ring and the title of *eques* were . . . shared by all citizens of free birth and equestrian census '.[58] In a stubbornly class-conscious society the uses of the *equestre nomen* and its privileges were both multiple and variable. A title adopted for show without substance is liable to debasement by new-comers, and its connotations alter as the prouder elements of the class find ways of marking their superiority. Some change and complication appears in the Principate before the higher *equites* were graced as *illustres*, or by later courtly epithets. Already in Cicero's day, when the class was old enough to demarcate its social strata, we have traced three homonymous grades : *equites* (*equo publico*), *equites* (*alias tribuni aerarii*), *equites* (' si ex censu spectas '). But this was not the first stage of its history or its name.

## IV. Postcript on Beginnings

This section presents no clinching argument, but an open question : When did the *iudices Gracchani* claim or acquire the title of *equites* ? In the dark age from the Gracchi to Sulla primary sources are too few and ambiguous for a plain answer, but the alternatives can be defined.

The title was current by 88 B.C. at the latest, for Cicero in 80 or 79 described the Marian régime as *equester splendor*.[59] His rhetorical allusion to *equites* and *tribuni aerarii* as *ordines* of 100 B.C. cannot be pressed.[60] Pliny implies that the *equestre nomen* was used before Cicero, in 63, ' finally stabilized ' it,[61] but he seems to regard it as post-Gracchan. The *ordo* (he says) was first designated by the name of *iudices*, which was then disputed ' vario seditionum eventu ', and for some time (*aliquamdiu*) the class was called *publicani*. From this evidence the safest conclusion is that the equestrian title was adopted sometime between 121 and 88.

Yet there is room for doubt. The *seditionum eventus* that cancelled the name of *iudices* was most probably Sulla's victory, which transferred the *iudicia* to the Senate ; but by then the title of *equites* was also in common use. It is possible that before Sulla, as after 70 B.C., the names of *iudices* and *equites* were used alternatively and concurrently.

Pliny—for this period a remote secondary source—quotes a passage of Junius Congus Gracchanus on a disputed title of the Roman cavalry. The ' Gracchanus ' is adducing an honourable and warlike etymology for the rude name of *trossuli* which the *equites* of his time resented.[62] It is a piece of antiquarian nonsense ; yet antiquarian nonsense began from the first *superba usurpatio* of the *equestre nomen*, and is so typical of the new *ordo equester* that it stirs a vague suspicion. Why was the learned friend of C. Gracchus so interested in the past history of the Roman cavalry and in disputes, past or present, over their title ?

Not much, however, can be made of the Gracchanus. A more positive sign of contemporary interest is the *plebiscitum* concerning the *equitum centuriae* soon after 129 B.C.—only some twenty years before Cicero, who records it, was born into the new *ordo*. ' Quam commode ' (says his Scipio) ' ordines descripti, aetates, classes, equitatus, in quo suffragia sunt etiam senatus, nimis multis iam stulte hanc utilitatem tolli cupientibus, qui novam

[57] Suet. *DJ* 39 (Laberius) ; Hor. *Epod.* IV (the reward of fighting for Octavian).

[58] A. H. M. Jones, *JRS* 1955, 16.

[59] *Pro Rosc. Am.* 140. The choice of date is immaterial.

[60] *Pro. Rab. perd.* 27.

[61] l.c., c. 34. As Pliny explains, the *equester ordo* was then inserted beside *Senatus Populusque*—presumably in some *SC* concerning Catiline's conspiracy or the *concordia ordinum* of 63.

[62] *Trossulus*, an obscure word, is clearly a diminutive of contempt. The town of Trossulum, linked by Gracchanus (ibid. c. 35–6) with some ancient or legendary exploit of the cavalry, is mentioned only by the antiquarians.

largitionem quaerunt aliquo plebiscito reddendorum equorum.'[63] 'Scipio' is somewhat inhibited by his dramatic date, but the passage can only mean (as is generally agreed) that the Senate was expelled from the *equitum centuriae*. It is to be noted incidentally that these centuries, if they had previously contained the *suffragia* of the whole Senate, must already have cast off the age-limit of the cavalry.[64]

The highest voting-group of the *comitia*, then, was being reformed by some *popularis largitor*—whether C. Gracchus or a close predecessor. Is this a coincidence, unconnected with judiciary reform? We now know that in A.D. 5 the *iudices* called *equites* were formally related to the top group of centuries in the *comitia*; and it has been argued above (after Last's initiative) that in 70 B.C. the judicial *decuria equitum* was in the same way related to the eighteen equestrian centuries. If so, it is tempting to suppose that the Gracchan *iudices* were already based on the reformed *centuriae* of *equites equo publico*. 'Scipio' does not prophesy how these centuries were to be composed after the expulsion of senators, but if (*ex hypothesi*) they constituted the new judicial class, they may have been qualified by non-senatorial status and equestrian census.

This hypothesis does not claim direct proof, but only the attraction of coherence. If the Gracchan centuries of *equites equo publico* were coextensive with the Gracchan class of *equester census*, it would become a matter of minor importance whether the title or the census were to be supplied as the lost qualification of *iudices* in the Lex Acilia, ll. 12 and 16. The new *equester ordo* could be consistently dissociated from the archaic cavalry, and its initial identity with the census class would explain why its equestrian title invariably presupposes the census in all its later connotations.

The ambiguity of these connotations justifies a final summary of the conclusions here suggested.

1. Whether the equestrian title dates from Gracchan times or later, in 70 B.C. an *élite* of the new judicial class was distinguished from the larger class of equestrian census by enrolment in the eighteen centuries of *equites equo publico*, from which the Aurelian *decuria equitum* was drawn. The Aurelian *tribuni aerarii*, also of equestrian census, formed another *ordo* of the *comitia centuriata*. Both they and other free-born citizens of equestrian census were commonly known as *equites Romani*.

2. Caesar as Dictator abolished the category of *tribuni aerarii*, and included all non-senatorial public *iudices* in one *decuria equitum*.

3. Augustus recreated an *élite* of *equites equo publico*, with the right of the gold ring, in his new *turmae*, outside the *decuriae*. His four *decuriae* of public *iudices* (including the composite *nongenti*) were incorporated in the reformed *comitia centuriata* of A.D. 5 with the title of *equites*, but were elsewhere known as *iudices*, and did not (unless they were also *equo publico*) acquire the gold ring until A.D. 23. Other free-born *cives equestri censu* were still known as *equites Romani*.

## Additional Note

This note can attempt no more than a general warning of uncertainties not always admitted.

About the *comitia centuriata* ancient authors seem less confident than modern. We may infer a third-century reform from the combination of Livy I, 43 xii and XXIV, 7 xii, but we have no evidence that Livy ever described or dated it: he merely notes some causes for the difference, evident to his readers, between the Servian Army and the *comitia* of his day. Nor can we say that Dionysius, in *AR* IV, 21 iii, is more than 'vaguely conscious of a change' (Brunt, *JRS* 1961, 82). Still less is it to be supposed that Cic. *De r. p.* II, 39 f. represents the result of a reform. Cicero gives one antiquarian reconstruction of the Servian system: Livy and Dionysius later follow another. The discrepancy merely reflects

[63] *De r.p.* IV, 2. Stein (o.c., n. 1, 2) oddly imagines that the *senators* wanted this *plebiscitum*; but *largitio* refers, as often, to a *popularis* measure (cf. C. Gracchus in *De off.* II, 72 and *Tusc.* III, 48).

[64] It is not necessary to determine exactly when the old cavalry disappeared from the army, since it may before that time have lost connection with the political *comitia centuriata*. Its survival 'ultra C. Gracchum' seems, however, to be merely Pliny's own tentative inference from Gracchanus (ibid., c. 36).

speculation and uncertainty about the past. Our scanty evidence points not only to early but to recent changes. (*a*) The reform of Cic. *De r.p.* IV, 2, soon after 129 B.C., cannot be denied, however it may be interpreted. (*b*) A more comprehensive reform by C. Gracchus is probably misunderstood, but not necessarily invented, by ps.-Sall. *ad Caes.* II, 8. (*c*) A 'restoration' of the Servian centuriate system by Sulla, though doubtless misdated to 88 B.C. by App. *BC* I, 59, appears credible in 81–80, and would account for the later speculations as to what the Servian system really *was*—for Sulla restored what he *chose*. The electoral experiments of the eighties with the Italian franchise, involving some tribal changes (Sisenna fr. 17), may have affected the form as well as the composition of the *comitia*. For all this the extant sources are notoriously poor, but they do not regard the *comitia centuriata* as an immutable or fossilized institution; neither do Livy and Dionysius. Against that assumption the Tabula Hebana should be a fresh warning. Antiquity shows no surprise at the innovations of A.D. 5 (Syme, *Tacitus*, 756 ff.).

## APPENDIX

This is the index of the inscriptions classified above (p. 65). The sample is confined to *ILS*, where readers can conveniently check it; further additions would not significantly enlarge our fraction of a lost total of many thousands. Future senators are excluded; also members of the *iuventus* (but *ILS* 1313 is doubtful). 'Iudex' here means a *iudex* of the (IV or V) Roman *decuriae* (or of the *selecti*).

| | (i) *Equo publico* (not *iudex*) | | | | (ii) *Equo publico* also *iudex* | (iii) *Iudex* (not *equo publico*) | (iv) *Eques Romanus* (not *equo publico*) | | |
|---|---|---|---|---|---|---|---|---|---|
| *ILS*: | 411 | 3952 | 6642 | 6980 | 2730 | 1320 | 533 (2) | 6141 | 7122 |
| | 1013 | 4326 | 6645 | 6983 | 2733 | 1397 | 1033 | 6173 | 7127 |
| | 1143 | 4873 | 6646 | 7127 | 2739 | 1403 | 1318 | 6188*a* | 7129 |
| | 1147 | 4946 | 6656 | 7132 | 5006 | 1419 | 1371 | 6264 | 7131 |
| | ?1313 | 4949 | 6664 | 7133 | 5012 | 2713 | 1383 | 6333 | 7163 |
| | 1314 | 4956 | 6665 | 7136 | 5016 | 4093 | 1390 | 6334 | 7188 |
| | 1315 | 5019 | 6666 | 7147 | 5274 | 6542 | 1990 | 6447 | 7742*a* |
| | 1368 | 5058 | 6678 | 7364 | 6457 | 6616 | 1991 (2) | 6448 | 7742*b* |
| | 1381 | 5272 | 6691 | 9188 | 6523 | 6674 | 2669 | 6484 | 7744 |
| | 1391 | 5473 | 6696 | | 6572 | 6747† | 2751 | 6494 | 8068 |
| | 1415 | 5501 | 6715 | | 6573 | 6764 | 2754 | 6495 | 8091 |
| | 1423 | 5533 | 6716 | | 6644 | 6772 | 2758 | 6496 | 8092 |
| | 1436 | 5551 | 6730 | | 6713 | 6863*a* | 2766 | 6574 | 8113 |
| | 1443 | 5679 | 6738 | | 6726 | 6982 | 2767 | 6630 | 8510 |
| | 1466 | 5755 | 6740 | | 6744 | 6989 | 3168 | 6648 | 8534 |
| | 1910 | 6138 | 6745 | | 6747* | 7122 | 4513 | 6717 | 8558*a* |
| | 2667 | 6139 | 6760 | | 6862 | 9394 | 4947 | 6765 | 8833 |
| | 2711 | 6148 | 6770 | | 6936 | | 5054 | 6810 | 8853 |
| | 2727 | 6472 | 6815 | | 6981 | | 5056 | 6835 | 8859 |
| | 2735 | 6523 | 6856 | | 9406 | | 5484 | 6838 | 8995 |
| | 2748 | 6598 | 6858 | | 9407 | | 5597 (2) | 7021 | 9018 |
| | 2759 | 6639 | 6942 | | | | 5712 | 7108 | 9041 |
| | 3742 | 6640 | 6954 | | | | 5728 | 7116 (2) | |

* Second part. † First part.

# IV

*P. A. Brunt*

# The Equites in the Late Republic

# THE EQUITES IN THE LATE REPUBLIC

by

P. A. Brunt
*(Oriel College, Oxford)*

A conspicuous feature of politics in the late Republic is the discord between Senate and Equites. Its extent and causes are not so clearly evident. The Equites in a broad sense comprised all free-born citizens outside the Senate worth 400,000 HSS or more[1]; like the senators they were thus men of property, and they were often linked with them by social intercourse[2], common pursuits such as jurisprudence and oratory[3],

1. First attested for 67 BC (Porphyry on Hor. *ep.* I 1, 62). Not a high qualification; a gentleman needed 600,000 *a year* to live in luxury, 100,000 with economy, Cic. *Parad.* 49. All eminent Equites must have had far more than the minimum. The term 'Equites' also of course denotes holders of the public horse, and it may be that the Gracchan *iudices* were drawn only from this narrower class (including perhaps past holders). This distinction is generally ignored in my paper, and does not (I think) affect the argument. But see p. 120, n. 4.

2. M. Antonius, *cos.* 99, and L. Crassus, *cos.* 95, had equestrian friends (Cic. *Brut.* 168; *de orat.* II 2-3; Val. Max. IX 1, 1). Figures such as Atticus and Balbus need no comment.

3. They were supplanting senators as jurists in the late Republic (W. Kunkel, *Herkunft u. soz. Stellung der röm. Juristen* [1952], 50 ff). For orators of equestrian status or origin, like Cicero himself and Caelius, *Brut.* 131; 167-8; 205; 241-2; 246; 271; 280 ff, cf. *Fam.* XIII 12,2; 22,1.

and even marriage ties [1]. Now the Republic was brought down by ambitious generals who were able to play on the social discontents of a rural proletariate from which the army was recruited, discontents which had earlier given rise to the agitations of "popular" leaders [2]. But most Equites had no more sympathy than most senators with the grievances of the poor; they too were attached to the preservation of order and property rights. Hence they had opposed Tiberius Gracchus [3] and turned against Gaius Gracchus when he resorted to violence [4], and later they united with the Senate against Saturninus [5] and Catilina [6]. Civil war, the natural result of the ambitions of military leaders, was also repugnant to their interests. Cicero's ideal of "concordia ordinum" was calculated to appeal both to the class from which he had sprung and that to which he had risen [7]. It is true that it comprised the maintenance of the Republican constitution, that is to say of senatorial authority, and Equites, who did not share in the political privileges of the senators, were more apt than they to seek "otium" at any price, even at the price of "regnum" [8]. Still, it might seem that there was more to unite the orders than to divide them. In fact the area of conflict was in my view more restricted than is often supposed. The Equites, in the sense defined, did not constitute an united pressure group with economic interests opposed to those of the Senate; it is only the publicans who can at times be seen in this light. Moreover the disputes that occurred turned as much perhaps on claims to rank and social and political recognition as on desire for profits, and they died away precisely in the crucial period, the age of Pompey and Caesar.

. . . . . . . . . . . . . . . . . . . . . . . . . . . . . . . . . . .

We can detect the origin of conflicts in Polybius' analysis of the

1. Cf. Cic. *Sulla* 25; *Planc.* 27 for equestrian *cognati* of the Manlii Torquati and Appulei Saturnini; the mother of L. Piso, *cos.* 58, from Placentia was doubtless of equestrian family (Cic. *Pis.* fr. 9-11).

2. See Brunt, *JRS* LII (1962) 69 ff.

3. *Per.* Livy 58; Vell. II 3,2.

4. Sall. *BJ* 42; presumably the Senate made it clear that they would not tamper with his judiciary legislation but allow the Equites so much share in the government ('spes societatis'). Opimius' acquittal, by the timocratic centuries, confirms Sallust.

5. Cic. *Rab. Perd.* 20-27.

6. e.g. Cic. *Cat.* IV 15.

7. See generally H. Strasbuger, *Concordia Ordinum* (1931)

8. Cic. *Att.* VII 7,5: 'An publicanos (bonos putas) qui numquam firmi sed nunc Caesari sunt amicissimi, an faeneratores, an agricolas, quibus optatissimum est otium? nisi eos timere putas ne sub regno sint qui id numquam, dum modo otiosi essent, recusarunt'. The remark is applicable to all classes mentioned. Cf R. Syme, *Roman Revolution* [1939] 14 citing Sall. *Hist.* I 55, 9 M; Cic. *Cluent.* 153; *Rab. Post.* 13.

reasons which made the people dependent on the Senate; by the people he of course means the Equites. [1] Firstly, almost all of them (so he says) were engaged in public contracts, and those contracts, when they were allegedly burdensome, could be cancelled or modified by the Senate. And secondly, senators were judges in most of the important criminal and civil cases (VI 17). The Equites were thus controlled by a body to which they could rarely rise. [2] This control must have been a source sometimes of economic loss, and often of irritation. In the pre-Gracchan period more than one dispute had occurred between the publicans and the senate or magistrates. [3] Gaius Gracchus did not create a cleavage between the orders, as hostile sources suggest, [4] rather he found such a cleavage in existence, and sought equestrian support by enhancing the power of the order. His new regulation of the taxes of Asia, which became the model for that of eastern provinces acquired later, gave the publicans new opportunities for profit and added to their influence, since the State relied heavily on the taxes they collected. [5] Gracchus did not touch the Senate's control over contracts, [6] but he made it more likely that it would be responsive to the claims of the Equites by giving them jurisdiction. They obtained a monopoly of seats in the *repetundae* court, where they could sit in judgement on senators themselves, and even Cicero admits that this made governors subservient to the publicans. [7] (Curiously enough we know of at most only two men, Rutilius and perhaps Gabinius, on whom equestrian jurors vented their wrath for checking equestrian oppression in the provinces. [8])

1. VI. 17, cf. F. W. WALBANK *ad loc.* Cicero too virtually equates people and Equites in I *Verr.* 38; *Cluent,* 151; *Phil.* IV 15; VIII 8.

2. But among *novi homines* note P. Rupilius (*cos.* 132), once a servant of the publicans, Val. Max. VI 9,8.

3. Appendix 1.

4. e.g. Varro *ap* Non. Marc. 728 L; Diod. XXXIV-V, 25,1; *Per.* Liv. 60.

5. Cic. *de imp. Cn. Pomp.* 17: 'Publicani... suas rationes et copias in illam provinciam (Asiam) contulerunt, quorum ipsorum per se res et fortunae curae esse debent. Etenim si vectigalia nervos esse rei publicae semper duximus, eum certe ordinem qui exercet illa firmamentum ceterorum ordinum recte esse dicemus. *Planc.* 23: Flos enim equitum Romanorum, ornamentum civitatis, firmamentum rei publicae publicanorum ordine continetur'. These statements were largely true, until Rome could adopt a different method tax collection. Cf. *Prov. Cons.* 11.

6. Cf. *Schol. Bobb.* 157 St. on the petition made in 61 'lege Sempronia'.

7. II *Verr.* 3,94 (a damaging admission in view of his pro-equestrian bias, cf. I *Verr.* 38); cf. Diod. (Posidonius) XXXIV-V 2,31 (anachronistic); 25.

8. RUTILIUS, GREENIDGE and CLAY, *Sources for Roman History* 125 ff; Cicero (*Fam.* I 9,26 cf *Planc.* 33) implies that Q. Scaevola too suffered from equestrian malice, but we do not know how. For the publicans' hatred of Gabinius see Cic. *Prov. Cons.* 11-12; *Pis* 41; *Qu. fr.* III 2,2; extricated by Pompey's influence from the charge of *maiestas*, he was convicted of *repetundae.*

In my view Gracchus went further still; he gave Equites a share in other criminal jurisdiction and extended their share in hearing civil suits, thus relieving them of that dependence on senatorial courts which Polybius had stressed. I have argued this in Appendix 2.

These new rights guaranted the material interests of the Equites; they also assured them of a place of splendour and dignity in the republic. [1] We should not underrate the importance they attached to this, nor their craving for *gratia*, *auctoritas* and even *honores* [2]. From two well-known passages in Cicero's speeches (*Cluent.* 150 ff; *Rab. Post.* 13 ff) it might be concluded that the prominent Equites of the pre-Sullan epoch were men who had abjured the advantages and risks of political life and preferred the quiet and security of private enrichment. But this was only true of some among them. Cicero himself describes them as men "qui summum locum civitatis *aut non potuerunt* ascendere aut non petiverunt" (*Cluent.* 151). As early as 111, if we may believe Sallust (*BJ* 31), Memmius was declaiming against the nobility's monopoly of office, and in the next decade Marius was not the only man of equestrian origin who rose to high office. [3] Sallust also says that at this time the plebs preferred new men (*ibid.* 65), but elections to the consulship and praetorship were decided by the votes of the rich, and in any case the electors could not have shown this preference, unless there had been candidates drawn from the Equites who sought high office. It was not a meaningless gesture when Drusus, in depriving Equites of their control of the courts, proposed to enrol many of them in the Senate. Sulla actually carried out his plan; the enlarged senate thereafter had room for many more men of equestrian origin, and from Caesar's time they swarmed into the *curia*. [4] This is unintelligible except on the assumption that many

1. Cic. *Rab. perd.* 20 ('omnem dignitatem iudiciorum'); the optimates could not endure this 'equestrem splendorem' (*Rosc. Amer.* 140).

2. 'Splendor', *Sest.* 137; 'dignitas', *Att.* I 17,9; *Prov. Cons.* 10; *Pis.* 41; *Cael.* 3 ('quaecumque in equite Romano dignitas esse possit, quae certe potest esse maxima'); Nepos, *Att.* I, 1; 6,2 (cf. last note, and Brunt, *JRS* LI (1961) 76 on social privileges which illustrated equestrian rank.) 'Gratia' and 'auctoritas', see e.g. *Planc.* 32; *Att.* I 2,2 Nepos, *Att.* 6,2. Equites claimed, and Optimates objected to, unfettered freedom of speech, *Planc.* 33 ff.

3. Cn. Aufidius, C. Billienus, C. Flavius Fimbria and Cn. Mallius Maximus happen to be known.

4. Cf. H. Hill, *CQ* XXVI (1932) 171 ff; R. Syme, *PBSR* XIV 1 ff; *Rom. Rev.* ch. vi; E. Gabba, *Origini della guerra sociale* (extract from *Athen.* 1934 (1954), ch. vii. Hill is surely right in thinking that Sulla recruited his new senators chiefly fom the 18 centuries, but not in equating them with nobles or even men of old senatorial family. The 18 centuries cannot have consisted mainly of such men; given the low rate of reproduction in senatorial families, which were constantly dying out, there cannot have been six members of such families outside the Senate

Equites did not share Atticus' attachment to "honestum otium". [1] In his defence of the younger Plancius Cicero makes it plain that the father of his client was not the only Eques who desired a political career for his son. [2] To some extent equestrian resentment of the arrogance of the nobility underlay the occasional discord of the orders. [3]

It is, however, much more clearly attested that between 123 and the time of Sulla the gravest disputes arose from the use the Equites made of their judicial powers and from the efforts of the Senate to dislodge them from the courts. At last in 70 the lex Aurelia effected a compromise. Thereafter we hear no more of conflicts, except in 61 to 59 when the refusal of the Senate to reduce the liabilities of the Asian publicans and a proposal to make equestrian jurors subject to penalties for corruption caused a new breach. [4] This was temporary. In the trials of the Ciceronian age both senatorial and equestrian jurors were often divided between condemnation and acquittal; they did not always vote in blocks. [5] In 49 the richest Equites were at first Pompeian in sentiment, [6] and if some of them later changed

before Sulla for every member in it. *Comm. Pet.* 33 assumes that the 18 centuries will follow the lead of the *ordo equester*, i.e. probably of the publicans, the flower of the order (*Planc.* 23). For publicans etc. in the 18 centuries see Livy XLIII 16. For Caesar's senators see especially Cic. *Phil.* III 15, and note Aelius Lamia, 'princeps equestris ordinis' (*Fam.* XI 16, 2), and aedile in 45.

1. Cic. *Att.* I 17,5; Nepos, *Att.* 6. He could clearly have obtained office, if he had wished it. The Senate was full of men of his type even before Caesar (cf. Cic. *Sull.* 24; *Planc.* 17), often helped by votes of their fellow *municipales* (*Planc.* 19 ff) and especially by publican influence (*ibid.* 23).

2. *Planc.* 24.

3. Hence attacks on the *pauci* (not the Senate) by Cicero (II *Verr.* 5, 180 ff; *Cluent.* 152 etc.) and by Sallust (eg. *BJ* 41), reflecting the feelings of the class from which they had come.

4. Cic. *Att.* I 17. 8-10; 18, 3 and 7; 19,6; II 1,8; 16,2; *Planc.* 35; *Off.* III 88; *Qu. fr.* I 1, 33; Schol. Bobb. 156 St.; Suet. *Caes.* 20,3; App. *BC* II 13; Dio XXXVII 7,4. We must not suppose that because Caesar's law reducing the publicans' liabilities won them over in 59, they remained on his side thereafter, cf. n. 6; p. 122, n. 1. It is interesting that Metellus Nepos' law abolishing Italian *portoria* in 60 is not mentioned as another equestrian grievance; it seems only to have evoked senatorial complaints (Dio XXXVII 51; Cic. *Att.* II 16,1). The publicans who collected these dues were vexatious (*Qu. fr.* I 1,33), but probably not very powerful; all Equites (as well as senators) not directly profiting from the contract would have welcomed relief from duties on their imports and exports.

5. Note especially the cases recorded in *Qu. fr.* II 4,6 and Asconius 55 C. Divisions within decuries are also recorded or implied in e.g. Ascon. 28; 53; 56; 61; Cic. *Att.* I 16,5; IV 15,4; *Qu. fr.* III 4,1; the last text shows that not all non-senatorial jurors were against Gabinius at his first trial. We have to allow for bribery and pressure, and also for some respect for evidence and justice.

6. *Fam.* VIII 14,3. Cf. Broughton p. 154 ff. *infra*.

their attitude, it was only because they had come to think that Caesar's victory would be more likely to preserve their lives and property. [1] Moreover senators as well as Equites were more or less equally divided in the civil war. [2] On each side men made a personal choice: there was no struggle between the orders as such. [3] In the last crises of the Republic their discord was not an important factor.

. . . . . . . . . . . . . . . . . . . . . . . . . . . . . . . . .

The earlier disputes had arisen mainly over public contracts and control of the courts, and concerned the publicans, who also dominated equestrian juries (p. 123 n. 6), rather than all Equites. In addition, the exclusiveness of the nobility exacerbated the feelings of many members of the order. But were there also, as is often supposed, more fundamental divergencies of economic interest? Were the Equites the "business class", and did their business activities, or more specifically, their trading interests determine their political attitudes and underlie their quarrels with the Senate?

The Equites (in the sense defined at the beginning of this paper) were certainly a mixed lot. They cannot all or mostly have been traders or, more vaguely, "businessmen". In Italy the chief source of wealth was not trade or manufacture but agriculture. Most Equites must, like the senators, have been landowners, even before the enfranchisement of the Italian gentry in the 80s, and still more thereafter. Land was the safest as well as the most respectable investment. [4] The publicans themselves had to find securities in land for the due performance of their contracts. [5] The leading publican of Cicero's day, Gnaeus Plancius, was a man of hereditary distinction in the flourishing rural district of Atina. [6] The successful merchant did well to invest his gains in land, [7] a course that even freedmen such as Isidorus or Trimalchio followed. [8] Most Equites were probably no

1. T. Frank, *ESAR* I 311 gives a selection of evidence; add esp. Cic. *Att.* VIII 1,3; 13, 1-2; 16, 1-2; IX 1,2; 7, 4-5; 8,1; 9,2; 10,2; 13, 4-6. Caesar's conduct on his entry into Rome in 49 and the warnings of Curio (X 4,8) and Caelius (*Fam.* VIII 16,1) revived fears of his intentions, cf. *Att.* X 8; 14,1. Dio XLI 18,6 says, that most senators *and Equites* ultimately joined Pompey; 40 distinguished Equites fell fighting for him (App. *BC* II 82).

2. For senators see D. R. Shackleton Bailey, *CQ* 1960, 253 ff.

3. Cf. Cic. *Att.* VII 7,5.

4. Cato, *de agric. pr.;* Cic. *Off.* I 151.

5. Polyb. VI 17 (οὐσίας); Lex. Put. (*FIRA* III no. 153) I 7; III 13; Cic. II *Verr.* I, 142-3; Lex. Malac. (*FIRA* I no. 24) 63-4; Ps-Ascon. 252 St. *Praedia* had to be in Italy, Cic. *Flacc.* 79-80 and Schol. Bobb. 106 St.

6. *Planc.* 32 cf. 21-2 on his equestrian friends from the neighbourhood.

7. Cic. *Off.* I 151.

8. Plin. *NH* XXXIII 135; I assume that as a freedman Isidorus made his money in trade or industry. Cf. Petron. 76-7.

more than country gentlemen, "domi nobiles", like Cicero's father. [1]

Such people had their social and political importance, contributing officers to the army, [2] controlling the attitudes of their home towns, attending the elections where their votes counted for much in a timocratic assembly, [3] and occasionally demonstrating (as in 59) in the conservative cause. [4] But when we read of the Equites as a political force, it is hardly of them that we should think, but rather of men whose estates permitted them to bid for the public contracts, but who derived from those contracts a far higher return on capital than agriculture could yield. These publicans Cicero calls the "flower of the equestrian order"; [5] more than once he simply equates equestrian jurors with them, [6] and when the Senate quarrelled with the publicans in 60, the " concordia ordinum " was shattered thereby. [8]

The importance of the publicans is easy to comprehend. They performed functions which were vital to the State (p. 121, n. 1), and from which senators were debarred by law. [7] Senators had to take account of their interests, yet did not share them. The large profits naturally attracted the richest of the non-senators, [9] and the capital required was so great that the co-operation of many such men was indispensable. [10] The publicans alone formed joint stock companies in which

1. Cic. *Leg.* II 3.

2. SYME, *Roman Revolution* 70 f; R. E. SMITH, *Service in Post-Marian Roman Army*, 1958, ch. v; details in J. SUOLAHTI, *Junior Officers of Roman Army in Republican Period* (1955). Augustus' use of Equites in the army was no innovation.

3. Cf. p. 121, n. 1.

4. *Att.* II, 19,3. The Equites who demonstrated against the triumvirs cannot be the same as those who had benefited from remission of the publicans' liability; rather conservative country gentlemen who had come up for the games and elections.

5. See p. 119, n. 5, cf. II *Verr.* 2,175; *Rab. Post.* 3: 'C. Curtius, princeps equestris ordinis, fortissimus et maximus publicanus.'

6. II *Verr.* 2, 174; 3, 94 and 168: 'si publicani, hoc est si equites Romani iudicarent'. Cf. p. 119, n. 8 on Rutilius' condemnation, esp. *Per.* Liv. LXX. Florus II 5 rightly identifies the equestrian opponents of Drusus ('robora populi Romani', Cic. *Cluent.* 153) with the publicans.

7. *Att.* I 17,9. Cf. p. 128 with n. 2. Cicero speaks of the terror of the Equites in 58 (*Dom.* 55; 96), alternatively of 'timor publicanorum' (*Qu. fr.* I 4,4).

8. Cf. Ascon. 93 C; Dio LV 10,5; LXIX 16, and comparable municipal rules, *Dig.* L 2,6,2 (Mommsen *StR*³ III 509 ff; 898 ff). Diod. XXXIV-V 38 describes Marius as once a publican; the context shows that this was before he held office, not after his praetorship (*contra* T. F. Carney, *A Biography of Marius* 23-4).

9. The losses of a publican mentioned in Cic. *Fam.* XIII, 10 may be connected with the civil war in 49-8 (cf. Caes. *BC* III, 31).

10. Asia paid perhaps 15,000,000 denarii, Bithynia, Cilicia and Syria certainly 35,000,000 (*ESAR* I 322 ff). The tax-farmers had to provide securities for these sums.

numerous investors could take shares, [1] and though these companies were not permanent in law but subsisted only to fulfil contracts let every five years, much the same group of *socii* may usually have obtained renewals of the right to farm the taxes; [2] how could rivals have carried on the work vithout the services of the large and experienced staff of freedmen and slaves which the old company had employed? [3] These companies then probably endured more or less continuously; their head offices were at Rome and there they met in conclave under *magistri* [4] and passed *decreta*, sometimes on political questions which did not directly relate to their business. [5] The Equites as such had no effective corporate organization, and it was therefore these companies which were deemed to express the common sentiments of the order as a whole [6].

No one will deny the power of the publicans. But it is not so clear that their interests brought them into continuous opposition to the senate, except when equestrian jurisdiction was in question. It was of course the duty of the government to let contracts on terms most favourable to the treasury and to prevent extortion from the taxpayers. If it had zealously performed these duties, disputes would have been common. They did indeed occur; yet instances known to us are rare. [7] It is a natural supposition that the publicans wished to extend the field of their operations, and that they favoured the annexation of new provinces to exploit. I shall revert to this question later, but it may be recalled that as late as 70 they had not even secured the contracts for the tithe of Sicilian grain, which were still let locally within the province, often to Sicilians. [8]

Now building contracts were surely less lucrative to the publicans

1. Polyb. VI 17 etc. Cf. Cic. *Fam.* XIII 9,2 on the Bithynian company—'quae societas ordine ipso et hominum genere pars est maxima civitatis; constat enim ex ceteris societatibus'. I cannot deal here with legal issues; for bibliography see Berger, *Encyclopaedic Dict. of Roman Law* s.v. Publicani. For a good description of the Asian publicans see T. R. S. Broughton, *ESAR*, IV, 535 ff (cf. my article in *Latomus* XIX 17 ff); for the system in Sicily V. Scramuzza, *ESAR* III 237 ff; 311 ff.

2. But see Liv. XLIII 16; Cic. II *Verr.* 1, 143; *de imp. Cn. Pomp.* 18. Presumably competition forced up the bids of the Asian tax-farmers in 61.

3. *De Imp. Cn. Pomp.* 16.

4. II *Verr.* 2, 182.

5. Cic. *Sest.* 32; *Vat.* 8; *Dom.* 74; 142 (relating to Cicero's exile and recall). Decrees honouring governors, II *Verr.* 2, 172.

6. The 18 centuries did indeed adopt L. Antonius as patron in 44, Cic. *Phil.* VI 13; VII 13. Even this action was unprecedented.

7. See Appendixes 1 and 3; p. 119 n. 8, p. 120, n. 1, p. 121, n. 4.

8. In 74 they were granted the contracts for quotas on fruits, but under the term of the lex Hieronica, II *Verr.* 3, 18.

than tax-farming, at least after 123, [1] and it may be thought that tax-farming does not lie within our subject here; it cannot be described in a natural sense as trade. The tax-farmers themselves, however, are known to have been concerned in trade and moneylending, [2] and in any case, if we exclude tax-farming from consideration, it is not at all plausible to explain the conflict of the orders in terms of divergent economic interests, as commerce in itself was far less important, and it may be doubted if it *could* have divided Senate and Equites.

It is indeed well known that in the east both before and after 88 Italian *negotiatores* were numerous; [3] and very probably there were just as many in the west, [4] where we lack copious epigraphic testimony and depend chiefly on casual literary allusions; for instance we hear that only fifty years after its occupation Gallia Transalpina was packed with Roman *negotiatores*, [5] who shared in every business transaction, while sherds of Italian pottery reveal a vigorous trade in wine even beyond the confines of the province. [6]

But who were the *negotiatores?* Before 90, in the east [7] and probably in the west too, [8] most of these *Italici* were not citizens, much less Equites, and their interests cannot account for the quarrels of the orders, just in the period when those quarrels are most conspicuous. [9]

Again, the Roman law of *societas* never permitted the formation of

1. See Appendix 1 and cf. p. 123, n. 10.

2. Trade, cf. *FIRA* I no. 11; the terms are not quite appropriate to an inland city (Termessus) and we must assume that they represent a standard form (D. MAGIE, *Roman Rule in Asia Minor* 1176 n. 34). Moneylending, Cic. II *Verr.* 2, 186-7; perhaps Plut. *Luc.* 20. For their interest in the slave trade see M. ROSTOVTZEFF, *SEHHW* 782 on Diod. XXXVI, 3.

3. See especially J. HATZFELD, BCH XXXVI, 1912, 5-218 (Delos) and *Les Trafiquants italiens dans l'orient hellénique* (1919).

4. Evidence in *ESAR* III, 334 ff (Sicily), IV 26-32 (Africa, cf. S. GSELL, *Hist. Anc. de l'Afrique du Nord* VII, 1928, 58-73), III 135-7; 143-4 (Spain cf. E. GABBA, *o.c.* in p. 120 n. 4, ch. x); C. JULLIAN, *Hist. de la Gaule* III (1920), 128-30.

5. Cic. *Font.* 11.

6. See C. A YEO, *Finanzarchiv* XIII (1952) 335 ff for conspectus and bibliography (cf. esp. O. BOHN, *Germania* 1923, 8 ff; 1925, 78 ff); for more recent evidence, J. HEURGON, *Par. del Pass.* 1952, 113 ff and articles by F. BENOIT and N. LAMBOGLIA in *Riv. St. Lig.* XVIII, XXI and XXIII; the wine trade seems to have gone back to early in the second century.

7. HATZFELD, *Trafiquants* 238 ff.

8. Note the name 'Italici' (Sall. *BJ* 26; 47; CIL I² 612; Diod. XXXIV 2, 27-34, where 31 is anachronistic, cf. FRANK, *ESAR* I, 297).

9. Against Gabba's view (*o.c.* in p. 120, n. 4, ch. IV, supported by E. T. SALMON, *Phoenix* XVI [1962] 107 ff) that Italian commercial interests influenced the policy of the ruling class among the allies who revolted in 90 see J. P. V. D. BALDSON, *Gnomon* (1954) 343; A. N. SHERWIN-WHITE, *JRS* XLV, 168 ff, and see further Broughton p. 155 ff. *infra.* I regard the objections as decisive.

trading companies with limited liability and more or less permanent duration, in which many could hold shares and which by the accumulation and concentration of capital that they represented could exercise powerful influence on the government. Nor were there any equivalents to Chambers of Commerce or Shipping, or Federations of Industry, or cartels. The *negotiatores* were unorganized individuals. [1]

They were not all traders; the term *negotiatores* includes men whose business was in land, and bankers and moneylenders. [2] It is of such people that Cicero is mainly thinking when he speaks of the *negotiatores* in Sicily [3] or Gaul [4] Now the old principle " omnis quaestus patribus indecorus visus" (Liv. XXI 63, 4) no longer excluded senators from such investments. Cato's prejudice against moneylending was extinct. [5] Senators as well as Equites acquired provincial estates [6] and lent money at interest. [7] In fact the largest creditors known to us are Crassus and Pompey, and the most notorious usurer, Marcus Brutus. He was certainly not the only senator to make his loans through an equestrian man of straw. [8] It was natural enough that senators should take part in this business. The profits of war and government had made Italians the creditors of the world, and none enjoyed more of them than the senators. Even commerce in the strict sense was not a matter of indifference to them. The principal imports

1. The 'conventus civium Romanorum' in many provincial towns could perhaps exert some influence on governors, but probably only if some of their members had powerful patrons at Rome.

2. Cic. *Font.* 46: 'omnes illius provinciae publicani, agricolae, pecuarii, *ceteri* negotiatores'. For inclusion of business relating to land cf. *Fam.* XIII 53,2: 'commendo negotia eius, quae sunt in Hellesponto, primum ut obtineat id iuris in agris quod ei Pariana civitas decrevit et dedit'. This is perhaps unusual; in II *Verr.* 2, 153 and 168 and *Font.* 12 'negotiatores' and 'aratores' are distinguished; II *Verr.* 2, 188 enumerates 'mercator an negotiator (banker or moneylender) an arator an pecuarius', cf. *Planc.* 64 for distinction of 'negotiatores' and 'mercatores'. For 'negotiatores' as bankers and moneylenders see also II *Verr.* 1, 14; 5, 155; *Font.* 11; *Fam.* XIII, 56; as traders *Att.* II, 16,4. Many landowners and moneylenders in the provinces resided in Rome (*de imp. Cn. Pomp.* 18) and used procurators.

3. II *Verr.* 2,6; examples, 3,36; 60-2; 5, 15 and 165, cf. Diod. cited p. 125 n. 8.

4. *Font.* 11 shows primary importance of moneylending (cf. *Mur.* 42; Sall. *Cat.* 40); 12 and 46 refer to land-owners (cf. *pro Quinctio*). For other provinces see *ESAR* I, 388; 391-2.

5. *De agric. praef.*

6. e.g. II *Verr.* 3, 93; 97; 152 (Sicily); *Fam.* I 9,24 (Cilicia); perhaps *Fam.* XII, 21 (Africa).

7. *ESAR* I, 351; 388-9 for evidence, cf. also Sall. *Cat.* 48,5 (Crassus). The notable moneylender, Q. Considius (*Att.* I 12,1; Val. Max. IV 8,3) is probably the senator named in Plut. *Caes.* 14; I *Verr.* 18; Cic. *Cluent.* 107; *Att.* II, 24,4.

8. Besides the notorious Scaptius, note his agents in Cappadocia, *Att.* VI, 1,4, and M. Cluvius, an agent for Pompey, *Fam.* XIII, 56. Cf. also *Fam.* XIII, 57 for a senator's *negotia* in Asia.

of Italy were grain, slaves and luxury articles, and senators were clearly among the chief purchasers of the costly products of the east and of the slaves they needed for their sumptuous households and vast estates. [1] In so far as Italy did not pay for these imports out of the spoils of empire, she balanced her accounts by exporting wine and oil, [2] much of which must have come from senatorial plantations. Marks on the amphorae of this period designate as producers not only men of equestrian or municipal note but a great Roman noble, Appius Pulcher, perhaps the consul of 38. [3] This is no more than we might expect. If Rome ever banned the planting of vines and olives in Gaul, the ban was as much in the interests of senatorial producers as of any others. [4] Their commercial advantage tended to merge with that of other Roman capitalists.

Of course producer and middleman need not be in accord. Traders as such might have had interests conflicting in some degree with those of senators. But we hear of no such conflict. Moreover traders do not seem to have been powerful or influential. Trade was a strenuous but precarious occupation. [5] In 49 when Cicero enumerates the various types of "boni", that is to say, "locupletes", he mentions publicans, moneylenders and farmers, not traders. [6] He never alludes to the loss they would sustain from Pompey's projected blockade of Italy. [7] In 70 he calls the merchants of Puteoli "homines locupletes et honesti", [8] but he also describes overseas traders as "homines tenues, obscuro loco nati"; [9] he remarks that such people rarely visited

1. See Frank's discussions of trade, sources of income etc. in *ESAR* I.

2. *ESAR* I, 276; 284; 355. Cf. p. 125, n. 6.

3. A. Oxé, *Germania* 1924, 80 ff. Bohn, *Germania* (1925) 83, adds the names of two Augustan consulars, L. Tarius Rufus (cf. Plin. *NH* XVIII, 37) and M. Herennius Picens. See also p. 128, n. 4. For other names see literature cited p. 125, n. 6.

4. Cic. *de rep.* III, 16. If the dramatic date, 129, is taken seriously, Frank's view (*ESAR* I, 172 ff) that the ban was imposed only on Ligurian production and in the interest of Massiliote, not Italian producers must be accepted. But the passage may be an anachronistic allusion to a ban imposed after the formation of the province of Transalpina c. 120, and perhaps after Posidonius' visit, since Diod. V, 26,2; 39,4 and Strabo IV, 1,2, who probably depend on his account, know nothing of it and explain the paucity or absence of viticulture by the cold climate. If it was ever effectively enforced, it was no longer in operation in and after Tiberius' reign (Celsus IV 12; cf. Plin. *NH* XIV 14; 18; 26-7; 43; 57; 68; Colum. III 2,16 and 25). Against Frank see esp. L. Bellini, *Mem. Acc. Linc.* (1948), 387 ff.

5. Cato *de agric. praef.*

6. See p. 118 n. 7. In *Comm. Pet.* there is no specific mention of traders, as of publicans (3; 50) and the 18 centuries (33), but cf. 29: multi homines urbani industrii, multi libertini (!) in foro gratiosi.

7. *Att.* IX 7,4.

8. II *Verr.* 5, 154.

9. *Ibid.* 167. 'Tenuis' is a relative term; an income of 100,000 HSS a year is 'tenue vectigal', *Parad.* 49. The actual ship-owners might be little men, financed

Rome; [1] if this be so, they could hardly exert pressure on the government there. In 59 he was ready to sacrifice to the publicans the interests both of Italian *negotiatores* engaged in the Asian coastal trade and of the whole province—"ne optima causa pereat". The "optima causa" of "concordia ordinum" is harmony between Senate and *publicans.* [2] Trade on a small scale Cicero regards as sordid: it is only the man with a large import and export business who is respectable, especially if he invests his gains in land. [3] Rabirius Postumus was perhaps such a man, but it is his activities as publican and moneylender that Cicero stresses. [4] I doubt if we can name a single prominent Eques who was primarily a merchant. [5] Atticus was surely representative of the richer and more influential members of his class; his wealth derived from town property at Rome, estates in Epirus, and banking and moneylending. [6] Traders were of little account, and manufacturers of still less; for industry was not much developed [7] and largely in the hands of freedmen. [8]

In the 80s most Equites were perhaps on the Marian side. [9] This has been connected with the credit crisis of the time. [10] The argument runs thus. The optimate Drusus debased the coinage: the Marian Gratidianus restored it. Moneylenders murdered with impunity a praetor who tried to protect debtors, and Sulpicius enacted that that no one with debts of over 2000 denarii might sit in the Senate; Frank suggests that he hoped that if the nobility could be kept from going into debt they would not interfere with the business of the

by bottomry loans. Cf. Plut. *Cato Maior* 21; Petron. 76, and see Broughton p. 161 ff *infra.*

1. II *Verr.* 3, 96.
2. *Att.* II 16,4 (cf. *OU. fr.* I 1, 6). I prefer Tyrrell and Purser's explanation to that of Constans (*Rev. de Phil.* 1931, 236 and in Budé edition); the 'optima causa' is certainly not the publicans' demand for a revision of their contract, which was already granted (*Att.* II, 16,2).
3. *Off.* III 151 (but cf. *Parad.* 46).
4. *Rab. Post.* 4. On this man see H. Dessau, *Hermes* XLVI 1911, 613 ff. Amphora marks (including one found at Koblenz, Bohn, *Germania* [1923], 8 ff) show that he exported the produce of his estates. His shipment from Alexandria (*Rab. Post.* 40) arose from special circumstances.
5. Cf. *ESAR* I 394. *Negotiatores* of high standing in Sicily (II *Verr.* 2, 69 cf 3, 148; 4, 42-3—the father of a senator; 5, 161) need not be traders.
6. Nepos, *Att.* 14,3 is not quite exact; for banking and moneylending cf. Cic. *Att.* I 13,1; IV 15,7; 16,7; V 13,2; VI 1,25; IX 9,4 etc.
7. *ESAR* I, 374 ff cf. V, 185-217.
8. See Gummerus, *RE* s.v. *Industrie u. Handel;* Duff, *Freedmen in Roman Empire,* 1958, 111 ff. Most Capuan manufacturers mentioned by M. W. Frederiksen, *PBSR* XXVII (1959), 107 ff, are freedmen, though they may have been financed by *ingenui* (as he supposes).
9. Ascon. 89 C; Cic. *Cluent.* 151.
10. Evidence in *ESAR* I 266-71.

forum. Sulla revoked his measure and did something to ease the burden on debt. All this makes a pretty picture of conflict between moneyed Equites and indebted landowners in the Senate. But it was the Marians who passed in 86 an even more drastic law scaling down all debts to one fourth, and this act was effective until the *Sullan* regime. Our picture is defaced. It never had more than superficial charm. In the 80s Equites no less than senators must have suffered from devastation or depreciation of their estates—lands which might be pledged to the treasury for fulfilment of their contracts—and they were far more likely to be ruined as publicans or *negotiatores* by the Mithradatic war. [1] Were there not debtors and creditors among both Marians and optimates, as in 49 when some men on both sides hoped to escape their financial embarrassments by victory, proscriptions and confiscations, and capitalists were fearful of both factions alike? [2] In so far as Equites espoused the Marian cause, it was surely because Drusus' judiciary law had exacerbated their relations with the Senate, and if Sulla took vengeance on the "veteres iudices" (Cic. *Cluent.* 151), probably men who had provoked resentment by the part they had taken in proceedings under the lex Varia, and doubtless on other rich men as well, it was partly because he needed lands and money to reward his own partisans. [3] These actually included Equites—from whom be filled up the Senate. The young Eques, Cicero, will not have been alone in his order in welcoming Sulla's victory, while deploring its abuse. [4] Perhaps Sulla sold the Spanish mines, hitherto leased to publicans, [5] but if so, it was surely to get ready money. He certainly did not deprive the publicans of the Asian contracts. [6] It was their political privileges that he was determined to annul. The "pauci", as Cicero was later to say (*Cluent.* 152), wished to bring the Equites once more under their power, to revive the situation that Polybius had described.

. . . . . . . . . . . . . . . . . . . . . . . . . . . . . . . . . .

It has often been thought that some phases of Roman aggrandisement can be explained by commercial motives. Wars obviously meant profits for army suppliers, [7] and conquests gave publicans new taxes

1. Cf. *de imp. Cn. Pomp.* 19 (perhaps refers to 74).
2. See evidence cited p. 122, n. 1.
3. Pompeians threatened to emulate Sulla by proscribing all who did not take their part, cf. *Att.* IX 7, 3-4; 10,2; 11, 3; X 14,1; XI 6,2. App. *BC* I, 96 implies that not all Sulla's rich victims had been active Marians. Cf. *Comm. Pet.* 9; *Cluent.* 188; *Rosc. Amer. passim.* The Triumvirs who surely had no political animus against the Equites behaved similarly, cf. Nepos, *Att.* 12,4; Broughton n. 4, p. 133.
4. *Rosc. Amer.* 136-7; 142; 153-4; cf *Brut.* 227; *Off.* II 27.
5. *ESAR* I 257 cf III 166-7.
6. Brunt, *Latomus* XIX 17 ff.
7. See e.g. App. *Lib.* 115 ff; Sall. *BJ* 44,5; Caes. *BG* I 39; VI 36; *B. Afr.* 75,3.

to collect and *negotiatores* better protection from the Roman government in foreign markets. Expansion must often have been welcome to such people, and on occasion the government did act to protect the lives and property of Italians overseas. But was commercial greed ever a decisive or even an influential factor in bringing about wars or annexations? The Senate generally displayed a cautious reluctance to assume new commitments. When this caution broke down, need we assume that equestrian pressure had triumphed? None stood more to gain from wars or government of provinces than individual senators, and solid or plausible reasons of state could often be found to veil their greed or ambition. Of this Caesar's conquest of Gaul is only the most signal example.

Tenney Frank rendered a great service in rebutting theories that Roman expansion before the Gracchi should be explained by commercial motives, and I shall not repeat his arguments which have not been refuted. [1] It may seem more plausible to suppose that in the post-Gracchan era, when the Equites were stronger, they were better able to influence foreign policy for their own economic ends. This view still has its adherents, but the weakness of their case can be seen in their own exposition of it: they are never able to produce direct testimony, but rely on combinations and conjectures. This is all the more remarkable because so much of our evidence derives from senatorial sources, and if the Senate often had to oppose policies inspired by sinister commercial purposes and contrary (in the opinion of the Optimates) to public interest we might expect to have some explicit allegations to this effect. For instance, it is clear that Plutarch's statement that Marius desired to stir up a war with Mithradates in 98 in order to secure a command for himself and win new glory and wealth (*Marius* 31) comes from a hostile, senatorial writer; but it is odd, if modern scholars are right in thinking that he then represented equestrian interests, that there is not so much as a hint of this in Plutarch's account.

We are still told that the conquest of the later Narbonensis was prompted by the desire to open up new domains to Roman capitalists. [2] But, as Frank rightly observed, in 125, as in 154, Rome acted primarily to defend Massilia, the conquest begun by Fulvius Flaccus was completed by optimates, and the limited annexation, excluding the territory of the defeated Arverni, could be justified as necessary

1. *Am. Hist. Rev.* 1912/3 233 ff, cf. *Roman Imperialism* 1925 *passim;* cf. *contra* G. de Sanctis, *St. d. R.* IV 26 n. 58; 554 n. 161 and E. Gabba. *op. cit.*, p. 120, n.4, ch. III, who cites the authority of Rostovtzeff. But Rostovtzeff came to agree with Frank, see *SEHHW* 737-8 (treatment of Macedon and Rhodes), 787-8 (Corinth and Carthage); he concedes economic motives only in connexion with piracy (784-6).

2. e.g. J. Carcopino, *Hist. Rom.* (1940), 244; 284 ff.

to secure the land route to Spain; it is significant that the building of the via Domitia followed at once. [1] Gaul too proved to be a valuable source of grain for armies operating in north Spain. [2] In 118 Narbo was founded. The Senate opposed it, and some have inferred that it was desired by the Equites. [3] This is not attested, and we may doubt if even the advocates of the new colony foresaw that it would become a great emporium. Lucius Crassus spoke for the foundation in the *popular* interest, that is to say as a successor of Gaius Gracchus, the founder of Junonia; and the title Martius indicates that it was intended to be (in Cicero's words) "specula populi Romani ac propugnaculum[4]." But a popular initiative was distasteful to the Senate, which may also have disapproved overseas colonization on the ground that it dissipated Italian manpower.

The Jugurthine war is also supposed to have had an economic motive. [5] But what could it have been? The extension of Roman territory? When the peace settlement was made, Marius who enjoyed equestrian support was at the height of his authority, and yet there was probably no enlargement of the province. [6] It is true that Equites insisted on vengeance on Jugurtha after he massacred Italians at Cirta, pressed for the replacement of Metellus by Marius on the ground that Metellus was protracting the war, and punished leading senators whose readiness to accept compromises with Jugurtha was ascribed to corruption, perhaps wrongly. But there is no mystery about all this. It was natural for people to feel indignation at affronts to Roman prestige, and at reports of incompetence or corruption in high quarters.

We can well believe that from the 90s opinion in Rome was divided

1. *Roman Imperialism* 254 ff.
2. Cic. *Font.* 8; 13.
3. C. H. Benedict, AJP LXIII (1942) 38 ff.
4. Crassus 'voluit adulescens in colonia Narbonensi causae aliquid popularis attingere' (Cic. *Brut.* 160). He was later criticized for his inconsistency in attacking the Senate in this speech and praising it, when advocating Caepio's law in 106; on that occasion he violently attacked the Equites, but we are not told that he had spoken on their behalf in 118 (*Cluent.* 140). Military purpose of Narbo, *Font.* 13. Gabba, *Athen.* XXIX, 1951, 220, denies it on the ground that Velleius I 15, does not classify it as a military colony, but it should be clear that Velleius means by a military colony one founded for veterans. P. Fraccaro, *Opuscula* II 77 ff, conjectures that Fulvius Flaccus had been responsible for citizen settlements in Piedmont; if this be so, Narbo represents an extension of the same policy.
5. So Gabba *op. cit.*, p. 120, n. 4. Cf. de Sanctis, *Problemi di Storia Antica* 186 ff. In his recent *Biography of C. Marius* (1962) T. F. Carney makes out that Marius consistently stood for equestrian interests.
6. P. Romanelli, *St, d. provincie romane dell' Africa* (1959), 82 ff. (I believe with S. Gsell, *op. cit.*, p. 125, n. 4, VII, 10, that the Marian towns in Africa consisted of Gaetulians.)

on the policy to be adopted towards Mithradates, and that Marius desired war for personal ends. In 88 Nicomedes 'aggression provoked Mithradates' attack; he was in debt to "Romans" in the suite of Manius Aquillius, who doubtless included Equites. But does this prove in default of all express testimony that Marius, Aquillius etc were the instruments of equestrian designs? Aquillius himself had been promised bribes by Nicomedes which could be paid only out of booty. [1] His irresponsible greed and rashness is parallelled by that of many other governors who had stirred up wars in Spain and elsewhere. Was there indeed a Marian party in the Senate backed by the Equites? Before we accept all the combinations on which this theory depends, it would be well to look carefully at the conduct of leading senators in the 50s, where we have abundant evidence showing that it would be far too simple to divide them into optimates and Pompeians, or to hold that each of them acted in a consistent manner, which we could predict from their past affiliations or their connexions of blood and marriage.

Even Frank thought that in 66 the Equites preferred Pompey to Lucullus because they knew that he would annex Cilicia and Syria, reversing Lucullus' decisions. [2] This theory depends partly on the fallacious assumption that Pompey had earlier shown his partiality to their interests by restoring to them the tax-farming of Asia (p. 129, n. 6), partly on a conjecture that before the Manilian law he had given an indication of his intention to annex Cilicia, though it was part of the Seleucid kingdom and Lucullus had recognized a new Seleucid king. [3] Granted that this is true, what of it? The last Seleucid king had been unable to win even the consent of his subjects, and in the light of his incompetence, unknown to Lucullus when he was recognized, strategic considerations now rendered it desirable to make the Euphrates the Roman frontier, in order to control Tigranes and keep the Parthians at a safe distance. [4] The Equites did indeed desire the removal of Lucullus, but their hostility was not decisive; his long

1. App. *B. Mith.* 11.
2. *Cl. Phil.* IX (1914) 191 ff.
3. Tigranes had ruled Syria c. 83-69 (Magie 1177 n. 35); when he allied with Mithradates, Lucullus recognized Antiochus XIII (App. *Syr.* 49; Justin XL 2,2). But in Cilicia his authority was probably never respected (cf. Magie 1178, n. 37), and in Syria, though Armenian forces were withdrawn, he could not maintain control; the confused evidence is given by Magie 1228 n. 19. This was probably realized by Pompey (and others) when Pompey settled ex-pirates in Cilicia (Magie 1180, n. 43). Frank thinks that this was tantamount to a declaration of his intention to annex Cilicia. I am uncertain of this, but if it were true, it is questionable if Pompey's action was known at the time of the lex Manilia.
4. Cf. Rostovtseff, *SEHHW* 870.

tenure had aroused the envy of his colleagues, and his apparent failure made his supersession inevitable. [1]

Bithynia, Cilicia and Syria yielded the treasury 35,000,000 denarii. [2] Cicero estimated the revenues of Egypt at 12,500 talents, a sum perhaps equivalent (allowing for the depreciation of Egyptian currency). [3] Here was an even richer field for Roman exploitation, and since 80 Rome had had a pretext for annexation. It was proposed in 65 by Crassus, but there is no indication that he had powerful support. [4] In 59 the triumvirs promoted the recognition of Ptolemy Auletes. [5] The enormous profits of this transaction [6] enured not to the equestrian order but to the triumvirs and to a few rich men who lent the king money. It was these few creditors alone who favoured proposals in 56 to restore Auletes. [7] If the equestrian order as a whole had been interested either in the annexation of Egypt or in the restoration of the king, we could hardly have failed to hear of it from Cicero's intimate letters, all the more as he was himself a persistent advocate of their interests. No doubt the king's creditors such as Rabirius were behind Gabinius' restoration of him in 55, [8] but the most important members of the order, the publicans, hated Gabinius for his treatment of them in Syria (p. 119, n. 8). In the story of Rome's relations with Egypt at this time we can discern no trace of any pressure exercised by the equestrian order in favour of the expansion of Roman territory or control.

Of course Equites supported the lex Gabinia against piracy. But the history of Rome's dealings with the Cilician pirates does not bear out the hypothesis that commercial interests determined Roman foreign policy. [9] For fifty years Rome tolerated or even encouraged the growth of the evil. It has been reasonably conjectured that the activity of the pirates in making slaves was actually beneficial to Roman *latifondisti*. [10] At last about 100 some action was taken or

1. Appendix 3.
2. Plut. *Pomp.* 45.
3. Strabo XVII 1,13. See S. L. Wallace, *Taxation in Egypt* p. 343 and n. 26.
4. Broughton, *MRR* II, 157 gives evidence.
5. *Ibid.*, 188.
6. Suet. *Caes.* 54 reports a bribe of 6000 Talents.
7. Cic. *Fam.* I 1,1 cf 7,6.
8. But see Cicero, *Rab. Post.* 19-21 (unconvincing).
9. Evidence and bibliography in Magie ch. xii. Cicero says (*de imp. Cn. Pomp.* 11): 'Maiores nostri saepe pro mercatoribus aut naviculariis iniuriosius tractatis bella gesserunt.' This statement was not verified in Rome's dealings with the pirates. Of course it is no proof of the importance of commercial interests if Rome had at times protected her citizens against injury abroad.
10. Cf. Strabo XIV 3,2; 5,2. Rhodes remained strong by sea even after 167 (Rostovtzeff, *SEHHW* 773 ff) and might have taken action but for apprehensions of Rome.

projected, avowedly for the protection of Roman and Italian seafarers. [1] It was ineffective or abortive, [2] a display of hostility that only served to make the pirates take the side of Rome's enemies. They assisted both Mithradates and Sertorius. [3] The campaigns of Servilius Isauricus and the appointment of Antonius Creticus were natural results. It is significant that Antonius was given his command in 74, the very year when war again broke out with Mithradates. His incompetence and failure cannot have been envisaged, or designed. The Senate itself recognized the need to put down the pirates when they had become a menace to Rome's security. It did not deny the need in 67, though fear of revolution made it oppose the grant of extraordinary powers to Pompey. [4] In Cicero's retrospective justification of the Gabinian Law we can see the reasons that made Pompey's appointment popular. The interests of Roman traders are mentioned only in a single sentence; [5] emphasis is rather placed on those of the publicans, which were in this case identical with those of the treasury, on the danger of famine and on the menace to Rome's security and the affronts to her prestige. [6] Commercial interests were not decisive.

. . . . . . . . . . . . . . . . . . . . . . . . . . . . . . . . . .

In the late Republic, then, Equites did not form an united pressure group, continuously advocating policies contrary to the wishes and interests of the senate. Rather, their aims were limited and not all were shared by the order as a whole. The publicans certainly sought to preserve their profits from the State contracts. This objective might actually lead to clashes with the traders proper, who had much less political influence. All Equites surely valued whatever promoted the independance and dignity of their order. Control of the courts was desired partly for this reason and not simply for the pressure which it enabled them to bring on the magistrates and Senate in pursuit of profit. And if many Equites were well satisfied with a private station, others resented the exclusiveness of the nobility and welcomed opportunities to attain office. After Sulla such ambitions were progressively realized, and it is surely no accident that once they had recovered their juridical rights in 70, the conflict between the orders became progressively less acute.

1. *FIRA* I, no. 9 B 5 ff (Delphic law against piracy).
2. M. Antonius accomplished little, and no action under the 'Delphic law' is recorded.
3. App. *B. Mith.* 63; Plut. *Luc.* 2,5; *Sert.* 7,3; 21,5.
4. Dio XXXVI 31 ff (Catulus' speech).
5. *De Imp. Cn. Pomp.* 32 cf. perhaps 54.
6. *Ibid.* 30-34; 44; 54; 64. But see Broughton p. 150 ff *infra*.

This analysis is confirmed by the role that Equites played after Caesar's victory in the civil wars. Though in 59 Caesar had conferred important benefits on the Asian publicans, and in 49-8 had ultimately won over the moneyed men outside the senate, he did not think it necessary to oblige the publicans or the creditor class in Italy. The publicans were never commissioned to collect the direct taxes in Gaul, and they were deprived of the contracts for such taxes in Asia and the East generally. [1] In Italy considerable relief was given to debtors. [2] We do not hear that these measures created a dangerous hostility to his rule in the equestrian order. To the great majority it was probably more important that he restored peace and order and that he gave them advancement in the Senate.

It will not be disputed that in the Principate Equites enjoyed a much higher position in the state than they had achieved under senatorial government. [3] Augustus opened up to them new positions of power and emolument in the public administration. In the new era a man of equestrian status counted as more than a plebeian. [4] To an ever increasing extent Augustus' successors relied more on Equites than on senators, until in the third century they almost displaced senators in governmental posts. No doubt Equites seemed more trustworthy because they lacked the corporate unity which made the Senate always a potential, if often latent, repository of traditions inimical to despotism. Yet the emperors can hardly be shown to have favoured the commercial interests of Equites. Caesar's new regulation of the direct taxes in the east was not disturbed; indeed, over a long period, the part played by publicans in collecting revenue was steadily reduced. [5] Nor did the government ever do much to promote the interests of Italian traders. Hatzfeld showed long ago that it was precisely under Augustus that the importance of such people in the east began to decline. [6] Italy's share in imperial commerce gradually diminished, and though Domitian's abortive measure in favour of

1. Asia: Dio XLII 6; App. *BC* V 4; Plut. *Caes.* 48; Judaea : F. Heichelheim, *ESAR* IV 232-3. There is no direct evidence for other eastern areas; elsewhere, but perhaps only in Africa (cf. *ILS* 901), publicans were still collecting direct taxes in grain as late as Tiberius, cf. Tac. *Ann.* IV 6.

2. Evidence in Broughton, *MRR* II 257; 273; 286-7. Cicero displays some resentment in *de off.* II 84.

3. See A. Stein, *Der röm. Ritterstand, passim,* with some modifications in Brunt, *JRS* LI (1961) 76 ff. I agree with Broughton's account of the Equites in the Principate.

4. Hor. *ep.* I 1,58; *Res Gestae* 35 etc. (Yet contrast *ILS* 112.)

5. For instance *portoria*, cf. S. J. de Laet, *Portorium*, ch. xvii.

6. *Trafiquants*, 148 ff.

Italian viticulture [1] must not be forgotten, it was presumably prompted as much or more by the interests of landowners than of traders (if indeed any sharp distinction between these classes may be drawn). But if the emperors relied so much on Equites, and if they had truly been a class of "businessmen", it is odd that so little attention was now paid to their business interests.

Historians are always too apt to recreate the past out of the experience of their own day. Hence a danger of anachronistic interpretations. The vast growth of trade and industry in modern times and the consequential discovery of the abstraction of economic man by thinkers of the 18th and 19th centuries may often have led us astray in interpreting the conditions in the ancient world and the motives from which Greeks and Romans acted. It would of course be absurd to deny that their conduct was often influenced or determined consciously by economic considerations. But it may well be that these considerations were not so dominant as they are sometimes supposed to be to-day. In antiquity there were far less opportunities for the profitable investment of capital and the indefinite accumulation of wealth. Various explanations may be assigned, scientific and technological backwardness, poor communications and inadequate transport, inappropriate legal institutions, shortage of fuel, reliance on slave labour, but whatever the causes, in the prevailing conditions capitalists were naturally disposed to use their wealth, not so much to increase it still further, as to promote non-economic aims, to satiate their pleasures or maintain their status by the ostentatious consumption which Romans called "luxuria", and to enhance their power and fame in life and preserve their memory after death. Crassus was one of the greatest capitalists of his day; he is reported to have said that no man could be esteemed rich who could not support an army from his own resources. [2] The remark betrayed the bent of his mind, and it was thoroughly Roman. All over the Hellenistic and Roman world capital was dissipated in benefactions which rarely promoted economic progress; in Greek they bore the significant name of "philotimiai". This love of fame or glory was not, as has been suggested, [3] an "irrational motive" for the ancients; even in the philosophical schools only Epicureans and Cynics would have endorsed this description.

1. Suet. *Dom.* 7,2; 14,2; Stat. *Silv.* IV 3,11; Philostr. *v. Soph.* p. 520; *v. Apoll.* VI 42.

2. Cic. *de off.* I 25 etc.

3. F. A. Lepper, *Trajan's Parthian War*, 1948, 198. Desire for glory would not, as he implies (190 ff), have been thought discreditable in Trajan. Cicero, *de off.* I 38 allows that wars may be fought for conquest and glory if there are good legal pretexts.

Given the conditions which limited the scope of human endeavour in the economic field, it was indeed perfectly reasonable. Thucydides, an acute observer of human behaviour, suggested that three motives decided men's actions, profit, fear and glory. [1] We are too apt to leave the third of this triad out of account. If the arguments in this paper are sound, it has some relevance to explaining the political role (or roles) played by Equites. [2]

1. I 75-6.

2. Help of various kinds has been given me by Mr. M. Frederiksen, Mr. M. K. Hopkins, Mr. G. M. Paul, Mr. G. E. M. de Ste Croix and by those who took part in the discussion at the Conference, notably Prof. Broughton and Prof. Tomsin. I alone am responsible for the views expressed and for any errors.

# APPENDIX I

## The Publicans before 123 B.C.

Tenney Frank is disposed to minimize the importance of the publicans before they secured the tax-farming of Asia. Thus he suspects Livy of anachronism when he speaks of men enriched by public contracts in 215 (XXIII 48,10). He even suggests that Polybius' account of their multiplicity and of the large number of citizens engaged in them (VI 17), written about 150, 'would not apply to any earlier period' (*ESAR* I 102; 148), though on his own showing (149 ff) the contracting business should have been important for about a generation before 150. He maintains (157) that in 150 the capital invested in it still did not amount to over 2% of the national wealth (cf. also 75 f.) This is a mere guess. But evenif it is roughly correct, it does not follow that the proportion of the national wealth so invested was not significant. It would have been a far higher proportion of the liquid capital, and may well have yielded profits far greater than could be obtained from land.

In some respects Frank has underestimated the amount and range of the publicans' business.

*a*) He seems to think (84-5) that it was a novelty in 215 for publicans to furnish army supplies. But the novelty of which Livy speaks (XXIII 48) is that they furnished supplies on credit, proof incidentally of their financial strength. Abuses in this system came to light, (XXV 3) and Frank conjectures that the state did not continue the publicans in this service thereafter (102). But it is again attested in 195 (XXXIV 9,12) and 167 (XLIV 16, 3-4, as shown by 'locavit'). It is not very easy to see what other system could be used, except requisitioning.

*b*) He conveys the impression that the publicans did not get any building contracts except from censors (149-50). But building works supervised by other magistrates or generals must have been put out at contract in the same way (cf. Mommsen, *StR*³ II 426 f). Use of the verb 'fecit' does not mean that the subject hired the labour and bought the materials etc: it is short for 'faciendum curavit' (cf. Fest. 258 L). Hence it is used of censors too (Vell. II 3,1; Strabo V 1,11 cf. *de vir. ill.* 72,8). See also Plut. *C. Gr.* 6, 3-4. In every case the person who had the 'cura' of the undertaking had the 'probatio' (e.g. Degrassi, *Inscr. Lib. Rei Publ.* 464-465a; lex Put. = *FIRA* III no. 153 iii 6 ff). It was thus his building. In assessing the amount of building contracts between 200 and 150 we must therefore take into account all the works listed by Frank 183 ff as well as censorial contracts, remembering that our chief source, Livy, is manifestly incomplete.

*c*) Frank argues that the Spanish mines were only let to publicans after 179 and that till then they were exploited directly by the state. It is hard to see how this could have been practicable. Frank infers it from the fact that the sums of booty which are reported to have been brought to the treasury by returning governors were large only until 178. As laconically observed by D. Kienast, *Cato der Zensor* 1954 n. 70, his own tabulation of the sums does not support this. (i) Almost as large sums are reported from Further as from Hither Spain, though at this time mines were worked only in the latter province. (ii) The sums reported vary greatly from year to year, and in many there are no returns. It does not look as if they represent regular revenue. Nor do they bear out Livy's statement that the wealth of the province 'daily increased' after 195 (XXXIV 21, 7). On Frank's own calculation, the average is only 1,700,000 *denarii* against 9,000,000 in the time of Polybius (XXXIV 9), when the mines were undoubtedly in the hands of publicans. (iii) If booty is reported on only one occasion after 178, that can be due to the incompleteness or loss of Livy's record, and to the greater infrequency of wars during the remaining years for which his narrative is extant. I therefore think it best to hold that it was Cato who first leased the mines to the publicans in 195, cf. Livy XXIV 21,7: 'vectigalia magna instituit ex ferrariis argentariisque'. I do not see what other form of *vectigalia* he can have devised. Cato's opposition to publicans on other occasions (XXXIV 9,12, and see below) was due to his zeal for the treasury, and it was the treasury's interest that the mines should be exploited, which could not be done without the use of publicans (cf. Liv. XLV 18).

The Spanish mines and the building contracts were doubtless the most lucrative activities of the publicans before 123. We cannot estimate the capital employed in the first; there is little value in Frank's conjectures (p. 155). For building operations censors were allowed in 179 and 169 respectively a year's *vectigal* or half that sum, spread over five years (p. 152). I suspect that Frank has rather underestimated the size of this (p. 153); in any event it represents a considerable proportion of state expenditure. In 184 the censors probably spent 6,000,000 *denarii* on the sewers (p. 184) and in 144 45,000,000 were voted for the Aqua Marcia (pp. 258 f). These were extraordinary commitments, and they are not comparable with the value of the Asian taxes, 10-15,000,000 each year. But we must recall that the contractors had to give security perhaps in full, and this makes it evident that substantial interests were already engaged in the public contracts. The facts thus support the judgement of Polybius.

Several disputes between the publicans and the magistrates or Senate are reported. Already in 211, according to Livy XXV 3, the Senate was afraid to take action against a fraudulent army contractor, and when tribunes did so, the *ordo publicanorum* caused a riot in his defence, though without success. In 184 the censors Cato and Valerius Flaccus 'vectigalia summis pretiis, ultro tributa infimis locaverunt' (Livy XXXIX 44). Evidently their predecessors had been more complaisant and the publicans, abetted by Cato's political enemies induced the Senate to annul the contracts; however the censors excluded from the new auction 'qui ludificati priorem locationem erant' and 'omnia eadem paulum imminutis pretiis locaverunt' (cf. also Plut. *Cato* 19; *Flam.* 19). In 169, when the censors Tiberius Gracchus and Gaius Claudius excluded from the auction all who had obtained contracts in 174, a tribune was induced to propose cancellation of the new contracts and even to prosecute the censors; Claudius was nearly condemned, after many of the centuries of the richest citizens had voted against him (Liv. XLIII 16). It is clear that the publicans had become an important body, with influence where their interests were directly prejudiced.

In 167 the senate refused to lease the Macedonian gold and silver mines to the publicans and closed them altogether, on the ground that it was not safe to let the natives work them and that publicans would prove oppressive. We have this not only from Livy (XLV 18 cf 29,11) but from Diodorus XXXI 8; Polybius is probably the common source and should be credited. It may well be that the publicans could only operate under the protection of an army of occupation which the Senate had no mind to instal. We do not even know that they protested. In 158 the mines were re-opened (Cassiodorus, *Chron. Min.* ed. Mommsen II 130), but not necessarily leased to Roman publicans. The profits may have gone to the local governments which issued much silver in the next few years (Gaebler, *Z.f. Num.* 1902, 143-4). Rome had perhaps become less apprehensive of Macedonian resurgence. (The *censoria locatio* of the old royal lands attested in 63, ic. *de Cleg. agr.* I 5; II 51 need not antedate the annexation in 148.)

We also hear from Pliny that a *lex censoria* forbade publicans to employ more than 5000 men in the gold mines near Vercellae (*NH* XXXIII 78) and that an old decree of the senate forbade all mining in Italy (*ibid*, cf. III 138; XXXVII 202); this decree certainly did not affect the iron mines of Elba (Strabo V 2,6). E. Pais (*Dalle Guerre Puniche* 1918, II 595 ff) gives reasons for thinking that this decree would have affected the mines in Vercellae, although strictly they were not in Italy but in Cisalpina; in this case the censors' regulation is an earlier restriction. Both probably fall within this period. Pais ascribes them to a moralistic preference for agriculture, while Frank (180) conjectures that the publicans who operated the Spanish mines were jealous of Italian competition and that the senate may have wished to conserve native ores. We cannot assume conflict between the orders in this case.

# APPENDIX II

## Gaius Gracchus' Judiciary Legislation.

Our sources are in notorious conflict. [1] On the one hand Plutarch (*C. Gr.* 5,2 cf 6,1; *Comp.* 2,1) records a judiciary law whereby Gracchus constituted a mixed *album* of 300 senators and 300 Equites, the last selected by himself. This version is apparently garbled in the *Perioche* of Livy LX where Gracchus is credited with a law adding 600 Equites to the Senate and thus trebling its size. [2] On the other hand the other sources more or less clearly state that Gracchus transferred the 'iudicia' to the Equites, and it is generally thought that they are confirmed by the extant *repetundae* law, preserved on the Tabula Bembina, which must be Gracchan, [3] whether or not it be identified with the lex Acilia, [4] and which explicitly excludes senators and their connexions from the *repetundae* court. According to Fraccaro the evidence of this document is decisive, since there was no Gracchan judiciary law other than the law *de repetundis.* [5] In recent years his opinion has been widely accepted. The most notable dissentient is Gelzer, who accepts Plutarch's version of the judiciary law and distinguishes from it the lex Acilia inspired by Gracchus, which he equates with the Tabula Bembina and dates either to 123 or 122. [6] Gelzer has not argued his case in detail, and I shall here seek to show that he is right; I believe, further, that both laws belong to 123, but I express no opinion on the proposed identification of the lex Acilia with the Tabula Bembina.

It is quite clear that none of our authorities limit the scope of Gracchus' judiciary legislation to the *repetundae* court alone. This is admitted by Fraccaro, except that he thinks that Appian (*BC* I 22) connects it solely with *repetundae* by referring to the fact that Gracchus reproached senatorial

1. See Gabba's edition of App. *BC* I, 338 ff; for some recent discussions E. Schönbauer, *Anzeiger Akad. Wien* 1956 13 ff.

2. The Epitomator is notoriously unreliable in reporting Livy; in my view he makes the reverse confusion over Drusus' judiciary proposal. It is hard to believe that a proposal by Gracchus to enlarge the Senate left no other clear trace in the tradition. Certainly no such proposal became law; the Senate was not enlarged before Sulla.

3. As proved by J. P. V. D. Balsdon, *PBSR* XIV (1938) 108 ff.

4. For the present state of this controversy see E. Badian, *Historia* XI 203 ff.

5. *Opuscula* II 255 ff.

6. *Kl. Schr.* I 222 = *Gnomon* XXV 319.

*iudices* with the wrongful acquittal of governors accused of misgovernment. But he fails to point out that Appian expressly says that Gracchus' legislation made Equites judges of *all* Romans and Italians, including senators, on matters concerning property, loss of civic rights and banishment. Now only senators could be defendants in the *repetundae* court; rightly or wrongly then, Appian like the other writers thought that Gracchus' legislation was more extensive. On the present view, it cannot be an objection to this that Appian in his very brief narrative drew special attention to *repetundae* cases, since I do not deny that for these cases Gracchus did pass a specific law, totally excluding senators from the courts.

The Epitomator of Livy states that the lex Aurelia of 70 BC transferred the courts to the Equites. In fact we know that under this law senators still constituted one third of the *iudices*. His mistake illustrates how easy it was for careless writers to make out that senators had lost the whole of their juridical rights when they had merely lost a monopoly of jurisdiction. [1] The mistake was all the easier, when senators were outnumbered by Equites in a mixed *album;* this will have been the case in 123, if we suppose that the Epitomator was right (as the number of *iudices* in the Tabula suggests) in holding that Gracchus added 600 and not 300 Equites to the senators for the purpose of jurisdiction. Moreover, on the present hypothesis Gracchus did remove senators altogether from the *repetundae* court, and as Fraccaro himself has stressed, it was the composition of this court, and of others established later on the same model, for instance the court set up *ad hoc* by the Mamillian law [2] and the *quaestio maiestatis* set up by Saturninus' law, which were to become the focus of political controversy; it was, therefore, natural enough that late writers, giving very summary accounts of what happened, spoke of a transference of the courts to the Equites and overlooked the existence of a mixed *album*, from which judges were drawn in other cases. By contrast, it is not easy to see how Plutarch and Livy should have been led into the error of inventing such a mixed *album*, or how Plutarch came to add the circumstantial detail that the first Equites were enrolled on this *album* by Gracchus himself [3]. It is certainly unsatisfactory to reject their account without even trying to explain the error. Hence most scholars who have adopted the same view as Fraccaro have held that Plutarch and Livy refer to an abortive project of Gracchus: this I hope to refute later.

It is vital to Fraccaro's case to hold that the version given by Plutarch and Livy must be rejected because no jurisdiction was reserved to senators except in cases of *repetundae*. *Prima facie* this contention is refuted by the testimony of Polybius (VI 17,2), that the 'people' were dependent on the Senate, most of all because 'the judges are taken from its members in the

1. Tac. *Ann.* XII 60, makes the reverse confusion over Caepio's law, cf. Balsdon (*op. cit.* p. 141, n. 3) 102 ff.

2. 'Gracchani iudices' in the context of Cic. *Brut.* 128, *means* only '*iudices* whose sympathies were Gracchan'; but presumably they were Equites, cf. *de Orat.* I 225, with U. Ewins *JRS* L (1960) 103.

3. I suppose that this was authorized by the law.

majority of trials, whether public or private, in which the charges are heavy' (Shuckburgh's translation). Fraccaro rightly stresses that Polybius does not claim that senators had an absolute monopoly of juridiction; he speaks only of the majority of the most important cases. Fraccaro adds that from the context it can be seen that he is thinking of administrative cases, and perhaps of trials *de repetundis*. This cannot be accepted. It is true that Polybius has just described the hold that the Senate had on the 'people' because of its right to vary public contracts. But he is now proceeding to mention a second and even stronger hold, which it is arbitrary to link closely with the first. There is no reason at all to suppose that he has in mind primarily cases arising out of public contracts which the censors might hear with a senatorial *consilium*. Least of all can he be concerned with *repetundae* trials in which only senators could stand in the dock and in which citizens were not usually the aggrieved party. Read in its natural sense, Polybius' text means that senators were judges in most important cases, public and private, in which non-senators were plaintiffs (or prosecutors) and defendants. This meaning fits Plutarch's statement that Gracchus' judiciary law 'did most to curtail the power of the senators; for (till then) they alone judged cases, and for this reason were feared by the people and the Equites.' This too is unintelligible if senators had a monopoly of jurisdiction only in the *repetundae* court. Plutarch plainly thought that Gracchus first gave Equites a share in jurisdiction in cases in which non-senators might be defendants. And Appian agrees.

Why did Fraccaro reject this evidence? He held firstly that there were as yet no permanent *quaestiones* except for *repetundae*. Others have thought that the rest were due to Sulla. Badian has shown that this last opinion is contrary to the evidence, but he too does not admit that any other *quaestio* existed in 123.[1] Cicero (*Brut.* 106), however, not only shows that the *quaestio de repetundis* set up in 149 was the first of its kind but indicates that others were established when C. Carbo (*cos.* 120) was a young man.[2] Whatever be made of this, the orthodox view rests on this argument: there is no clear evidence that such *quaestiones* yet existed; therefore they did not. This is a fragile proof. In the meagre evidence of these years which survives could we expect to hear of laws or trials concerned with non-political crimes, like murder? Charges of *repetundae* or *maiestas* affected men of note, and the laws raised political issues; yet here too evidence is fragmentary, and the lex Junia *de repetundis* remains an enigma. Should we hear of the kind of proceedings taken against a peasant accused o stabbing his unfaithful wife? The common notion that his fate was decided,

1. *Op. cit.* (p. 141 n. 4) 206-9, cf. Ewins, *op. cit.* (p. 142 n. 2), n. 42. Add perhaps (a) Sall. *BJ* 35,7 to evidence for murder tribunal; (b) Cic. *Rab. Post.* 14, which seems to show that in Glaucia's time proposals to set up permanent *quaestiones* which could judge all citizens were familiar. We can never be sure that a criminal lex Cornelia did not have an antecedent law on the same subject, like the lex Cornelia *de repetundis*.

2. 'Nam et quaestiones perpetuae hoc adulescente constitutae sunt quae antea nullae fuerunt; L. enim Piso tr. pl. legem primus de pecuniis repetundis Censorino et Manilio consulibus tulit'.

after *provocatio*, by the *comitia centuriata*, ought, however, to strain credulity.

Fraccaro also held that senators could have had no monopoly of the function of the *unus iudex* in civil cases. By origin, he held, the *unus iudex* was an arbitrator and he was always chosen by the parties from among all citizens. Even when the choice was left to the praetor, he was not bound to select a senator, though obviously he would do so in the most important cases. This is rather a large admission, for we must suppose that when the parties did not agree on a name, the praetor must have been able in one way or another to impose his own choice; and this may well have been of common occurrence. But Fraccaro's views on the *unus iudex*, though enunciated *ex cathedra*, would not command universal acceptance. Lévy-Bruhl has recently written that the view that the *unus iudex* was originally an arbitrator is now hardly held. [1] In the nature of things, such views can never be more than hypotheses. However this may be, what of the parties' freedom of choice to select an *unus iudex?* Had they in fact the right to select any one they pleased, or was their freedom restricted to an *album*, and perhaps in Polybius' day to senators? It is well-known that in imperial times the *iudices* of the *album* acted in civil as well as in criminal cases, and though some texts have been adduced to prove that the parties could none the less choose some one whose name did not appear on the *album*, all are susceptible of a different interpretation. [2] Imperial evidence cannot, however, be safely used, one way or another, to establish the practice in the second century BC. It is more relevant that Cicero claims that 'neminem voluerunt maiores nostri non modo de existimatione cuiusquam sed ne pecuniaria quidem de re minima esse iudicem nisi qui inter adversarios convenisset' (*Cluent.* 120). He evidently means to assert an immemorial tradition still valid in his own time. But his statement is certainly very loose. Many civil suits affecting property were decided by *recuperatores*, *centumviri* and *decemviri*, and they were not appointed by agreement between the parties. At most then his statement is true of the *unus iudex*. But given that he is speaking so loosely for rhetorical effect, can we press his words to imply that the parties could agree on any *iudex* they pleased, and not one to be taken from a specified list, whether of the Senate or of a mixed *album?* It should be clear that this piece of declamation cannot outweigh the evidence of Polybius.

Fraccaro also asserts that the other judges mentioned could not all have been senators. Mommsen, he says, admits that the magistrate could select any citizens as *recuperatores*. But Mommsen gave no proof, [3] and in one instance at least we know that the magistrate's freedom was limited: the *lex agraria* (v. 37) prescribes selection from the first class. The *centumviri*, *decemviri* and *tresviri* were, according to Fraccaro, all elected by the people.

1. *Recherches sur les actions de la Loi* (1960) 130 n. 2, cf. E. Wieacker, (*ZSS*), 1959, 590. Cf. F. La Rosa, *Labeo* IV (1958) 31 n. 63; 36 ff.; G. Broggini, *Iudex Arbiterve* (1957) 1-87. Further bibliography in these works, cf. also H. Jolowicz, *Hist. Introd. to Study of Rom. Law* 180-1 (older view maintained).

2. La Rosa, *op. cit.* 35 ff; Lévy-Bruhl, *op. cit.* (last note) 131 ff.

3. *Strafrecht* 178.

Now, as to the first, Festus states that 'terni ex singulis tribubus sunt electi ad iudicandum, qui centumviri appellati sunt' (47 L). It is not clear to me that 'electi' must mean 'elected' and not 'selected' (e.g. by the praetor), but even if it does, we do not know to what time Festus refers; indeed we do not know that the centumviral court yet existed. On one recent view, which asserts the great antiquity of that court, the system Festus described is roughly coeval with the lex Plautia of 89 and in Gracchus' day the *centumviri* were senators. [1] As for the *decemviri* and *tresviri*, they were minor magistrates, and therefore elected. [2] Just for that reason they were at least likely to be men of senatorial families, and it would be rather pedantic to treat their jurisdiction as constituting a substantive exception to what Polybius says of the authority the Senate derived from their jurisdiction. In any event, he does not claim that senators had a monopoly in *all* important cases.

This fact is also relevant to Fraccaro's contention that the senators were not sufficiently numerous to monopolize jurisdiction. Polybius does not say that they did. It might indeed be thought that they could not have manned the centumviral court, yet this court decided important suits concerning inheritances. [3] But in Pliny's day the *centumviri*, then numbering 180, were divided into four panels; [4] probably some such system had always obtained, [5] and the panels may have met in rotation. As for any permanent, pre-Gracchan *quaestiones*, we cannot say whether the *iudices* would have been as numerous as under Gracchus' *repetundae* law; it is relevant that the first cases of *repetundae* had been heard by only 5 *recuperatores* (Livy XLIII 2), a precedent that the Calpurrian law may have followed.

Under the Principate *iudices* on the *album* of less than equestrian status could decide only 'de levioribus summis' (Suet. *Aug.* 32). It might well be that custom or statutes in Polybius' day prescribed that only senators could adjudicate when large sums were at stake. (The provision cited from the *lex agraria* shows how statutes might fix the qualifications for jurisdiction, in this instance a lower qualification than that which on my view Gracchus' law demanded.) It is idle to try to define the criteria by which important and less important suits were then differentiated; because we do not know what they were, we are not, however, entitled to empty Polybius' testimony of its meaning.

It may be said that granted that Gracchus sought to relieve Equites of that dependence on the Senate of which Polybius wrote we might expect him to have transferred to Equites all jurisdiction hitherto reserved to senators. Why indeed should he have adopted this course only for the *repetundae* court? Perhaps an answer is not hard to provide. Experience had shown that senators were manifestly biased in favour of their peers and thus

1. La Rosa *op. cit.* 27 ff.
2. On all these courts see Lévy-Bruhl, *op. cit.*, 147 ff.
3. Cic. *de orat.* I 173; 180.
4. Plin. *ep.* I 18,3; VI 33,3; cf. Quint. XII 5,6.
5. Cf. Val. Max. VII 7,1.

incompetent to sit in the *repetundae* court. But there was no such good reason for excluding them from other jurisdiction. Indeed, since most or all jurists were as yet senators, it would have been contrary to the general convenience if no senator had been permitted to act as *unus iudex* even by consent of the parties. The course here attributed to Gracchus was thus perfectly defensible, and for reasons already given it does more to account for the apparent discrepancy of the sources than the hypothesis that Gracchus excluded senators from all jurisdiction. (It is also clear that on the present view, assuming that the two laws were roughly contemporaneous, the qualifications for sitting in the *repetundae* court could not have been defined by reference to the judiciary law.)

It remains, however, to consider the theory that Plutarch and Livy describe an earlier stage in Gracchus' legislation and that in the end he transferred jurisdiction to the Equites. Such a theory can take various forms. It can be held either that Gracchus proposed but did not pass a law of the kind described by the Epitomator (p. 141 n.2) or that he proposed but did not pass Plutarch's judiciary law or that he actually passed it, but then proceeded later to modify it in a more extreme sense. To the first and second versions it can be objected that both the Epitomator and Plutarch speak of a law and not of a mere bill, and though this objection probably has little weight, [1] it can be added that all three versions are confronted with the difficulty that there is no hint of any change of plan in any of our sources. This argument from silence has much force; for Plutarch at least, who has a good deal to say of Gracchus' withdrawal of the *rogatio de abactis*, would have found it of supreme biographical interest if Gracchus had changed his views on a matter of far greater moment and proceeded from a moderate proposal to one much more extreme. [2]

The question of dating is also relevant. It has been argued that Appian places the judiciary legislation either in Gracchus' second tribunate or at least after his re-election in the summer of 123. But Fraccaro [3] and Münzer [4] have independently demonstrated that Appian's order of narrative is not temporal at all: his account is useless for chronology. [5] Last gave other arguments for dating the legislation in its final form to 122. [6] (a) Fannius' loyalty to Gracchus could not have survived the blow struck at senatorial rights. This will not do: we know far too little of Fannius to be sure that he was not the merest time-server, who associated with Gracchus only to get his backing in the elections. (b) Last identified the Tabula Bembina with the lex Acilia and concluded, on the basis of the mention in *IGRR* IV 1028, of a lex Rubria et Acilia, that the nominal author of the lex Acilia was the

1. Plut. 5,1 speaks of a νόμος συμμαχικός.
2. Last's theory (*CAH* IX 51 ff) that he similarly changed his mind on enfranchisement of the allies is refuted by Badian, *Foreign Clientelae* 299.
3. *Opuscula* II 20 ff.
4. *RE* IIA 1 383 ff.
5. Cf. Badian, *Foreign Clientelae* 300-301 on the inadequacy of Appian's chrono logy for 122-1.
6. *CAH* IX 891-6.

colleague of that Rubrius who proposed the colony of Junonia. As he dated the lex Rubria to 122, it followed that the lex Acilia was in the same year. But the lex Rubria must in fact be placed in 123, [1] and granting all Last's other premisses, his conclusion cannot follow. But Tibiletti has since shown that the phrase 'lex Rubria et Acilia' implies that a Rubrius and an Acilius were not colleagues at all, but that Rubrius held office in an earlier year. [2] It might then seem that Last's conclusion could be reached by another route. If the author of the *law about Iunonia* was tribune in 123, the lex Acilia *de repetundis* cannot be before 122. But this argument contains too many uncertain equations. We cannot identify with any certainty either the lex Acilia with the Gracchan *repetundae* law, or the authors of the lex Rubria et Acilia with two Gracchan tribunes. [3]

General probabilities have more cogency. It is natural to think that Gracchus sought to consolidate support among all classes outside the Senate at the very beginning of his tribunician career, and that his projects of reform apart from his *rogatio de sociis* (which, as he must have known, was more likely to alienate than secure goodwill), were launched at once. The judiciary legislation should then be early. But, though it was well calculated to gain him equestrian support, it was not widely popular. We learn from Diodorus XXXIV/XXXV 27 (cf XXXVII 9) that it passed by only one tribal vote. In 122 Drusus would surely not have hesitated to veto it, as he did veto a proposal to extend the citizenship (App. I 23); he need not have apprehended the fate of Octavius in such circumstances. Moreover Fraccaro produced a good reason for holding that the Tabula Bembina cannot be very late nor very early in either year, since it follows from vv 12 and 16 that the praetorian provinces had already been allocated for the current year. [4] On the plausible time-table for events in 122 given by Badian [5] this law could then only be fitted into that year after Gracchus' return from Africa, when his influence had been subverted. This cannot be believed. The extant law, and presumably the judiciary law proper, should then be placed in 123, and perhaps in the late spring; it is provided in the Tabula Bembina that the peregrine praetor should impanel 450 *iudices* for the current year, but also that no charge may be preferred under the new procedure after the 1st September (vv. 12 with 7-8). If September had already been close at hand, there would have been little purpose in setting up the new court until the following year. [6]

1. Appian *BC* I, 24 and Plutarch 10,2 put Gracchus' visit to Africa in 122, but refer to the passing of the law in genitive absolute clauses which give no indication of date, cf. also *Per.* Liv. LX. Much planning and preparation should have preceded the moment when the *deductio* could begin. Vell. I 15 and two writers drawing on Livy (Oros. V 12 and Eutrop. IV 21) date the colony to, 123; this must be the date of the lex Rubria. Cf. also n. 6 below.
2. *Athen.* 1953 5 ff.
3. Cf. Badian, *op. cit.* (p. 141, n. 4) n. 31.
4. *Opuscula* II 30.
5. *Foreign Clientelae* 301.
6. If the lex Rubria mentioned in v. 22 is that concerned with Junonia, it must then be earlier in 123.

Thus the judiciary legislation should be in the first half of 123; indeed in general Gracchus' laws should be placed here, as later in his first tribunate he must have been pre-occupied with administration, and in 122 Drusus was able to thwart him. Chronologically, there is little room for a change of plan. If indeed A. H. M. Jones [1] is right in accounting for the fact that the panel of *iudices* available to try charges of *repetundae* numbered 450 by the hypothesis that Gracchus had once thought that it should comprise 150 senators and 300 Equites, it would certainly appear that he changed his mind on one point. But an overt modification of his published programme, as distinct from an alteration in private planning is improbable, since we should expect it to have been recorded.

To sum up, the hypothesis that Gracchus did more than exclude senators from the *repetundae* court and that he also constituted a mixed *album* of Equites and senators for other important criminal and civil cases does most to reconcile, and account for the apparent conflict of, our sources; it accords with their unanimous testimony that he was concerned with the 'iudicia' in general and with the probability that he wished to free the Equites from that dependence on the Senate which Polybius ascribes in part to the monopoly of jurisdiction in important cases, affecting non-senators, which the senators had hitherto enjoyed. [2]

# APPENDIX III

## Lucullus and the Equites.

Lucullus became governor of Cilicia, and soon afterwards of Asia, in 74; after Cotta's return in 70 he was also in sole control of Bithynia. He retained Asia till 68 and Cilicia till 67 (*MRR* II 106 ff; 146). In 67 a lex Gabinia ordered the discharge of the Valerian legions and replaced him in Bithynia and Pontus by the consul, Manius Glabrio. As the Valerians argued that he had no right to command them, not only because they had been discharged but also because his provinces had been assigned to others (Plut. *Luc.* 35,3), and as he himself made no effort to defend Cappadocia on the plea that Glabrio was near (Dio XXXVI 17,1), it would seem that Glabrio

1. *Proc. of Camb. Philol. Soc.* (1960) 39 ff. I am not much perturbed by the drafting anomalies which Jones detects; they can be explained (to use his own words) by 'legal caution' or by 'mechanical repetition' from earlier laws.

2. The *lex ne quis iudicio circumveniatur* (on which see U. Ewins, *op. cit.* p. 142 n.2 and N. J. Miners, *CQ* 1958, 241) also becomes easier to understand if senators retained some criminal jurisdiction. Cicero *ap.* Ascon. 79 C, cannot invalidate my thesis, cf. Balsdon, *op. cit.* (p. 141, n. 3) 101, for its correct interpretation. This thesis, however, requires me to modify Badian's view of Caepio's law, *op. cit.* (p. 141, n. 4) 207-9 which cannot have introduced mixed juries but can only have applied the principle of the lex Sempronia to *repetundae* trials and to any such special courts, like that set up by the Mamillian law, as might thereafter be constituted.

was intended to take command of his army in the war, and when Cicero averred in 66 'L. Lucullum ... ab eo bello discedere,' and that he had discharged his troops or handed them over to Glabrio (*de imp. Cn. Pomp.* 5 and 26), he was describing what should have happened. Thus Lucullus was legally in charge of the war for seven years and in practice for eight, as in fact Glabrio did not take over, and it was only in 66 that he was relieved by Pompey. Cicero says of the *lex Gabinia* (*ib.* 26) that the people thought that 'imperi diuturnitati modum statuendum.' Probably many senators shared this opinion. The *Senate* had appointed successors to him in Asia and Cilicia. Except for certain generals in the Hannibalic war, for Marius and Sulla and most recently for Metellus and Pompey in Spain, no one had been in continous command for so long. It was alleged that he was trying to prolong the war (Plut. *Luc.* 33,4; Dio XXXVI 2). This charge was not made only by Equites: it was proclaimed by the Optimate proconsul of Asia in 67 (App. *Bell. Mith.* 90). Certainly so long a tenure could be justified only by extraordinary success. But by 67 he seemed to have failed; Mithridates had revived, and it was urgent to replace a general who could not keep his own troops loyal. [1]

No one will deny the animosity of many Equites to Lucullus. The publicans and moneylenders whom he had aggrieved by his reforms in Asia in 71-0 are said to have instigated influential tribunes to work against him (Plut. *Luc.* 20). But this agitation had no visible effects till the Senate was ready to move in 68, and to deprive him of Asia. The same men were anxious for his replacement in 66. Cicero explains this by saying that they feared a new invasion of Asia (*de imp.* 4-5). That seems wholly plausible, though past grudges doubtless continued to rankle. But if his equestrian enemies now had their way, it was because all were agreed that Lucullus had to go. Their enmity was not in itself decisive. In 54 Cicero was to remind Lentulus Spinther of the harm the publicans had done to Scaevola (*Fam.* I 9,26). Why not to Lucullus, a more recent and telling instance, if he could have used it? [2]

1. The mutiny in the army was aggravated by the agitation against him at Rome, but not wholly due to it; his troops had been ill-disciplined from the first (Sall. *ap.* Plut. 33,3)

2. But see Broughton p. 154 *infra*.

# V

*T. R. S. Broughton*

Comment

# COMMENT

by

T. Robert S. Broughton
*(Bryn Mawr College)*

With the chief propositions in Mr. Brunt's thoughtful and comprehensive discussion I am almost fully in agreement, though inclined to think that the Roman Equites were not so completely uninterested in trade or, on occasion, so ineffective in politics. Men of senatorial and of equestrian rank should have had much in common, and, like the senators, the great majority of the equestrian order, as Gelzer believes, based their fortunes on property in land. [1] It also seems difficult to find equites who were themselves active in the grain trade or engaged personally in sea-borne commerce. They were not a consistent or a united political party (Were there any such in Roman politics?) even when they were strong enough to rally in defence of financial or political and judicial interests. Nor can it be claimed that they were a decisive influence in favor of Roman imperial expansion. But I think that we should allow a little more latitude at some points for their influence to be felt in trade and politics. In the next few

1. M. Gelzer, in his review of H. Hill *The Roman Middle Class*, now in *Kleine Schr.* 1.222-228, esp. 225 f.

pages I attempt to discuss a few of these points, but will use the greater part of my time to point out factors which were available for Augustus to use in creating the equestrian order of the early empire.

Senatorial and magisterial supervision of public contracts had frequently caused friction, and would naturally continue to do so. Yet even at moments when dissatisfaction was strong, as in 184 or even in 169, when feeling against the censors extended to many centuries of the first class, [1] such matters tended to refer to groups within the order and to be episodic. Nor is the case for senatorial exclusiveness, though good, overwhelming, in spite of the small number of new men who attained the consulship in the century before Gaius Gracchus. Our quite imperfect record, especially so after 167, still reveals about seventy-five new family names among the lower magistrates and officers. [2] Acceptance of military functions by equites continued steadily, and prepared the way in all periods for a fairly continuous infiltration of members of the order into the Senate, however much both processes may have been changed and accelerated in the first century after the Social War and the enfranchisement of the Italian allies.

For both orders the feeling expressed by Cicero [3] that petty trade was sordid probably remained generally effective; yet the possibility of considerable interest in sea-borne commerce remained great, even exclusive of the interest of the owners of great estates in acquiring gangs of slaves. Agricultural products (grain, and in Italian commerce, predominantly wine and oil) naturally constituted a high percentage of the goods transported, even when one grants that industrial products maintained their share. If senators could hardly be immune to an interest in the marketing of their products, and the Lex Claudia made provision for it, how much less the equites, who remained unrestricted by the law. Even Cato found a way to circumvent the Lex Claudia. He used to loan money, says Plutarch, [4] in the most disreputable of all ways, on ships. He had borrowers bring many others into partnership with them, and when there were fifty partners, and as many ships for security, he took a share through his freedman Quintus, who engaged in business personally and sailed

1. On Cato, Liv. 39.44; Plut. *Cato Maior* 19; on Gracchus, Liv. 43.16. See Broughton, *MRR* 1.323 f., 374 f., for other sources.

2. M. Gelzer, "Nobilität der römischen Republik," in *Kleine Schr.*, 1.59 f., lists the *novi homines* known up to 63 B. C. The number 75 is only approximate, based on a search in the Index of Broughton, *MRR*. On the junior officers and their promotion, see J. Suolahti, *The Junior Officers of the Roman Army in the Republican Period* (Helsinki, 1955), esp. pp. 169-187, 288-295.

3. Cicero *De Off.* 1.150-151.

4. *Cato Maior* 21.5-6.

along with the borrowers. Here is described a pattern of participation which has found its analogues in many periods: a financial interest, the distribution of risk, and the use of agents. It was probably common among the Roman equites and their Italian associates or allies before the Social War.

It is also of some significance that when the question of possession of ships was raised against Verres in his trial in 70 Hortensius argued that the Lex Claudia was practically a dead letter. Cicero's remarks [1] show that it was still technically in force, but, speaking to a jury drawn from the Senate to which Sulla had added three hundred equites, he makes little of the point. The possibility of a considerable interest of this kind is not to be excluded, even though there is so little evidence that the members of the equestrian order were personally engaged in the work of shipping and distribution, or sailed the seas themselves. The great bankers and lenders, too, Atticus or Egnatius, worked mostly through agents. [2]

Two other factors limit our evidence. The fact that Cicero's relationships were mainly with leaders of the order would itself diminish the references to the activities of the lesser members, while he and his brother in their provinces naturally had more to do with the publicans and the money-lenders. And second, the word *negotiator* is a term that includes many activities, while the word *mercator*, which is infrequent, would be avoided because of the greater social stigma. References to ordinary commercial activity would naturally be fewer, and we should allow for the possibility that some of the less "splendid" equites, the type that could be referred to as *homo levis ac sordidus sed tamen equestri censu*, were so engaged. [3] Yet cases are rare. The Cossutii, [4] for example, known in Delos and in Greece, dealt in objects of art, but perhaps on a sufficient scale to escape the stigma: Julius Caesar's early *fiancée* was a Cossutia, of equestrian family, and *praedives*. Yet land and finance remained the chief interests. Rostovtzeff [5] and others are right and reasonable in holding that the profits made in other ventures by members of the equestrian order, as well as freedmen and other traders, tended to be

1. *Verr.* 2.5.45-46 : antiquae sunt istae leges et mortuae, quem ad modum tu soles dicere, quae vetant. See J. R. Hawthorne, "The Senate after Sulla," *Greece and Rome*, 9 (1962) 53-60, esp. 57 f.

2. On agents of Atticus, see, for example, Cicero *Ad Att.* 4.16.7; 5.9.1, and 13.2; and on Egnatius, Cicero *Ad Fam.* 13.43, and 44, and 73, and 74. See T. Frank, *Econ. Survey Anc. Rome*, 1.351.

3. Cicero *Ad Quint. Frat.*, 1.2.6.

4. J. Hatzfeld, *Les trafiquants Italiens dans l'Orient hellénique*, 228; Suet. *Iul.* I.1; *RE*, s. v. Cossutius, 1673 ff.; cf. R. Syme, review of Gelzer's Caesar, *JRS* 34 (1944), 93 f.

5. Cf. Rostovtzeff, *SEHRE* 17 ff.

invested in land and used to enhance the respectability of the families concerned. And it is clear in the early Empire that the privileges [1] granted to the *navicularii* were designed to satisfy mainly people of lower status, freedmen and Junian Latins for the most part though freemen are included.

It is justifiably claimed that the equites were not a well-knit political party with a program but rather a group that rallied when tax-contracts and other privileges were involved. Was even the Senate likely to rally consistently or with a fair degree of unanimity except in defence of privilege, dignity and property? In fact, the combined effect of the two Gracchan bills, on the collection of tributes in Asia and the constitution of the juries, may not have been readily foreseeable or realized immediately, and the equites may have learned their power in practice. Hence the interval before they began to take vengeance on governors and the fewness of the cases known, even granting that others escaped by being pliable or collusive. It is significant that the attack on Rutilius came at a time when Marius, who had been termed a publican in contemporary political attacks, and his partizans were gathering their strength. [2] Moreover, political relationships tended to be personal, and no order acted as a unit, yet it is probable that enough of the equestrian order followed Marius and Cinna to justify Asconius' statement (89 C) and Sulla's vengeance. [3]

Their political power could express itself both in the courts and in the assemblies. The case of Gabinius shows that even after 70 they continued to be influential in the courts if the interests of a considerable number of their leaders were at stake. [4] One is aware of the note of warning when Cicero urges his brother to restrain his remarks against even lesser equites in Asia—and a threat of prosecution did eventuate in 58—, and of Cicero's own relief that agreements for the payment of tribute by the towns of the province were completed before his own arrival in Cilicia [5]. In the centuriate assembly their number

1. Suet. *Claud.* 19.2; cf. ROSTOVTZEFF, *SEHRE* 158 f., 607 f.

2. See discussions in E. BADIAN, "Quintus Mucius Scaevola and the Province of Asia," *Athenaeum* 34 (1956) 104 ff., esp. 111 ff.; *Foreign Clientelae*, 210, 215; "Caepio and Norbanus," *Historia*, 6 (1957) 318-346. Cf. Plut. *Marius* 45.7; Diod. 34.38; T. CARNEY, *A Biography of Marius* (*Proc. African Class. Assoc.*, Sup. 1) 22 ff., esp. 22-24, 48 ff.

3. Cf. Cicero *Cluent.* 151: "pro illo odio quod habuit in equestrem ordinem"; Ascon. 89 C.

4. On Gabinius' relations with the publicans, see Cicero *De Prov. Cons.* 9-12, and the discussion by E. M. SANFORD, "The Career of Aulus Gabinius," *Trans. Am. Philol. Assoc.*, 70 (1939), 64-92, esp. 80 ff.

5. Cicero *Ad Quint. Frat.* 1.2.6, cf. 1.1.32; 1.3.7; 1.4.2; and on the contracts in Asia, *Ad Att.* 5.13.1.

in the first class made them important, especially when they gathered from all Italy, as on the occasion of Cicero's recall from exile in 57. But this assembly was rarely used except for the election of the higher magistrates, and Cicero's plans for his candidacy for the consulship show that while a good following among the equites was helpful it was far from decisive. In the tribal assemblies, where they were greatly outnumbered, they must have needed many allies in order to secure elections or legislation that they wished, and have had to watch for the situation and arguments that would secure them: popular or senatorial, as occasion required. [1]

Accordingly, in the agitation that led up to Pompey's great commands and the supersession of Lucullus in Asia, it would perhaps be preferable to leave more scope for Pompey's intrigues and the influence of the equites. In view of the recent lengthy commands of Servilius Isauricus, Metellus Pius, and Pompey himself, [2] the duration of Lucullus' command need not have seemed so invidious. Consider the succession of events. The ordinances of Lucullus for reform of the debts in Asia were promptly followed by loud outcries from the money-lenders in Rome, "who bribed leaders of the people to move against him, men of great influence, who had made many of the active politicians their debtors. [3] " Then arose the criticism that he was prolonging the war in order to prolong his command, and the withdrawal of the province of Asia from his command in the course of 69, perhaps even before the arrival of news of his victory over Tigranes. Our sources do not say expressly whether the withdrawal of Asia was an action of the Senate. Note the technique of Marius' attack on Metellus Numidicus in 106: per publicanos aliosque in Africa negotiantes criminatus Metelli lentitudinem. [4] Was the same sort of campaign in use again against Lucullus?

In 68 Cicilia was assigned to Marcius Rex, and in 67 the Lex Gabinia assigned Bithynia and Pontus and a part of Lucullus' army to Acilius Glabrio, while dismissing the Valerian legions. The continued criticisms were made by popular leaders (δημαγαγοί), of whom the most influential was a praetor L. Quinctius, a popular leader and an old opponent since his tribunate in 74. In fact, Lucullus had tried

1. Cicero *Ad Att.* 1.1; *Comm. Pet.* 3-4. See L. R. TAYLOR, *Party Politics in the Age of Caesar* 50-75, on the functioning of these assemblies.

2. See BROUGHTON, *Magistrates of the Roman Republic*, under these names.

3. Plut. *Luc.* 20: "καὶ χρήμασιν ἀνίστασαν ἐπ' αὐτὸν ἐνίους τῶν δημαγωγῶν, μέγα δυνάμενοι καὶ πόλλους ὑπόχρεως πεποιημένοι τῶν πολιτευομένων"; cf. 33.3-5; including a citation of Sallust. On the withdrawal of Asia and Cilicia, Dio 36.2 On the Gabinian law giving Bithynia and Pontus to Glabrio and dismissing the Valeriani, see esp. Sallust 5.13 M, and other texts in Broughton, *MRR* 2.143, 144.

4. Vell. Pat. 2.11.2.

to buy him off. [1] Meantime, all the factors worked together to favor a demand for Pompey, who had, moreover, made such a special display of his status as an *eques* until 70: the insolence and vastly increased strength of the pirates, who had become particularly menacing in league with Mithridates and had shut off the *commercium annonae*, created the overwhelming combination of popular and equestrian support that was required. The points that were stressed in the debate do not minimize the support of the equites. They are the points that would appeal most to voters in the tribal assembly in 67 and continued to appeal in 66 along with the glamor of Pompey's success.

We may now revert to the question of the relationship between the Roman equites and the Italian allies. Eight years ago Professor Gabba [2] advanced the view that the equestrian business men, in view of their status and their position in the courts had gained a marked advantage over their Italian rivals in the markets of the provinces, and that this advantage had been the final factor in deciding the leaders of the Italian communities to demand equality through acquisition of Roman citizenship or to revolt. This attractive view has had further support recently from Professor Salmon. [3] It is true that Italici from Apulia, Lucania and other regions, mainly in southern Italy, who were numerous at Delos and active in the provinces would feel such rivalry, if it existed, and undoubtedly there was serious discontent and some military preparations in 91 in the relevant regions of Italy. [4] But many who had long been in business with the Italians came from towns such as Cumae and Puteoli which ranked as Roman, and the actual outbreak of hostilities began in Picenum, while the bitterest and most stubborn resistance persisted among the Marsi and Paeligni and in northern Samnium, precisely the regions in which our present evidence attests the smallest number of Italian business men and there was a history of anti-Roman feeling. [5] The case is not fully made. When there were so many causes of irritation one or two incidents would be sufficient to set off a great explosion. Such as series may be found in the expulsion of the Italians from Rome in 95 and the assassination of their champion in Rome, Livius Drusus, in 91, and the failure of his legislation. [6] In fact, it is quite

1. Plut. *Luc.* 33.3-4; Sall. 4.71 M; cf. 4.70 M.
2. *Athenaeum* 32 (1954), 41 ff., esp. 53-61.
3. *Phoenix* 16 (1962),107-119.
4. Appian *BC* 1.38.173; 1.41.182; Liv. *Per.* 72; 73; Diod. 37.13.1. See SALMON, *op. cit.* (note 22)114.
5. See reviews of Gabba's work by BALSDON, *Gnomon* 26 (1954), 343 f.; and SHERWIN-WHITE, *JRS* 45 (1955), 168-170. Data on the place of origin of Italian traders in the East may be found in HATZFELD, *op. cit.* (note 9), 52 ff., and esp. 238 ff.; also *Bull. Corr. Hell.* 36 (1912).1 ff.
6. Note particularly Ascon. 67-68 C; cf. BROUGHTON, *MRR* 2.11.

possible that, far from being bitter rivals in business, Romans and Italians abroad were cooperating, and that the publicans had been using the experience and skill of many of the large number of mostly new, and, it would seem, still unregistered, citizens who were massacred at the command of Mithridates in 88. [1]

The enfranchisement of the Italian allies probably made no great change in the general orientation and interests of the equestrian order. Gabba has shown that some began to be active in political life very soon, and Suolahti that in the late Republic there was a considerable number of new family names among the junior officers,—an anticipation of the situation under Augustus. [2] Apart from the dispossessed or people in such greatly devastated regions as northern Samnium [3] the leading families of the Italian towns cannot have differed greatly in their interests from the Roman equites or in range of possessions from the knights whom Sulla promoted to the Senate or a Roscius of Ameria, who claimed to have been a Sullan supporter, down to a Catienus, *homo levis ac sordidus sed tamen equestri censu*, and various clients of Cicero of barely an equestrian census. [4] But the process of assimilation was not easy or swift. Many in the coloniae and the municipia, *domi nobiles*, were ready to support Catiline in 63, and there is evidence of unrest then in Picenum, among the Paeligni and in the south, as well as in Etruria. But it had gone far enough to bring major support to Cicero from the leading elements of most of Italy in 57. [5]

Two texts from 50 B. C. yield an indication of the chief interests and attitudes of the equestrian order at that time. In a letter of September, Caelius Rufus declares that the senate and *qui res iudicant* i. e. the leaders among the equites, will support Pompey. But in a letter to Atticus on the eve of the outbreak Cicero divides them into three groups, the publicans, never reliable and now very friendly toward Caesar, the *faeneratores* and the *agricolae*, whose first desire is peace and quiet. [6] These are the ones who count, the trader is not on the list.

1. T. Frank, *op. cit.* (note 7), 1.277 f. Hatzfeld, *op. cit.* (note 9), 238 ff., notes the difficulty Greeks felt in distinguishing between Romans and Italians. On the new citizens, see Posidonius in Athenaeus 5.213a. On the number, Memnon in *FGrH* IIIB, 252, no. 434, 22.9; Val. Max. 9.1.3; Plut. *Sull.* 24 makes it 150,000.

2. Gabba, *Athenaeum* 32 (1954), 98-108; cf. R. Syme, *Rom. Rev.* 78 ff., esp. 88; 349 ff. Suolahti, *op. cit.* (note 3), 109-138, 160-166, 181-184, 283-286.

3. Strabo 5.4.11, 249-250 C.

4. Texts are cited in Broughton, *MRR* 2.74, at no. 1 under Sulla. On Roscius, see Cicero, *Rosc. Amer.* 15-16, 20-21, 24-25, 126. On Catienus, Cicero *Ad Quint. Frat.* 1.2.6; and others, *Ad Fam.* 9.13.

5. Sall. *Cat.* 17; 27, 2; Oros. 6.6.7. On Cicero and *cuncta Italia*, see L. R. Taylor, *op. cit.* (note 16) 61 ff., and R. Syme, *Rom. Rev.* 88 ff.

6. Caelius Rufus in Cicero *Ad Fam.* 8.14; Cicero *Ad Att.* 7.7.5.

The tumultuous period of the Civil Wars emphasized the factors that led to the formation of the equestrian order of the early Empire. Caesar's abolition of the farming of the tithe [1] shifted the emphasis to other interests, and removed one of the chief causes of union for political pressure. His advancement of the families of former Marians, and his recruitment of officers, assistants, and, indeed, considerable numbers of his enlarged Senate, from among the knights of all Italy and some of the provinces, completed the process of assimilation among them and fostered it in the Senate. [2] Most of them were men of property and often conservative in tendency. It was of Caesar's enlarged Senate that Cicero in February, 43, when moving against Mark Antony and trying to encourage Trebonius, remarked: *Habemus fortem senatum, consulares partim timidas, partim male sentientes.* [3] Above all, the times enhanced the military potential of the order, many of whose members served as officers of combat or supply for years on end. [4] The proscriptions meant a considerable change in the ownership (The property of over two thousand knights was taken. [5]) and to some extent in the concentration of property in land, but the interests of new owners could not differ greatly from the old. Frequently equites, as regular aides and close advisors of the military leaders, held great power and influence, and were even entrusted with important commands. [6] This is not to say that before Actium all those in Italy were as yet loyal followers of Octavian. War levies were severe, and interest rates, which fell to one-half after the winning of Egypt, reflect the uncertainty of the time. Dio wryly remarks that Octavian brought great numbers of senators and equites to Brundisium during the Actium campaign, in order to enhance the appearance of unity, and to keep the dissidents from making trouble. [7]

In the new order of Caesar Augustus the military, judicial, and financial functions of the equites were gradually channelled and organized in the service of the state, while their private fortunes inevitably benefitted from peace, recovery, and the great expansion in the early Empire of trade, industry, and property values. The order had, however, to be reorganized and brought under greater control. Revival of the procession and the *probatio* gave control of the *equites*

1. Plut. *Caes.* 48.
2. R. Syme, *Rom. Rev.* 78 ff.
3. *Ad Fam.* 10.28.
4. Examples: Volusenus Quadratus, Mamurra, P. Ventidius; see R. Syme, *Rom. Rev.* 70 ff.; 80 ff.
5. Appian *BC* 4.5; cf. Dio 47.6 and 17.
6. For example, Oppius, Balbus and Matius (See Tacitus *Ann.* 12.60: *praevalida nomina*), and, in the triumviral and early Augustan periods, Vedius Pollio. See R. Syme, *Rom. Rev.* 71 ff., and on Vedius, *JRS* 51 (1961) 23-30.
7. Dio 50.10-11.

*equo publico* and placed a much desired emphasis on military service. *Equites selecti* served in the *decuriae* of jurors, and apparently made up a large part of the centuries that carried through the *destinatio* o*ι* magistrates described in the Tabula Hebana. [1] Behind these were the large numbers scattered throughout the Empire of Roman citizens of free birth for two generations who possessed the equestrian census. There were said to be five hundred of these each in Gades and Patavium alone. [2] The processions, the sevirate and corresponding municipal celebrations alike emphasized association with the Princeps and served to encourage a military career, and perhaps also, as with the preliminary senatorial offices, to aid in recruiting and selecting officers for future promotion. [3] I doubt if the order of the late Republic was sharply diminished or interrupted, and agree with De Laet that Augustus anticipated in generous measure the enrollment in the provinces which Dio attributes to Gaius. [4] The new army benefitted from the new emphasis: many equestrian military careers extended over many years, and the presence of some barbarian names among them indicate that they were given the rank for this purpose. [5]

The tithe was no longer farmed and the major tributes were collected directly, but in the collection of the indirect taxes the societies of publicans were only slowly superseded. [6] Some compensation was given through the channelling of the financial and administrative abilities of the equites into salaried positions in the service and appointment of the emperor. These often enabled them to vie with senators in power and influence, if not in *dignitas*, and were not, it seems, devoid of opportunities for additional profits. Prejudice against personal service kept them for a time out of the imperial household, but the financial procuratorships in imperial provinces made many of them collectors and paymasters for wide areas, while personal

1. A. Stein, *Röm. Ritterstand* 54 ff., and cf. Gelzer's rev. in *Klein. Schr.* 1.228 ff. A. H. M. Jones has shown that a distinction must be made between *equites equo publico*, *equites selecti*, and the *ordo equester* in general: "The Elections under Augustus," in *Studies in Roman Government and Law*, 29 ff., esp. 39-45, a study to which Mr. Brunt kindly called my attention.

2. Strabo 3.5.3, 169 C; 5.1.7, 213 C; on processions in Rome, Dion. Hal. 6.13.4. Large numbers of Romans of equestrian census are attested for the region of Corduba in Spain in 48-47, Caes. *Bell. Alex.* 56.

3. See L. R. Taylor, *JRS* 14 (1924) 169 ff.; E. Birley, "The Equestrian Officers of the Roman Army," in *Roman Britain and the Roman Army*, 133-153.

4. Dio 59.9.2. S. J. De Laet, "La composition de l'ordre équestre," *Rev. Belge Philol. Hist.* 20 (1941) 509-531.

5. See particularly, De Laet's list, *op. cit.* (note 42), or, for examples, Ehrenberg and Jones, *Documents Illustrating the Reigns of Augustus and Tiberius*, nos. 224, Q. Octavius Sagitta; 233, T. Iunius Montanus; and 241, Staius Vobenus, son of Esdragass.

6. See, for example, on the customs dues, S. J. De Laet, *Portorium* (Gand, 1944) 363 ff.

procurators of imperial possessions in senatorial provinces were useful and at times too eager sentinels there. Prefectships, of Egypt, of the praetorian guard, the watch, the grain supply, the fleets, and some minor military provinces extended their functions. In a real sense the administrative system of the new order depended on the equites [1]. Their judicial funtions have been mentioned. There were highly placed individuals, a Maecenas, a Proculeius, or a Sallustius, as once a Matius or a Vedius, *praevalida nomina*, who chose to remain equites, and held an influential place in imperial counsels as the emperor's *amici* [2]. Thus Augustus developed elements of a pattern which had begun to appear under Pompey and Caesar and gradually welded it into a hierarchical yet socially mobile system in which the fundamental administrative elements were attached closely to himself.

Did this administrative importance give the equestrian order a share in the making of policy or make their interests an important factor in the expansion of the Empire? Apart from the influence of a few individuals there was little opportunity. There was no organization of the order as a whole, and its empire-wide distribution would have made it ineffective. Formal actions attributed to them in Rome appear to be largely ceremonial in character: a share in acclaiming Augustus *pater patriae*, in giving the title *princeps iuventutis* to Gaius and Lucius, in mourning for them, and in apotheosizing Augustus. Their demonstrations against the Julian marriage and inheritance laws took place from their section in the games. [3]

There were doubtless economic factors involved in the expansion of the Empire under Augustus, but there is little suggestion that equestrian interests were particularly served. It was desirable to exploit the gold and other metals of north-western Spain, but there was an uneasy and unpacified frontier to settle, a new army to be trained, and, though this may be merely a result, a fresh reserve of military man-power to be tapped. [4] The excavations at the town on the Magdalensberg in Noricum reveal a lively trade with Italian centers, particularly Aquileia, during the late Republic and the

1. R. Syme, *Rom. Rev.* 355-360; cf. A. H. M. Jones, *op. cit.* (note 39) 4 f.

2. Tacitus *Ann.* 12.60. See J. Crook, *Consilium Principis*, chapters 3 and 4, esp. pp. 21 ff.

3. Actions of the Equites; Augustus, *pater patriae*, *Mon. Anc.* 45, and Ovid *Fasti* 2.127; Gaius and Lucius, *Principes Iuventutis*, *Mon. Anc.* 14; mourning for them, Cenotaph of Pisa, Dessau 139; apotheosis of Augustus, coins in H. Mattingly *Coins Roman Empire Brit. Museum* 155, 160, with inscription, *consensu senat. et eq. ord. p. q. R.*; cf. also, Dio 58.2.7; Suet. *Claud.* 6.1; Dio 59.6.6, for other such actions. On the protests against the Lex Papia Poppaea, Dio 56.1; Suet. *Aug.* 34.2.

4. Van Nostrand, in T. Frank, *op. cit.* (note 7), 3.150 ff.; Sutherland, *The Romans in Spain* 133 f., 143.

early Empire. Trade in the iron of Noricum had long been active, and, as Professor Egger has pointed out, uninterrupted and friendly intercourse resulted in incorporation without the usual tale of Roman exactions and native revolt,—unlike the experience of neighboring Pannonia and Dalmatia. [1] The natural resources and the man-power of the northern frontier regions were doubtless welcome, but the main point was strategic: expansion to natural frontiers, security and economy in defense, and establishment of land communications between the eastern and the western halves of the Empire. Bato's remark, that the Romans had sent not dogs or shepherds to guard their flocks, but wolves, suggests that, like Licinus in Gaul, the robbers in Dalmatia were imperial officials. [2]

Augustus' attempt to conquer the Sabaeans is the most probable example of an action motivated by the desire to control trade. If successful he would have held the Red Sea, the coast of Arabia, and controlled the access of both the Egyptians and the Nabateans to Indian and African trade. The careful collection of information on communications, products and ships by those who were engaged is significant. It is not clear that equestrian interests were involved. The equestrian prefects of Egypt were natural choices for command either on the Red Sea or in the Nile valley, but the trade itself remained largely in the hands of Greeks and natives. [3] Annius Plocamus, the long-term contractor for the Red Sea revenues, may perhaps have been an eques, but it was his freedman who was coasting about Arabia when he was blown off to Ceylon. [4] When spices and frankin-cense were so expensive and in such general demand the desire to control the trade in them was natural enough. [5]

What then were the financial opportunities that remained outside of official careers? In an age of internal peace and recovery they must have been many at home and abroad, both for the successful speculator and the careful investor. First may be mentioned the opportunities for contractors during the great period of imperial

1. T. Frank, *op. cit.* (note 7), 5.114 f., 287 ff.; Calderini, *Aquileia Romana* 467 ff; R. Egger, *Die Stadt auf dem Magdalensberg. Ein Grosshandelsplatz* (Wien, 1961).

2. Dio 56.16.3; and on Licinus, 54.21; Suet. *Aug.* 67. See *Cambridge Ancient History* 10, 347 ff.

3. Strabo 2.5.12, 118 C; 16.4.22-24, 781-782 C; Plin. *NH* 6.160-162; Dio 23.29; *PIR*² 1, 27, no. 179, on Aelius Gallus; *RE* s. v. Petronius, no. 21, on Petronius. See Rostovtzeff, *SEHRE* 53, 94; E. H. Warmington, *The Commerce between the Roman Empire and India*, 78 ff.

4. Plin. *NH* 6.84-97; on the two recent inscriptions, D. Meredith, *JRS* 43 (1953) 38-40. See C. Starr, *Class. Philol.* 51 (1956) 27-30.

5. On production and trade of frankincense and myrrh, see Plin. *NH* 12, 51-84; and see Gus. W. Van Beek, "Frankincense and Myrrh," *The Biblical Archaeologist* 23 (1960) 70-95.

building, new construction and repairs in Rome, Italy and the provinces. Mines remained for some time in private ownership, and the working of imperial properties on contract was profitable. [1] Above all, there was money-lending and investment in land. The panic of 33 A. D., though soon forgotten, was at least a temporary lesson to those who had put too small a portion of their capital into the more modest returns from agriculture. [2] The prejudice against petty trade remained: note the Sempronius Gracchus who sustained himself by means of *sordidas merces* and was accused of supplying Tacfarinas with grain. [3] Although the financing of shippers and traders cannot have been neglected in these times of safe and expanding commerce, information remains scanty. Equites are not mentioned among the *navicularii*, nor among the names of shippers on the second and third century sherds from Gaul and Spain in Monte Testaccio. Perhaps the provincial equites who were chided under Nero for staying at home instead of coming *e longinquis provinciis* to their duties in Rome were more commercially minded. And one might ask whether a knight of Sabratha who dwelt in Italy was living on the income from estates in Tripolitania or on the proceeds of Trans-Saharan trade. [4]

The numerous inscriptions found recently, scratched on the walls of the trading center in the town on the Magdalensberg in Noricum, give a good picture of who these traders were. Large lots of iron vessels of various kinds, as many as five hundred in a lot, are listed, and several small loans in connection with the trade are recorded. The names of the traders, some 250 in all, consist almost wholly of those of freedmen agents or native producers, while none indicate a higher status than ordinary free citizens. Several, such as Barbius and Statius, suggest groups already known at Aquileia and several cities in Pannonia and Dalmatia. But even this is doubtful, since, as Dr. Panciera has warned us, not all of the persons with these names found in a large area over a considerable period remained in close connection. No Barbius or Statius from Aquileia appears in *PIR*, and the one which De Laet found to put in his list of knights of the early Empire records a military career. [5] Similarly, Tacitus describes

1. See, on the mines of Sextus Marius in Spain, Tacitus, *Ann.* 6.19.
2. Tacitus *Ann.* 6.17.
3. Tacitus *Ann.* 4.13.
4. See Suet. *Claud.* 18-19, and cf. Rostovtzeff, *SEHRE*, Index, s. v. Navicularii. On Monte Testaccio, see T. Frank, "Notes on Roman Commerce," *JRS* 27 (1937) 72-79. On knights in provinces, Tacitus *Ann.* 16.27. On the knight of Sabratha, Suet. *Vesp.* 3.1.
5. R. Egger, *op. cit.* (note 49); cf. Calderini, *Aquileia Romana*, 467 ff.; S. Panciera, *Vita economica di Aquileia in Età Romana* esp. 94 ff.; and on the knight of Aquileia, De Laet, *op. cit.* (note 42), p. 515 note.

the Romans at the court of Maroboduus in Bohemia as *lixae et negotiatores*. [1] The anonymous Roman knight who travelled the amber route to the Baltic under Nero was sent by Nero's procurator in charge of games, and the amber he brought back was used for imperial display,—hardly a commercial proposition. [2] And Ptolemy has not told us the status of Maes who was also called Titianus, the Syrian merchant whose man ranged the roads of Asia to Tashkurgan in modern Turkestan. [3]

In fact, Roman thinking was largely bounded by interest in agriculture and finance, and the equites, whatever their origin, tended to move into these activities. Although they were administratively the most important element in the regime of the Early Empire, as a group, apart from a few important individuals, they probably had little political influence. There is equally little evidence that they engaged actively in trade: the freedmen, the Greeks and the Syrians were already in possession. [4]

In conclusion, three passages appear to epitomize the difference between the equites of the late Republic and those of the Empire. To Cicero they were the *publicani*, the *faeneratores* and the *agricolae*. Seneca mentions among the interests of a typical rich man his fine household and his splendid house, and adds "multum serit, multum faenerat." And Tacitus in his characterization of Seneca's brother Mela says: "He had refrained from seeking public office because of an inverted ambition to attain the influence of a senator while remaining a Roman eques; he also believed that a shorter road to the acquisition of wealth ran through procuratorships for the administration of the emperor's affairs." [5]

1. Tacitus *Ann.* 2.62.
2. Plin. *NH* 37.45. See CHARLESWORTH, *Trade Routes and Commerce* 176 (where he has confused the names); WHEELER, *Rome Beyond the Imperial Frontiers* 21 ff., esp. 29 f.
3. Ptolemy, *Geog.* 1.11; CHARLESWORTH, *op. cit.* (note 60), 103; M. CARY, *Class. Quart.* 6 (1956) 130-134.
4. T. FRANK, *op. cit.* (note 7) 5.27 off., 279 ff., for a discussion who the shippers were. Similarly, Warmington holds that the Indian trade was largely in the hands of natives, Greeks and Syrians, *op. cit.* (note 51) 78.
5. Cicero *Ad Att.* 7.7.5; Seneca *Ep. Mor.* 41.7; Tacitus *Ann.* 16.17.

# VI

*J. P. V. D. Balsdon*

## The History of the Extortion Court at Rome, 123–70 B.C.

# THE HISTORY OF THE EXTORTION COURT AT ROME, 123–70 B.C.



## I. Nature of the Problem [1]

The available evidence concerning the history of the Extortion Court, the *quaestio repetundarum,* at Rome is tabulated opposite page 114.[2] In view of the bulk of this evidence, it is at first sight surprising that this should be one of the most confused chapters of Roman history. Indeed, it is improbable that all Roman historians would agree upon any more precise statement of certainty than the following: that C. Gracchus, whether by a *lex Sempronia iudiciaria,* or by a *lex Sempronia de repetundis,* or by a *lex Acilia de repetundis* which may, or may not, be reproduced in the *lex repetundarum,* fragments of which are preserved at Naples and at Vienna (*CIL* $1^2$, 583), established *equites* (selected either from owners and past owners, within certain age limits, of the *equus publicus,* or from all those who possessed the equestrian *census*) *either* in place of, *or* in association with, senators as jurors in the *quaestio de repetundis;* that Q. Servilius Caepio, probably in his consulship in 106 B.C., proposed, and perhaps carried, a judiciary law in the interest of the Senate; that C. Servilius Glaucia either in 111 (Mommsen [3]), 108 (Carcopino [4]), 104 (Last [5]) or 101 B.C. (Niccolini [6]) carried a *lex repetundarum*

[1] The clearest and fullest history of the court is to be found in Th. Mommsen, 'Lex Repetundarum,' *Ges. Schr.*, 1, 1–64 and 'Über die leges iudiciariae des vii Jahrhunderts bis zur lex Aurelia,' *Ges. Schr.* iii, 339–355; A. H. J. Greenidge, *The Legal Procedure of Cicero's Time* (Oxford, 1901), 433–504; J. L. Strachan-Davidson, *Problems of the Roman Criminal Law* (Oxford, 1912), ii, 75–152. This paper is written with the object of examining the theory put forward by J. Carcopino in Bloch-Carcopino, *Histoire Romaine* (Paris, 1935) 248–251, 311 f., 317 and, in greater detail, in his book *Autour des Gracques* (Paris, 1928), especially on pp. 205–235. In case my criticisms of this theory should convey an impression of ungraciousness, I must state that no book on ancient history has ever stimulated or excited me more than *Autour des Gracques.*

[2] Where detailed references are not given in the text or notes of this paper, they can easily be discovered by reference to this table. Asconius throughout is cited by the pages of A. C. Clark's edition (Oxford, 1907) and other Ciceronian scholiasts by the pages of the edition of Th. Stangl (Leipzig, 1912).

[3] *Ges. Schr.* i, 18 f.

[4] *Autour des Gracques*, 230.

[5] Professor H. M. Last in *CAH* ix, 162 f.

[6] G. Niccolini, *I fasti dei tribuni della plebe* (Milan, 1934), 195 ff.

and perhaps other judiciary laws in which he *possibly* either gave for the first time, or restored, to the *equites* complete possession of the juries and *certainly* effected two reforms in procedure, (*a*) by legalising the prosecution not only of recent magistrates and pro-magistrates, but also of their accomplices and (*b*) by introducing the form of 'double action' known as *comperendinatio*;[7] that M. Livius Drusus, as tribune in 91 B.C., endeavoured unsuccessfully to establish, or to re-establish, as the case may be, mixed juries of senators and *equites*, and to make equestrian as well as senatorial jurors liable to prosecution for accepting bribes; that in 89 B.C. by a *lex Plautia* of the tribune M. Plautius Silvanus mixed juries were established, certainly for trials of *maiestas*, and perhaps for *repetundae* too. After this, the way is clearer. Sulla re-established senatorial juries, which survived until 70 B.C., when, by the *lex Aurelia*, jurors were selected from three panels—from senators, *equites* and *tribuni aerarii*.

Mommsen[8] held that C. Gracchus handed over the courts, lock, stock and barrel, to the *equites*; that the law by which this change was accomplished was sponsored not by Gracchus himself, but by a fellow-tribune, M'. Acilius Glabrio; and that this is the law of which fragments survive on the Naples tablets.

Carcopino[9] has revived the theory that C. Gracchus established *mixed* juries of senators and *equites*, and that it was Glaucia who first recruited jurors exclusively from the *equites*. Glaucia's law, the *lex Servilia repetundarum*, is, on this view, the extant law of the Naples tablets. Flaws in Carcopino's argument have already been indicated by others,[10] but, none the less, it has found favour in certain quarters. E. Cavaignac, for instance, writes of the Naples law as 'la loi *repetundarum* maintenant fixée (*sic*) en 108.'[11]

This paper is written with the object of examining closely the evidence concerning Acilius, Caepio and Glaucia, who are the three 'mystery figures' in the history of the extortion court, in the belief that Carcopino's theory is untenable and that the Naples law is still firmly fixed where Mommsen placed it, as the *lex Acilia*, part, and a leading part, of the legislation of C. Sempronius Gracchus.

## II. Character of the Evidence

Though the evidence concerning the courts in this period may be large in bulk, in character it has no more homogeneity than the contents of a magpie's nest. Cicero could have given us all the information that we need; but, un-

[7] Or *comperendinatus*, *Verr.* ii, 1, 26.
[8] *Ges. Schr.* i, 20 ff
[9] *Autour des Gracques*, 205 ff.
[10] E.g. by H. M. Last in *JRS* xviii, 1928, 231 f.
[11] *Revue de philologie*, 1934, p. 73.

fortunately, he has not done so. Livy, too, probably gave this information in the missing books of his *History*; but Livy's evidence survives only in disparate fragments and at second hand, in the *Periochae* or in later writers most of whom consulted, not Livy's complete History, but some, though not necessarily the same, epitome of that History.[12]

We possess three narrative histories which cover the whole of this period, supplied respectively by Livy's epitomator, by Velleius Paterculus and by Appian in Book i of the *Civil Wars*. The only legislators in the field of judiciary legislation of whom any of them know are, in this period, C. Gracchus, Livius Drusus, Sulla and L. Aurelius Cotta. That C. Gracchus handed the courts over to the *equites* is stated by Velleius Paterculus[13] and by Appian; the epitomator, who says nothing about the courts, declares—what may or may not be relevant—that C. Gracchus drafted 600 *equites* into the Senate. The laws of Acilius, Caepio and Glaucia are ignored by all three writers. Of Livius Drusus, Velleius says that he wished to restore the courts to the Senate, Appian that he wished to draft 300 *equites* into the Senate and to hand the courts over to a Senate thus enlarged, the epitomator that he actually carried—*pertulit*—a law establishing mixed juries, and he says nothing of its repeal. The restoration of the courts to the Senate by Sulla is recorded by Velleius Paterculus, but ignored by the other two writers. Not one of the three gives us the truth about the *Lex Aurelia* of 70 B.C., of which we have certain knowledge from Cicero and his scholiasts. Appian ignores the law completely; Livy's epitomator misunderstands it—he says that the courts were handed over to the *equites*—and Velleius Paterculus, mentioning mixed juries, but ignoring the *tribuni aerarii*, alone comes within striking distance of the truth.

In the case of the legislation, proposed or carried, by Livius Drusus, Sulla and L. Aurelius Cotta, we are on the fringe of the Ciceronian period,[14] and Cicero and his scholiasts enable us, in this small part of the field, to apply a valid test of accuracy. Velleius Paterculus alone emerges from the test with credit.[15] Appian is only $33\frac{1}{3}$ per cent. accurate and, for the rest, if not ignorant, at least not explicit. The epitomator of Livy cuts the poorest figure of all. Unlike the other two, he does not even achieve a $33\frac{1}{3}$ percentage of accuracy; he is careless, or misinformed. This fact might well be borne in mind by those who place unquestioning faith in his account of the drafting of 600 *equites* into the Senate by C. Gracchus.[16]

[12] See p. 104, n. 29 below.

[13] See p. 98, n. 2 above.

[14] See Strachan-Davidson, *op. cit.* ii, 77 f., for some very trenchant observations on the comparative value of Cicero and our other authorities.

[15] Strachan-Davidson, *loc. cit.*, on Livius Drusus, 'My own opinion is that Appian does not on this occasion win the crown promised to the one-eyed in the country of the blind, but that it must fall to Velleius.'

[16] *E.g.* W. Judeich, *Hist. Zeitschr.*, 3te. Folge, xv, 1913, 491 ff.; E. von Stern, *Hermes* lvi, 1921, 281 ff.

## III. Mixed Courts

Cicero has bequeathed to us one remark which covers the period from C. Gracchus to Sulla. He states in the *Verrines*[17] that the *equites* sat on the jury 'annos prope quinquaginta continuos.' He does not state that they sat *alone* on juries during these fifty (or, to be strictly accurate, just over forty[18]) years, and his remark,[19] while it excludes a complete interruption of equestrian tenure of jury service during this period, is not incompatible with the existence, within this period, of mixed senatorial and equestrian juries. Nor does Cicero's remark in the *Pro Cornelio*, 'cum primum senatores cum equitibus Romanis lege Plotia iudicarent,' necessarily suggest that, in Cicero's opinion, mixed juries had never existed before 89 B.C. *Cum primum* might mean 'when for the first time in history'; on the other hand, it is far more likely to mean no more than *simulac*, 'as soon as the lex Plautia established mixed juries.'[20] It is therefore to be remarked that Cicero nowhere firmly denies the creation—and subsequent abolition—of mixed juries before 89 B.C.

The 'mixing' of senators and *equites* could be effected in either of two different ways, between which the historian must make a careful distinction. On the one hand (*a*) fresh blood, in the form of *equites*, might be infused into the body of the Senate and the courts be held by the Senate thus re-constituted. In this case, though the personnel of the Senate was enlarged, the courts were, technically, in the hands of senators. On the other hand, (*b*), the *album iudicum*, the list of qualified jurors, might consist, half and half, or in some other proportion, of senators and *equites*. In this latter case juries would be 'mixed' in the proper sense of that term.

The frequency with which, according to one or other of our authorities, these changes were proposed or effected in our period is little short of startling. The evidence can best be presented in tabulation:

(*a*) Admission of *equites* to the Senate.

1. Gaius Gracchus (Livy, *Per.*).
2. Proposed, but not achieved, by Livius Drusus (Appian).
3. Sulla (Livy, *Per.* 89, Appian, B.C. I, 100, 4, 468. Cf. Dionys. V, 77, 5 and Sallust, *Cat.* 37, 6).

(*b*) Constitution of Mixed Juries.

1. Tiberius Gracchus (Plutarch).
2. Gaius Gracchus (Plutarch).
3. Q. Servilius Caepio (Cassiodorus and Obsequens).
4. Proposed, but not achieved, by Livius Drusus (Livy, *Per.*; *De viris illustribus*?)
5. Lex Plautia of 89 B.C. (Cicero)
6. Lex Aurelia of 70 B.C. (Asconius, *In Pisonianam.*)

[17] I, 38.

[18] There is some indication of an alternative figure in the MSS. of *Verr.* I, 38, but pseudo-Asconius *ad loc.*, p. 218, confirms 'quinquaginta.' He himself elsewhere, *ad Div.* 8, pp. 188 f., gives forty years for the length of this period.

[19] And, incidentally, the comments of pseudo-Asconius to which reference was made in the previous note.

[20] See R. Kühner, *Grammatik der lateinischen Sprache*² (Hanover, 1914), II, ii, 352 ff. For this reference, and for valuable assistance on this matter, I am indebted to my colleague, Mr. E. A. Barber. I am surprised to find that this point does not appear to have attracted the attention of previous historians. Nearly all historians (*e.g.* Mommsen, *Ges. Schr.* iii, 342) treat Cicero's remark as firm evidence that mixed courts cannot have existed, in Cicero's opinion, before 89 B.C., though Professor H. M. Last states (*CAH* ix, 162, n. 3) that 'he does not share the prevailing confidence with which conclusions are drawn from this passage.'

## IV. Acilius, Caepio and Glaucia

Except for the mention, by Valerius Maximus, of a man under trial 'lege Servilia,' the laws of Acilius and Glaucia are recorded by no ancient authority whatever, apart from Cicero and his scholiasts. Caepio's 'law' is mentioned by Cicero—with one exception, in his oratorical works, and always in works on which there are no scholia—and also, in puzzling, indeed contradictory, language by Tacitus, Obsequens and Cassiodorus. As Acilius, Caepio and Glaucia are the three 'mystery figures' of the period, the evidence concerning their laws calls for careful examination.

M'. Acilius Glabrio, author of the *lex Acilia,* which he carried, presumably, during his tribunate, was father of the *praetor repetundarum* who presided at Verres' trial in 70 B.C. His tribunate, therefore, for whose date no other certain evidence exists, may well have been roughly, even exactly, contemporary with that of C. Gracchus.[21] Cicero refers twice in the *Verrines* to this law, on both occasions, as was to be expected, in complimentary terms. In *Verr.* 1, 51 he states, 'Qua lege populus Romanus de pecuniis repetundis optimis iudiciis severissimisque iudicibus usus est,' which Mommsen takes to refer to the first introduction of equestrian jurors in 123 or 122 B.C., and pseudo-Asconius makes the comment, 'M'. Acilius Glabrio legem Aciliam tulit de pecuniis repetundis severissimam'—it is not hard to trace the origin of that epithet[22]—'ut qua ne comperendinari quidem liceret reum.' In the last part of this sentence pseudo-Asconius appears to have made a definite contribution to our knowledge. The appearance is deceptive, for the information is derived from the second passage (*Verr.* ii, 1, 26), in which Cicero refers to the law: 'Verum, ut opinor, Glaucia primus tulit ut comperendinaretur reus; antea vel iudicari primo poterat vel amplius pronuntiari. Utram, igitur, putas legem molliorem? Opinor, illam veterem. . . . Ego tibi illam Aciliam legem restituo. . . . Puta te non hac tam atroci, sed illa lege mitissima causam dicere.' This language is hard enough to reconcile with a *lex* which is *severissima* in any other sense than that accepted by Mommsen, that it introduced *severissimi iudices.* In his commentary on this second passage pseudo-Asconius states of the *lex Acilia,* 'Quae lex neque comperendinationem ⟨*neque*⟩ ampliationem habet.'[23] The accuracy of this comment may be considered later.[24]

[21] Mommsen, *Ges. Schr.* i, 18. An inscription (*I.G.R.R.* iv, 1028), which proves the existence, earlier than 105 B.C., of a Lex Rubria Acilia, suggests that Acilius' tribunate may have been exactly contemporary with one of the tribunates of C. Gracchus. See H. M. Last in *CAH* ix, 892.

[22] I cannot see why the fact that the first part of this statement 'répond quasi littéralement' to the sentence in the *Verrines* on which it is a comment is thought by Carcopino (*op. cit.*, 215) to increase its value. Carcopino's translation, 'une loi dite Acilia, qui est la plus sévère de celles dont les crimes de concussion aient été l'objet,' would, I suspect, have given pseudo-Asconius something of a shock.

[23] p. 231.

[24] See p. 113, below.

Next, Caepio and Glaucia. Both, unfortunately, possessed the *nomen* Servilius. The laws of both, therefore, were *leges Serviliae*. When Tacitus writes, however,[25] 'Cum . . . Serviliae leges senatui iudicia redderent,' the *leges Serviliae* to which he refers are certainly the law, or laws, of Caepio. Caepio was, like the Livii Drusi, father and son, 'patronus senatus';[26] Glaucia was notoriously its enemy. Tacitus declares then, that, thanks to Caepio, the Senate recovered the exclusive right of filling the jury, which it had lost earlier to Gracchus. If this was in Caepio's consulship, it was in 106 B.C.[27]

A record, not that Caepio restored jury service to senators, but that, in his consulship in 106 B.C., he established *mixed* juries of senators and *equites*, is preserved, and preserved very strangely. Cassiodorus, in his *Chronicon*, records, of this year, 'Per Servilium Caepionem consulem iudicia equitibus et senatoribus communicata,' and Obsequens, 'Per Caepionem consulem senatorum et equitum iudicia communicata. Cetera in pace fuerunt.' Nowhere do the uncomely parts of ancient historiography show greater comeliness. Cassiodorus, writing in A.D. 519, rarely interrupts his list of consuls to insert any historical happening. Indeed, between 133 and 70 B.C. he records only six historical facts: the founding of Aquae Sextiae (as happening in 122 B.C.), the removal of actors from Rome by the censors of 115 B.C., Caepio's law in 106 B.C., Ptolemy, 'king of Egypt's' bequest to Rome in 96 B.C. (a mistake, which Obsequens makes also, for Ptolemy Apion's bequest to Rome in this year), Sulla's division of Asia into forty-four 'regiones' in 84 B.C., and the burning of the Capitol in 83 B.C. Why these six facts, and these only, should have seemed to him worthy of record, it passes the wit of man to imagine; but as, of the five other facts, four are reasonably accurate and one right except for the confusion of Egypt and Cyrene, the statement about Caepio does not seem likely to be seriously wrong.

Obsequens, whose date is uncertain—some have thought him as early as Hadrian, others as late as Honorius—composed, as a devotee of Roman paganism in its later days, a list of recorded prodigies in Roman history, from the year 249 B.C. onwards. To these he appended, from time to time, facts of historical importance, as he thought, directly related to them, for instance disasters following on the appearance of prodigies. From 133 to 70 B.C. he mentions a limited number of episodes in the domestic history of Rome, the death of Tiberius Gracchus in 133 B.C., 'dissensio' concerned with M. Fulvius Flaccus the triumvir in 129 B.C. (the passage is corrupt), 'tumultus

[25] *Ann.* xii, 60, 4.

[26] Valerius Maximus vi, 9, 13.

[27] Strachan-Davidson, *op. cit.* ii, 80 n. 2, thinks it likely to belong, not to Caepio's consulship, but to 111 B.C., repeating Mommsen's error of thinking that the Naples law must have been repealed in that year. See, on this, p. 114, below. Strachan-Davidson does not attach sufficient importance to the question of the origin of the information possessed by Cassiodorus and by Obsequens, whom he summarily dismisses as 'late chroniclers.'

in urbe, Graccho leges ferente' in 123 B.C., the death of C. Gracchus in 121 B.C., the scandal of the *equites* and the Vestal Virgins in 114 B.C., Caepio's law in 106 B.C., the banishment of a slave of Q. Servilius Caepio in 101 B.C. and the attempt of Livius Drusus to legislate in 91 B.C. Here again, though the choice of subjects is *macabre*, the general standard of accuracy, where it can be tested, is high and there is an *a priori* probability that the statement about Caepio is correct. The significant addition of the words 'cetera in pace fuerunt' to the notice about Caepio's law indicates that something of a *tumultus* attended its passing. Hence Obsequens' interest in Caepio and his law.

Both Cassiodorus and Obsequens derive their knowledge of Roman history of this period, wholly or in part, from an epitome of Livy. That there were other *epitomae* of Livy as well as the familiar extant *Periochae* was conjectured by Niebuhr, and has since been demonstrated by the discovery at Oxyrhynchus of the fragments of a previously unknown *epitome* of Livy for the years 190–179 and 148–137 B.C.[28]

Now, these *epitomae* have as their basis, in all probability, a table of contents—'eine Inhaltsangabe'—of the books of Livy. To this skeleton of facts was added, from time to time, material whether culled from the full text of Livy or from some other source. This is established clearly by A. Klotz, in his examination of the subject.[29] Now, in the case of Obsequens, it is not conceivable that any table of contents, or indeed any 'potted Livy,' should have reproduced in detail anything of such small historical importance as the list of prodigies given regularly by Livy;[30] yet Obsequens repeats them, as we can see from the period in which we can check his account against Livy's, almost *totidem verbis*. It is clear, therefore, that Obsequens, or his source, had combed the *full* text of Livy for prodigies—not in itself a very difficult operation, since they occur regularly in connexion with the assumption of office by magistrates at the beginning of each year—and had probably used this in combination with a skeleton table of contents of the whole work, a skeleton table which looks very much as if it were the same as that used by Cassiodorus.

The discovery of the Oxyrhynchus *epitome* has already damaged a little the credit of the compiler of the familiar *Periochae* of Livy; though his account is longer, it lacks the chronological precision of the Oxyrhynchus account, and is less informative on matters of domestic history.[31] We have already seen the

[28] *P. Oxy.* iv, 668.

[29] A. Klotz, 'Die Epitoma des Livius,' *Hermes* xlviii, 1913, 542–557; 'Zu den Periochae des Livius,' *Philologus* xci, 1936, 67–88. *Cf.* Th. Mommsen, 'Die Chronik des Cassiodorus Senator vom J. 519 n. Chr.,' *Abh. d.k. Sachs. Ges.*, phil.-hist. Kl., iii, 1861, 547–697, esp. 551–558.

[30] A. Klotz, *Philologus* xci, 74, 'Denn es ist unmöglich dass irgendein Auszug aus Livius den Text der Prodigia, falls sie überhaupt im einzelnen aufgenommen wurden, so wenig verkürzt haben sollte, wie dies bei Obsequens der Fall ist.'

[31] See A. Klotz, *loc. cit.*, and B. P. Grenfell and A. S. Hunt, *P. Oxy*, iv, pp. 92 f. A comparison of the surviving books of Livy with their *Periochae* makes evident the haphazard and careless manner in which the author of the *Periochae* produced his work.

weakness of its description of the *repetundae* courts from 91 to 70 B.C. Its author, or his source, was in fact negligent and but slightly interested in domestic legislation. The *argumentum ex silentio* is always a dangerous one. In the case of the *Periochae* of Livy and in face of the conflicting evidence of Obsequens and Cassiodorus it is not merely dangerous; it is illegitimate.

In face of the evidence, therefore, it is extremely difficult to avoid the belief that Livy recorded, as passed in the year 106 B.C., a law by which jury service in the *quaestio repetundarum* was shared between senators and *equites*. And, as between Livy's statement and the statement of Tacitus that the courts were restored exclusively to senators, Livy is to be followed.[32] Appian asserts that in 91 B.C. Livius Drusus regarded the restoration of the courts to the Senate as an object impossible of achievement, and proposed the establishment of mixed courts only as an ingenious *pis-aller* (τεχνάζων. . . ὧδε[33]). *A fortiori*, in 106 B.C. the transfer of the courts to the Senate would have been out of the question. With Marius in Africa, the stock of the Populares stood high—so high, indeed, that in the election to the consulship for 105 B.C. Q. Catulus, whose personality and prestige tempted his supporters to regard him as a safe candidate, was defeated by the outsider, Cn. Mallius.[34] In these circumstances the passing of Caepio's bill was in itself a triumph. Its success was largely due to the speech delivered in its favour by the thirty-four-year-old P. Licinius Crassus, the future consul of 95 B.C. Cicero's numerous references to Caepio's law are concerned, with two exceptions,[35] with this speech of Crassus, a great panegyric of the Senate, and, quite evidently, a *tour de force*. The young Cicero regarded it as a model speech.[36] Indeed, we possess a small fragment of the speech itself, 'Eripite nos ex miseriis, eripite ex faucibus eorum, quorum crudelitas nisi nostro sanguine non potest expleri; nolite sinere nos cuiquam servire, nisi vobis universis, quibus et possumus et debemus,' a passage which M. Antonius admired, but which P. Rutilius Rufus thought, 'non modo parum commode, sed etiam turpiter et flagitiose dicta.'[37]

Apart from a reference to the *Servilia lex* by Valerius Maximus,[38] our knowledge of Glaucia's law is derived entirely from Cicero and his scholiasts. From this evidence it is clear that Glaucia was the originator of the system of *comperendinatio*, that is, the division of a trial into two parts, separated by an

[32] Mommsen, misled, as I have endeavoured to show (p. 101, n. 20 above) by Cicero, *Pro Cornelio*, quoted by Asconius, p. 79, finds the truth in a combination of Tacitus' account and that of Cassiodorus and Obsequens. He writes (*Ges. Schr.* iii, 342), 'Livius hebt auch hier wieder mehr das Princip hervor, während Tacitus sich streng an den Wortinhalt hält—jene Angabe ist eine historische, diese eine antiquarische.'

[33] *BC* i, 35, 3, 157.

[34] Cicero, *Pro Plancio* 12, *Pro Murena* 36.

[35] *De Invent.* i, 92, *De Oratore* ii, 199 f.

[36] *Brutus* 164, 'Mihi quidem a pueritia quasi magistra fuit.'

[37] *De Oratore* i, 225 ff. G. L. Hendrickson has argued (*CP* xxviii, 1933, 158) that the words 'parum commode' mean 'unsuccessfully,' and that this should be treated as evidence that the law was not passed; but his argument is clearly not valid.

[38] viii, 1, 8.

interval, in each of which parts both counsel spoke—prosecution first, defence second—and witnesses were heard.[39] This system was confirmed by Sulla, and so determined procedure in 70 B.C., when Cicero prosecuted Verres. It applied to the *quaestio repetundarum*; and there is no evidence to show whether it applied to any other court.[40] Glaucia's law allowed prosecution of accessories to the crime, as well as of the main culprit himself.[41] The law was still valid in 91 B.C.[42] The jurors by this law were *equites*[43] and, just as Caepio was 'patronus senatus,' so Glaucia 'equestrem ordinem beneficio legis devinxerat.'[44]

Nowhere are we told that Glaucia established equestrian juries. If, as Carcopino maintains, Glaucia established exclusive equestrian juries for the first time in Roman history, this silence of our authorities must appear very surprising indeed.

## V. The Chronology of Acilius, Caepio and Glaucia

Caepio's law, as we have seen, was a consular law, and Caepio was consul in 106 B.C. That is our only certain date. The laws of Acilius and Glaucia were certainly tribunician, and from the evidence of *Verr*. ii, 1, 26, where the *lex Acilia* is described, in relation to Glaucia's law, as 'illa vetus lex,' it is certain that Acilius was earlier than Glaucia. Caepio, then, can be dated absolutely, Acilius and Glaucia only relatively to each other.

Now, on one point Mommsen and Carcopino are in agreement: both place Acilius' *and* Glaucia's laws *before* the *lex Servilia* of Caepio. Both date Acilius to 123 or 122 B.C.; Mommsen places Glaucia's tribunate in 111 B.C., Carcopino in 108 B.C.[45] In both cases the dating is dependent on an interpretation of the Naples laws. Of the two laws on the Naples tablets, the *lex agraria* can be dated with certainty to 111 B.C. Mommsen, considering the *lex repetundarum* on the reverse of the tablet to be the earlier of the two laws, argued that, since it could be turned to the wall after 111 B.C., it had been repealed not merely *by*, but *in*, 111 B.C., and therefore dated Glaucia's law to this year. Carcopino, on the other hand, claiming that the *lex agraria* was the earlier of the two laws on the tablet, that this was the *second* of the agrarian laws mentioned by Appian in B.C. 1, 27, 2, 122, and that it was rescinded by the '*lex Mamilia Roscia Peducaea Alliena Fabia* of 109 B.C.',[46] considered that it was the *agrarian* law whose face was turned to the wall in 109 B.C., and that the later *lex repetundarum* was in-

[39] See p. 113, n. 62, below.
[40] *Verr*. II, i, 26; Greenidge *op. cit.*, p. 501.
[41] *Pro Rab. Post.* 8 f.
[42] Asconius *in Scaurianam*, p. 21.
[43] Cicero, *Pro Scauro* i, 2.
[44] *Brutus* 224.
[45] See p. 98, notes 3 and 4.
[46] The view of E. Fabricius (*Heidelberger Sitzungsberichte*, phil.-hist. Kl. xv, 1924–5, part i) which cannot, surely, survive the criticisms of E. G. Hardy (*CQ* 1925, 185 ff.).

scribed, and therefore passed, by Glaucia in the following year, 108 B.C. This is, in both cases, an extremely fragile process of reasoning. The tablet may, after all, have lain idle for five, ten, indeed for any number of years, before some economical person decided to use the other side and so to avoid the expense of procuring a new sheet of bronze.[47]

To both Mommsen's and Carcopino's dating of Glaucia's tribunate the gravest *a priori* difficulties suggest themselves. On Mommsen's theory the *equites* possessed exclusive rights to jury service by the *lex Acilia* from the time of C. Gracchus. What, then, can Glaucia have added to their privilege which justified Cicero's strong language, 'equestrem ordinem beneficio legis devinxerat'? This difficulty does not arise in the case of Carcopino's theory, because he thinks that the *equites*, who received only two thirds of the places on juries from Gracchus, gained exclusive possession of the courts for the first time from Glaucia. But of both Mommsen and Carcopino it may be asked, Who rescinded the legislation of Caepio? The *equites*, without question, were in undisturbed possession of the courts in 91 B.C., and they held this control 'lege Servilia.'[48] It is a feeble and unconvincing escape from a difficult dilemma to suggest, as historians who follow Mommsen or Carcopino must suggest, that Caepio's law, if it was ever passed at all, was revoked, and Glaucia's law revived, by some unknown act of legislation soon after 106 B.C. Why, in that case, did the 'unknown legislator' not give his own name to his law? Why in 91 B.C. was this law still the *lex Servilia*?

*A priori* everything points to Glaucia following Caepio and by his legislation annulling the legislation of Caepio. And there is evidence to support this conjecture. The only way of making sense out of the confused and erroneous sentence in Appian B.C. 1, 28, 3, 127 is by assuming that Glaucia was tribune in the year preceding the first or the second tribunate of Saturninus—that is, in 104 or 101 B.C. Niccolini prefers the date 101, Last the date 104 B.C.[49]

Tacitus might, with hesitation, be employed to support a date for Glaucia's tribunate later than the consulship of Caepio. After stating in *Ann*. xii, 60, 4 that Caepio handed the courts over to the Senate, he continues, 'Mariusque et Sulla olim de eo (*sc*. the question of the constitution of the juries) vel praecipue bellarent,' an odd, and, as far as Marius is concerned, an unconfirmed assertion. Now elsewhere (*Ann*. xi, 22, 9) Tacitus states that Sulla 'senatui . . . iudicia tradiderat.' The two passages can only be reconciled by the hypothesis that, in Tacitus' opinion, Marius had restored to the *equites* the control of the courts which they had lost to Caepio. Glaucia having been a

[47] See further, on this point, p. 114, below.
[48] Asconius *in Scaurianam*, p. 21.
[49] See p. 98, notes 5 and 6.

*popularis* and an associate of Marius, it may have been of Glaucia's legislation that, admittedly in a very confused manner, Tacitus was thinking.

## VI. Is the 'Lex repetundarum' of the Naples Tablets Part of the Gracchan Legislation, or is it the 'Lex Servilia' of Glaucia?

Carcopino has revived the theory that the Naples law is the *lex Servilia* of Glaucia. Serious objections to this theory have been noticed elsewhere,[50] and the present discussion will concern only one part, but that a fundamental part, of Carcopino's argument. This concerns *comperendinatio*. Cicero states in *Verr.* ii, 1, 26, 'Glaucia primus tulit ut comperendinaretur reus,' and there is no valid reason for disputing the truth of his statement. Carcopino claims that the process of *comperendinatio* is defined among the regulations for procedure in the Naples law (lines 46 ff.). If he is right, then the Naples law cannot be earlier than the law of Glaucia; it cannot be the *lex Acilia*.

*Comperendinatio*, at least by the time of the *Verrines*, was a compulsory division of a case into two parts, known as the *actio prima* and *actio secunda* (or *altera*).[51] The moment at which the praetor called upon the jurors to vote (*mittit in consilium*) was at the end of the second *actio*.

Side by side with *comperendinatio*, we have to consider *ampliatio*. This was an adjournment for fresh hearing in cases where more than a certain proportion of the jury—by the Naples law, more than a third—were not prepared to vote Guilty or Not Guilty (*Condemno* or *Absolvo*), but voted instead Not Proven (*Non Liquet*). Now, by the Naples law the number of times that jurors could follow this craven path with impunity was restricted, on Mommsen's restoration of lines 46 ff., to twice, on Carcopino's—equally plausible—restoration, to once. After this, on all subsequent occasions when more than a third of the jury voted N.L., each offender was to be fined HS 10,000. Here, Carcopino thinks, was *comperendinatio* in embryo.

To illustrate that this single *ampliatio* was the first embryo and beginning of the system of *comperendinatio*, he points to Cicero's procedure against Verres, as described in the all-important passage, *Verr.* ii, 1, 26. Cicero 'destroyed the force of' the *comperendinatio*—'adimo enim comperendinatum'—*i.e.* he reduced the hearing from two *actiones* to one *actio*. In this, Cicero says, he reverts to practice in the days of the *lex Acilia*—'ego tibi illam legem Aciliam restituo.' The *lex Acilia*, according to the scholiast, whom Carcopino believes to speak truth,[52] 'neque comperendinationem ⟨*neque* ampliationem habet.' And so

[50] See p. 99, note 10.

[51] Pseudo-Asconius ad *Verr.* II, i, 75, p. 242, notices that in trial before a provincial governor's *consilium*, if a case was adjourned (*ampliatio*), the re-hearing could be called *actio altera*, like the second part of a trial under the *comperendinatio* procedure at Rome.

[52] P. 231.

Carcopino states his theory, that adjournments—*ampliationes*—without limit in number and, presumably, without penalty of fining, were allowed from 149 to 123 B.C., that by the *lex Acilia* of 123 B.C. they were rigorously prohibited, and that by Glaucia's law the prohibition was lifted to this extent, that *one* (unpenalized) *ampliatio* was allowed, and one only. *Comperendinatio* had been invented.

Now, this theory is open to serious objections.

In the first place, there is clearly a *formal* difference between a compulsory division of a hearing into two parts (*comperendinatio*) and, on the other hand, mere adjournments which are permitted, but, beyond a certain point, penalized, their number being restricted, not by law, but by the scruples of jurors, or their uncertainty whether the defendant's agents will continue to re-imburse them the amount of their fines.[53]

Secondly, the known facts of Verres' trial militate against Carcopino's explanation of the Verrine passage.[54] Cicero's first anxiety was to save time and to ensure that the trial was not made to drag out through the whole of the last five months of the year. This object he could achieve only by a risky act of self-sacrifice, by not speaking himself and by relying on the bare evidence of his witnesses to establish Verres' guilt. The *actio prima* opened. Cicero delivered the short speech which survives, an explanation, chiefly, of the reason for which he was taking the unusual, but not unexampled,[55] course of dispensing with a detailed denunciation of the prisoner's guilt. By this act he saved a great deal of time, not only the time of his own speech, but also the time that would have been taken by the full speech of the defending counsel, Hortensius; for the prosecution not having formulated any detailed charges against the prisoner, the defence, clearly, was not in a position to rebut those charges. As pseudo-Asconius informs us, 'Qua arte ita est fatigatus Hortensius, ut nihil contra quod diceret inveniret.'[56] The witnesses were heard, and their evidence of Verres' guilt was overwhelming. The adjournment (*comperendinatio*) was then moved. Cicero had ready a speech to deliver at the opening of the *actio secunda*, to which Hortensius would, presumably, have essayed a reply, after which further witnesses would have been heard, and the jury would have retired to vote. At the time of the *actio prima* Cicero had no reason to anticipate

[53] Though I do not deny that the imposition of a fine for excessive adjournments 'ist schon der Beginn der Entwicklung, aus welcher die *comperendinatio* hervorging'; P-W i, cols. 1979 f., s.v. *ampliatio*; cf. iv, col. 790, s.v. *comperendinatio*.

[54] The phrase 'illam Aciliam legem, qua lege multi semel accusati, semel dicta causa, semel auditis testibus condemnati sunt' (*Verr.* II, i, 26) does not warrant Carcopino's interpretation (*op. cit.*, 216), 'Selon Cicéron, la loi d'Acilius prescrivait de juger sur *un* (Carcopino's italics, not mine) réquisitoire.' Again, on p. 213, it is only thanks to the omission of a vital sentence in the text of Cicero that Carcopino can force the passage, 'Glaucia primus tulit . . . condemnati sunt,' to support his argument.

[55] It had been employed earlier by L. and M. Lucullus against L. Cotta, *Verr.* I, 55 and pseudo-Asconius *ad loc.*, p. 222.

[56] P. 205; stated also on pp. 230, 232.

that the *actio secunda* would not take place; his own words make that fact transparently clear.[57] In fact, however, his tactics succeeded better than he had hoped: Verres abandoned his defence and retired into exile. The court did not re-assemble, and the case was never formally concluded. Cicero, however, wrote up and published the speech that he had prepared for delivery at the *actio secunda*, and that is the second Verrine oration which survives, and which contains the passage with which our argument is concerned. It must be read in its imaginary context, *i.e.* as being spoken in the *actio secunda* against a prisoner who had not abandoned his defence.

When, therefore, Hortensius is represented as likely to object to Cicero's tactics on the ground, 'adimo enim comperendinatum,' the act to which he objects is not Cicero's *dispensing with* the *comperendinatio* (because that, clearly, was a thing which Cicero had not the power to do—procedure in court is determined by existing law and cannot be altered to suit a barrister's whim), but, on the contrary, Cicero's defeating the *intention* of the *comperendinatio* procedure. This, as Cicero admits, he has done, because, while *comperendinatio* allowed of *two long* set speeches from both counsel—one in the *actio prima*, and one in the *actio secunda*—Cicero's tactics have allowed of *one* only from each side, his own (second) speech, and Hortensius' anticipated reply.

In this *actio secunda* Cicero looks forward to the voting of the jury. He says, 'testibus editis ita mittam in consilium ut, etiamsi lex ampliandi faciat potestatem, tamen isti turpe sibi existiment non primo iudicare.' Now this sentence bristles with difficulties. Is the *lex*, as Carcopino thinks, the *lex Cornelia*, under which Verres was being tried, or is it, as scholars whose advice I have been privileged to enjoy are unanimous in thinking, the *lex Acilia*, to which earlier in the paragraph Cicero had referred?[58] And how is 'etiamsi . . . faciat potestatem' to be translated? Is the meaning (*a*), '*Even if* the law allowed *ampliatio* (which it doesn't)' or (*b*), 'Even if in fact the law *does* allow *ampliatio*'?

If the first alternative, (*a*), is correct, then there was some law, either the *lex Cornelia* or the *lex Acilia*, which did not allow *ampliatio* at all. If this were the *lex Acilia*, then Carcopino's point would be proved, and with it the existence of a very odd legal system which did not recognise honest doubt as a legitimate psychological state for a juror or allow, as in Scotland, a verdict of Not Proven or, as in England, the right of a jury to announce that it is unable to

[57] *Verr.* I, 34, 'Tua ratio est ut secundum binos ludos mihi respondere incipias, mea ut ante primos ludos comperendinem.' I am grateful to Dr. A. B. Poynton for emphasising to me the importance of this passage.

[58] Carcopino, *op. cit.*, 218, with whom, partly on the strength of the meaning of *lex* in section 25 and in the first sentence of section 26 in *Verr.* II, i, I agree. On the other hand, Dr. A. B. Poynton and Professor H. M. Last, to whom I owe thanks for his kindness in revising the manuscript of this article, consider, as Greenidge considered (*The Legal Procedure of Cicero's Time*, 501 n. 2), that by *lex* Cicero meant the *lex Acilia*.

agree on a verdict. But Carcopino has not chosen this easy means of reinforcing his own contention. By *lex* he understands the *lex Cornelia*, and thinks that the *lex Cornelia* allowed one *ampliatio* only—in the form of *comperendinatio*. If this were right, then we should have evidence, which otherwise we lack, that *ampliatio* was forbidden in extortion cases after the introduction of *comperendinatio*.[59]

If the second of the alternative meanings of 'etiamsi lex ampliandi faciat potestatem' is the right one, then the 'law,' whatever it was, allowed *ampliatio*. If the 'law' be the *lex Acilia*, Carcopino's case is put straight out of court. But it may be the *lex Cornelia*. Of the—as I think—four possible ways of taking the sentence, this is the only one which Carcopino notices, although it is one which suits his thesis badly. He translates, 'Bien que la loi *Cornelia* leur donne le pouvoir de demander un supplément d'information.' He thinks that 'adimo comperendinatum' means, not 'I make a farce of,' but 'I dispense with' the adjournment, *i.e.* 'I call on the jurors to vote straightway—etiamsi lex ampliandi faciat potestatem'—although the law allows *one ampliatio*, in the form of *comperendinatio*. To this there are two altogether fatal objections. The first, noticed above, is that barristers cannot at will play fast and loose with regulations, as determined by law. The second is that the imaginary setting of the second speech against Verres is after, not before, the adjournment. On Carcopino's own translation, therefore, the jurors of 70 B.C. have the right to vote Non Liquet at the end of the *actio secunda*. That is to say, *comperendinatio* is not, as Carcopino claims, the equivalent of a single *ampliatio*.

The facts can be stated simply. *Comperendinatio* was introduced by Glaucia and was retained by Sulla. There is no mention of it in the extant fragments of the Naples law. *Ampliatio*, on the other hand, is a feature of trials whose existence is recognised and for which definite regulations are made—whether or not for the first time, we cannot say—in the Naples law. That it survived the introduction of formal *comperendinatio* by Glaucia is probable in itself, but cannot be proved by definite evidence.

If these considerations make it unlikely that the Naples law should be the *lex Servilia Glauciae*, one passage in the Naples fragments is strong enough to establish that it *cannot* be that law even if, with Carcopino, one dates Glaucia's tribunate to 108 B.C. In line 74 (repeated in line 81) of the Naples law it is expressly stated that judgments under the earlier *lex Calpurnia* (of 149 B.C.) and *lex Iunia* (of date unknown) are not to be disturbed by this law. The relevant fragment of the tablet—(Quibusquom ioudicium) fuit fueritve ex

[59] Very little evidence exists of *ampliatio* at all, and none of its employment in the *quaestio repetundarum*, in the Ciceronian period; Greenidge, *op. cit.*, 499 ff.

lege, quam L. Calpurnius L.f. tr. pl. rogavit, exve lege quam M. Iunius D. f. tr. pl. rogavit, quei eorum eo (ioudicio . . .)—shows clearly enough that the list of preceding laws has been concluded before the break. Why is there no mention of the Gracchan law—or, according to Carcopino, laws—of 123–2 B.C.? This question is surely unanswerable on any other hypothesis than that of Mommsen, that the Naples law is part of the Gracchan judiciary legislation.

## VII. The 'Lex Acilia,' in the Light of 'Verr.' ii, 1, 26 and the Verrine Scholia.

Before we can re-affirm, with Mommsen, that the Naples law is the *lex Acilia* of 123 or 122 B.C., we must examine the view that the *lex Acilia* altogether prohibited *ampliatio*. The improbability of such a prohibition from a legal point of view, whether in 123 or at any other time, has already been indicated.

Carcopino's argument depends on the extremely difficult and confused passage, *Verr*. ii, 1, 26. In this passage Cicero states that 'in destroying the point of *comperendinatio*,' he is, in effect, restoring the practice of the courts in the days before the introduction of *comperendinatio*, that is to say, before Glaucia. In so doing, he says explicitly, 'ego tibi illam Aciliam legem restituo.' He is anticipating Hortensius' objection that, by his refusal to make a set speech at the *actio prima* and by depriving Hortensius thereby of the opportunity of making a set speech in reply, he has reduced the set speeches on either side from two to one—the one of the *actio secunda*. Hortensius could claim that there was a danger of the jury giving a verdict on insufficient information: 'causam, inquit, cognosci oportet.' Cicero replies with a cunning logical trick, by using an improper disjunction. Under the *lex Acilia*, he says, a judgement might be given after a single hearing, or the case could be adjourned—'vel iudicari primo poterat vel amplius pronuntiari.' This is a true alternative. So, he continues, the innocent could have their agony cut short; the guilty, on the other hand, could, as we should say, be given a long run for their money—'vel cito absolvi vel tarde condemnari licebat.' The trap is baited. In apparent innocence Cicero has substituted 'cito absolvi' for 'iudicari primo,' 'tarde condemnari' for 'amplius pronuntiari.' He proceeds: 'Ego tibi illam Aciliam legem restituo, qua lege multi semel accusati, semel dicta causa, semel auditis testibus. . . .' The court would expect, 'absoluti sunt.' Instead they—imaginatively—heard, 'condemnati sunt, nequaquam tam manifestis neque tantis criminibus quantis tu convinceris.' Cicero was carefully working for this effect; no doubt in court he would have paused for a moment after the word 'testibus,' in order to heighten the emphasis. There is nothing here to indicate that the *lex Acilia* forbade *ampliatio*; on the contrary, the passage can only be understood on the assumption that the *lex Acilia* allowed it.

Carcopino's interpretation of 'antea vel iudicari primo poterat vel amplius pronuntiari' as meaning, 'from 123 to 108 B.C. *ampliatio* was completely forbidden, while in the previous twenty-six years it was allowed, without any restriction,' is, in Latinity, of doubtful possibility.

As for the scholia, in the first place the epithet 'severissima,' applied to Acilius' law, is patently borrowed from the phrase 'severissimi iudices,' on which pseudo-Asconius was commenting, and the epithet was applied by Cicero to the *iudices* established by Acilius, as being *equites*, not senators. In his second comment it has simply to be assumed that, in stating that the *lex Acilia* did not allow *ampliatio*, the commentator has made a mistake, through failing to understand the Verrine passage on which he was commenting. After all, in his comments on this same paragraph[60] he makes two other mistakes. He writes, 'comperendinato iudicio dicit prior defensor,' a remark repeated by him elsewhere,[61] but contradicted by many of Cicero's statements in this same speech.[62] Again he writes, 'Ante legem Glauciae de comperendinatione aut statim sententia dicebatur, si absolvendus esset reus, aut amplius pronuntiabatur, si videretur esse damnandus,' a remark which he contradicts elsewhere by a correct statement of the law.[63] It may be noticed that this latter observation, on his attitude to which Carcopino is silent, does not indicate that pseudo-Asconius, on whom he chiefly relies, shared his own view that in the fifteen years preceding Glaucia's legislation *ampliatio* was not in any circumstances allowed.

As between different judgements on the value of these scholia concerning the *lex Acilia*, between Mommsen's—'merae nugae sunt neque aliunde fluxerunt nisi ex ipsis Ciceronis verbis pessime lectis'—and Carcopino's—'elles en respectent le sens et elles l'éclaircissent'[64]—Mommsen may speak harshly; but there can be little doubt that he speaks the truth.

## VIII. Conclusion

Glaucia's tribunate, then, is probably to be dated to 104—possibly to 101 B.C.—and his legislation, in as far as it concerned the constitution of juries in the *quaestio repetundarum*, is to be understood as cancelling the legislation of Caepio, which was passed in 106 B.C. and accurately recorded by Cassiodorus

[60] Ad *Verr.* II, i, 26, p. 230.
[61] P. 224.
[62] *Verr.* II, i, 71; ii, 177; v, 32, etc. *Cf.* Greenidge, *op. cit.*, 501, n. 1.
[63] Ad *Verr.* II, i, 74, p. 242.
[64] Mommsen, *Ges. Schr.* i, p. 18; Carcopino, *op. cit.*, 215.

and by Obsequens.[65] For the rest, however, Mommsen's interpretation of the Naples law is as certain now as it was when he first propounded it; that law is the *lex Acilia* of 123 or 122 B.C., by which the *quaestio repetundarum* was handed over, exclusively, to the knights. In the great chorus of ancient witnesses who attest that this was the achievement of C. Gracchus, the contradictory voice of Plutarch and the silence of the Epitomator of Livy (inaccurate as he is elsewhere, as we have seen, on the history of the court) need not disconcert the historian. And as for the trio of Gracchan laws so ingeniously elicited by Carcopino, a *lex Acilia* which abolished *ampliatio*, a lex *Sempronia iudiciaria* which established an *album iudicum* of six hundred *equites* and three hundred senators, and a *lex Rubria* or *Rubria Acilia* which excluded big business men from jury service—if the Naples law is not identified as the *lex Servilia* of Glaucia, they lose, all three of them, their *raison d'être*.

The *lex Acilia* appears to have held the field from 123/2 to 106 B.C. How, then, are we to explain the engraving, on the reverse of the Naples tablet, of the *lex agraria* of 111 B.C.? Many suggestions may be made: for our present purpose two will suffice. Though the agrarian law was passed in 111 B.C., this copy of it may not have been set up in Campania until after 106 B.C. Alternatively, the side bearing the *lex repetundarum* may never have been posted publicly at all. It is defaced by a piece of carelessness on the part of the engraver, lines 72–78 being repeated in full in lines 79–85. From the start, therefore, it was a faulty copy, and may have been judged unfit for posting. In which case the agrarian law gives us no clue at all to the date at which the *lex Acilia* was rescinded.[66]

J. P. V. D. Balsdon

[65] F. Münzer, P-W xiii, col. 258 (L. Licinius Crassus, no. 55); iiA, cols. 1783 f. (Q. Servilius Caepio); cols. 1796 f. (C. Servilius Glaucia); *Römische Adelsparteien*, pp. 287 f., believes in the historical reality of Caepio's legislation, as described by Cassiodorus and by Obsequens, but he follows Mommsen in placing Glaucia's tribunate in 111 B.C.

[66] As it will be some time before the work that I was doing in Rome in the spring of 1937 will be ready for publication, I should like to take this opportunity of expressing my gratitude for the privilege of residing at the British School and of using both its library and the Bibliothek des deutschen archäologischen Instituts at Rome.

# VII

*A. N. Sherwin-White*

# Violence in Roman Politics

# VIOLENCE IN ROMAN POLITICS

By A. N. SHERWIN-WHITE

To speak of Roman politics in the late Republic without touching on violence would hardly be possible.[1] But my real theme is concerned with methods of interpreting Roman history. We have seen in the last hundred years some three general attitudes or schools of thought about the study of the later Republic. It all begins with Mommsen, of course. First there were those who, following Mommsen, tended to explain Roman history in terms of the nineteenth century. The conflict of Optimates and Populares tended to be assimilated to the forms of conflict in parliamentary countries ; parties, programmes, even democrats and conservatives were brought in. Then came a swing away. The stress was laid more and more on the generals and their ambitions. The terminology of parliamentary democracy was discarded as unsuitable, and the history of the late Republic was seen as an inevitable procession of great Imperatores, each foreshadowing the next. Even the Scipios were involved, then Marius, Sulla and so forth. Much less stress was laid on the popular movement. Apart from the Gracchi the tribunes were treated as tools of the Imperators and nothing more. The politics of the generation before the Social War were explained in terms of the Ciceronian age. One might cite the great chapters of the *Cambridge Ancient History*, and Meyer's *Caesars Monarchie* as characteristic.

Meantime a third school was coming into being, that of Münzer and family history. The details of aristocratic organization were minutely studied—which family backed which—who married whom. Terms such as *clientela* and *factio* began to dominate discussion. Roman politics were explained in terms of complicated combinations of family interest and Roman history took on an eighteenth century air. What happened at sessions of the Comitia and Senate was regarded as subject to a law of family determinism. The groups arranged it all beforehand. Families mobilized their vast *clientelae* to pass this law or that Senatusconsultum, to elect this or that man consul. The two preceding schools had not been unaware of the importance of family arrangements in Roman politics. Their exponents all knew why Pompey married Julia, and some knew that Tiberius Gracchus had powerful friends. But never before had such preponderance been given to the mechanics of social organization in politics. The new school was also very strong in the matter of power. The object of these family arrangements was to secure power for the family members. The bigger the group the more power it gets. Roman politics were seen to have reached the merger stage in the Ciceronian age. Gigantic family combinations produced gigantic personal commands. One thinks of the 200 senators at the so-called Conference of Luca.

Now these two latter schools have contributed much to the explanation of Roman history, and in varying combinations—since they are far from exclusive—may be said to dominate the present scene. But they suffer from certain defects in method. In the one case each decade or phase is explained in terms of the next ; the interpretation is evolutionary to the point of anachronism. Events are not studied sufficiently in relation to their own setting, but are illuminated by the light of a later age. The Münzer school falls into the opposite vice. Roman politics are represented as static ; methods are taken to be the same after the Social War and the unification of Italy as before it. The age of Pompey is explained by the mechanisms of the age of Marius, and vice versa. One cannot do without these methods. For the broad sweep of events nothing is more illuminating than the representation of the series of great Imperators. The lines of perspective lead the historical eye inevitably to Caesar and the Principate. Equally in examining a particular moment of history we must know all about the family and personal relationships of the persons of the drama. But, when searching for the contemporary significance of events, actions should be judged by their own evidence and in their own context, without *parti pris*, and without forcing the future to appear in the past, and equally without the assumption that the rules of the family game were always kept—that no one ever changed his opinions or his side.

[1] This paper was read at the conference arranged by the Committee of the Joint Greek and Roman Societies at Oxford in August, 1955. The sources are well documented in Greenidge and Clay, *Sources for Roman History* B.C. 133–70 (Oxford, 1926), and in T. R. S. Broughton, *Magistrates of the Roman Republic* (New York, 1951). Here references have been added to the original text only at places crucial for the argument.

Not every marriage is significant, and if the Romans made political marriages one should remember that they also enjoyed a very lax system of divorce.

I propose to analyse two historical situations—in order to show how differently things appear in their own light when the illumination of a later age is removed, and rather more attention given to the immediate past than to the remoter future. First is a discussion of the career of Marius, and after that the events of the first consulship of Pompeius and Crassus are investigated.

## THE CAREER OF MARIUS

Marius is commonly represented as the prototype of the military despots of the late Republic. Backed by his legionaries he wrests repeated consulships and agrarian laws from the teeth of aristocratic opposition, and as leader of a violent popular movement he breaks the authority of the senatorial government. But was it really like that at the time? Or does his career make better sense when explained in terms of the previous two generations than by those of the post-Sullan age?

The second century B.C. had seen a series of distinguished *novi homines*, men born outside the circle of aristocratic consular families, who by personal ability had reached the headship of the State, the consulship and Censura, and had themselves founded a noble family, in the technical sense of *nobilitas*. M. Cato was the most famous of these. Among the more recent was the first Pompeius, consul in 140 B.C. and censor in 132, and P. Rupilius, a remarkable man who began life as a *publicanus* and secured his advancement under the wing of Scipio Aemilianus. It was the custom of the great houses to adopt promising 'new men' in this fashion. Relatively few reached the consulship—there were but two consuls a year—but many became Praetor. So too Marius. He was the son of a wealthy magnate of Arpinum, as is shown by the stories of his lavish bribery. He began under the wing of the great family of the Caecilii Metelli, who helped him to a tribunate in 119, in which he made a little display of independence, to put up his price. Such displays were part of the stock-in-trade of new men long before the age of the Gracchi. He just managed to secure a praetorship in 115, and performed moderately in his Spanish province. Six years later he went to the Numidian war on the staff of his protector, Q. Metellus.[2] This was his first such legateship. So far his career had developed with a slowness equalled only by its lack of distinction. He was 47 years old and had done nothing of note. When he informed Metellus in the course of 108 that he intended to stand for the consulship that year, Metellus thought the man mad, not without reason, and made the famous if tactless reply: 'It will be time enough to think of standing when my son is candidate.' It was the fashion of the second century for *novi homines* to become consuls thus in conjunction with a member of their protecting family. So Laelius with L. Scipio, and Cato with Valerius Flaccus. But Marius was not prepared to wait, and abandoned his connection with the Metelli. He had other irons in the fire.

So far Marius had taken no part in the politics of the radical group at Rome which had begun to agitate about certain scandals, first in the affair of the Vestals and then in the supposed abuses of the Jugurthan war. Sallust, the detailed source for the troublesome tribunates of Memmius and Mamilius, in 110–109, and for the electoral campaign of Marius in 108, makes a significant distinction. The politics of Memmius and Mamilius were concerned with the *plebes* and only the *plebes*. The so-called equestrian classes held aloof from popular politics, and supported the Senate, after abandoning Gaius Gracchus in 122, down to 108. Then Marius brought them into politics on the popular side in his electoral campaign, by the promise of a speedy end to the war if he were made consul. Such is Sallust's account. He may oversimplify. Such men as Memmius were themselves men of equestrian standing. But the distinction between equestrian and plebeian interest remains the key to Roman politics from 108 to 100, and in the main Marius supported and was supported by equestrian interests.[3] Before 108 the plebeian radical

[2] On the circumstances of Marius' legateship see Vell. Pat. II, 11. Plut. *Mar.*, 7. Diod. 35, 38.

[3] Compare Sallust, *BJ* 27, 30, 31–3, 40.3–5, with 64; 65, 4; 73. For the rift between equestrians and *plebes* after Gaius Gracchus, ibid. 42, 1.

wing had been noisy, but of limited effect. Then there is a coalition of what Sallust calls *plebes* and *equites Romani*, and much progress is made. When this coalition breaks up in 100 the popular movement collapses. But meanwhile Marius exploited plebeian and equestrian dissatisfactions which he turned to his personal advantage. Thus he won a consulship, and by a freak of fortune a succession of consulships. But he at no time supported any radical programme of reform; when Saturninus produced such a programme in 100 Marius parted company with him.

Before Saturninus there was no such programme. Memmius and Mamilius had revived the Gracchan tradition in a narrower field. Such leaders as Memmius, and the troublesome Cassius and Norbanus in 106–5, confined themselves to criticism and prosecutions. They set themselves up as watch-dogs over the consular-senatorial administration, ready to bark and bite whenever consuls misbehaved or lost a battle. The Jugurthan affair and the disasters in Gaul at the hands of the Cimbri provided plenty of material. The tribunes had a merry time setting up tribunals for the correction of consulars. They were very rough with Q. Servilius Caepio, the proconsul who precipitated the disaster of Arausio in 105. But there was nothing beyond this. There was no attempt to diminish the role of the Senate in the government of Rome, and no Gracchan programme of social reform, no corn law, no agrarian bills.

All this suited Marius very well. He was able to exploit the *invidia nobilitatis*, just as Cato had once exploited the *invidia Scipionis*. He made a great show as the blunt but able soldier, kept out of the chief command by the jealousy of the nobles. But there is much exaggeration in the modern view that Marius stood for the *principle* of the career open to talent, and in the implication that he breached the fortress of the *nobilitas* for the benefit of all and sundry. Sallust is taken too literally. He may well be right in saying that the *nobiles* reckoned the consulship polluted if held by anyone but themselves. But he also states as a fact that Marius was the first *novus homo* to hold the consulship 'post multas tempestates'.[4] How long is a *tempestas*? Is it a generation, or a decade, or only a year? Rupilius, the consul of 132, only twenty-four years before, was indisputably a 'new man'; and there is a strong case for putting the consuls of 124 and 116, C. Sextius Calvinus and C. Licinius Geta, in the same category. It is difficult to think that Marius believed greatly in consulships for other 'new men'. In the nine years of his dominance Flavius Fimbria was the only other *novus* to be elected consul. Cicero remarks in the Brutus that the predominance of Marius prevented another good 'new man', G. Billienus, from securing the office.[5]

So far Marius' career was in the tradition of M. Cato, who at the beginning of the century had shown similar skill in exploiting popular discontent to secure his own advancement. Having won his consulship by intrigue, and ousted Q. Metellus from the command in Africa, Marius set about earning it by coping with Jugurtha. Then came the Cimbric crisis on the European front. Marius was elected in his absence, contrary to the Lex Annalis, to a second consulship. This resembles the case of Scipio Aemilianus at the time of the Third Carthaginian war, when the people swept aside the Lex Annalis and the allocation of provinces to make Aemilianus consul and commander *ante tempus*, when he was not even a candidate. Plutarch says that this very parallel was quoted at the time.[6] So too in 108 the people by plebiscite had altered the Sempronian allotment to send Marius to Africa.[7] Now they set aside the Lex Annalis in 105 to send the best man against the Germans. This could all have happened in the pre-Gracchan period. The use of the second consulship was a favourite device to deal with military crises. One thinks of Marcius Philippus, Aemilianus Paulus, and again Aemilianus. The exceptional thing in Marius is the series of consulships from 104 to 100. For this there was no parallel since the war against Hannibal. But the motive was the same and the Epitomator of Livy, who is not noted for his popular bias, states as much: 'his consulship was continued for several years because of fear of the Cimbri.' The Epitomator also makes it clear that this was done

[4] ibid., 73.

[5] For the origins of Rupilius see Val. Max. VI, 9, 8. For Billienus, Cic. *Brutus* 175. Mallius Maximus, consul in 105, was *ignobilis* but not *novus*, Cic. *pro Plancio* 12.

[6] Plut. *Mar.* 12, 1.

[7] Sall. *BJ* 73.

*ex senatusconsulto*, i.e. the Senate ratified the setting aside of the Lex Annalis. It is known from Sallust that the original allocation of Gaul to Marius was *ex s.c.*[8] Had the war not lasted so long Marius would not have had so many consulships. He owed them to the failure of the Cimbri to turn up and fight when expected. But why did not the Senate simply prorogue the second consulship of Marius for as long as the war lasted? There was good reason. The great disaster of Arausio had been caused by the failure of a proconsul and a consul to co-operate on the same battlefield. The proconsul Caepio had disobeyed the consul Mallius and caused a crushing defeat. If Marius was to be generalissimo, he must at least be consul, or he might be found under the orders of another consul commanding another army in the same area; for no one could tell where in the north the campaign would be fought. There was at this date no other way round this constitutional difficulty. So Marius had to be re-elected consul until the Cimbri and Teutones were finished off.

But what about the consulship of 100? Surely that was unnecessary? The fighting in 101 was all over before the elections. Here at least one might see the military man supported by the soldiery making his bid for power with the help of his sinister henchman, Saturninus. The sources tell a different tale. They say in remarkable agreement that Marius was given his sixth consulship as the reward of his merits with the approval of the hitherto suspicious *nobilitas*, who admitted that he had saved the State. Only Rutilius Rufus, friend of the affronted Metellus and therefore enemy of Marius, muttered in his memoirs, not of violence and soldiery at the hustings, but of the bribery of voters.[9] The truth is that Marius was steadily drawing closer to the consular class in these years. This appears also on his reluctance to stand for his fourth consulship, a well-known story, and in the voluntary sharing of his triumph at the end of 101 with his optimate colleague, Catulus. But there remained the persistent opposition of the Metelli. At this juncture Plutarch says straight out that Marius was particularly afraid of Quintus Metellus, who was keeping a close watch on his activities.[10] That is why Marius had to turn to Saturninus and the radicals to secure allotments of land for the war heroes who had defeated Jugurtha and the Cimbri. Even so the land was to be found not in Italy but overseas, a conciliatory gesture to the landed proprietors.

The story of Saturninus and Marius is a tale of misalliance. Saturninus is the real innovator of these years. He was fostering a scheme that would secure a great extension of the effective power of tribunes, a scheme that would enable tribunes not merely to pass general legislative reforms, as formerly, but also to intervene extensively in ordinary administration, and to subject the upper magistracies to a detailed control of their activities in a way that smacks of government by *psephisma*. This concerns Saturninus rather than Marius, and cannot be discussed at length here. The essence of the plan appears in the famous oath which Saturninus attached to his agrarian legislation in 100, and to the lengthy document known as the ' piracy law ' of 100 by which Saturninus seems to have sought to control Asiatic affairs in considerable detail. The object of the oath was to use the Senate as an instrument by binding all senators and magistrates to carry out plebiscites, instead of neglecting them if contrary to their own ideas. The oath was not necessary for Marius and his veterans, and had not appeared in the first Marian land bill, that of 103. Marius nearly broke with Saturninus when he heard of this oath; as presiding consul he brought it up for discussion in the Senate, and proposed a means of avoiding its effect. Only a singularly skilful intrigue on the part of Saturninus kept Marius with him for some time longer. Saturninus cunningly used the oath to effect the downfall and exile of Marius' arch-enemy Metellus.[11] The consummation of the vendetta may have comforted Marius. But during the year the equestrian element became more and more dissatisfied with the dodges of Saturninus, culminating in the astonishing murder of the senior and respected

[8] Livy, *Ep.* 67. Sall. *BJ* 114.

[9] Vell. Pat. II, 126. Livy, *Ep.* 68–9, gives both sides of the picture. Plut. *Mar.* 28, 5, gives the Rutilius version. Cf. Dio's statement on the ' consensus omnium ' at the elections of 102, *fr.* 92.

[10] Plut. *Mar.* 28, 4.

[11] App. I, 30, 3–6. Plut. *Mar.* 29, 2 and 4. The bias of the source is apparent. Marius could not have known beforehand that Metellus alone of all the senators would refuse to take the conditional oath. Saturninus' trick could only be devised after the final taking of oaths.

radical leader, Memmius, at the consular elections. This was too much for Marius and his equestrian friends. The popular coalition dissolved into its component parts. Marius intervened as consul under the authority of the Senate, and with the help of a posse of Roman knights he eliminated the too enterprising leader of the *plebs*.[12]

Where in all this is the political general, the first of the military despots in disguise? At this stage of Roman history neither generals nor legionaries were ready to support one another with armed violence in the civil sphere. It is not as organized legionaries but as citizens that the discharged veterans make their contribution in the year 100. The point of Marius's actions is not that he calls upon his veterans to support his interests. He does no such thing. But he supports *their* interests. The Marian army reforms took a sinister turn only when a general appealed to his troops to help *him* against the Senate or the Comitia. That happens from 88 B.C. onwards, but not before the Social War. The story of Sulla's *coup d'état* shows that it never occurred to Marius and his associate, Sulpicius Rufus, that the consul Sulla might refuse to obey the plebiscite that legally deprived him of his eastern command. Metellus in 107 had obediently gone home when deprived of Africa, and they expected Sulla to do likewise in 88. He did not, and thereby the violent phase of the late Republic began.

Marius in 88, and still more in 100, was conditioned by the political habits of the second century. However much in retrospect he may seem the prototype of the political Imperators of the later age, the analogy is misleading. These things lay as seeds in the womb of time. The Social War fertilized the Marian army reform and begot the Revolution. But that was not yet. Marius was an unimaginative child of his age. He wanted to be a second Cato, or a second Q. Pompeius. It is characteristic that in the period after 100 he was ambitious to hold the censorship of 97 with his friend and former fellow consul, Valerius Flaccus. So too some ninety years before old Cato had been censor with his friend and former colleague, an earlier Valerius Flaccus. Marius feared a defeat at the censorial elections, and in the end he did not stand.[13] But the ambition, and the disappointment which he is said to have felt, was characteristic. Marius wanted to end his days as *vir censorius*, like the other great worthies among the *novi homines* of the second century.

## POMPEIUS IN 71–70 B.C.

English historians have a short way with the events of 71–70 B.C. Professor Syme in the *Roman Revolution* says: 'Pompeius combined with another army commander and carried out a peaceful *coup d'état*.' The *Cambridge Ancient History* takes the same line: 'the two marshals now advanced on Rome, where the Senate was even more defenceless than in 77 B.C.' The whole story of 71–70 is then represented as a dictate.[14] Pompeius under threat of civil war takes an illegal consulship and overthrows the constitution of Sulla. I know of no voice that dissents from this view. It may be the truth but it is not the whole truth, and in its tones and overtones and in certain essential details it is a modern invention.

The sources for the politics of 71–70 are remarkably brief for such great events. A collection of sundry sentences in various writers bears on the legislation of 70, but the continuous narrative of events appears only in the last page of Appian *Bellum Civile* I, and in a page-and-a-half of Plutarch's life of Pompey, repeated more briefly in his Crassus.[15] Plutarch is the more detailed. He says that when Pompey, after finishing off the revolt of Spartacus, marched towards Rome, there was some fear and suspicion because men were afraid that he would not disband his army, but would wade through arms and despotic power against the settlement of Sulla. Hence as many came out to greet him through fear as through gratitude for his victories. But he dispelled this fear by declaring that he would disband his army after his triumph. After that pronouncement the only complaint against him was that he was too much on the popular side, in that he had decided to restore the

[12] Plut. *Mar.* 30, 3. Cic. *pro Rab. perd. reo.* 20, 27. Cf. Orosius v, 17.
[13] Plut. *Mar.* 30, 4.
[14] R. Syme, *Roman Revolution*, 29. H. M. Last in *CAH* IX, 332.
[15] App. *BC* I, 121. Plut. *Pomp.* 21, 3–23, 2. *Crass.* 12.

tribunician power. And that, says Plutarch, *really* was true ; ὅπερ ἦν ἀληθές. Now it is known from Velleius that Pompey celebrated his triumph on the last day of 71.[16] Plutarch indicates that Pompey kept his word, and the army was disbanded, and that of Crassus also, straight away. Besides, how could he retain his army after crossing the Pomerium ?

In Appian there is a slight difference, which is the basis of the modern version. Speaking of 71 down to the consular elections he says that Crassus would not disband his army because Pompey did not do so, and that they continued to keep their armies in being after the elections, Pompey using the excuse that he was waiting to share his triumph with Metellus Pius. Appian then describes a scene which he seems to place during the consulship of the two men in 70—and this is the only description of 70 that he gives. The People, fearing a civil war between the two, persuade them to accept a formal reconciliation, and after this to disband their two armies. Now this reconciliation is described with more detail by Plutarch, who does not connect it with the question of the armies, already dismissed, but relates it to a long series of quarrels between the two during their consulship, names the chief agent of the agreement, and dates it to the last day of 70.

It is apparent that Appian has made one of his famous muddles. He has telescoped the triumphal celebrations and dismissal of armies at the end of 71 with the reconciliation scene at the end of 70. Hence Plutarch is right, and there were no armies in being round Rome during the year 70. But it is even more remarkable that neither historian makes the threat of armed force the immediate cause of the consulships and legislation of 70. Plutarch dismisses the threat as unreal, and Appian regards the armies of the two men as aimed not at the State or the Senate, but at one another. Neither gives the modern version, the march on Rome and the dictate. This might be due to a later whitewashing of the tradition about Pompey. But several considerations suggest that the threat of force in 71 was remote. Who after all was Pompey, why did he want a consulship, exactly how illegal was this desire, and what use did he make of his consulship ?

The young Pompeius had certainly had a strange career, post on post, and all without regard for the Sullan Lex Annalis : the commission under Catulus against Lepidus followed by the *imperium* against Sertorius, ' non proconsule sed pro consulibus.' But this had been done as Cicero said of Sulla ' pro optimatibus '. For ten years Pompeius commissioned by Sulla or the Sullan Senate had been slaughtering the leaders and other ranks of the *populares*, in Sicily and Africa, in Cisalpine Gaul and in Spain. Thanks to him the Optimates and their henchmen slept snug in their beds, and Sullan *possessores* enjoyed their ill-gotten gains. A strange candidate this for the leadership of an anti-Optimate coup at Rome. True, the man had had difficulties during his war with the clique that ran things in the post-Sullan decade. Supplies, with or without excuse, had been kept in arrears. It had ever been the way of the Roman oligarchy to prune the tallest poppies, and there may have been those, now as later, who wanted to take Pompey down a peg. But all that Pompey required in 71 for himself was the regularization of his position. In a famous scene he reported to the censors of 70 that he had done all his military service *se imperatore*. This rubbed in the incongruity of his position the year before. Not for him now to toil through the lesser magistracies. One stride to the consulship, and he would be in the place due to his *dignitas*, as the son of a consular, ' tantis rebus gestis.' As with Catalina and Caesar later it boils down to the very Roman question of *status dignitatis*. Pompey wanted the consulship, not to secure a new command, but to be *consularis*. He and Crassus both refused provinces at the end of the year, and he did nothing else for himself in 70 at all. But men who want to be consular are by definition not men who want to start revolutions.

What, next, about the supposed illegality of his consulship under the Sullan rules ? Pompey was not asking for the office itself, but for a dispensation from the Lex Annalis regulating candidatures which the Senate under the Sullan system was perfectly competent to grant.[17] Such dispensations for individuals, sometimes loosely called *privilegia*, played a marked part in the senatorial intrigues of the post-Sullan decade—so much so that the

[16] Vell. Pat. II, 30.

[17] Pompey was granted dispensation to hold his triumph in 71 by the Senate, Cic. *de Imp. Pomp.* 62. The *sc.* allowing *ratio absentis* would be at the same time.

tribune Cornelius in 67 brought in a bill aimed at the abusive grant of such privileges. Sulla meant the Senate to govern the Roman State, and left it with the power to take xtraordinary measures if they were necessary. The constitution did not crumble in 74 when Lucullus managed to change his consular province for the command against Mithridates, or when the worthless Antonius was given wide powers to deal with pirates. It was no worse to dispense a man in the odd position of Pompeius from the formal requirements of the Lex Annalis. It is the modern doctrine of precedent that makes the step seem revoluionary. One such concession, and the Lex Annalis is annulled. So we think, but that was not the Roman way of thinking, least of all of legal thinking. During the next two decades he Lex Annalis continued to mould the careers of men unchallenged, and notably that of Julius Caesar.

But, say the objectors, Pompey was no friend of the Senate. What about Lepidus in 79–78, and the army at the gates in 71, and the laws of 70? The remarkable thing about the ntrigue of Pompey with Lepidus is that the moment that Lepidus revealed a really revolutionary intention, Pompey turned away from him and supported the Optimates. It is a well-known fallacy by now to speak as though the Senate were a coherent political party. No Roman politician ever had the whole Senate, or even all the Optimates, on his side. Pompey had friends and enemies, in the Roman sense, like anyone else. His friends had secured him notable concessions in recent years, not only the commands of 78–77 but such enactments as the consular law of 72 which confirmed his grants of citizenship to persons in Spain. And now his friends secured him two decrees allowing him to celebrate a triumph and to stand for the consulship, in return for his notable services to the Optimate cause. What less could they have done? One thinks of Marius and his sixth consulship, *praemium meritorum*.

But, they say, this was under the threat of armed force. No such thing. Pompey and Crassus did not march on Rome, they marched to Rome, as they were entitled to do, to hold well merited triumphs. They were elected in technical absence to consulships, disbanded their armies, and entered the city. So too in the year 180 B.C. Livy records that the praetor, Q. Fulvius Flaccus, returned from Spain with an army and a great reputation, and while he was outside the city because of his triumph he was elected consul though *absens*, and a few days later entered the city with his troops in a formal procession of triumph.[18] In 71 the thought of civil war existed according to the only source that discusses the matter, not in the intentions of Pompey but in the minds of the Roman population, and was false. No doubt Pompey played a little on this fear and exploited the psychosis of the age. But it fits neither the character nor the circumstances of Pompey in 71 that he contemplated an armed seizure of Rome *against* the Optimates. One needs more than an army for such a move. Pompey with an army and the backing of the Optimates, or Caesar with an army and the backing of equestrian interests, may try to solve political problems by force. But for the *aduluscentulus carnifex* fresh from the butchery of Sertorius to start a civil war against the Optimates makes nonsense. Besides, what would Crassus and Metellus and their not inconsiderable armies do while Pompey was seizing Rome?

Next for Pompey's part in the legislation of 70. Pompey promised his support for the restoration of the tribunate before the elections. It was his bid for votes. The Comitia Centuriata was largely under the influence of the Optimate families, as always, among whom Pompey had many enemies. He offset this by cashing in on a promising situation, as Plutarch remarks. The agitation for the restoration of the tribunate was at its height; Pompey added his support, and his election was secure. With the Optimate influence divided, and the popular vote estranged, it was necessary to make some electoral gesture. Pompey quickly redeemed his legislative pledge in 70, but only after consulting the Senate in a debate at which the arch-Sullan Catulus conceded that this was a necessary change; and the bill was passed *ex senatus consulto*. Cicero reveals this in the First Verrine.[19]

The judiciary law, which altered the Sullan system of political juries, was a careful bill which gave the control to a body that was constituted very differently from the old Gracchan panel. There is evidence that Pompey was not greatly interested, though he

[18] Livy XL, 43, 4–5.

[19] Cic. *I in Verr.* 44.

touched on the question in his *contio* as consul designate. Cicero in the Verrines insists that this bill was the child of L. Cotta, not ' one of us ', he says, but a *homo nobilissimus*. Plutarch significantly remarks that Pompey *allowed* the bill to go forward : περιεῖδεν τὰς δίκας μεταφερομένας. The dates support this. While Pompey's bill had been quickly passed, the jury bill was still under discussion in August 70.[20]

Those who take the mailed fist view of these events usually concede that the mailed fist was duly gloved in velvet. But even they have difficulty in explaining why Pompey did nothing for his all important army. Some have suggested that something must have been done, though not recorded. But Cassius Dio in a little noticed passage reporting a speech of Pompey in 59 B.C. has a reference back to 70.[21] Pompey says that formerly the Senate itself proposed a distribution of land to the veterans of Pompey and Metellus, but that the proposal was not carried out, ' quite reasonably,' because the Treasury was then short of cash. A queer warlord this, who so lightly lets a Senate which is supposed to be terrified of him, cheat his precious troops out of their due. In fact the incident reveals a very different, and much more political, situation at Rome in 70. At every crucial moment we find Pompey working through, not in defiance of, the Senate, as he had done since the beginning of his career. It had served his purpose in the past, and might do so again.

True, Pompey freed the tribunate from the shackles of the Sullan legislation. To the modern view this means the downfall of the Sullan system and, what is taken for the same thing, the near collapse of the Republic. But men like the Aurelii Cottae, who first broached the matter, and Cornelius the tribune, who carried on the work of 70 in 67, would say not that they were destroying the Republic, but that they were restoring it. Hence also the revival of the censorship at this time.

Pompey emerges, not the blunt man of action drawing a gun on the Senate, but as we meet him in Cicero's letters, the cunning prevaricator, Mr. Facing-both-ways, who makes haste slowly, who is ever ready to cash in on a promising situation, but never goes too far. This is the Pompey of the debates on the restoration of Ptolemy Auletes, the Pompey who allowed the recall of Cicero. Not Magnus but Catus. He would bluff up to the limits of legality, but he never marched on Rome or crossed a Rubicon in his life. He disbanded his legions at Brundisium on his return from the East. In his own phrase he would take a sword, but only if the consuls placed it in his hands ; if someone else drew a sword he would raise a shield.

As for the damage to the Sullan system, it was less extensive than is commonly assumed. A great part of Sulla's aim had been to give the Senate effective power over the administration. The Lex Annalis and the penal laws, the treason law and the extortion law, were the main instruments. These remained in full force despite the concession to Pompey, and the penal laws were meant to be enforced more, not less, vigorously by the new jury panel. The weakness of the post-Sullan Senate lay not in the fact that it took extraordinary measures to deal with extraordinary situations—that was its job—but that it failed to enforce the public laws in its own court impartially upon big men and little men alike. This failure was apparent before 70, as Catulus publicly admitted and Cicero fully documented in the Verrines and the *pro Cluentio*. Metelli and Luculli go unchecked in their extortions and malpractices, while a Fidiculanius or Septimius falls into trouble. The legislation of 70 came too late. The greatest names remained immune from the controls whereby before the Social War the proconsuls had been kept in some subservience to the State. The Senate's failure as a corporate body lies not in its weak reaction to external pressures, but in its acquiescence in the corruptions of the Optimate cliques within. It was because they would not discipline themselves that they were in no position to discipline Pompey. The condemnation of some great Optimate in the seventies would have gone far to instill caution into those who murmured : ' Sulla potuit, ego non potero ? '

[20] For the author and date of the Aurelian rogation see o.c. 46, 11 ; *in Verr.* II, 174 ; III, 223. Plut. *Pomp.* 22, 3. For Pompey's *contio* see *I in Verr.* 45.

[21] Dio 38, 5, 1–2. Professor R. E. Smith in a forthcoming article, which he kindly communicated to me, links this with the obscure *lex Plotia* that formed the model for the agrarian rogation of Flavius in 60 B.C. Cic. *ad Att.* I, 18, 6.

## CONCLUSION

So much for Marius and Pompey. If these two analyses have established anything apart from a salutary reminder not to forget the sources in the spinning of theories, it is that each decade or age should be interpreted by its own light rather than by that of a succeeding age, and that by this difference of emphasis, such as it is, a new look can be given to the series of episodes that make up the history of the later Republic. The value of this new look is that, if the job is properly done, one comes closer to the texture of the ancient world ; one tries to see events not in retrospect, not even through the eyes of Sallust or Tacitus, as is so fashionable nowadays, but through the eyes of the actors themselves. This is seldom very easy, given the nature of our sources. But however erroneous some of the preceding arguments may be in detail, something of importance emerges. This is not the whitewashing of an age in which violence could not be always avoided, but the underlying legality of the Roman outlook. There has for long been a sad divorce between the study of Roman politics and of Roman law. It sometimes seems impossible to believe that the despotic figures who appear in modern studies could belong to the folk who produced—who were already producing—the Roman civil law.

Professor A. H. M. Jones has salutarily remarked in his recent article on the Principate of Augustus [22] that there was a numerous element in the municipalities of Italy who were disgusted by the methods of the Triumviral period, and insisted if not on law at least on legality. He might have gone further. The leaders themselves seem to have little taste for their own revolutions. They lack the gusto of a Central American politician for the method of violence. These things were sometimes forced upon them by the logic of events, but they did not enjoy them. This makes sense of Roman history as a whole. A genius for civil law, for civil administration, for municipal government, for compromise in the handling of provincial subjects, all these qualities fit very oddly with an unabashed preference for power politics. Sulla and Octavian were the exceptions. Marius and Pompey, like many another, instinctively took the path of law and custom.

[22] *JRS* XLI, 1951, 112.

# VIII

*Z. Yavetz*

# The Living Conditions of the Urban Plebs in Republican Rome

# The Living Conditions of the Urban Plebs in Republican Rome

*Illas binas aut amplius domos continuare nobis larem familiarem nusquam ullum esse*
(Sall., *Cat.*, 20)

In his work on population in Greco-Roman antiquity (1) Julius Beloch came to the conclusion that the population of Rome in the first century B. C. did not exceed 800.000 people in all. In 1902, Nissen (2) contested Beloch's calculations on the grounds that in his opinion the term *civium capita* was not to be understood as meaning all the citizens of Rome who possessed full civic rights, but only the *iuniores* among them, i.e. men between the ages of 16 and 46. Beloch's very convincing rejoinder (3) that *civium capita* meant *seniores* as well as *iuniores* is generally accepted among scholars. After certain corrections the great majority of scholars have tended to accept the view that the population of Rome in the last stages of the Republic reached approximately the 1 million limite (4). There is general agreement (even among those who feel sceptical towards the scanty statistical evidence) that the city was then heavily overpopulated. Several modern works give a vivid picture of the living conditions of the various classes of the population. In particular, Friedländer, Carcopino and Homo (5) have made full use of the existing literary and

(1) J. Beloch, *Bevölkerung der Gr. Röm. Welt*, 1886.

(2) H. Nissen, *Italische Landeskunde*, II, p. 99 ff.

(3) J. Beloch, *Bevölkerung Italiens im Alterum* in *Klio*, III, 1902, 3, p. 470.

(4) E. g. Rice Holmes, *The Roman Republic*, I, pp. 360-3 ; A. H. M. Jones, *Ancient economic history*, passim. Against this view, however, see : A. von Gerken in *Römische Mitteilungen*, 1940 (1943), whose conclusion is that Rome's population did not exceed 600.000. See also W. J. Oates, *Population of Rome* in *Class. Phil.*, 1943, vol. 29, p. 101, with some very valuable critical remarks on Beloch's calculations, and F. G. Maier, *Römische Bevölkerungs-Geschichte u. Inschriftenstatistik* in *Historia*, 1954, p. 318 ff. Maier deals mainly with imperial Rome (*op. cit.*, p. 320).

(5) L. Friedlaender, *Darstellungen aus der Röm. Sittengeschichte*, Ed. X, passim. J. Carcopino, *Daily life in ancient Rome*, 1941, *passim*. L. Homo, *Rome impériale et l'urbanisme dans l'antiquité*, 1951.

epigraphic material, dating from the early and late Empire. With regard to the Republican period, however, they have been satisfied with a few general remarks. Robert Pohlmann's very illuminating study (1) deals mainly with the Empire (especially the later period) and the density of population in Constantinople and Alexandria. While the former works are intended in the first place to be descriptive, it is obvious that Pohlmann's outlook is profoundly social and educational, a fact which is in no way detrimental to the scholarly value of the work. After describing the deplorable standard of living of the so called « Lumpenproletariat » in the big cities of the ancient world, Pohlmann warns us of the overcrowded cities of our own days. London is a nightmare for him (2) and he gives vent to his distress that Berlin has become the « magnet for all those elements that have declared war on society » (3). The logical conclusion is obviously that excessive density of population in the big cities leads not only to unemployment, unbearable hygienic conditions, and thus a high death — rate, but also to political disaster. About the Republican period, Pohlmann has a few highly important things to say, which, however, I propose to examine from a different point of view.

Miss Ruth Whiterstine, though devoting her article (4) to the period under consideration in this work, makes no mention of the Plebs urbana. She declares explicitely that it is her intention to examine the living conditions of « important Romans » (5). W. W. Fowler arrived — from my point of view — at correct conclusions ; his book (6) however, is of too general a character, and does not enter into a discussion of the many and complicated problems that arise (7).

I shall here try to describe briefly the living conditions of the urban Plebs, as they become apparent from sources of the first century B.C., in the hope that this may prove helpful in making certain social and political phenomena appear in a new light. Part of my conclusions are based on an analysis of Vitruvius' books « On Architecture », in spite of the indisputable fact that Vitruvius cannot be considered a pure Republican author. The early humanists readily accepted the statement appearing in the introduction to his first

(1) R. Pohlmann, *Übervölkerung der antiken Grosstädte*, 1884.

(2) *Op. cit.*, p. 51.

(3) *Op. cit.*, p. 54, against this view see Kromayer, *Wirtschaftliche Entwicklung Italiens* in *Neue Jahrbücher für Klass. Altertum*, vol. XXXIII-IV, 1914, p. 146.

(4) Ruth Whiterstine, *Where the Romans lived in the first century B. C.* in *Class. Journal*, XXI, p. 566.

(5) *Ibid.*

(6) W. W. Fowler, *Social life at Rome in the age of Cicero*, 1908.

(7) See specially pp. 24ff.

book, that Vitruvius lived in the days of Augustus, to whom his work is dedicated. With the further development of textual criticism, however, many philologists believed that Vitruvius belonged to a far later period. Some of them held that his book was composed in the time of the Emperor Vespasian, others made him a contemporary of Constantine, and certain scholars even wished to place him as late as the 10th century A. D. Most of these deliberations were based only on linguistic analysis which showed that the language used by Vitruvius resembled that of Apuleius rather than that of Caesar and Cicero. Philologists of the beginning of our century return to the view originally advocated by the Humanists of the Renaissance i.e. that Vitruvius' work was composed in the time of Augustus (1). They rightly stress that Vitruvius' style should not mislead us, as his subject naturally required a linguistic treatment different from that of Cicero, and Vitruvius himself apologizes for his way of writing (2). Furthermore our attention is aroused by the astonishing fact, that Vitruvius has a great deal to tell us about buildings that were put up in the days of Augustus, but knows nothing at all about outstanding edifices of a later time. For two reasons I venture to conjecture that Vitruvius wrote in the early days of the Augustan period.

a) Vitruvius speaks mainly about *lateres*, while in Augustus' later days there already existed in Rome magnificent marble buidings (3).

b) In his books Vitruvius attacks a certain condition that had arisen in the field of house construction and hopes that Augustus will put an end to certain misdeeds. He therein refers to the period of building speculation initiated by Crassus and his followers. In what follows I shall try to show that these assumptions are entirely borne out by the facts. However, whether Vitruvius lived and wrote at the beginning of the Augustan era or towards its end, it seems legitimate to make full use of his writings for the elucidation of our problem.

Such quotations as are adduced here from Juvenal and Martial serve only as striking illustrations, if a similar state of affairs is confirmed by Republican sources. These quotations are nowhere meant

(1) Ludwig Sontheimer, *Vitruvius u. seine Zeit* (Diss. Tübingen, 1908), p. 88 ; W. Dietrich, *Quaestionum Vitruvianarum specimen* (Diss. Leipzig, 1906). Both dissertations were published at almost the same time. Dietrich and Sontheimer, without collaborating, or even knowing of each other, reached the same conclusions. See also L. Homo, *Rome impériale*, p. 5.

(2) Vitr., *De arch.*, I, 1, 18. Sontheimer even concludes that Vitruvius' style is similar to that of the author of the Bellum Africanum.

(3) Suet, *Aug.*, 28, see also Dio C., LVI, 30 and Dietrich, *op. cit.*, note 14.

to bear the burden of a proof. Livy too has been cited very cautiously with explanatory comments.

The extant historical sources abound in information about the conditions under which the more well-to-do classes of Rome (Senators and Knights) lived. Cicero, for example, finds infinite delight in the description of his villae suburbanae (1) ; Vitruvius, who devotes a considerable portion of his books to public buildings and temples (*aedes sacrae*), knows that quite different houses are fitting for aristocrats on one hand and for bankers and moneylenders on the other (2). The poor quarters hold no interest for Vitruvius. Even the country-houses of the rich are more prominent in his books (3) than the *tuguria pauperum* (4) though the latter were certainly far more numerous than the villae.

It seems safe to say that the class differences, as far as lodging houses are concerned, were enormous. Moreover, if we accept as trustworthy the statement that the house of Lepidus (which in 78 B. C. was said to be still the most magnificent in Rome) never reached the height of splendour displayed in the days of Caesar by the villas of other aristocrats, we may well be entitled to conclude that the economic conditions of the masses of Rome deteriorated, while the luxury and splendour of the life of the ruling classes increased (5). While Cicero, the owner of 8 villas and 4 deversoria, was prepared to incur further debts for the acquisition of an additional house (6), so as not to appear less well-off than the *piscinarii* (for whom he intertained such a contemptuous hatred), while the pleasure walls of Lucullus and Sallust extended over enormous areas, the process of cramming the sentina rei publicae into the *insulae* steadily continued. Of what life was like in these poor quarters we hear but little. Such scanty information as has been preserved does not permit us to determine with any appreciable precision the extent to which these *insulae* were overpopulated ; we are left to mere conjecture (7).

(1) Cic., *ad. Att.*, V. 2. 2 : *Habuimus in Comano quasi pusillam Romam* ; Locus classicus : *de Domo*, 109.

(2) Vitr., *op. cit.*, I, 2, 9 : *non item feneratoribus, aliter beatis et delicatis*, etc. While the former stand more in need of houses that are safe from the danger of burglary, the latter require large and elegant apartments. On private houses see especially book VI, passim.

(3) *Op. cit.*, VI, 6.

(4) Liv., III, 13, 10.

(5) Plin., *Nat. Hist.*, XXXVI, 50.

(6) Gell., *N. A.*, XII. 12.

(7) For figures for the days of Constantine see BELOCH, *Bevölkerung*, p. 405 : Within the walls 23.726 insulae and 959 domus ; outside the city walls 20.754 insulae and 823 domus. For the definition of insulae in those times, see RICHTER in *Hermes*, XX, p. 91 ff. FIECHTER's article *Insula* in P. W., *R.E.*

It is impossible to determine the exact number of people who lived in one flat, and therefore we are equally in the dark as to the number of the inhabitants of one *insula*, since we hear that a certain number of the tenants of an *insula* used to sleep in a *taberna* that happened to be on the ground floor of their house (1). The information that comes from Valerius Maximus, stating that 16 people were living in a domuncula (2), does not help us much, for even a small

and L. Homo, *op. cit.* pp. 100-3 ; 552 ff. The following statistical items, from the available sources, speak for themselves, even if we do not wish to draw final conclusions from them :

a) In the days of Augustus the majority of the plebs was still living within the Servian wall. It was only in the time of the Empire that Rome extended beyond this wall, but even during the reign of Constantine the density of population in the old city was far greater than in the suburbs, although the area outside the wall was twice that within its precincts (see Beloch, *op. cit.*, p. 405 for an exact list of the 8 districts within and 6 districts outside the wall).

b) Cicero's annual income from his insulae amounted to 80.000 sesterces. (see Cic., *ad. Att.*, XVI, 1, 5 ; XV, 17, 1, 20, 4).

c) Sulla in his youth had to pay a yearly rent of 3000 sesterces (Plut., *Sull.*, 1).

d) In a flat or room still worse than Sulla's a freedman paid 2000 sesterces annually (Plut., *Sull.*, 1).

e) In Caesar's time an annual rent of 2000 sesterces in Rome and of 500 sesterces outside the city was considered reasonable (see Dio C., XLII, 51 ; XLVII, 9 ; Suet. *Caes.*, 9 ; Cic., *de off.*, II, 83.

f) At times, more than 16 people were huddled together in one flat (*in una domuncula* : Val. Max., IV, 4, 8 ; Plut. *Aem. Paul.*, V, 6). *Insula* is usually used as opposed to *domus*. *Domus* is a one-family house, while an *insula* contained a number of families. The flats in an *insula* were let for rent. The question therefore arises : What was the numeral proportion between the inhabitants of the *domus* and those of the *insulae*, towards the end of the Republic ? Beloch's figures (see note 7, p. 503), however, are only of very doubtful value for a clarification of our problem, since the term *insula* got an entirely different meaning in the time of the Emperors, which explains why Festus 111 explicitly says « *Insulae proprie dicuntur* » (see Richter, *op. cit*). In an aristocratic *domus* lived all the *familia urbana*. It is well known that during the last stages of the Republic « Sklavenluxus » flourished in the city, so much so that it was not considered proper that one and the same slave should perform various duties (Cic., *in Pis.*, 27). It follows that at least part of the city population lived in *domus*. But even if we estimate the number of the *domus* inhabitants (including slaves) as amounting to 200.000 — 300.000 souls, there remain 700.000 — 800.000 people domiciled in *insulae*.

(1) Asc., p. 37, *in taberna dormientem* ; Tac., *Hist.*, I, 86. see also Nissen, *Pompejanische Studien*, p. 600 ; *dig.*, XXXII, 7, 7.

(2) See note 7, p. 503.

sized house is more spacious than a room in the upper storey of an insula. What is reported about the Gens Aelia is regarded as an exception, and Plutarch explicitly mentions the fact that Aemilius' daughter did not hesitate to marry into such a poor family. We do not know whether Cicero's fructus insularum (1) refers to a gross or nett income. If we knew that much, we would be able to determine the number of Cicero's tenants (2). One thing however is certain, namely that the inhabitants of the poorer quarters were crowded together in the upper storeys of the insulae, which were utterly unfitted for a normal and orderly family life. We shall in the following pages deal in detail with some of their vital problems.

> *Magni reditus urbanorum praediorum, sed pericula sunt longe maxima. Si quid autem posset remedii fore, ut ne tam assidue domus Romae arderent, venum hercle, dedissem res rusticas et urbicas emissem* (Gell., *N. A.*, XV, 1. 3).

Rome was built without any plan, and if we may believe tradition in this matter, it was done after the Gallic invasion (3) in the 4th century B. C. so that the ruins were hurriedly repaired and the houses erected without any sort of town planning.

Slowly and gradually more aristocratic quarters became distinguishable from poorer districts, and in the first century B. C. most of the plebs urbana was concentrated on the Aventine the Caelian (the centre of the retailers and small merchants) and Argiletum (the centre of the shoemakers and booksellers) (4). Naturally, this division was not absolute, and we know of highly important and even wealthy people residing in the poorer quarters. Thus we are told, for example, that Pompeius continued to live in Carinae (5) (a district between the Caelian and Esquiline) ; that Julius Caesar, before being elected Pontifex Maximus, lived in Subure (6) ; and of Sulla (7) and Augustus (8) we hear wery much the same story. The value of these pieces of information should not be exaggerated. We have to keep in mind that C. Gracchus (9) moved from the Palatine into the neigh-

(1) *Ibid.*

(2) *Ibid* : from Cic., *De off.*, II, 83, it may be deduced that the rent paid by every single one of Cicero's tenants did not exceed 2000 ses. since he complains bitterly of Caesar's law on *remissio habitationum* ; see also Madwig : dans *Philologus*, II, 143.

(3) Liv., V, 55 (2-5) ; Dio C., XIV, 116, 8 ; Tac., *Ann.*, XV, 43, 1 : *post Gallica incendia nulla distinctione nec passim errecta* ; for a further discussion see L. Homo, *op. cit.*, pp. 48 ff.

(4) *C. A. H.*, vol. I, X, p. 781 ff.

(5) Cic., *Harusp. Resp.*, 49 ; Vell. Pat., II, 77 ; Suet., *Tib.*, 15.

(6) Suet., *Jul.*, 46.

(7) Plut., *Sull.*, 1.

(8) Suet., *Aug.*, 72.

(9) Plut., *C. Gracchus*, 12.

bourhood of the Forum. This was an act of an eminently political character, and it appears possible that many demagogues of aristocratic origin went to live in the poor districts, so as to win thereby the sympathies of the poorer classes. A person's residence was therefore sometimes a matter of political significance. To begin with, let us see when and why many-storeyed buildings were put up in Rome and from what time onward we are entitled to speak of *Insulae*.

Very early in the history of Rome a second floor was added to the ordinary *domus* and there the servants were generally put up (*cellae servorum*). These cellae were never above the *atrium*, as long as the light could penetrate only through the compluvium. This difficulty, however, was soon overcome, the atrium was covered, and another storey was raised on top of it (1). Most scholars accept as trustworthy the story of the ox that climbed up to the third floor of a house (2) in the 3rd century B. C. Vitruvius explains that because of the great density of population in town and the high prices for building plots, new storeys were added to already existing houses (3). That might well have happened at the end of the third century B. C. or at the beginning of the second century, when a great number of people streamed into Rome as a result of the economic crisis which then beset the city. The results can easily be imagined. Between 181 and 171 B. C. there were many terrible outbreaks of the plague, in and around Rome (4). We know of one plague that lasted for three years. Dead bodies were then lying in the streets of the plague-ridden city, for the hand of the disease was quicker than those whose duty it was to bury its victims. The mobilization authorities were hampered in their work, as a number of those who had to enlist were stricken by the plague (5). Vitruvius' description of the growing demand for flats, and Livy's, of the concentration of townspeople and dispossessed villagers in arta tecta, fit this period exactly. At the same time the *contabulatio* or *contignatio* began. Then rents began to rise (6), and in the first century B. C. Cicero could say : *Romam in*

(1) P. W., *R. E.*, art. *Römisches Haus* ; MARQUARDT, *Privatleben der Römer*, Ch. I, passim.

(2) Liv., XXI, 62.

(3) Vitr., II, 8, 17.

(4) Livy's description of the plague in 463 B. C. ; see III, 6 (2-3) : *Ea conluvio mixtorum omnis generis animantium et odore insolito urbanos et agrestem confertum in arta tecta aestu et vigiliis angebat, ministeriaque in vicem ac contagio ipse volgabant morbos*, might well illuminate the situation in the second century B. C., when people streamed into the town not for the sake of a temporary shelter only, but in order to settle there permanently.

(5) Liv., XL, 19, 3 ; 36, 14 ; XLI, 21, 5 ; Val. Max., I, 8, 2. On hygienic conditions generally see POHLMANN, *op. cit.*, ch. III. ; HEITLAND, *Roman Republic*, I, p. 182.

(6) Diod. (Dindorf), 31. 8, see below p. 514.

*montibus positam et convallibus coenaculis, sublatam atque suspensam, non optimis viis, angustissimis semitis...* etc. (1). Augustus soon realized the dangers inherent in the prevailing methods of house construction and prohibited the erection of houses beyond a maximum height of 70 feet (2). Presumably also in those days some men knew better than others how to evade the law (3), and Trajan had to issue a further decree forbidding the construction of high houses (4). Some poets of the Empire have left us descriptions of the chamber doors in the attic that were so low that one had to stoop in order to be able to enter (5). We know also of a poor teacher, who came to Rome in Cicero's days. He taught *maiore fama quam emolumento* and had to live *sub tegulis*, exactly as in the days of Juvenal (6) If the period of the Republic had known poets and writers of an outlook like Juvenal and Martial, they too might have called a flat in an insula a *miserabile hospitium* (7). During the Republic, the inhabitants of the insulae were faced with two very serious problems :

a) The collapse of houses and frequent conflagrations owing to irresponsible building.
b) The payment of rent.

Builders and architects at Rome flourished particularly in the first century B. C. Builders like Mutius (in the days of Marius) and Cyrus, (who was more than once employed by Cicero) (8), were well known, Vitruvius, who lived, as we have tried to establish, at the end of the first century, knew a great number of architects (9). The latter were greatly appreciated by the high and mighty of Rome, and Cicero considers architecture a very honourable profession (10). And yet houses collapsed and fire was a most frequent event in Rome (11). Are the architects to be blamed for it? Vitrivius attacks those *qui falso architecti nominabantur* (12). His demands are impressive indeed : every architect should be well versed not only in the subjects

(1) Cic., *De leg. agr.*, II, 96.
(2) Strab., V, 3, 7. (p. 235) and see on Rutilius' speech. *De modo aedificiorum.* Suet., *Aug.*, 89.
(3) Vitr., II, 8, 17.
(4) Aur. Vict., *Ep.*, 13, 13. Pohlmann, *op. cit.*, p. 143.
(5) Mart., II, 53, 8 : *si tua non rectus tecta subire posse.*
(6) Suet., *De Gramm.*, 9.
(7) Juv., III, 166.
(8) Cic., *ad. Att.*, II, 3 ; 5 ; 7 ; IV, 10, 2 ; *ad Qu. Fr.*, II, 2 etc.
(9) Vitr., VII. *Praef.* 18 : *nostra memoria satis multi architecti.*
(10) Cic., *De off.*, I, 150.
(11) Plut., *Crass.*, 2. 4.
(12) Vitruv., VI, *Praef.* 7.

directly connected with his profession, such as arithmetic, drawing, surveying etc. (1), but also in philosophy, optics, medicine, history, music, jurisprudence, astrology and climatology, for without knowing all these sciences, how could anyone build a proper house (2)? Vitruvius tries to reassure us that it is not too difficult to achieve such a high level of learning, since these subjects, which he considers indispensable for any architect, form a coherent whole. It is clear that only few would have been worthy to become architects if Vitruvius had had the practical decision in his hands.

In my introductory remarks, I said that Vitruvius' ten books on architecture are in my opinion not merely a technical manual. Occasionally the author gives vent to his dissatisfaction with regard to the existing conditions in Rome, and his pen picture of the « ideal architect » has an eminently practical purpose: it is his design to warn the niggardly landlords not to economize on the expenses of the architect by employing an ill-qualified and inexpert man, or worse, by themselves playing the part of the architect (3). If such things did really happen, the fault of the architects would be grievous indeed, and the lack of their technical knowledge would be the reason for the collapse of many houses. Though I would not wish to minimize the importance of this factor, there is further evidence to be considered, which may alter our outlook on the whole problem.

1) If a house collapses, not under the direct influence of the powers of nature, it appears that something in its construction was faulty. This is evident to Vitruvius, and he explains: *Firmitatis erit habita ratio cum fuerit fundamentorum ad solidum depressio, quaque e materia copiarum, sine avaritia diligens electio* (4). In other words the architect is to be blamed only if the foundations of the house he has put up were not sufficiently deep or solid. As far as the exaggerated economy, quantitavely and qualitatively of the building material is concerned, *the landlord is solely responsible* (5), a circumstance fully admitted by Vitruvius. He describes at great length the result of parsimony in connection with buildingmaterials (6). It would not be fair, however, to hold the landlord alone responsible, without taking into consideration certain natural and technical difficulties, which also had a bearing on the matter. Vitruvius, for example,

(1) *Op. cit.*, I, 1 (2-3).

(2) *Op. cit.*, I, 1, 10: *sine his enim rationibus, nulla salubris habitatio fieri potest.*

(3) *Op. cit.*, VI, *Praef.* 6.

(4) *Op. cit.*, I, 3, 2.

(5) *Op. cit.*, VI, 8, 9: *... quibus autem copiarum generibus oporteat uti non est architecti potestate.*

(6) *Op. cit.*, II, 3, 2; VI, 8 (1-9).

does not yet know of any better way of testing the quality of the stones, than to let them lie for two years in some exposed place. If they could stand the test of sun and rain, they were fit to be used in a building, but if they crumbled, they might be used for secondary purposes, but not for the erection of house walls (1). It is hard to see how, with such methods prevailing, the building work of the city could proceed at all, if we recall the constant and pressing need for new flats in Rome. In addition to that we have to take into account the difficulties in laying foundations on swampy ground (2), and the very considerable influence of rain water and innundations on on the lower part of the walls (3). And yet one thing is beyond doubt : Many landlords and building contractors took the greatest advantage of the existing natural and social difficulties, and the miseries of the masses supplied them with quite a substantial source of income. Great was the number of those who made a fortune by using inferior building materials, putting up extra-thin walls, or neglecting all the elementary rules of solid building (4).

2) Nor were the contractors slow to exploit the favourable situation. Taking advantage of the great demand for flats, they fixed a price before the building was begun ; by the time the house was ready, the price had risen by 50%. The results were that certain landlords could not meet those exorbitant demands, and the building was interrupted (5). But no general stoppage of building work followed. Sometimes a way was found to complete the building at somebody else's expenses. In this way the *avaritia copiarum* and the disregard for the rules and regulations regarding the construction of houses spread in town. We shall here cite but one example : a certain height of the house demanded a certain width of the walls (6). Many landlords ignored this fundamental principle. Soon the walls began to crack (7). The tenants demanded repairs, but in vain (8). The landlords paid no heed. On the contrary, the ever-growing demand for flats, not only because of the influx of new people into the town, but quite simply because of *the great number of houses that collapsed*, — offered

(1) *Op. cit.*, II, 7, 5.

(2) *Op. cit.*, III, 4, 2.

(3) *Op. cit.*, VI, 8, 5.

(4) *Op. cit.*, II, 8, 17.

(5) *Op. cit.*, X, *Praef.* 2.

(6) Corresponding to the height of the house, the width of the walls had to be between 1 1/2 feet (0,444 m), and 3 feet or 4 1/2 feet. On the Diplinthii and Triplinthii, see esp. FIECHTER, *op.cit.* and Vitr., II, 3, 3. ; Plin., *Nat. Hist.*, XXXV, 173.

(7) Vitr., II, 8, 1 ; Plin., *op. cit.*, XXXV, 172.

(8) Cic., *ad. Att.*, XIV, 9, 1 ; Catull., XXIII, 9 ; Juv., III, 194-5.

them an opportunity of adding further storeys on unstable foundations. This state of affairs is reflected in Vitruvius' work : *Nam si in pendentibus onera fuerint parietum aut columnarum, non poterint habere perpetuam firmitatem* (1).

Finally, let us have a look at an actual description in one of Cicero's letters (2). He tells his good friend Atticus that two of his tenement houses have altogether collapsed (3), and the rest are about to fall ; because of the mortal danger, all the tenants have left the place, and even « the mice have begun to emigrate from ». Only at this critical moment did Cicero call for Chrisippus (one of the architects) and ask him to undertake the necessary repairs. But the story does not end here. Cicero thought he would have to invest good money in the matter, but with the help of Vestorius (who was not only a banker, but used also to instruct workers how to build and make plans for buildings) he finds a way to turn loss into profit. If we add this story to the descriptions supplied by Vitruvius, particularly in the matter of *avaritia copiarum,* then the picture we get is complete : the landlord, the architect, the banker, all work hand in hand, with the aim of economizing on the cost of living quarters, and the inhabitants of the insulae had to put up with the results.

One trespass against the law is generally followed by another. Is it mere accident that we nearly always hear of collapses and conflagrations in close connection with each other? Livy's history is strewn with dozens of stories about fires in Rome at different times, and there is no reason to disbelieve him. In 213 B. C., for instance, a fire broke out that raged for two nights and a day. It razed to the ground the whole district between Salinae and the Carmentalis Gate where the vegetable market stood (4). Three years later, in 210 B. C. a fire broke out in the vicinity of the Forum — in various places at once, so that it could only be extinguished with considerable difficulty. This time damage was done mostly to the tabernae and the fish market. It is true there were efforts to put out the fire, but they were mainly directed towards saving the temple of Vesta from complete ruin (5). In 203 B. C. a street in the neighbourhood of the Aventine, one of the centre of the poor, was completely burnt down (6). Inundations accompained by fire and the collapse of houses also

(1) Vitr., VI, 8 ; see also Plin., *Hist. Nat.*, XXXV, 173.

(2) Cic., *ad. Att.*, XIV, 9, 1.

(3) *Ibid.* : *tabernae mihi duae corruerunt.* « *Taberna* » should here be translated as « tenement house » and not as workshop. See Cassiodor., *Com. Ps.*, 14. 1 : *maiores nostri domos pauperum tabernas appellaverunt.* In the same sense see Varro, *L. L.*, V, 160 ; Suet., *Nero*, 37, 1 ; Juv., I, 105 ; Horat., *Carm.*, I, 4, 13. On Cicero as landlord see the interesting letter *ad. Att.*, XII, 32, 2.

(4) Liv., XXIV, 47, 15.

(5) Liv., XXVI, 27 (1-3).

(6) Liv., XXX, 26, 5.

befell the city in 194 B. C. and at the beginning of 192 (1). In the second half of 192 Rome was visited by a twofold affliction — an earthquake, followed again by an enormous fire. This time the Forum Boarium was hit and houses and tabernae burnt down with all the goods in them (2). These were the very years in which great masses of people moved in to Rome from the country. Many slaves were set free at the same time, and the need for flats was tremendous. In no time new storeys were added to existing houses. It was indeed forbidden to cover the roofs with wooden tiles (scandulae), and tegulae or imbrices were used instead (3). However, in order to have more rooms to let, thin wooden partitions were put up, mainly in the upper floors. These were the partitions on which it was said: *Craticii ad incendia uti faces sunt parati* » (4). Vitruvius expresses his regret that they were invented at all. There existed it is true a special kind of wood, which was not easily inflamable, but that was expensive and nobody thought it necessary to use it in the construction of insulae (5). The reason for using wood for the upper floors of the houses was that the foundations and the ground-walls were so poorly built that no other material but wood was possible if one thought at all of adding another floor (6). In his way, it seems to me, one has to explain the opinion of the ancients, that the height of the building is the cause of the fire (7), for it was just here, in these upper storeys — that served the poorest part of the population as lodgings — that landlords and contractors permitted themselves to economize on the material and to build poorly and carelessly. The fear of conflagration had its clear and distinct effect on the life of the city, and various authorities were concerned about it (8). From the time of the Empire we have the combined evidence of Tacitus, Seneca, Juvenal and Martial about the shocking results of the conflagrations. However, I am inclined to think that in the days of the Republic, the state of affairs in this respect was far worse, for the following reasons:

a) Assuming that the height of the building had something to do with the frequent outbreaks of fire, we have to remember that only

(1) Liv., XXXIV, 44 (7-8); XXXV, 9 (3-4); 25 (4-5) etc...

(2) Liv., XXV, 40 (7-8).

(3) Pl., *H. n.*, XVI, 36, 42.

(4) Vitr., II, 8 (18-20).

(5) Vitr., II, 9, 16; VII, 1, 2. (on Larigna).

(6) See espec.: Sen., *Contr.*, II, 1, 1, 9, 1, also Tac., *Hist.*, III, 7 and *Ann.*, XV, 43.

(7) *Bell. Alex.*, I, 3: *Nam incendio fere tuta Alexandrea, quid sine contignatione ac materia sunt aedificia...*

(8) E. g. Haruspices suggested that a temple for Vulcan should be erected outside the city, so that Rome itself would be saved from the flames: (see Vitr., I, 7, 1).

under Augustus was the height of a house submitted to public regulations (1). In the Republic the landlords were entirely free and unrestricted in this respect.

b) We have mentioned above the speculations of those building-contractors who raised the price by 50% and more while the work was already under way. It seems that in Ephesus in Asia Minor these things were kept under control, and Vitruvius yearns to see supervision and control introduced in Rome too : *Utinam dii immortales fecissent ea lex, non modo publicis sed etiam privatis aedificiis esset constituta* (2). We have noticed the disastrous effects of those speculations on the building market, without any intervention on the part of the authorities. Only after the death of Augustus did Rome come to know some sort of supervision in this field. Under the new law, a landlord was entitled to demand in court the return of the sum originally paid, if the contractor had raised his price by more than 50%, after the work had begun (3).

c) When a fire broke out in Rome during the Empire, the *vigiles* were ready to extinguish it. 7000 men were specially trained for that purpose. Though we learn that in the Republic also the office of Tresviri Nocturni existed (4), their presence or activity was hardly felt. The plebs urbana in the time of danger, depended completely on the goodwill of some rich citizens, with a great number of slaves at their disposal. And indeed we hear of a certain Egnatius Rufus, who won his public reputation by means of the help he extended through his slaves, when a fire had to be put out somewhere (5). Only later did Augustus organize a fire brigade, thus putting an end also in this direction to the increasing activity of demagogues. (Conflagrations occured in Rome in the years 23, 14, 9 and 7 B. C. and then the fire brigade was established) (6).

In his article on building-laws in Rome, Moritz Voigt (7) summarizes the general tendency of these laws thus :

a) Control of building activity with particular emphasis on precautions against conflagrations.

(1) Strab., V, 7. 3.

(2) Vitr., X, *Praef.* 1.

(3) Sontheimer, *Vitruvius*, p. 82. from a responsum of Labeo Dig., XIX, 2, 60, 4.

(4) See : Reynolds, *The Roman vigiles*, p. 20, note 2. Mrs. Reynolds does not mention the quinquiviri. On them see Premerstein's articles in *Hermes*, 1919, vol. 39, p. 327 and in *Festschrift Hirschfeld*, 1903, p. 224.

(5) Dio C., LIII, 24, Vell. Pat., II, 91, 2.

(6) Dio C., LIII, 33, LIV, 24, 29 ; LV, I, 8.

(7) M. Voigt, *Römische Baugesetze* in *Ber. Ges. Wiss. Leipzig, Phil. Hist. Klasse*, vol. 55, p. 175.

b) To encourage the re-erection of demolished houses.
c) Control over building plots.

We should, however, point out that the laws mentioned by Voigt did not exist in the Republic. It was Augustus who first proposed to introduce law and order into the hitherto neglected field of building. Later on, in the days of Nero, the *Lex Neronis de modo aedificiorum urbis* was issued and was further enlarged by Vespasian, Trajan and Hadrian (1). If in spite of all these praiseworthy efforts and governmental control, Juvenal in the time of the Empire still had reason to long for a safe place for the night where there was no fear of night-alarms (2), and could exclaim : *Nos urbem colimus tenui et tibicine fultam magna parte sui* (3), if Seneca could go so far as to remark that in his time even the roofs of palaces were no safe places (4), adding with regard to poor quarters : *Parietes insularum exesos rimosos inaequales* (5) — we are left with one possible conclusion only : *If the position was so unsatisfactory in the Empire, it must have been far worse during the Republic, when building speculators of the type of Crassus had their day* (6). Towards the end of the Republic the city proletariate found themselves caught in a vicious circle ; the city population becomes even more dense, prices for building-plots rise, thus building becomes more expensive and speculation sets in ; economizing on building-material leads to frequent collapses and conflagrations, thousands remain without a roof over their heads, and thus the demand for the speedy completion of new living-quarters constantly increases. Building technique was unable to fulfil the demands of speed and solidity at one and the same time. Consequently there was careless building, which again led to the above mentioned instability of the houses and so forth in an endless sequence of cause and result. Catullus was able to remark cynically (7) that beggars had nothing to fear from fire, since they had nothing to lose. Yet these people possessed certain commodities : a bed, a table, kitchen utensils and some clothes were in every house. Obviously Crassipes, Cicero's son-in-law, lost more when in 54 he became the victim of an innundation (8), but it may safely be assumed that Crassipes found it easier to replace what he had lost than those *tabernarii* who together with him were hit by the flood.

(1) For references see Voigt, *op. cit.*
(2) Juv., III, 197-207.
(3) *Op. cit.*, III, 192.
(4) Sen., *Ep.*, 90, 43.
(5) Sen., *De ira*, III, 35.
(6) See : Plut., *Crass.*, 2.
(7) Catull., XXIII, 9. (written between 61 and 54 B. C.).
(8) Cic., *ad. Qu. fr.*, III, 7 : *L. Crassipedis ambulatio oblata horti, tabernae plurimae, magna vis aquae usque ad piscinam publicam.*

The writers and poets of the Republic did not go out of their way to talk of the difficulties of the poorer people in paying their rent. In the time of the Empire, on the other hand, house rent was a favourite topic of satire for Martial and Juvenal.

Are we allowed in this matter to draw conclusions from the later days for the earlier? Were there no men like Civis and Atestinus in the Republic, who did not have the means to pay their rent (1)? Did the dread of expulsion of the kind: *O Juliarum dedecus Kalendarum* », not hang over the heads of the poor in the Republic too (2)? I believe we may answer these question thus: the poems of Martial and Juvenal are of no great value for us if we wish to be enlightened about the problems of house rent in Republican times, but on the other hand, the absence of this motif from the literature of the Republic does not by any means show that such difficulties did not exist. In the Republican era, political life, as centred in the Forum, formed the main subject of general interest. The « litte man » did not enter into the literary limelight at all (3). That explains, in my opinion, the absence of such subjects from the literature of the Republic. And we must bear in mind besides the loss of the comedies of Novius and Pomponius.

And yet, a collection of hints and chance remarks of the period will give us a fairly distinct picture of the situation. In the foregoing paragraph I have tried to show that the movement of *contabulatio* or *contignatio* began towards the end of third, and increased in the beginning of the second century B. C. In the seventies of the second century the dethroned king Ptolemy VI of Egypt arrived in Rome, having fled from his country after a quarrel with his brother, Ptolemy VIII. Diodorus, apparently following Polybius, says quite plainly (4). that Ptolemy was compelled on account of the high rent to live in an attic. Attics were, of course, cheaper. We have no certain evidence what such a rent may have amounted to, in the second century B. C., but it appears that rents were constantly rising. Thus, for example, we learn that in the thirties of that century, the Censors Longinus and Caepio rebuked the augur Aemilius Lepidus for having paid 6000 sesterces for year house-rent. Velleius Paterculus, writing approximately 150 years after the event, observes that in his own day 6000 sesterces was considered a negligible sum, and if anyone paid only that amount for rent, he would hardly be considered a senator (5). This is confirmed by what we hear of Caelius, the friend

(1) Mart., III, 38; see also Juv., III, 162 ff.

(2) Mart., XII, 32, but see for Rep. times: Cic., *ad. Qu. fr.*, II, 3, 7.

(3) Val. Max., IV, 3, 13: *Exultat animus maximorum virorum memoria percurrens.* Valerius Maximus feels a particular deligth when he has the occasion of picturing for us the lives of great men.

(4) Diod. (Dindorf), 31, 18.

(5) Vell. Pat., II, 10, 1.

of Cicero, who living in an *insula* paid 10.000 sesterces rent yearly (1). Caelius' appartment was not characteristic of the situation in the *insulae*, but we know also that the rent there was not much more than 3000 sesterces ; Sulla who in his youth, lived in an *insula*, paid that amount for his rent, but a freedman living one floor above him paid only 2000 sest. (2) ; that was 40 years before Julius Caesar issued his decrees. In other words : though rents did rise one should not overrate the extent of this tendency. Fluctuations in the currency value have also to be taken into account. The increase will then no more appear quite so abrupt. But the most essential question remains : were the poorer classes capable of paying even the sum of 2000-3000 sest. for their rent ? Would we be justified in saying that it was precisely because of this item in their budget that the plebs urbana usually became involved in debt ?

Cicero says of Caelius that his only expenditure was the house rent (3). It is impossible, of course, to rely entirely on the arguments used by a lawyer in court, but Cicero's words demonstrate quite clearly that it was then considered very plausible in Rome that a man should contract debts on account of his house rent. But, as admitted before, Caelius may not be typical for the plebs urbana. What, then, about the ordinary inhabitants of the insulae? The rent was collected four times a year (4). The owner of the insula did not attend to it himself. A so called *insularius* was installed for that purpose, who was often a freedman, or sometimes an educated slave. The *insularius* was responsible for the maintenance of good order in the house ; he would settle disputes between tenants, and collect the rent at fixed times in the year (5). Severe measures were taken against those who were in arrear and the danger of *expellere*, *eiccere*, *repellere* was always hanging over their heads (6). There were tenants who in time of need, finding it hard to raise the necessary money for the rent, were prepared to give false evidence in court in support of some case of their landlord (7) ; but woe to those who got confused and harmed the whole case. Expulsion from their flat was the immediate result.

Such was the situation in ordinary days, but even then we hear of difficulties in collecting the rent in Cicero's *insulae* (8). In a previous paragraph we have stressed the fact that it is essential to take into

(1) Cic., *Pro Caelio*, VII, 17.

(2) Plut., *Sull.*, 1.

(3) Cic., *Pro Caelio*, VII, 17.

(4) Carcopino, *Daily life in ancient Rome*, p. 44.

(5) Cic., *ad. Att.*, XV, 17, 1.

(6) Pohlmann, *Aus Vergangenheit u. Gegenwart*, p. 110.

(7) Cic., *Pro Flacco*, 22.

(8) Cic., *ad. Att.*, XV, 20, 4. Cicero was prepared to let only to tenants who were able to pay in time : *ut sint qui ad diem solvant*.

account not only normal, everyday conditions in Rome, but also those catastrophes of nature which time and again rendered thousands of people homeless and stranded. May it not be assumed that it was precisely at times when those who were hit by disaster had to invest every penny they possessed in their new living quarters, that they were slow to pay the rent, and contracted debts? Let us examine the known facts. In 60 B. C., three years after Catiline's conspiracy, a great many houses in Rome collapsed (1), in 56 an earthquake overtook the city (2). The year 54 was the year of the great flood. The Tiber overflowed its banks so impetuously that not only the lower-city was affected, but also considerable portions of the upper-town (3). The water level did not fall for a number of days, and the houses that were mainly built of brick became torturated and naturally collapsed soon afterwards. Dio mentions the fact that even those people who managed to escape from the zone of danger in time had no great luck afterwards. They were put up in houses that were not affected by the flood; but those houses too collapsed a few years later. It is natural that building speculation flourished in those years, for the demand for flats grew from day to day. We have not the slightest evidence that the state authorities helped those affected by the disaster to find new lodging. The authorities merely organized the foodsupply. (Pompey was then responsible for the *cura annonae*, and he took the greatest care in this matter) (4). Here, however, trouble did not end. Hardly had people rallied after the flood, when, in 50, an immense fire broke out which destroyed no less than 14 vici. It was the greatest and most terrible fire in the history of the Roman Republic (5). And again the state did not come to the rescue of those who were left without a roof. Only in the days of Augustus were great sums of money invested in the reconstruction of the demolished houses (6). This is an additional example showing once more, as we have already seen above, that as regards living conditions the Republic was far more negligent than the Empire. In 49 B. C. there occured another earthquake followed by an outbreak of fires. This time the Temple of Quirinus burnt down as well as many living-quarters (7). The situation was desperate.

In the same year the tension in the relations between Caesar and Pompey reached its climax. It is no wonder, therefore, that the masses hoped to receive from Caesar *tabulae novae* — abolition of debts.

(1) Dio C., XXXVII, 58. 3.

(2) Dio C., XXXIX, 20, 2.

(3) Dio C., XXXIX, 61 (1-2).

(4) Dio C., XXXIX, 63, 3.

(5) Orosius, VI, 14 (4) (5).

(6) Orosius, VII, 2, 1: *Caesar Augustus ad reparationem eorum quae tunc exusta erant magna vim pecuniae ex aerario publico largitus est.*

(7) Dio C., XLI, 14, 4.

It was particularly the catchword « abolition of house rent » that was popular among the plebs urbana. The words Cicero had used for Athens seem equally applicable to Rome: *Credo sed Atheniensium plus interfuit firma tecta in domiciliis habere, quam Minervae signum ebore pulcherrimum* (1).

*Conclusion.* — The whole question of the dwelling conditions of the lower classes of the population in ancient Rome should not be studied as a mere problem of « Römische Privataltertümer ». It should be considered in close connection with other historical problems, and should not be studied apart from them. One example will suffice to justify this attitude. No research has yet been done on the problem whether the urban plebs was indebted or not. A common view expressed by modern scholars is that the slogan *tabulae novae* was not attractive to the urban proletariate, for these people had no assets, no credit and therefore no debts (2). This opinion, however, plausible as it seems at first sight, does not supply us with an answer to the question why the urban plebs joined those political leaders who promised a complete abolition of debts, or at least their reduction. Having dealt with this question at such length we may now sum up.

1) The heaviest monetary burden from which the urban plebs suffered was the necessity to pay their rents.

2) It will not suffice to estimate the rent they had to pay. Through frequent collapses and conflagrations, the urban plebs were time and again compelled to meet considerable expenses. With regard to lodgings no *largitiones* existed. Everybody had to manage his affairs entirely by himself.

In conclusion: the urban plebs might be deeply indebted as a result of the speculation then existing on the building market and of exorbitant rents. The Roman tabernarii, who needed some working capital in order to run their businesses, depended on credit too: *quorum res fidesque in manibus sitae erant* (Sall., *Jug.*, 73).

A further investigation of the connection existing between the abolition of debts (3) and the payment of rents would show that it was precisely in this field that an « unholy alliance » was established between indebted aristocrats and the plebs urbana against the Roman faeneratores and argentarii.

*The Hebrew University, Jerusalem.* Z. Yavetz.

(1) Cic., *Brut.*, 257.

(2) E.g.: *C. A. H.*, IX, 492.

(3) It may be interesting to stress that the item *tabulae novae* does not appear in the Pauly Wissowa, *R. E.*

* It gives me great pleasure to express at this opportunity the gratitude I feel for Mr. C. E. Stevens of Magdalen College Oxford who offered me most valuable advice and stimulating suggestions. Likewise I wish to thank my friend Mr. S. Krieger, Jerusalem, for helping me with the English text of the article.

# IX

*Ch. Wirszubski*

## Cicero's *Cum Dignitate Otium:* a Reconsideration

# CICERO'S *CVM DIGNITATE OTIVM*: A RECONSIDERATION

By CH. WIRSZUBSKI *

In his political Apologia, the letter *Ad Fam.* I, 9, addressed to Lentulus in the year 54 B.C., Cicero observed that, as he had repeatedly preached, the goal at which statesmen like himself and his correspondent ought to aim in the conduct of affairs of State was *cum dignitate otium*.[1] The obvious example of this preaching is the well-known passage in the *Pro Sestio*, 96 ff., which is Cicero's fullest extant statement of *cum dignitate otium* as the aim and purpose of the Optimates. The political import of this statement is, for the modern student at any rate, somewhat vague, its vagueness being due to the variety of different meanings of which both *dignitas* and *otium* admit. The modern student of the *Pro Sestio* is in fact faced with a number of questions on the answer of which his understanding of the meaning and purpose of *cum dignitate otium* will depend : Is *dignitas* in this phrase used in its political or moral sense ? And is it the *dignitas* of individuals or of the State ? Is *otium* private leisure or public tranquillity ? Does *cum dignitate otium* invariably mean the same thing ? Such questions have in fact been asked, and variously answered by modern scholars, with the result that their interpretations of *cum dignitate otium* still differ from one another.

In the opinion of E. Remy,[2] *cum dignitate otium* in the *Pro Sestio* applies to the State and the government, whereas in all other instances it applies to individuals.[3] As applied to the State, it represents the conditions of a happy political situation : the government ought to be strong and respected (*dignitas*), and the governed ought to enjoy real tranquility (*otium*). Thus Cicero's formula is equivalent to Le Play's ' la tranquillité volontaire et satisfaite (c'est *otium*) dans l'ordre établi (c'est *dignitas*) '.[4] In Remy's view Cicero in the *Pro Sestio* maintains that in the prevailing circumstances of the Roman State the defenders of the republican constitution ought to be more concerned for the strength and prestige of the government than for tranquillity.[5] Elsewhere in his interesting article, Remy observed that *dignitas* was to members of the ruling class what *libertas* was to the people.[6] But, unfortunately, he did not follow out this line of thought in the interpretation of the *Pro Sestio*, so that in spite of his excellent observations on the social meaning of *dignitas* he failed, among other things, to account sufficiently for Cicero's statement in the *Pro Sestio* that the Roman people is delighted ' otio suo et dignitate optimi cuiusque et universae rei publicae gloria ' (104).

Much less satisfactory is the explanation proposed by H. Wegehaupt.[7] He argues that *dignitas*, in the sense of ' greatness in the maintenance of personal rights and claims ', approaches the meaning of *salus* and contains the notion of political freedom. Considered in its undisturbed duration, *dignitas* corresponds to *otium*. Therefore *cum dignitate otium* is a uniform conception expressive of Roman conservatism.[8] In the *Pro Sest.* 96 f., *cum*

* My thanks are due to Professor Sir Frank Adcock, who kindly read the manuscript and made valuable suggestions for improvements of expression and substance.

[1] *Ad Fam.*, I, 9, 21 ' Accepisti quibus rebus adductus quamque rem causamque defenderim, quique meus in re publica sit pro mea parte capessenda status. De quo sic velim statuas, me haec eadem sensurum fuisse, si mihi integra omnia ac libera fuissent ; . . . numquam enim ⟨in⟩ praestantibus in re publica gubernanda viris laudata est in una sententia perpetua permansio, sed ut in navigando tempestati obsequi artis est, . . . sic, cum omnibus nobis in administranda re publica propositum esse debeat, id quod a me saepissime dictum est, cum dignitate otium, non idem semper dicere, sed idem semper spectare debemus.' Cicero's statement is applicable to statesmen in general. But as the context shows, he is primarily thinking of himself, so that in ' omnibus nobis ' he has primarily in mind Roman statesmen like himself and his correspondent.

[2] E. Remy, ' *Dignitas cum otio*,' *Musée Belge*, XXXII (1928), 113–27. It is noteworthy that, whereas Cicero's formula is *cum dignitate otium*, Remy usually quotes it in the form *dignitas cum otio* or *dignitas et otium*.

[3] o.c., 113.

[4] o.c., 117.

[5] o.c., 117 f.

[6] o.c., 125.

[7] Helmut Wegehaupt, *Die Bedeutung und Anwendung von dignitas in den Schriften der republikanischen Zeit*. Breslau Dissertation, 1932.

[8] ' In diesem Sinne (viz Grösse in der Behauptung persönlicher Rechte und Ansprüche) steht *dignitas* der Bedeutung von *salus* nahe, insofern *salus* den Zustand eines allgemeinen " Heilseins " bezeichnet, und u.a. auch den Begriff der politischen Freiheit enthält. *Dignitas*, in ihrer ungestörten Dauer betrachtet, entspricht dem Begriff des *otium*. *Otium cum dignitate* ist daher die Abstraktion eines völlig einheitlichen Gedankens, der Zeugnis ablegt von dem stark ausgeprägten konservativen Willen des Römers,' o.c., 53.

*dignitate otium* means the greatness (*dignitas*) of the State in the maintenance (*otium*) of its natural and historic conditions of existence, a state of natural perfection of the body politic in so far as it represents might against enemies, and justice towards gods, citizens, and allies.[9]

Like Remy before him, Wegehaupt appears to have missed the significance of ' dignitas optimi cuiusque ' in *Pro Sest.* 104. He also missed another crucial fact, namely that Cicero conceives *dignitas* and *otium* not as naturally complementary but as potentially conflicting : ' neque ullum amplexari otium quod abhorreat a dignitate ' (98).[10] It is further to be observed that, although both Remy and Wegehaupt assume that *cum dignitate otium* sometimes expresses the desirable end of the State and sometimes the desirable end of individuals, neither of them has squarely faced the question what, if any, is the relation between these two ends that are expressed by the same phrase.

This question was taken up by P. Boyancé,[11] whose interpretation of *cum dignitate otium* differs from those of his predecessors mainly in three respects : first, he assumes that *dignitas* and *otium* in the phrase *cum dignitate otium* in the *Pro Sestio* primarily apply to individuals ; secondly, he stresses the moral aspect of *dignitas* ; thirdly, he relates *cum dignitate otium* to Cicero's *De Re Publica* and, more especially, to Peripatetic philosophy. His thesis is briefly this : The so-called digression on the Optimates in the *Pro Sestio* is actually the central part of the whole speech, and Cicero is there concerned with the political programme only incidentally, that is, only in so far as it is related to the thing he had most at heart, namely moral philosophy.[12] Uppermost in Cicero's mind, from the very beginning of the *Pro Sestio*, was his concern for the moral education of future statesmen, and it was primarily to the aspiring youth that his ' digression ' on the Optimates was addressed.[13] The formula *cum dignitate otium* in para. 96 represents a kind of reconciliation between two conflicting philosophies of life : addiction to pleasurable tranquillity, on the one hand, and devotion to duty, on the other.[14] This reconciliation is possible, because *otium* in Cicero's formula does not mean selfish pursuit of pleasure, but rather the well earned leisure which crowns and rewards a long career of action and achievement.[15] At the same time *otium* also means tranquillity of the people as a whole, and is thus the end of societies as well as of individuals. Cicero in fact states a law of human nature which holds good for societies and individuals alike.[16] In this he was inspired by Aristotle's view of σχολή as the desirable end of the individual and the State.[17] And as for the reconciliation between *otium* and *dignitas* in the *Pro Sestio*, it owed its primary inspiration to the Peripatetic discussion of σχολή in connection with the controversy between Theophrastus and Dicaearchus concerning contemplative and active life.[18] ' La célèbre " digression " sur les optimates nous fait donc saisir sur le vif le politique philosophe que Cicéron a rêvé d'être. N'en chercher l'explication que dans la conjoncture romaine, c'est en méconnaître le sens et la portée.' [19]

As will be seen later, Boyancé is right in his contention against Remy and Wegehaupt that *dignitas* in *cum dignitate otium* in the *Pro Sestio* is the *dignitas* of individuals no less

[9] ' " *Otium cum dignitate* " bedeutet die Grösse (*dignitas*) des Staates in der Behauptung (*otium*) seiner natürlichen und historisch gewordenen Lebensbedingungen,. einen Zustand der natürlichen Vollendung des Staates, — in optima r.p. (de orat. I, I), entsprach einem " in imperio ac dignitate " (de leg. agr. 2, 9) — insofern er die Macht vertritt gegen äussere und innere Feinde (s. novarum rerum cupidi) und der Pflicht zur Gerechtigkeit gegen Götter, Bürger und *socii* unterworfen ist.' o.c., 63.

[10] This has been rightly stressed by P. Boyancé (see next note), 184 f.

[11] Pierre Boyancé, ' *Cum Dignitate Otium*,' *RÉA* XLIII (1941), 172–191.

[12] o.c., 178.

[13] o.c., 174–8.

[14] o.c., 185–9.

[15] o.c., 186.

[16] o.c., 183.

[17] ' Ce qui fait que pour notre formule nous pouvons parler sans paradoxe de soutenir en même temps les deux thèses opposées, c'est qu'en fait Cicéron se place à un point de vue plus élevé qui les domine, les rend toutes deux possibles. Il faut se souvenir que Cicéron est philosophe, élève de Platon. Platon identifie totalement dans la *République* la justice fin de la cité et la justice fin de l'âme. Ordre extérieur et ordre intérieur ne font qu'un. Mais, on va le voir, c'est surtout à Aristote qu'il faut ici songer. Dans le livre VII de la *Politique*, Aristote, fidèle en cela à Platon, revient plusieurs fois sur l'idée que l'individu et que l'État s'assignent la même fin, et c'est, on va le voir, dans les textes, qui, à l'un comme à l'autre, assignent comme but la σχολή — *l'otium*,' o.c., 183–4. See also 189 f.

[18] o.c., 190 f.

[19] o.c., 191.

than of the State (the precise meaning of *dignitas* is a different matter which need not concern us at present) ; he is also right in assuming a tension between *dignitas* and *otium* (although the nature of that tension is not what he believes it to be). But his interpretation of *otium* is largely mistaken, and his view that *cum dignitate otium* represents a reconciliation between two conflicting philosophies of life is untenable.

Boyancé's view of the nature of *otium* in *Pro Sest.* 96 f. is clearly inconsistent with *Pro Sest.* 139, where Cicero says that those who seek true glory ' aliis otium quaerere debent non sibi '. This fact did not escape Boyancé's notice, and he has himself candidly stated the resulting difficulty.[20] Nevertheless he argues that personal *otium* itself can be understood in two ways. ' Le § 138 (actually it is § 139 that matters most) exclut qu'il (namely l'*otium* individuel) puisse être une tranquillité égoïste, consacrée au plaisir, rendant impossible la vie active. Il n'exclut aucunement qu'il soit, au terme d'une carrière bien remplie, le loisir qui vient la récompenser et la couronner, le loisir du sénateur qui jouit de la *dignitas*, fruit des actions accomplies et des charges gérées. C'est le moment de nous souvenir du verbe *prospiciant* qui montre l'*otium* poursuivi par les optimates au loin, au terme de leurs efforts.' [21] The verb *prospiciant* shows nothing of the kind. Boyancé appears to have misunderstood *Pro Sest.* 98 : ' Neque enim rerum gerendarum dignitate homines ecferri ita convenit ut otio non prospiciant.' In accordance with Ciceronian usage, ' prospicere otio ' does not mean to look forward to *otium*, but to provide for *otium*, to take care of *otium*, and the like.[22] Moreover, if the aim of the Optimates, so far as *otium* is concerned, is the leisure that crowns and rewards a successful senatorial career, what are we to do with *Pro Sest.* 98 where Cicero declares that *cum dignitate otium* at which the leading Optimates aim is ' maxime optabile omnibus sanis et bonis et beatis ', and thereby are meant (as it appears from § 97) not only senators, but townspeople, farmers, businessmen, and even freedmen ? It is also to be observed that the kind of *otium* Boyancé has in mind, even if unselfish, is still *otium suum*, and does not square very well with Cicero's emphatic injunction ' aliis otium quaerere debent, non sibi '. The difficulty arising from Boyancé's view of *otium* thus remains unresolved, and the inconsistency cannot be explained away. On Boyancé's own showing this is enough to prove him wrong, so that it is not necessary to raise other objections.

Without the slightest intention to belittle the influence that Greek philosophy exerted on Cicero's mind, I submit that the explanation of the meaning and purpose of *cum dignitate otium* is to be sought in the first place in Roman politics and not in Greek philosophy, because *cum dignitate otium* in the *Pro Sestio* primarily belongs to the sphere of party political slogans, and not to political theory or ethics. We must not forget that the context in which *cum dignitate otium* appears in the *Pro Sestio* is eminently political, in the sense that it is primarily concerned with the actualities of contemporary Roman politics. Uppermost in Cicero's mind in the *Pro Sestio* is not the education of a πολιτικός, nor the question of βίου αἵρεσις, but the Optimate ' via ac ratio rei publicae capessendae ' (*Pro Sest.* 103. See also *ibid.* 100). Cicero treats Roman politics not as a philosopher but as a politician, and his party political attitude is well illustrated, among other things, by his choice of examples with which he drives home his political lesson. Having described the pursuit of *cum dignitate otium* as the desirable but arduous way in politics, he proceeds to give examples of statesmen who lived up to the ideal, and whose careers he recommends as illustrious, everlasting, and divine models to be imitated by all who seek *dignitas*, *laus*, and *gloria*. They are three undaunted leaders of the Optimates, made famous by persistent opposition to the Populares : M. Aemilius Scaurus (Princeps senatus, *cos.* 115 B.C.), Q. Caecilius Metellus Numidicus (*cos.* 109 B.C.), Q. Lutatius Catulus (*cos.* 78 B.C.).[23] These significant names throw much light on the purpose of Cicero's exhortations to the aspiring youth both

[20] ' Comment concilier ce § 138 (the decisive phrase occurs at the beginning of § 139) et notre § 96 ? Si les jeunes gens qui aspirent à suivre la carrière des optimates doivent au § 138 renoncer pour eux au bénéfice de l'*otium*, cet *otium*, qui est leur but au § 96, ne saurait être, comme nous le disions, un *otium* personnel, individuel, et nous nous sommes trompé sur ce point,' o.c., 186.

[21] ibid.

[22] Cf. Cic. *In Cat.* IV, 3 : ' qua re, patres conscripti, consulite vobis, prospicite patriae, conservate vos, . . . populi Romani nomen salutemque defendite.'

[23] See *Pro Sest.* 100–2.

here and elsewhere in the *Pro Sestio*, and are a warning against the assumption that ' on ne saurait sans contresens parler de programme politique '.[24]

Nor must we overlook another fact of no small consequence for our purpose, namely that not only *dignitas* but also *otium* belongs to the vocabulary of political life at Rome. Indeed, we have in Cicero enough contemporary evidence to show that *otium*, no less than *concordia* and *pax*, became at times a prominent political slogan. It is this aspect of *otium*, I suggest, that is of especial importance for the understanding of Cicero's *cum dignitate otium* in the *Pro Sestio*.

The word *otium* [25] has always been known to denote, *inter alia*, peace, and ' pax atque otium ' appears as a household phrase in Plautus.[26] Although sometimes used as the opposite of *bellum*,[27] *otium* seems more often to signify internal tranquillity as distinct from peace on the frontiers.[28] It is also to be noted that in some of the instances where *otium* is the opposite of *bellum*, the latter, as the context or circumstances imply, is to be understood as civil war.[29] The meaning of *otium* is well brought out by the fact that it is, on the one hand, associated with *pax*, *tranquillitas*, *quies*, *concordia*, and *salus*,[30] while, on the other hand, it is opposed to *tumultus*, *seditio*, and *novae res*.[31] Thus it appears that *otium*, in the sense of *commune otium*,[32] is conceived, by Cicero at any rate, as public tranquillity born of undisturbed political order.

Cicero, in fact, tends to identify *otium* with the preservation of a certain political order. A remark of his in the *In Pis*. 9 is very illuminating in this respect. Referring to Clodius' measure concerning *obnuntiatio* [33] he says : ' a fatali portento prodigioque rei publicae lex Aelia et Fufia eversa est, propugnacula murique tranquillitatis atque oti.' Why Cicero regards these laws as the bulwark of tranquillity and *otium* appears from *Post Red. in Sen*. II, where Cicero describes the same Lex Aelia et Fufia as measures ' quae nostri maiores certissima subsidia rei publicae contra tribunicios furores esse voluerunt '.[34] Equally revealing is the remark that Cicero put in the mouth of Lucullus (*Acad*. II, 15) : ' Nonne cum iam philosophorum disciplinae gravissimae constitissent tum exortus est ⟨ut⟩ in

[24] Boyancé, o.c., 178.

[25] Ernst Bernert, ' *Otium*,' *Würzburger Jahrbücher für die Altertumswissenschaft*, IV (1949–50), 89–99, is mainly (except p. 91) concerned with the non-political aspect of *otium*. I have not seen Marianne Kretschmar, *Otium, Studia litterarum, Philosophie und* βίος θεωρητικός *im Leben und Denken Ciceros*, Leipzig Dissertation, 1938, and know of it only from a review by A. Klotz, *Philol. Wochenschr*. LXI (1941), 76–80. H. Fuchs, ' Augustin und der antike Friedensgedanke ', *Neue Philol. Untersuchungen*, 3, Berlin, 1926, 185 ff., is interesting and suggestive.

[26] *Amph*. 206–10.

[27] Cic. *Pro Caec*. 43 ; Caes. *BC* II, 36, 1 ; Nep. *Timol*. 3, 2 ; *Hamilc*. 2, 5. Cf. also Plautus l.c. ; Cic. *Ad Att*. I, 20, 5 ; IV, 6, 2 ; Liv. III, 32, 4.

[28] See Cic. *De Leg. agr*. II, 9 where *pax externa* is distinct from *otium domesticum*. Cf. ' ubi militem donis, populum annona, cunctos dulcedine otii pellexit ', Tac. *Ann*. I, 2, 1. See also Cic. *De Harusp. Resp*. 4 ' videbam illud scelus (viz. Clodius' sacrilege) . . . non posse arceri oti finibus '.

[29] Cic. *Ad Att*. XV, 2, 3 ; *Ad Fam*. II, 16, 2 ; *Pro Mur*. 83 ; Sall. *Hist*. I, 77 (Orat. Phil.) 11 (M).

[30] Plaut. l.c. ; Cic. *De Leg. agr*. I, 23 ; II, 102 ; III, 4 ; *Pro Mur*. 78 ; 86 ; *Ad Q. Fr*. III, 5–6, 5 ; *Ad Att*. IX, 11a, 1 ; *Phil*. I, 16 ; V, 41 ; VIII, 10–11 ; *De Fato*, 2. Cf. *Comment. Petit*. 53. See also Cic. *In Pis*. 73, *Post Red. ad Quir*. 20, *De Dom*. 15 quoted in the following note.

[31] *Rhet. ad Heren*. IV, 15, 21 ' contentio est, cum ex contrariis rebus oratio conficitur, hoc pacto : . . . in otio tumultuaris, in tumultu otiosus es '. Cic. *Ad Att*. II, 1, 4 ' Ac nunc quidem otium est, sed, si paulo plus furor Pulchelli progredi posset, valde ego te istim excitarem. Verum praeclare Metellus impedit et impediet.' *In Pis*. 73 Cicero explains his ' cedant arma togae ' thus : ' non dixi hanc togam qua sum amictus, . . . sed, quia pacis est insigne et oti toga, contra autem arma tumultus atque belli, poetarum more locutus hoc intellegi volui, bellum ac tumultum paci atque otio concessurum.' Cf. *Post Red. ad Quir*. 20 ' quoniam illi arti in bello ac seditione locus est, huic in pace atque otio.' *De Dom*. 15 ' in meo reditu spes oti et concordiae sita videbatur, in discessu autem cotidianus seditionis timor.' Cf. *Pro. Mur*. 90 ; *Ad Fam*. XII, 1, 1 (as emended by Purser). Sall. *Jug*. 66, 2 ' nam volgus, uti plerumque solet et maxime Numidarum, ingenio mobili seditiosum atque discordiosum erat, cupidum novarum rerum, quieti et otio advorsum.'

It is interesting and illuminating to compare with these texts Cicero's statement on the origin of eloquence, Brut. 45 : ' pacis et comes otique socia et iam bene constitutae civitatis quasi alumna quaedam eloquentia ' ; and Tacitus' rejoinder, *Dial*. 40, 2 : ' non de otiosa et quieta re loquimur et quae probitate et modestia gaudeat, sed est magna illa et notabilis eloquentia alumna licentiae . . . comes seditionum, effrenati populi incitamentum, . . . quae in bene constitutis civitatibus non oritur.' These statements show well what kind of associations go with *otium* by way of similarity and contrast.

[32] Cic. *De Prov. cons*. 24 ; *De Re p*. I, 7 ; *Phil*. X, 3. Cf. *De Off*. III, 3 ; *Pro Sest*. 5 ; 15.

[33] See Cic. *Pro Sest*. 33 ; 56 ; Ascon. 8, 20 f. Clark.

[34] Cf. Cic. *In Vat*. 18 ' simul etiam illud volo uti respondeas, cum te tribuno plebis esset etiam tum in r.p. lex Aelia et Fufia, quae leges saepe numero tribunicios furores debilitarunt et represserunt '. See also ibid. 23.

optuma re publica Tib. Gracchus qui otium perturbaret sic Arcesilas qui constitutam philosophiam everteret.' Elsewhere he says that 'Ti. Gracchus convellit statum civitatis' (*De Har. Resp.* 41. cf. *In Cat.* I, 3). Especially significant is the connection of *otium* with 'hic rei publicae status'. *De Leg. agr.* II, 8 : 'omnia turbulenta consilia contra hunc rei publicae statum et contra vestrum otium partim iniri, partim nobis consulibus designatis inita esse dicebantur.' *Ibid.* III, 4 : 'caput est legis XL de quo ego consulto, Quirites, neque apud vos ante feci mentionem, ne aut refricare obductam iam r.p. cicatricem viderer aut aliquid alienissimo tempore novae dissensionis commovere, neque vero nunc ideo disputabo quod hunc statum rei publicae non magno opere defendendum putem, praesertim qui oti et concordiae patronum me in hunc annum populo Romano professus sum.' *Pro Sest.* 46, 'alii rem ipsam publicam atque hunc bonorum statum otiumque odissent et ob hasce causas tot tamque varias me unum deposcerent.' In the light of these statements it is easy to see why Cicero writes, in April, 44 B.C. : 'habes igitur φαλάκρωμα (viz. Matius) inimicissimum oti, id est Bruti.' [35] It is interesting to note that Brutus and Cassius express themselves in a somewhat similar manner : 'nos ab initio spectasse otium nec quicquam aliud libertate communi quaesisse exitus declarat.' [36]

It is understandable that Cicero tended to identify *otium* with the preservation of the established form of republican government. Viewed from the standpoint of the Optimates, Roman party politics after Sulla's death were largely a struggle for or against the established order. And since the established order is for its supporters the desirable order, it is understandable that they regarded it as the only way to ensure tranquillity and peace. Moreover, a politician who held such views might easily be disposed to regard as enemies of tranquillity and peace his adversaries who, he believed, were undermining the existing order. Cicero, in fact, often described Clodius, and, at a later date, the Caesarians as enemies of *otium*.[37] Others may conceivably have held similar views, and used similar language : the attitude is only too familiar in political and social struggles. Well might a saint reflect : 'Nam et illi qui pacem, in qua sunt, perturbari volunt, non pacem oderunt, sed eam pro arbitrio suo cupiunt commutari. Non ergo ut sit pax nolunt, sed ut ea sit quam volunt.' [38] But this is not, as a rule, the spirit of party political propaganda.

In Cicero's extant writings the use of *otium* as a political slogan can be traced from 63 to 43 B.C., and it is indeed in Cicero that we find the earliest known instance of *otium* so used. But the available evidence of political propaganda before 63 B.C. is so fragmentary and scanty that it is impossible to ascertain whether *otium* in Cicero derives, like the cognate *pax* and *concordia*, from the stock of current [39] political slogans, or was first introduced into political propaganda by Cicero himself, and thus represents his own variation on a traditional theme. On this question Sallust's [40] *Oratio Lepidi* (*Hist.* I, 55 [M]) is relevant, but quite inconclusive. We find in that speech 'quies et otium cum libertate' (§ 9) as well as 'otium cum servitio' (§ 25). But, since this speech cannot be safely assumed to represent more than Sallust's own view of what might have been said by an agitator against the Sullan régime, it does not follow from what Sallust represents Lepidus as saying that *otium* had in fact figured in the propaganda of 78 B.C. For we must take into account the possibility that Sallust, writing as he did after Cicero, deliberately recalled and countered Cicero's Optimate *cum dignitate otium* in *otium cum servitio*, a phrase of Sallust's own creation which he put into the mouth of the *popularis* Lepidus. Thus, since neither hypothesis can be adequately proved or disproved, it is better not to be dogmatic about it.

As has been said, the earliest known instances of *otium* used as a political slogan belong

[35] *Ad Att.* XIV, 2, 3. In 49 B.C. Matius was regarded as an 'auctor oti', *Ad Att.* IX, 11, 2.

[36] *Ad Fam.* XI, 2, 2 (addressed to M. Antonius, May, 44 B.C.).

[37] *De Dom.* 12 ; 137 ; *Pro Sest.* 15 ; *Phil.* X, 3 ; XI, 36 ; *Ad Att.* XIV, 2, 3 ; *Ad Brut.* I, 15, 4. A variation of the same theme is the substitution of fear for hatred : 'timent otium,' *Ad Att.* XIV, 21, 2 and 4 ; 22, 1 ; XV, 2, 3.

[38] Augustin. *Civ. Dei*, XIX, 12 (p. 372, 24 f. Dombart-Kalb).

[39] I think it is inconsistent with the available evidence to assume that *pax* and *concordia* were essentially Optimate slogans (as does H. Fuchs, o.c., 192, n. 2).

[40] Sallust's authorship of this speech has been denied, on insufficient grounds, by C. Lanzani, *Lucio Cornelio Silla Dittatore*, Milano, 1936, 367–73. Against this view see E. Bolaffi, 'L'orazione di Lepido nelle "Historiae" di Sallustio,' *Rivista Indo-Greco-Italiana*, XX (1936), 61–66.

to Cicero's consulship. Aware that tranquillity and peace born of civil concord were the most popular things at Rome, Cicero declared himself a popular consul in the sense that he intended to be a patron of peace and concord, and by promises of *pax*, *tranquillitas* and *otium* endeavoured to win the confidence of the people as well as its support for the rejection of Rullus' land bill.[41] Towards the end of his consulship, at the trial of consul designate L. Murena, *otium* is again prominent in Cicero's entreaties for Murena's acquittal.[42]

During the Catilinarian conspiracy *salus* understandably ousts *otium*, but *otium* soon reappears. Before Pompey's return Cicero wrote to him that he was much pleased by Pompey's dispatch ' tantam enim spem oti ostendisti, quantam ego semper omnibus te uno fretus pollicebar ' (*Ad Fam.* v, 7, 1). And of his own speech in the Senate after Pompey's return he tells Atticus : ' etenim haec erat ὑπόθεσις, de gravitate ordinis, de equestri concordia, de consensione Italiae, de intermortuis reliquiis coniurationis, de vilitate,[43] de otio. Nosti iam in hac materia sonitus nostros . . . ' (*Ad Att.* I, 14, 4). Thus Cicero himself classes *otium* with the stock themes of his political oratory. In subsequent years *otium* appears again and again in Cicero's letters and speeches after his return from his exile,[44] on the eve and in the beginning of the Civil War,[45] and after the assassination of Caesar.[46]

Enough has been said to show that throughout his political career Cicero used *otium*, frequently joined with *concordia*, *pax*, or *salus*, as a standing expression for tranquillity and peace at Rome. In this sense *otium* is also used in the beginning of the *Pro Sestio* : Sestius is eager for the preservation of ' salus communis atque otium ' (§ 5), whereas Clodius is the enemy of ' otium et communis salus ' (§ 15). With this in mind we can now approach *otium cum dignitate* in the *Pro Sestio*.

The passage in which *cum dignitate otium* is stated to be the aim of the Optimates follows the praise of Milo. Milo, says Cicero, had shown how a leading man in the State ought to act (§ 86) ; he embraced the cause of Cicero's recall, a cause supported by unanimous consent and complete concord (§ 87) ; nothing could deter or discourage him (§ 95). Here is indeed a living example of a true Optimate : ' nimirum hoc illud est, quod de me potissimum tu in accusatione quaesisti, quae esset nostra natio optimatium ' (96). Thus by way of answering the prosecutor's provocative question, Cicero created the opportunity for a piece of party political propaganda.[47]

The description of the Optimates as *natio* originated with Vatinius.[48] *Natio* is here used in a derogatory sense,[49] and is a word of abuse, analogous to Cicero's own ' gens ista Clodiana ' (*Pro Sest.* 81), and carrying the same invidious connotation as *factio* or *conspiratio*.[50] Applied to Optimates, *natio* inevitably lends a depreciatory colour to the former, so that ' natio optimatium ' has in the mouth of a *popularis* [51] the same emotive quality and disparaging character as ' factio paucorum ' (Caes. *BC* I, 22, 5). Cicero counters this taunt by a tendentious interpretation of the term ' optimates '. He identifies ' optimates ' with ' optimus quisque ', and by skilfully exploiting the flexibility of the latter term endeavours to show that the Optimates, far from being ' the clan of oligarchs ', are in fact the entire Roman people, regardless of classes, less ' the wicked '. But the essential fact must not be lost sight of that Cicero proceeds from, and continuously dwells upon, the

[41] *De Leg. agr.* I, 23 ; II, 9 ; 102 ; III, 4. Cf. *In Cat.* IV, 17.

[42] *Pro Mur.* 78 ; 83 (cf. 79) ; 86 ; 90.

[43] Vilitate *edd.* ; utilitate *M.* Vilitas, provided the reading is right, is here used in the same sense as in *De Imp. Cn. Pomp.* 44. See also *De Dom.* 14 (sub fin.) f.

[44] *De Dom.* 15 ; 17.

[45] *Ad Att.* VI, 1, 11 ; VII, 7, 5 ; VII, 18, 2 ; IX, 11, 2 ; 11a, 1.

[46] *De Fato* 2 ; *Phil.* I, 16. The moderate course advocated by Fufius Calenus for the sake of peace met with Cicero's disapproval, ibid. VIII, 11 f., and provoked him into saying, ibid. X, 3 : ' cur cum te et vita et fortuna tua ad otium, ad dignitatem invitet, ea probas, ea decernis, ea sentis quae sint inimica et otio communi et dignitati tuae ? ' — a remark worth remembering in the interpretation of *cum dignitate otium*.

[47] It does not very much matter for the present purpose whether this passage in its present form was or was not in the speech as delivered in court.

[48] See *Pro Sest.* 132 and Schol. Bob. *ad loc.*

[49] Cf. Schol. Bob. l.c.

[50] For the latter see Vatinius *ap.* Cic. *Ad Fam.* v, 9, 1.

[51] Whether actually so phrased or only implied. It is not certain whether Vatinius actually used the phrase ' natio optimatium ' or only referred to the Optimates as ' ista natio '. *Pro Sest.* 132 is consistent with either. A *popularis* might avoid calling his opponents ' optimates ', just as Caesar and Sallust did.

distinction and opposition between the ways and means to which the Optimates and the Populares resort in politics.

There have always been in Rome, says Cicero, two kinds of men who sought distinction in politics: the Populares and the Optimates. The Populares are those who in word and deed curried favour with the mob, whereas those who acted in such a way as to win the approval of 'optimus quisque' are the Optimates.[52] The fact that 'optimus quisque' admits also of the sense 'every good man', enables Cicero to argue: 'omnes optimates sunt qui neque nocentes sunt, nec natura improbi, nec furiosi nec malis domesticis impediti. Sequitur ut hi sint (quam tu nationem appellasti) qui et integri sunt, et sani, et bene de rebus domesticis constituti' (§ 97). Having thus established the identity of the Optimates and all good men, he goes on to say: 'horum qui voluntati, commodis, opinioni in gubernanda re publica serviunt, defensores optimatium, ipsique optimates gravissimi, et clarissimi cives numerantur, et principes civitatis' (*ib.*). Thus Cicero has made his point that, unlike the Populares who are demagogues, the Optimates are those statesmen who direct the affairs of State in accordance with the wishes and interests of all good men. The sequel to this definition of the nature of the Optimates is Cicero's statement of their aim. The Optimates as the helmsmen of the ship of State direct their course to the attainment of what all sound, good, and propertied people consider foremost and most desirable: *cum dignitate otium* (§ 98).

The vagueness of this phrase is part of its usefulness: it may be used for different purposes, because in different circumstances it will convey different meanings. The full import of *cum dignitate otium* in each instance cannot, therefore, be adequately deduced solely from the meaning of *otium* and of *dignitas*. Rather it is necessary in each instance to elicit from the context what it is that Cicero has chiefly in mind. I say 'chiefly' because both *dignitas* and *otium* not only carry overtones, but each of their several meanings or uses can easily, in fact imperceptibly, shade off into another. Thus in order to grasp what is most prominent in Cicero's mind we must turn to the context.

Having declared that the aim of the Optimates is *cum dignitate otium*, Cicero adds: 'hoc qui volunt, omnes optimates: qui efficiunt, summi viri et conservatores civitatis putantur.' Now, obviously if those who bring about *cum dignitate otium* are considered saviours of the State, the realization of *cum dignitate otium* is in some way related to the preservation of the State. Cicero, in fact, fully explains this relation. Leaving out one sentence which will be better discussed later, we find him saying: 'huius autem otiosae dignitatis haec fundamenta sunt, haec membra, quae tuenda principibus et vel capitis periculo defendenda sunt: religiones, auspicia, potestates magistratuum, senatus auctoritas, leges, mos maiorum, iudicia, iurisdictio, fides, provinciae, socii, imperi laus, res militaris, aerarium.' He then goes on to say (§ 99) that in the vast number of citizens there are many who are anxious for revolution, or who thrive on civil strife and sedition, or else who would perish in a common conflagration rather than alone. 'Qui cum auctores sunt et duces suorum studiorum vitiorumque nacti, in re publica fluctus excitantur, ut vigilandum sit iis, qui sibi gubernacula patriae depoposcerunt enitendumque omni scientia ac diligentia ut conservatis his, quae ego paulo ante fundamenta ac membra esse dixi, tenere cursum possint et capere oti illum portum et dignitatis.' Thus it appears that in order to have *cum dignitate otium* all the components of the republican form of government must be preserved, because that form of government is the condition under which alone the realization of *cum dignitate otium* is possible. Cicero in fact tends to identify the traditional form of government with 'otiosa dignitas' in the same way as elsewhere he tends to identify the preservation of that form of government with *otium* (see above, pp. 4–5). He describes the institutions in which that form of government consists as 'the foundations and components' of *otiosa dignitas*.[53]

[52] *Pro Sest.* 96: 'duo genera semper in hac civitate fuerunt eorum qui versari in re publica atque in ea se excellentius gerere studuerunt; quibus ex generibus alteri se popularis, alteri optimates et haberi et esse voluerunt. Qui ea quae faciebant quaeque dicebant multitudini iucunda volebant esse, populares, qui autem ita se gerebant ut sua consilia optimo cuique probarent, optimates habebantur. Cf. *De Off.* I, 85 alii populares alii studiosi optimi cuiusque.'

[53] A noteworthy parallel expression is *otiosa libertas* used in 44 B.C. by Trebonius *ap.* Cic. *Ad Fam.* XII, 16, 3.

It is indicative of the emphasis that Cicero places on *dignitas* that his substitute for *cum dignitate otium* in the *Pro Sestio* is ' otiosa dignitas ' and not ' honestum otium '. And since there has been a tendency to equate *cum dignitate otium* with ' honestum otium ' and to interpret the former as meaning honourable retirement,[54] it will be useful to observe that even ' honestum otium ' itself was at least once used by Cicero in much the same political sense as ' otiosa dignitas '. Some ten years after the *Pro Sestio* Cicero wrote : ' ego sum, qui nullius vim plus valere volui quam honestum otium idemque, cum illa ipsa arma, quae semper timueram, plus posse sensi quam illum consensum bonorum, quem ego idem effeceram, quavis tuta condicione pacem accipere malui quam viribus cum valentiore pugnare,' *Ad Fam.* V, 21, 2. This will only make sense if ' plus valere quam honestum otium ' here means what ' plus valere (*or* posse) quam res publica ' means elsewhere (e.g. *Phil.* V, 17). And if this is so, ' honestum otium ' here means very much the same as ' otiosa dignitas ' in the *Pro Sestio*. But, as I have said, this use of ' honestum otium ' is unique. And as for its usual meaning, it will be better to discuss it later.

The passage just quoted is noteworthy for the ease with which Cicero passes from ' honestum otium ' to ' ille consensus bonorum ', which shows that they are closely related in his mind. The relation is understandable in view of the fact that ' consensus bonorum ' (or, for that matter, ' concordia ordinum ') is the mainstay of the régime the preservation of which results in ' honestum otium ', or ' otiosa dignitas ', or *cum dignitate otium*. In the *Pro Sestio*, too, *consensus* is a very important theme. Cicero devoted a very long passage, §§ 106–27, to prove his view that ' nunc . . . in eo statu civitas est ut, si operas conductorum removeris, omnes idem de re publica sensuri esse videantur ' (106). In the restoration of consent and concord, as will presently be seen, lies the possibility for the restoration of the commonwealth (*renovare r.p.* 112 ; 147) and the realisation of the desirable *cum dignitate otium*.

The way to *otium* with *dignitas*, says Cicero, is admittedly difficult and dangerous (100–2). ' sed tamen haec via ac ratio rei publicae capessendae olim erat magis pertimescenda, cum multis in rebus multitudinis studium aut populi commodum ab utilitate rei publicae discrepabat. . . . Multa etiam nostra memoria, quae consulto praetereo, fuerunt in ea contentione ut popularis cupiditas a consilio principum dissideret. Nunc iam nihil est quod populus a delectis principibusque dissentiat : nec flagitat rem ullam neque novarum rerum est cupidus et *otio suo et dignitate optimi cuiusque* et universae rei publicae gloria delectatur. Itaque homines seditiosi ac turbulenti, quia nulla iam largitione populum Romanum concitare possunt, quod plebes perfuncta gravissimis seditionibus ac discordiis *otium amplexatur*, conductas habent contiones . . . ' (103–4).

I have so far deliberately refrained from considering what is the precise meaning of *otium* and *dignitas*. The time has now come to approach this question. Remy, Wegehaupt, and Boyancé are all agreed that *otium* and *dignitas* in *cum dignitate otium* are either both of them personal, i.e. the *otium* and the *dignitas* of the individual, or both of them collective, i.e. the *otium* and the *dignitas* of the State. But, as ' otio suo (viz. populi) et dignitate optimi cuiusque ' is here to remind us, this neat classification in symmetrical pairs cannot possibly contain the whole truth.[55] The assumption that the counterpart of collective *otium* is the *dignitas* of the State is true only in a very limited sense. It will not suit Cicero's own words in the *Pro Sestio*, 104, let alone the realities of Roman life. Cicero, it is true, sometimes uses the expression ' communis dignitas ' [56] as well as ' dignitas rei publicae '.[57] He sometimes combines ' communis dignitas ' with *salus*.[58] And if he could exclaim, on hearing about Caesar's preparations for civil war, ' o vix ullo otio compensandam hanc rei publicae turpitudinem ' (*Ad Att.* VII, 18, 2), there is no reason to doubt that he could very well think of *otium* in conjunction with ' rei publicae dignitas '. But we must not forget that ' r.p. dignitas ' or ' communis dignitas ' are vague abstractions, ' speciosa nomina ', the usefulness of which in the language of politics consists in their moral tone and emotional appeal. And the outward similarity of the expressions ' commune otium ' and ' communis dignitas '

[54] See Wegehaupt, o.c., 53 ; 76.
[55] See also Cic. *Phil.* X, 3, quoted above, n. 46.
[56] *De Leg. agr.* I, 27.
[57] e.g. *Pro Sest.* 7. The expression is common.
[58] *In Cat.* IV, 15.

ought not to mislead us into thinking that they represent things of the same order. One can truly speak of ' commune otium ' at Rome, because the tranquillity that reigns at Rome is *per se* the tranquillity of every Roman as such. The same applies also to ' communis libertas ' and ' communis salus ', but not to ' communis dignitas '. The dignity of Rome is not *per se* the dignity of every Roman as such, because at Rome *dignitas* is *not* a common possession of all Romans, nor was it meant to be otherwise.[59]

Therefore, as soon as one turns from abstractions to actual facts, and tries to express the social and political realities of Rome in terms of *otium* and *dignitas*, it becomes apparent that the counterpart of ' commune otium ' is the *dignitas* of those individuals who possess it. And Cicero's ' otio suo (populi) et dignitate optimi cuiusque ' shows that in the *Pro Sestio*, 96 ff., he has primarily in mind the tranquillity of all and the dignity of the ' best '. This is not to say that *cum dignitate otium* does not also mean tranquillity with honour in the general vague sense of honourable tranquillity, tranquillity consistent with the honour of the State. *Cum dignitate otium* may well mean both things at the same time, because ' rei publicae dignitas ' and ' dignitas optimi cuiusque ' are in truth not exclusive but complementary. Our habit of speaking about the State as a person makes us apt to forget that the State is not an actual being possessed of a dignity of its own, but that the dignity of the State is the dignity of those who personify the State, or else what those who personify the State consider to be its dignity : ' est igitur proprium munus magistratus intellegere se gerere personam civitatis debereque eius dignitatem et decus sustinere ' (*De Off.* I, 124. See also Cic. *De Dom.* 3 ; cf. *De Leg*, III, 12). And the perusal of *Post Reditum in Senatu* or, indeed, the *Pro Sestio* itself will prove to any attentive reader how easily Cicero identifies the ' res publica ' with his own person. Therefore, as regards *cum dignitate otium* in the *Pro Sestio* there is really no room for a clear-cut disjunction to the effect that *dignitas* means either ' rei publicae dignitas ' or ' dignitas optimi cuiusque '. I think myself that both are meant at the same time, and the real question is only which meaning matters most and is uppermost in Cicero's mind. As to that, there can be no doubt that he thinks of *cum dignitate otium* primarily in terms of the tranquillity of all and the dignity of the ' best '. This is indeed what the traditional form of aristocratic republicanism normally produced at Rome, and Cicero believes that that form of government can be restored and preserved because there is at the time no real cause for difference between the people and the *principes*.

Since this inquiry is only concerned with the meaning of what Cicero said, and not with the value of what he meant, we need not go into the question whether or not his reading of the political situation at Rome was correct. I should like to add only one remark which directly bears on the meaning of ' otiosa dignitas '. The list of the ' foundations and constituents ' of ' otiosa dignitas ' is indeed comprehensive, and looks very impressive, out of its context. But the *Pro Sestio* as a whole leaves no doubt that, so far as peace is concerned, Cicero's ' otiosa dignitas ' savours of ' otium urbanum ' — if I may borrow his own expression, *Ad Fam.* XII, 1, 1 — rather than of *pax Romana.* In the *Pro Sestio* Cicero is concerned with Roman party politics, and not with the Roman world, and he thinks of public tranquillity primarily in terms of peaceful relations between the ruling oligarchy and the Roman Plebs. His interest is largely confined to the elimination of intestine strife and civil discord. And it is with a view to this end that he enumerates the foundations and elements that must be preserved at all costs.[60] It is, therefore, going too far to suppose that *pax Augusta* is foreshadowed in the elements of Cicero's ' otiosa dignitas '.[61]

There remains still the omitted part of the third sentence in § 98. ' hoc (i.e cum dignitate otium) qui volunt, omnes optimates, qui efficiunt, summi viri et conservatores civitatis putantur ; *neque enim rerum gerendarum dignitate homines ecferri ita convenit ut otio non prospiciant, neque ullum amplexari otium quod abhorreat a dignitate.*' The italicised clause

[59] ' Iure, lege, libertate, re publica communiter uti oportet ; gloria atque honore, quomodo sibi quisque struxit,' Cato the Elder, Malcovati, *Orat. Rom. Frag.* I, 218, no. 249. ' Libertate esse parem cum ceteris, principem dignitate,' M. Antonius, the orator, see Cic. *Phil.* I, 34. ' ipsa aequabilitas est iniqua, cum habet nullos gradus dignitatis,' Cic. *De Re p.* I, 43.

[60] It is interesting, and sobering, to compare the elements of *otiosa dignitas* (*Pro Sest.* 98) with the recital of Clodius' crimes (ibid. 84. Cf. *De Harusp. Resp.* 60).

[61] See H. Fuchs, o.c., 192.

is not concerned at all with the ultimate ends of human endeavour; for although it refers generally to men, it applies only to those men who engage in the conduct of affairs. Clearly, therefore, Cicero has in mind statesmen, 'summi viri et conservatores civitatis,' and he formulates a principle of statesmanship and not a law of human nature. What he says is this: Neither ought men to be carried away by the dignity of their affairs to the point of neglecting tranquillity, nor to embrace tranquillity that is incompatible with dignity. This reflection was, I think, inspired principally by Cicero's personal experience since his consulship, and especially 'ex Metello consule' when circumstances compelled him to weigh his prestige against his safety. And his letters to Atticus of the year 60 B.C. as well as his retrospective remarks to Lentulus, written a few months after the trial of Sestius, provide some insight into the experiences and considerations that lie behind Cicero's maxim.[62]

There is also in the *Pro Sestio* a clear indication of the kind of thing contemplated in 'nec ullum amplexari otium quod abhorreat a dignitate'. Cicero explains (§ 100) why the Optimate way is difficult and dangerous: 'maioribus praesidiis et copiis oppugnatur res publica quam defenditur, propterea quod audaces homines ac perditi nutu impelluntur et ipsi etiam sponte sua contra rem publicam incitantur, boni nescio quo modo tardiores sunt et principiis rerum neglectis ad extremum ipsa denique necessitate excitantur, ita ut non numquam cunctatione ac tarditate, dum otium volunt etiam sine dignitate retinere, ipsi utrumque amittant.'[63] It seems to me unlikely that Cicero is here theorizing. Considering the fact that in the *Pro Sestio* the villain of the piece is Clodius, I suspect that the circumstance Cicero has immediately in mind is the attitude of certain *boni*, and even Optimates, to Clodius.[64] 'Num est igitur dubium—says Cicero not long after the *Pro Sestio*—ex iis rebus quas is (*sc.* Clodius) egit agitque cotidie quin ego in illo oppugnando rei publicae plus quam otio meo, non nulli in eodem defendendo suo plus otio quam communi prospexerint' (*De Prov. cons.* 24). Be that as it may, Cicero is only too well aware that in the prevailing circumstances of unrest, insecurity and factious strife the claims of *dignitas* may collide with the requirements of *otium*, so that neither of them can be properly maintained without regard for the other. Hence, *cum dignitate otium*: 'neque enim rerum gerendarum dignitate homines ecferri ita convenit ut otio non prospiciant, neque ullum amplexari otium quod abhorreat a dignitate.'

Here again the meaning of *otium* and *dignitas* fluctuates between personal *otium* and *dignitas*, on the one hand, and general *otium* and *dignitas*, on the other. But while the former meaning undoubtedly preponderates, it is, I think, true to say that, considering the kind of persons Cicero envisaged, the two meanings are, in his own mind at any rate, inseparable. And it is also true that he is more preoccupied with dignity than with tranquillity. The emphasis in *cum dignitate otium* is on *cum dignitate*.

At the end of his long statement Cicero returns to his opening theme: the difference between the Optimates and Populares, §§ 136–40. Loyalty to the traditional republic under senatorial supremacy is the only path of praise, dignity, and honour (137).[65] Those who defend that form of government to the best of their ability are Optimates, of whatever class they may be; 'qui autem praecipue suis cervicibus tanta munia atque rem publicam sustinent, hi semper habiti sunt optimatium principes, auctores et conservatores civitatis' (138). The rest of this paragraph and the beginning of the next, called in to support the view that *cum dignitate otium* represents a reconciliation between the pursuit of duty and the pursuit of pleasure, in translation is as follows:

> I admit, as I have said before (cf. 100 f.), that men of this kind (i.e. those whom he calls 'principes optimatium') have many adversaries, enemies, enviers; they face many dangers, suffer many iniquities, must bear and submit to great toil. But my entire discourse is concerned

[62] See *Ad Att.* i, 19, 6–8; ibid. i, 20, 2–3; ibid. ii, 3, 3–4; *Ad Fam.* i, 7, 7 and 10. cf. *De Orat.* ii, 334 'nemo est enim . . . posse retineri'; and *Ad Fam.* i, 9, 21 'cum omnibus nobis . . . sed idem semper spectare debemus'.

[63] The tone of this remark is somewhat reminiscent of certain passages in the *Oratio Philippi* in Sall. *Hist.* I, 77, 3 and 5.

[64] See *De Harusp. Resp.* 50 and *Ad Fam.* I, 9, 19. For an entirely different view of the significance of *Pro Sest.* 100 see K. Büchner, 'Der Tyrann und sein Gegenbild in Ciceros "Staat"', *Hermes*, LXXX (1952), 369.

[65] It is interesting that *otium* has dropped out. Perhaps because he is now addressing especially those who must seek *otium* for others.

with virtue, not with sloth; with dignity, not with pleasure; with those men who consider themselves born for their country, for their fellow citizens, for praise, for glory, not for sleep, and banquets, and delight. For if there are men whose motive is pleasure, and who have entirely given themselves up to the seductions of vice and the gratification of their desires, let them renounce public offices, let them stay away from the commonwealth, let them be content to enjoy their leisure that they owe to the exertions of brave men. But those who desire to be reputed good by good men, which alone can be truly called glory, ought to seek tranquillity and pleasures for others, not for themselves. They must toil for the advantage of the community, must incur enmities, must often face storms for the sake of the commonwealth, must fight with many audacious, wicked, and sometimes even with mighty opponents.

It is of course true that the pursuit of pleasure is here opposed to the pursuit of virtue, dignity, and glory; and in a sense it may even be said that Cicero envisages here an opposition between *dignitas* and *otium*, although the terms which he actually uses are *dignitas* and *voluptas*. But, as the context clearly shows, all this is only a sideline that does not affect his main argument. The voluptuaries and quietists are mentioned only to be dropped, because Cicero's real interest does not here lie in the opposition between a life of action and a life of pleasure. And that this is really so may easily be seen from the fact that he immediately proceeds to an entirely different set of opposites: 'neque eos in laude positos videmus qui incitarunt aliquando populi animos ad seditionem, aut qui largitione caecarunt mentis imperitorum, aut qui fortis et claros viros et bene de re publica meritos in invidiam aliquam vocaverunt. levis hos semper nostri homines et audacis et malos et perniciosos civis putaverunt. at vero qui horum impetus et conatus represserunt, qui auctoritate, qui fide, qui constantia, qui magnitudine animi consiliis audacium restiterunt, hi graves, hi principes, hi duces, hi auctores huius dignitatis atque imperi semper habiti sunt.'

Thus it becomes apparent that the opposition that really matters (and it is restated again in § 140) is between two political ways, and not between politics and pleasure or quietism. The sources of trouble are not the voluptuaries who shirk the hardships of politics, but the Populares who engage in politics of the wrong kind. It will be useful to recall the opening sentence of Cicero's statement on the Optimates: 'duo genera semper in hac civitate fuerunt eorum qui versari in re publica atque in ea se excellentius gerere studuerunt', etc. (§ 96). From a party political point of view, therefore, the opposite to the pursuit of *cum dignitate otium*, in so far as it represents the Optimate 'via ac ratio r.p. capessendae', is less the pursuit of *otium sine dignitate* than what Cicero called elsewhere 'iactatio cursusque popularis' (*De Prov. cons.* 38), or 'popularis levitas' (*Phil.* v, 49). *Iactatio* and *levitas* are disparaging words, but they belong to the contemporary vocabulary of political abuse, and need not be taken at their face value. Cicero knew only too well (see *De Prov. cons.* 38) that the Populares strove after *dignitas* as much as anybody else, but he deplored their ways. And it was primarily in opposition to the *cursus popularis*, and not to contemplative quietism or disreputable hedonism, that he described at the end of his statement what he believed to be 'the only path of praise, of dignity, of honour'.

To end this inquiry we may briefly consider what *cum dignitate otium* means in Cicero's own life. *Cum dignitate otium* represented for Cicero the achievement of a certain 'vitae cursus' (*De Orat.* I, 1) as well as the Optimate 'via ac ratio r.p. capessendae' (*Pro Sest.* 103, cf. *ibid.* 100), or 'id quod in administranda r.p. propositum esse debet' (*Ad Fam.* I, 9, 21), just as the traditional republicanism was for him a way of life (*vitae via*, *Pro Sest.* 140) no less than a form of government. This is so because for a man like Cicero his way of life is inseparable from his politics. How Cicero felt about it may be seen from the famous opening sentence of his *De Oratore*. 'Cogitanti mihi saepe numero et memoria vetera repetenti perbeati fuisse . . . illi videri solent, qui *in optima re publica, cum et honoribus et rerum gestarum gloria florerent*, eum vitae cursum tenere potuerunt, ut vel in negotio sine periculo vel in otio cum dignitate esse possent.' As the italicised clauses show, the envisaged way of life is dependent upon the excellence of the form of government and the distinguished position that the fortunate man—or rather statesman—holds in the State by virtue of present office and past achievement. *Cum dignitate otium* is, therefore, inseparable from the *res publica* and the *honores*, in the sense that it depends upon them.

The dependence of *cum dignitate otium* on the *res publica* and the position that the statesman holds in it may be clearly seen from Cicero's letter *Ad Fam.* I, 8, 3–4 :

> me quidem etiam illa res consolatur, quod ego is sum cui vel maxime concedant omnes, ut vel ea defendam, quae Pompeius velit, vel taceam vel etiam, id quod mihi maxime libet, ad nostra me studia referam litterarum ; quod profecto faciam, si mihi per eiusdem amicitiam licebit. Quae enim proposita fuerat nobis, cum et honoribus amplissimis et laboribus maximis perfuncti essemus, *dignitas* in sententiis dicendis, libertas in re publica capessenda, ea sublata totast, nec mihi magis quam omnibus ; nam aut adsentiendum est nulla cum gravitate paucis aut frustra dissentiendum.
>
> Haec ego ad te ob eam causam maxime scribo, ut iam de tua quoque ratione meditere. Commutata tota ratio est senatus, iudiciorum, rei totius publicae ; *otium* nobis exoptandum est, quod ii, qui potiuntur rerum, praestaturi videntur, si quidam homines patientius eorum potentiam ferre potuerint ; *dignitatem* quidem illam consularem fortis et constantis senatoris nihil est quod cogitemus ; amissa culpa est eorum, qui a senatu et ordinem coniunctissimum et hominem clarissimum abalienarunt.

Cicero implicitly admits that under the new régime he is no longer free even to embrace *otium* at his own discretion.[66] But while he hopes that his *otium* may be conceded by the potentates, he considers his *dignitas* completely lost as a consequence of those political mistakes that made possible the changes that took place in the State. Now *dignitas* that is lost, and regained,[67] through political changes is evidently political standing, and not moral nobility. Under Caesar's dictatorship Cicero was once congratulated by a friend on having retained his *dignitas*. His illuminating reply is relevant to our purpose : ' ego autem, si dignitas est bene de re publica sentire et bonis viris probare quod sentias, obtineo dignitatem meam ; sin autem in eo dignitas est, si, quod sentias, aut re efficere possis aut denique libera oratione defendere, ne vestigium quidem ullum est reliquum nobis dignitatis ' (*Ad Fam.* IV, 14, 1).

Clearly, then, Cicero conceived his *dignitas* primarily in terms of political prestige, influence, and worthiness, and not in terms of integrity of character and devotion to duty. *Dignitas*, it is true, always (and especially in Cicero) carries moral overtones of honesty and a sense of duty. But it is a fact never to be lost sight of that *dignitas* at Rome implies less what its possessor owes to others than what he claims as due to himself. Therefore *cum dignitate otium*, whether it represents an aim or an achievement, is essentially inseparable from the *res publica*, and is never devoid of political implications, even when *otium* itself means no more than leisure devoted to letters.

This is indeed what distinguishes *cum dignitate otium* from ' honestum otium '. The adjective in the latter expression only marks off this *otium* from sheer idleness, or unbecoming pursuits,[68] but does not by any means carry the same connotation as *cum dignitate*.[69] This may easily be seen from the fact that ' honestum otium ' is applied by Cicero to a life of retirement, voluntary or enforced, from the conduct of affairs of State and from public office,[70] whereas *cum dignitate otium* signifies in the life of the statesmen leisure enjoyed in the midst of an active and successful political career.[71] Thus the personal situation envisaged in ' honestum otium ' and *cum dignitate otium* respectively is quite different. And it is precisely the personal situation that matters most. His own *otium* that he devoted to literary pursuits during his retirement from politics Cicero regarded as a ' honestissimum otium '.[72] Nevertheless, he felt that it was rather less than what he

[66] Cf. *Ad Att.* IV, 6, 1 f. ; *Ad Fam.* VII, 33, 2.

[67] Cicero regarded his recall from exile as a reinstatement to his former *dignitas*, see *De Dom.* 9, and *Pro Sest.* 52.

[68] See Cic. *Brut.* 8 ; *Acad.* I, 11 ; *De Off.* II, 2 and 4.

[69] Cicero, it is true, says in his letter to M. Marcellus (*Ad Fam.* IV, 9, 3) ' honesto otio tenueris et statum et famam dignitatis tuae.' But if this courteous remark is weighed against Cicero's other utterances it will be found insufficient to bear out the identity of *honestum otium* and *cum dignitate otium*. A Roman statesman cannot retain his ' status dignitatis ' in exile, even if it is voluntary exile, and no one knew it better than Cicero.

[70] *Ad Att.* I, 17, 5 ; *Ad Fam.* IV, 4, 4 ; IV, 9, 3 ; VII, 33, 2. Cf. *Brut.* 8 ; *Acad.* I, 11. *Pro Sulla*, 26, is very illuminating for the difference between *honestum otium* and *cum dignitate otium*.

[71] Cf. *De Orat.* I, 1 with *De Off.* III, 2–3.

[72] *Ad Fam.* VII, 33, 2 ; IV, 4, 4 ; *Acad.* I, 11 ; *De Off.* II, 4.

deserved : ' et otio fruor non illo quidem quo debeat is qui quondam peperit otium civitati ' (*De Off.* III, 3). Wistfully he thought of the *otium* enjoyed by the Elder Africanus, and on comparison with it found his own *otium* wanting : ' nam et a re publica forensibusque negotiis armis impiis vique prohibiti, otium persequimur . . . Sed nec hoc otium cum Africani otio . . . (comparandum est). Ille enim requiescens a rei publicae pulcherrimis muneribus otium sibi sumebat aliquando . . . Nostrum autem otium negoti inopia, non requiescendi studio, constitutum est ' (*De Off.* III, 1 f.). The difference between Cicero's and Scipio's *otium* lies principally in the former's political situation, and not in the content of his *otium*. The essential characteristic of *cum dignitate otium*, in so far as it represents the achievement of a ' vitae cursus ', thus appears to be the distinguished position in the State held by the statesman enjoying *otium* rather than the intrinsic value of the pursuits to which his *otium* is devoted.

As I have repeatedly said, *cum dignitate otium* is a vague phrase that lends itself to different interpretations ; and vagueness tends to invite speculation. One can argue with some plausibility that *cum dignitate otium* is to be viewed in the light of the controversy about active and contemplative life,[73] or in the light of the tension between the strong individual and the peaceful community.[74] But it is hard to see how such interpretations can survive the confrontation with all relevant texts. My own view is that the principal meaning of *cum dignitate otium* is most satisfactorily explained if we take *dignitas* and *otium* in the sense they usually bear in the language of Roman political life. I consider this the most satisfactory explanation simply because it squares with all known instances of *cum dignitate otium* and fits their contexts. *Cum dignitate otium* appears in the years 56–54 B.C., and is to be viewed against the background of Roman domestic politics since the formation of the First Triumvirate, and especially in the light of Cicero's own standing in Roman politics before and after his exile as well as before and after the Conference of Luca. *Cum dignitate otium* was for Cicero above all tranquillity with dignity in the Roman State as well as in his own life. What these two aspects of *cum dignitate otium* actually mean, and how they relate to each other, I have tried to explain in the foregoing pages.

[73] See Boyancé, o.c., 190.

[74] See Büchner, o.c., 369.

# X

*P. A. Brunt*

# 'Amicitia' in the Late Roman Republic

# 'AMICITIA' IN THE LATE ROMAN REPUBLIC[1]

## I

In describing a close political union Sallust observes *haec inter bonos amicitia, inter malos factio est* (*BJ* 31, 15).[2] This remark may be taken as a text for a fashionable interpretation of *amicitia* in the late Roman Republic. Professor Lily Ross Taylor writes that 'the old Roman substitute for party is *amicitia*' and that 'friendship was the chief basis of support for candidates for office, and *amicitia* was the good old word for party relationships'.[3] Again, Sir Ronald Syme says that '*amicitia* was a weapon of politics, not a sentiment based on congeniality' and he maintains that 'Roman political factions were welded together, less by unity of principle than by mutual interest and by mutual services (*officia*), either between social equals as an alliance, or from superior to inferior, in a traditional and almost feudal form of clientship: on a favourable estimate the bond was called *amicitia*, otherwise *factio*'.[4] On this view, if a Roman called a man *amicus*, it meant that he was a political ally, or a member of what in eighteenth-century England could have been described as the same 'connexion'.

This sort of relation is one described by Cicero as *non amicitia sed mercatura quaedam utilitatum suarum* (*ND* I, 122). His own account differs strikingly. True friendship, he holds, arises not from our consciousness of our own deficiencies or from our need for reciprocal services: it springs rather from natural affection and benevolence from which in turn reciprocal services result.[5] This affection is one of the bonds that unite any human society, but in an intenser form it subsists only between two or at most a few men. Between them it is certain to last only if they are good men, whose character and views do not 'alter when they alteration find'.[6] It is only on the foundation of virtue that genuine and durable affection can be based, a friendship inspired by mutual good faith (*Amic.* 65) and goodwill and by reciprocal recognition of merits (*ibid.* 20), and cemented by similarity of character (*mores*) and pursuits (*studia*) (*ibid.* 27 and 74); the friends are frank, though courteous to each other, loyal and unsuspecting (65–6); they share, and ought to share, each other's joys and sorrows (22; 45–8);

[1] This paper, of which I read a version to the Cambridge Philological Society in 1964, was suggested by reading F. Lossmann, *Cicero u. Caesar im Jahre* 54, *Stud. z. Theorie u. Praxis der röm. Freundschaft* (1962), cf. my review in *Cl. Rev.* XIV (1964), 90 f. I have also been helped by the valuable collection of material in J. Hellegouar'ch, *Le Vocabulaire latin des relations et des partis politiques sous la République* (1963).

[2] Cf. *BJ* 41, 6: *nobilitas factione magis pollebat, plebis vis soluta atque dispersa in multitudine minus poterat*; Cic. *Rep.* I, 44; 69; III, 44 and esp. 23: *cum autem certi propter divitias aut genus aut aliquas opes rem p. tenent, est factio, sed vocantur optimates.* Alluding to the doctrine that *amicitia* subsists only between *boni*, Sallust insinuates that the self-styled *boni* merely form a *factio*; these men are the nobles (cf. *BJ* 40–1; *Hist.* I, 12), between whom and the people the state is torn (cf. Cic. *Sest.* 96); neither he nor Cicero knows of factions of the Metelli, etc., within the nobility. See also Hellegouar'ch 99 ff.; M. I. Henderson, *JRS* XLII, 115.

[3] *Party Politics in the Age of Caesar*, 7–8.

[4] *Roman Revolution*, 157; cf. ch. II.

[5] *Amic.* 19–32; cf. 51.

[6] *Ibid.* 18–20; 50; 65; 79–84; cf. Arist. *EN* 1156b 6 ff.

they serve each other without keeping an account of profit and loss (58); a man will do more for his friend than he would do for himself, and should even deviate from the strict path of justice, if his friend's life or reputation is imperilled,[1] though naturally he will do, and will be asked to do, nothing absolutely shameful (56–61; cf. 40); in short the true friend is an image of oneself (23), or indeed a kind of second self—'tamquam alter idem' (80; cf. 92).[2]

In this essay Cicero was presumably drawing on Greek philosophy, and W. Kroll, who held that *amicus* means in the everyday language of the time no more than a political follower, was content to explain that we find Roman practice in the strongest contradiction with Greek theory.[3] Cicero's source or sources cannot be identified with certainty;[4] he does not here name any source, in the way that he names Panaetius in the *de officiis*, and neither internal evidence nor Gellius' statement[5] that he had apparently used Theophrastus on friendship proves who the writer or writers were that he was following; it is obviously possible that he was not slavishly following any source, even though he was influenced by one or more Greek philosophical treatments of his subject.[6] It is true that he was not an original thinker and that where he is concerned with the more abstract philosophic themes, metaphysics, physics and the like, he perhaps does no more than expound the doctrines of others, whether or not he indicates his own approval or dissent. But it is another matter to suppose that he adopted the same procedure when writing of practical morality or politics. Here he expressly claims independence. 'It would be very easy', he says in *de legibus* (II, 17), 'to translate Plato, which I would do if I did not wish to express myself.' Even in the *de officiis*, where he avows that he is mainly following Panaetius, it is plain that he does so only because and in so far as he can adopt the views of Panaetius as his own, and confirm and illustrate them from Roman experience.[7] This was possible because Panaetius himself had written not about the duties of the ideal *sapiens*, but about those which should be performed by men who could conventionally be regarded as good in the workaday world (I, 46). So too in the *Laelius* Cicero makes it clear that the good men who alone can enjoy true friendships are not necessarily philosophic sages but men who are good in the plain man's sense;[8] he cites models from Roman history.

[1] F. Schulz, *Principles of Roman Law*, 237, aptly cites *Verr.* II, 3, 122 and 152.

[2] For *mores* cf. Nepos, *Att.* 5, 3; though Atticus' sister married Quintus Cicero, he was more intimate with Marcus, *ut iudicari possit plus in amicitia valere similitudinem morum quam affinitatem.* Common *studia*, *v. infra*; cf. also *Cluent.* 46: *iam hoc fere* scitis omnes *quantam vim habeat ad coniungendas amicitias studiorum ac naturae similitudo*; examples, *Lig.* 21 (Tubero); *Fam.* I, 7, 11; 9, 23–4 (Lentuli); III, 13, 2 (App. Claudius); V, 13, 5; 15, 2 (Lucceius); XIII, 29, 1 (Plancus); *de fato* 2 (Hirtius); *Ac. praef.* and I, 1 (Varro). Hellegouar'ch, 174 ff., misses the common sense of intellectual pursuits. Frankness, *Fam.* XI, 28, 8. Courtesy in complaints, III, 11, 5. Image: Lossmann, 33 ff., compares Arist. *MM* 1213a 7 ff. Second self: *Fam.* VII, 5, 1 (Caesar); *Att.* III, 15, 4 (Atticus); *ad Brut.* 23 (= I, 15), 2 (Brutus); *Att.* IV, 1, 7 (Pompey on Cicero); cf. Lossmann, *loc. cit.*

[3] *Kultur der ciceronischen Zeit*, I, 55 ff.

[4] *RE* VII A, 1163 ff. (Philippson).

[5] I, 3, 11; *contra* Philippson (1164) he clearly held that Cicero used Theophrastus, but he need not be right.

[6] Cf. V. Pöschl, *Röm. Staat u. gr. Staatsdenken bei Cicero*, 23, n. 27 on the *de Republica*.

[7] Panaetius, the main source of I–II (cf. III, 7: *quem nos correctione quadam adhibita potissimum secuti sumus*; *Att.* XVI, 11, 4), is criticized explicitly in I, 7; 9–11; 152; 161; II, 16; 86; III, 33.

[8] *Amic.* 18–19; 21.

The doctrine of the *Laelius* was certainly not the mere product of Cicero's philosophic studies in old age. In a youthful work he defines friendship as 'the will that good things should enure to the man loved for his own sake, combined with a like will on his part' and adds that 'as we are here speaking of lawsuits, we take into account not only friendship but also its fruits, so that it would seem to be sought for their sake as well'. 'There are some', he proceeds, 'who think that friendship should be sought only for its utility, others for its own sake alone, others again who value it on both counts.'[1] This distinction which reappears not only in the *Laelius* but also in a letter to Appius Claudius (*Fam.* III, 10, 7–9) between two types of friendship, not mutually exclusive, is somewhat different from Aristotle's, who had held that friendship was of three kinds: what attracted us in a man might be either the good, the useful or the pleasant.[2] But the pleasures of friendship also constituted a theme well known at Rome; it was a rhetorical *topos* that *maximum bonum est amicitia; plurimae delectationes sunt in amicitia* (*de invent.* I, 95; cf. *Amic.* 22); such terms as *iucundus* and *suavis* are often used to describe friendly relations, and Aristotle's classification underlies Cicero's explanation of the fact that Catilina had so many friends; in the *pro Caelio* (12–14) he says that Catilina was able to do them services, his company gave them pleasure and to all appearances he was a man of many virtues.

A sharp contrast between Greek theory and Roman practice is indeed out of place in Cicero's day. Roman thinking was already permeated by Greek ideas. Like many others of his class, Cicero had been versed in Greek philosophy long before he began to write on it more or less systematically,[3] and he could take such knowledge for granted in others; thus in writing to Appius Claudius long before he composed the *Laelius*, he can refer to the books of learned men on friendship as a matter of common knowledge (*Fam.* III, 7, 5; 8, 5). Cicero himself took the moral and political principles he had adopted from Greek thought so seriously that in 49 B.C., for instance, he examined over and over again how he should act in accordance with them; as Gelzer remarks, 'this way of thinking sprang from his deepest convictions'.[4] At the same time it is implausible to suppose that the Romans, whose word for friendship (as Cicero points out)[5] derives from *amo*, had no native acquaintance with genuine affection of a non-sexual kind. Cicero contended that in general the Romans were better practitioners in moral and political life than the Greeks,[6] and that the experience of a Roman statesman gave him special competence to write on political theory,[7] although the virtue Romans drew from nature, tradition and experience could be matured and

[1] *de invent.* II, 167; cf. 157.

[2] *EN* 1156b 16 ff. It is characteristic of one difference between Greek and Roman society that Cicero does not bring up Aristotle's point that friendship for utility is proper to the business man.

[3] *Rep.* I, 7; 13; *Fam.* IV, 4, 4; *Brut.* 308, etc.; for later studies in leisure *Ac.* I, 11; *Att.* II, 16, 3, etc. For other Romans see E. Zeller, *Phil. d. Griechen* III 1[4], 550–6 with numerous references, esp. *Ac.* II, 4 f. (Lucullus); *Fam.* IV, 3, 3, cf. 2, 2 (Ser. Sulpicius); XV, 4, 16 (M. Cato, whom in *Fin.* III, 7 Cicero depicts in Lucullus' library *multis circumfusum Stoicorum libris*).

[4] *RE* VII A, 995.

[5] *Amic.* 26. Cf. Hellegouar'ch, 146 f., for *amor* as equivalent to *amicitia*, e.g. *Att.* XIV, 13 B, 1.

[6] *Tusc. Disp.* I, 1–3; cf. *Rep.* III, 7; *Leg.* II, 62.

[7] *Rep.* I, 13; *Leg.* III, 14.

deepened by the study of Greek doctrines.[1] Thus in his view Romans had a special aptitude for ethics and politics, the most important parts of philosophy.[2] It would be strange then if Cicero, holding as he did to the superiority of Romans in practical morality, would have been content in his old age merely to copy out Greek doctrines from a book, if they were totally irrelevant to the actualities of Roman life as he knew them in a long career. The *Laelius* is constantly illustrated from Roman life and it should be taken seriously as an expression of Roman experience.

The passage I have already cited from the *pro Caelio* is only one of many in the speeches and letters in which *amicitia* is not restricted to a connexion founded solely on mutual services and common interests, still less to membership of the same faction. It is easy but one-sided to quote such statements as Cicero's *idcirco amicitiae comparantur ut commune commodum mutuis officiis gubernetur.*[3] Even when only utility is mentioned, what is stressed is often not so much the services actually rendered as the constant and known will or readiness to render them,[4] and the sense of *amicitia* is not exhausted by *officia*; thus Trebatius is not only *plenus offici* but also *utriusque nostrum amantissimus* (*Fam.* XI, 27, 1). And *amicitia* often purports to describe sincere affection based on a community of tastes, feelings and principles and taking the form, where opportunity permits, of continuous and intimate association (*vetustas, familiaritas, consuetudo*).[5] It is immaterial for my present purpose whether such affection always existed where it was professed: I am concerned for the present only with the meaning of the term.

Here Cicero's correspondence with Appius Claudius is of special interest. It needs no proof that their *amicitia* was purely political, a matter of expediency. It is therefore the more striking that Cicero chooses to represent it as something more. He tells Appius that if it is the mark of the greatest shrewdness *omnia ad suam utilitatem referre*, nothing could be more useful to him than a union with a man of such ability and influence as Appius, but he proceeds: *illa vincula, quibus quidem libentissime astringor, quanta sunt, studiorum similitudo, suavitas consuetudinis, delectatio vitae atque victus, sermonis societas, litterae interiores.* Even to Caelius Appius is represented as 'suavis *amicus et studiosus studiorum etiam meorum*'.[6] Thus their friendship is depicted as more than a political connexion: it is based on their common intellectual pursuits and the delight they take in each other's conversation and company. He later writes to Appius in the spirit of the *Laelius*: *propono fructum amicitiae nostrae ipsam amicitiam, qua nihil est uberius* (*Fam.* III, 13, 2). Similarly he tells Lucceius that he would greatly

[1] *Rep.* I, 13; III, 4–6. Hence it is a public service to expound Greek doctrines, *ND* I, 7; *Divin.* II, 1–4; *Fin.* I, 10; *Offic.* I, 155.

[2] *Rep.* I, 33; *ND* I, 7; *Offic.* III, 5.

[3] *Rosc. Am.* 111.

[4] E.g. Sall. *Cat.* 20, 4: *idem velle atque idem nolle, ea demum firma amicitia est*; *Fam.* V, 2, 3; V, 7, 2; XI, 28, 1 (Matius refers to *perpetua benevolentia*); *Planc.* 5, etc. Cf. Hellegouar'ch, 181 ff.; but his view (183): '*Voluntas* est donc le terme propre à désigner la notion d'"opinion politique"' is at once too narrow and too weak; *voluntas* connotes the will to realize one's opinions and they need not be political.

[5] On these and other such terms see Hellegouar'ch's analyses, 68 ff. *Consuetudo* could naturally be hampered by separation, cf. *Fam.* XV, 14, 2 and p. 5 on Matius.

[6] *Fam.* III, 1, 1 (Appius dear to Cicero *propter multas suavitates ingenii, officii, humanitatis tuae*); 10, 9–10; II, 13, 2.

desire to live in his society; *vetustas, amor, consuetudo, studia paria; quod vinclum, quaeso deest nostrae coniunctionis?* (V, 15, 2), and in 62 he writes to Pompey that if his services have not yet brought them close together, politics will certainly cement their union; he hopes that on his return Pompey will allow him *et in re publica et in amicitia adiunctum esse*, to be united to him *both* in politics *and* in friendship; a similar distinction is often made.[1] By his own account these hopes were fulfilled; in 61 he refers to their *multa et iucunda consuetudo*; in 56 he publicly claims not only political co-operation but *hanc iucundissimam vitae atque officiorum omnium societatem*; in 50 he speaks not only of Pompey's services to himself but of *consuetudinis iucunditas*; their union is marked by *amoris atque offici signa*;[2] and in 49 he regards himself as bound to Pompey by *merita summa erga salutem meam*, by *familiaritas* and by *ipsa rei publicae causa*. Similarly in the *Brutus* (1–2) he recalls how much he lost by the death of his friend Hortensius in 50—*consuetudo iucunda, multorum officiorum coniunctio*, and wise advice in the political crisis. The *officia*, when distinguished from political collaboration, must refer to personal or private services; the sense of loss on the death of a man from whose intimacy Cicero claims that he derived pleasure and private profit was enhanced (*augebat molestiam*) by the fact that he was also a political associate.

*Sermo, litterae, humanitas* (cf. *Fam.* III, 9, 1) were recognized as qualities which might make even a disreputable man a welcome associate on whom the name of friend could be bestowed (*Verr.* II, 3, 8). I need hardly do more than refer to Cicero's relations with Caelius, Cornificius or Papirius Paetus with whom he might indulge in rallies of wit.[3] From Trebatius he derived *non mediocri...voluptate ex consuetudine nostra vel utilitate ex consilio atque opera tua* (*Fam.* VI, 17, 2).[4] Cicero represents his friendship with Matius, who as early as 53 is described as *suavissimus doctissimusque* (*Fam.* VII, 15, 2), as beginning not with reciprocal services but with mutual affection (*amor*), which at first did not ripen into intimacy only because their different ways of life kept them apart;[5] then came the time when Matius rendered valuable help to Cicero in the civil war, and at last, after his return to Italy, they lived on terms of familiarity; they often spent many hours *suavissimo sermone*, and Matius encouraged Cicero to write philosophical works. *Omnia me tua delectant*, says Cicero, *sed maxime maxima cum fides in amicitia, consilium, gravitas, constantia, tum lepos, humanitas, litterae* (*Fam.* XI, 17).

Above all of course there is Atticus whom Cicero says that he loves for his virtues next to his brother; Atticus is the partner of his studies; they share the same joys and griefs; when Atticus is away, Cicero lacks not only his advice but *sermonis communicatio quae mihi suavissima tecum solet esse*, and yet even then he sees him as if he were present, so clearly does he perceive the fellow-feeling of his love.[6] In the same way he

[1] *Fam.* V, 7; cf. *Fin.* III, 8 on Lucullus *mecum et amicitia et omni voluntate sententiaque coniunctus*; *de orat.* I, 24: *M. Antonius, homo et consiliorum in re p. socius et summa cum Crasso familiaritate coniunctus*; *Fam.* XII, 15, 2 (Lentulus writes): *homo mihi cum familiaritate tum etiam sensibus in re p. coniunctissimus* (Hellegouar'ch, 70, misinterprets both the last texts); *Planc.* 95, etc.

[2] *Att.* I, 16, 11 (cf. 17, 10); *de domo* 28; *Fam.* III, 10, 10; *Att.* VIII, 3, 2.

[3] *Fam.* II, 12, 1; VIII, 3, 1; XII, 18, 2; IX, 15, 1–2.

[4] For Trebatius cf. also *Att.* IX, 9, 4; X, 11, 4; *Fam.* VII, 19–20; XI, 27, 1; *Topica* 1–5.

[5] Cf. *Fam.* XV, 14, 2.

[6] *Att.* I, 17, 5–6; V, 18, 3; VIII, 6, 4; *Fam.* VII, 30, 2.

tells Lucceius that even when parted, they will seem to be united *animorum coniunctione iisdemque studiis* (*Fam.* v, 13, 5). One is reminded of the dictum in the *de amicitia* (23): *amici et absentes adsunt.* Atticus, so Cicero believes, cares for his interests more than for his own (*Att.* xii, 37, 3), just as Laelius is made to say that a friend should. *Quid dulcius quam habere quicum audeas sic loqui ut tecum?*, asks Laelius (*Amic.* 22). Cicero could speak with Atticus as with himself (*Att.* viii, 14, 2); indeed Atticus is a sort of *alter ego.* The phrase was borrowed from the Greeks, but it was in common use; Cicero applies it also to Caesar and to Brutus, and Pompey used it in public of Cicero.[1]

It is a similar relation between Laelius and Scipio that Cicero portrays in the *de amicitia.* 'In Scipio's friendship', says Laelius, 'I found agreement on politics, advice in private affairs and repose full of delight.' They shared the same house, the same life, the same campaigns, the same travels; they were occupied in leisure in the same philosophical inquiries. They enjoyed 'that in which lies the whole strength of friendship, the most complete agreement of wills, pursuits and opinions'.[2] Kroll cites one of these texts to justify his statement that 'Cicero makes Laelius say that for his friendship with Scipio political agreement was essential'. This distorts Cicero's meaning; he is rather suggesting that the political agreement which did subsist between Scipio and Laelius itself flowed from their perfect accord in character, which was the main basis of true friendship. Of course Laelius emphasizes that such friendship is uncommon; the bonds of affection can unite only two or at most a few persons (*Amic.* 20) and there is no certainty that such affection will endure unless the friends are good men, a doctrine that Cicero alludes to in writing to Appius (*Fam.* iii, 10, 7; 13, 1–2). But the rarity of true friendship is not a peculiarity of Roman society; it is probably true among all peoples, and in all ages.

In professing his renewed friendship for Crassus Cicero writes to him: *has litteras velim existimes foederis habituras esse vim, non epistulae* (*Fam.* v, 8, 5). Professor Taylor cites this to support her statement that 'friendship for the man in politics was a sacred agreement'. Although in fact many political friendships were short-lived and insincere, there is no doubt that she has hit off the meaning of the term *foedus.* Treaties were ratified by solemn oaths and to break them was perjury. But it is wrong to confine the sacredness of friendship to political connexions. Catullus uses the same metaphor of his relations with Lesbia, in a passage where *amicitia* stands for *amor*, just as *amor* may replace *amicitia* (p. 3, n. 5); he prays

*ut liceat nobis tota perducere vita*
*aeternum hoc sanctae foedus amicitiae.*[3]

According to Sallust, indeed, it was one mark of the depravity of his age that *ambitio multos mortalis falsos fieri subegit, aliud clausum in pectore, aliud in lingua promptum habere, amicitias inimicitiasque non ex re, sed ex commodo aestumare, magis-*

[1] *Att.* iii, 15, 4; cf. p. 2, n. 2.
[2] *Amic.* 15; 79; 103–4.
[3] Catullus 109; cf. 76, 3; 87, 3. Many parallels for such *foedera* can be found in *TLL* vi, 1004–6. Cf. Hellegouar'ch, 38 ff., for *foedus* being cognate with *fides*, on which *amicitia* rested (*Amic.* 65).

*que voltum quam ingenium bonum habere* (*Cat.* 10, 5). This indictment of the political morality of his times is not even intended to be of universal application; we are not to suppose that there were not also some, or many, Romans who recognized that *amicitia* involved sacred obligations.[1] The common practices of private life, not least the frequency with which men rewarded with legacies the services they had received in life, show how strongly the *fides* on which *amicitia* was based still worked on men's minds; the prevalence of *fides* in business life explains many of the institutions of Roman law. A friendship contracted *ex commodo* could easily involve the recipient of benefits in an obligation to repay them in circumstances when it was no longer his interest to do so. A friend has a duty to give good advice (*Att.* III, 15, 4) and when necessary to lend money (*Fam.* XIV, 1, 5; 2, 3), or to perform all manner of other services. The recognized moral element in political friendship made it possible for Cicero to appeal to Caesar as his friend in 49 to let him prove himself *bonus vir*, *gratus*, *pius* in his relationship with Pompey (*Att.* IX, 11 A, 3). But those who were guided in any measure by a sense of obligation could easily recognize that their obligations to their friends were transcended by their obligation to their *patria*; and this in turn made it natural for seeming friends to excuse political differences with a plea that covered a divergence of their own interests.

In its highest form, true affection between good men, *amicitia* was durable even among politicians because they were *ex hypothesi* men who shared the same moral and political principles. Others aspired or pretended to such a genuine and lasting intimacy, when in reality they were linked only by common tastes and interests; and the hollowness of their connexion was not exposed unless their interests diverged. In the meantime this secondary form of friendship might assume a close familiarity, as between Cicero and Caelius, and involve obligations to render mutual services. But not all who called themselves friends were so closely bound together. Wherever courtesies and services were interchanged, the urbanity of social etiquette extended the use of the term *amici* to persons with whom no sort of intimacy subsisted. *Amicitia* had imperceptible gradations in quality and degree;[2] yet even the *ambitiosae fucosaeque amicitiae*[3] which *fructum domesticum non habent* took their name by external analogy from the true affection, which is the primitive significance of the word.

Like ourselves,[4] the Romans might politely describe as a friend a person with whom they had no familiarity, but to whom they had, or professed to have, nothing but goodwill at the time. Cicero calls both the censors of 70 B.C. his friends, but in almost the same breath remarks that he was intimate with only one of them

[1] Cf. F. Schulz, *Principles of Roman Law*, ch. XI (of which Professor P. W. Duff reminded me); M. Gelzer, *Kl. Schr.* I, 70 ff.

[2] Cf. *de invent.* II, 168: *amicitiarum autem ratio, quoniam partim sunt religionibus iunctae, partim non sunt, et quia partim veteres sunt, partim novae, partim ab illorum, partim ab nostro beneficio profectae, partim utiliores, partim minus utiles, ex causarum dignitatibus, ex temporum opportunitatibus, ex officiis, ex religionibus, ex vetustatibus habebitur.*

[3] *Att.* I, 18, 1. The qualities of his friendship with Appius listed on p. 4 above were 'domestica' (*Fam.* III, 10, 9).

[4] The *New Eng. Dict.* (1901), IV, 545–6, recognizes that 'friend' may be 'applied to a mere acquaintance, or to a stranger, as a mark of goodwill or kindly condescension on the part of the speaker', and that it may mean 'one who is on good terms with another, not hostile or at variance'.

(*Cluent.* 117). In 43 he declared that there was no consular (not even his old enemy, L. Piso) *quin mecum habeat aliquam coniunctionem gratiae, alii maximam, alii mediocrem, nemo nullam* (*Phil.* VIII, 20). It was surely the merest commonplace, understood by all, that *consuetudines victus non possunt esse cum multis* (*Mil.* 21). In letters he bestows the name of friend on far too many people to warrant the supposition that he even expected his correspondents to think that they were all his close associates.[1] The author of the *Commentariolum* observes that a candidate may be free with the title of friend and give it to anyone who manifests his support; but from such supporters is to be distinguished *quisque domesticus ac maxime intimus*, though others may be confirmed in allegiance, *adducenda amicitia in spem familiaritatis et consuetudinis* (16–23); even if he be not Q. Cicero, the writer was well versed in the manners of the age. Many who belonged to the governor's *cohors*, or who paid morning visits of respect to the great houses, were *amici* only by courtesy.[2] More accurately, some were clients, but this was an appellation resented like death by all with any pretensions to rank or affluence (*Offic.* II, 69).

Such *amici*, drawn from the *plebs*, may well be regarded as political followers, yet it may often have happened that no ties of either interest or obligation bound them closely to any one political leader, and that they owed but a shifting allegiance. In the higher ranks of society, while the term *amicus* no more implies cordiality than that of 'honourable friend' in the House of Commons, it does not even denote political association, as the latter does. Courtesy or expediency often required that one senator should style another as his friend, despite serious disagreements in politics, merely because he had no wish for a personal quarrel, and at times because a genuine personal liking subsisted among those who were not in political accord. Moreover, in the network of relationships between leading senators men incurred obligations to different *amici* whose policies and interests subsequently diverged, and were then confronted with a conflict of duties,[3] or if they preferred to act *ex commodo* rather than *ex fide*, with a difficulty of deciding where their own advantage lay. These considerations alone, to say nothing of the fact that the welfare of the state still weighed heavily with some, make it no less inadequate to equate *amicitia* with party in the real world of political life than to hold that the meaning of the term is exhausted if it is described as a connexion for mutual convenience. In the second part of this paper I propose to illustrate the complexity of *amicitia* in political affairs.

## II

Courtesy often outstepped the bounds of even temporary political co-operation. In May 44 Cicero privately described Antony's conduct as negligent, dishonourable and pernicious, at the same time that he assured him that he had always loved him and that in the present political juncture he regarded no one as more dear (*Att.* XIV, 13, 6; 13A). Thus covert enmity and opposition were veiled by polite professions of concord and amity. In his speech of 2 September Cicero still claimed to be Antony's

[1] *Fam.* XIII, 71: *etsi omnium causa quos commendo velle debeo, tamen cum omnibus non eadem mihi causa est.*

[2] M. Gelzer, *Kl. Schr.* I, 102 ff.

[3] *Ibid.* 164 f.

friend while openly criticizing his conduct of affairs (*Phil.* I, 11–12). This was indeed too much for Antony; he made an insulting reply (*Phil.* V, 19–20). Cicero professed surprise: *quid est dictum a me cum contumelia, quid non moderate, quid non amice?* (II, 6; cf. I, 27). He expected his readers to accept that political opposition was compatible with friendship, if there were no abuse. In demonstrating how much further he could go when provoked, he adds: 'I made serious complaints on policy, but said nothing of the man, as if I had been contending with Marcus Crassus, with whom I had many grave disputes, and not with the most worthless of cut-throats' (II, 7).

The allusion to Crassus is interesting. Crassus believed that it was Cicero who prompted the charges made against him in 63 of complicity in Catilina's plot (Sall. *Cat.* 48, 9), and Cicero thought that Crassus worked against his return from exile and intrigued against him before Luca.[1] But this mutual hostility was hardly ever avowed. In 61 Crassus tickled Cicero's vanity with a deceitful encomium (*Att.* I, 14, 3–4), and in 58 it was Clodius who said that Crassus was an enemy to Cicero, not Crassus, who was content with declining to use his good offices on Cicero's behalf; it was, he said, for the consuls to act (*Sest.* 39–41). Thus there was no overt quarrel, and in exile Cicero could advise his brother, if accused of *repetundae*, to ask Crassus to defend him (*Qu. fr.* I, 3, 7); on his return there was no need for formal reconciliation with Crassus, still less with Pompey, as Plutarch (*Cic.* 33, 5) and Dio (XXXIX, 9) wrongly assert; Cicero had only to repress his sense of the wrongs Crassus had done him, until at last Crassus insulted him personally in defending Gabinius; then his pent-up wrath broke forth, and it was this sudden breach that had to be formally healed (*Fam.* I, 9, 20), a breach caused by mutual abuse. Thereafter, Cicero who still regarded Crassus as *hominem nequam* (*Att.* IV, 13, 2) could write to him, not implausibly, of their *vetus necessitudo* (*Fam.* V, 8). It may be added, as a curiosity to those who think that political ties were hereditary, that Crassus' son, Publius, was an ardent admirer of Cicero.[2]

Again in 43, when Cicero was trying to galvanize the senate into resisting Antony effectively, the reprobate still had his friends and spokesmen in the house, notably Q. Fufius Calenus (*Phil.* V, 6; XII, 18, etc.). Cicero had never had a good opinion of the man, once a *levissimus tribunus plebis* (*Att.* I, 14, 1 and 6) and an apologist for Clodius (*Phil.* VIII, 16), though he had admired his father (*ibid.* 13) and in the very year of his tribunate had used influence with him on behalf of P. Sestius (*Fam.* V, 6, 1); even in 49 he received him in his villa (*Att.* IX, 5, 1). Calenus was perhaps hostile to Cicero's pardon in 47 (if his name may be read in *Att.* XI, 8, 2); at any rate there was an open quarrel, which Calenus sought to make up in a letter which Cicero found tasteless (XV, 4, 1), but to which he must have replied with polite assent. For now Calenus is *vir fortis ac strenuus, amicus meus* (*Phil.* VIII, 11), and if Cicero attacks his views, he professes to do so more in sorrow than in anger; he is careful to avoid abuse (VIII, 17; 19) and to express pleasure when for once their opinions coincide (XI, 15). He only fears that *ita saepe dissentio ut...id quod fieri minime debet, minuere amicitiam nostram videatur perpetua dissensio* (X, 2). Thus, if the courtesies were observed, a

[1] *Fam.* XIV, 2, 2; *Ibid.* I, 9, 9.

[2] *Ibid.* V, 8, 4; XIII, 16, 1; *Qu. fr.* II, 8, 2; Plut. *Cr.* 13.

nominal friendship might survive political disagreements, unless they were too continuous, or degenerated into personal assaults. In the same spirit Cicero could reject the suspicion that he had differed from Appius *animorum contentione*, *non opinionum dissensione*; *nihil autem feci umquam neque dixi quod contra illius existimationem esse vellem* (*Fam.* II, 13, 2).

A closer familiarity was still more likely to outlast political divergencies. In 56 Cicero claimed that political dissension had not ended his old *familiaritas* and *consuetudo* with Caesar: *ita dissensi ab illo ut in disiunctione sententiae coniuncti tamen amicitia maneremus.*[1] His complimentary language to Caesar even in the debate on the fate of the Catilinarians, his hope that his influence might render Caesar 'meliorem' at the end of 60, and the offers of posts Caesar made to him in 59 confirm that they were in some sense friends, but even if Cicero's claim was false, it cannot have seemed nonsensical to assert that political opponents could remain *amici*. Cicero's rejection of Caesar's offers in 59 (cf. *Att.* IX, 2A, 1) and Caesar's part in Cicero's banishment (e.g. *Prov. Cons.* 41–2) resulted in an *inimicitia*, which Cicero renounced professedly *rei publicae causa* and in fact, no doubt, because Caesar's goodwill was necessary to his return from exile and future safety; at the same time it is hard not to feel some sincerity in the warmth with which he speaks of Caesar in the private correspondence of 54; perhaps, little as he approved of the politician, he could not help liking the man.[2] Again even in the clash of arms in 49 he kept up friendly correspondence with Caesar himself for a time and with several of his partisans;[3] they looked after his interests while he was with Pompey and helped to secure his restoration,[4] and for years both before and after Caesar's assassination they lived on terms of close familiarity and seeming cordiality.[5] No doubt both they and Cicero were at times angling for political advantage with each other; but this does not alter the fact that outwardly there were all the marks of affection in their intercourse and that a community of cultural interests seemed to transcend differences of political outlook.

It was not only Cicero who behaved in this way. Varro in Spain commanded a

[1] *Prov. Cons.* 25 ff. (cf. Gelzer, *Kl. Schr.* I, 165 ff.), esp. 40; *Qu. fr.* II, 14, 1; *Fam.* I, 9, 12.

[2] *Cat.* IV, 9; *Att.* II, 1, 6; 18, 3; 19, 4–5; *Prov. Cons.* 41, cf. Lossmann's book and my review (p. 1, n. 1).

[3] Correspondence with Caesar, *Att.* VII, 22, 3; VIII, 2, 1; 3, 2; 11, 5; IX, 6A; 11A; 16, 2; their meeting, IX, 18. Relations with Balbus and Oppius, VII, 3, 11; VIII, 15A; IX, 7A and B; 13A; X, 18, 2; with Trebatius (*a quo me unice diligi scio*), VII, 17, 3–4; *Fam.* IV, 1; *Att.* IX, 9, 4; 12; 15, 4 and 6; 17, 1; X, 1, 3; 11, 4 (still in early May *vir plane et civis bonus*); with Matius, IX, 11, 2 (and often linked with Trebatius); *Fam.* XI, 27, 3; with Caelius, *Fam.* VIII, 15–16; *Att.* X, 9A; with Antony who professed the warmest affection, X, 8A; 10, 1; XI, 7, 2, and visited him, X, 11, 4, as did Curio, X, 4, 8, cf. 16, 3. In Pompey's camp he received a letter from his son-in-law, Dolabella, written in Caesar's, *Fam.* IX, 9.

[4] *Fam.* XI, 27, 4 (Matius); 29, 2 (Oppius); XV, 21, 2 (Trebonius); for Antony, Balbus, Oppius, Hirtius, Pansa, Trebatius, Vatinius cf. *Att.* XI, 5, 4; 6, 3; 7, 2; 8, 1; 9, 2; 14, 1; 18.

[5] *Fam.* XI, 27–8 (Matius); 29, cf. *Att.* XVI, 12, 1 (Oppius); *Fam.* VII, 19, 1; XI, 27, 1; *Top.* 1 ff. (Trebatius). *Fam.* VI, 12, 2 (46 B.C.): *omnis Caesaris familiaris satis opportune habeo implicatos consuetudine et benevolentia sic ut, cum ab illo discesserint, me habeant proximum. hoc Pansa, Hirtius, Balbus, Oppius, Postumius plane ita faciunt ut me unice diligant*, cf. IX, 16, 2 (their *amor* is genuine); VI, 10, 2; 14, 3. References to his teaching rhetoric to Hirtius and Pansa are particularly common. In 44 he hoped to turn Hirtius into an optimate, *Att.* XIV, 20, 4; 21, 4; but for distrust of Hirtius, Balbus and Matius at this time see XIV, 1, 1; 21, 2; 22, 1; XV, 2, 3.

Pompeian legion but *amicissime de Caesare loquebatur*; like Cicero, he had old ties with each of the rivals and could make no decided choice (Caes. *BC* II, 17). In negotiations with the Pompeians Caesar made use of men who had friends in the opposing camp (Caes. *BC* I, 26, 3; III, 57, 1); similarly as a friend of both Antony and Octavian, L. Cocceius Nerva was able to reconcile them at Brundisium (App. *BC* V, 60 ff.). The Pompeian Scribonius Libo found it easier to negotiate with Caesar than Bibulus could have done, for Bibulus *inimicitias habebat etiam privatas cum Caesare* (Caes. *BC* III, 16, 3); so too Octavian distinguished between his private enemies and others who had held out against him at Perusia (App. *BC* V, 38; 40; 49). Even when Caesar was aware that Cicero would not countenance his acts, he still appealed to him in the name of their friendship not to join Pompey and thus inflict *amicitiae graviorem iniuriam* (*Att.* X, 8 B); thus Cicero's refusal to take his side was in his eyes an injury, but not fatal to their amity.[1] Like Balbus (*Att.* VIII, 15 A, 1), Caesar complained that his old enemies had driven a wedge between Pompey and himself *invidia atque obtrectatione laudis suae* (*BC* I, 7); in his later narrative he was careful not to confuse Pompey with his personal enemies (I, 3–4; 7), and he persisted in efforts to secure reconciliation,[2] while for his part Pompey begged Caesar *ne ea quae rei publicae causa egerit in suam contumeliam vertat* (I, 8). In August 44 Brutus and Cassius formally protested to Antony in terms rather like those of a diplomatic note sent by one state to another with which it preserves technically 'friendly relations'; they declared that though they regarded their own freedom as more valuable than his amity, they did not mean to invite him to become their enemy.[3] Avowed political adversaries, they were not yet *inimici*. Courtesies were kept up on the brink of civil war—or even beyond.

But if *amicitia* may connote no more than outward courtesy, it can also indicate readiness to render effectual aid. When Cicero describes two consular candidates of 65 as 'destitute of friends and reputation' (*Att.* I, 1, 2), he surely means only that they lacked real support; one of them, D. Silanus, was returned for 62. None of the consulars, he told Lentulus Spinther in 56, was his friend besides Hortensius, Lucullus and himself; some were covertly unfavourable, others did not conceal their anger against him (*Fam.* I, 5B, 2; 7, 3). But it can hardly be supposed that the *obscurius iniqui* or even the *non dissimulanter irati* were abusive of Lentulus; the latter actually included the consul Marcellinus who made it clear that except on the Egyptian question he would vigorously defend Lentulus' interests (*Fam.* I, 1, 2). The term *amicitia* is indeed ambiguous within a wide range. To determine its exact nuance in any particular context requires tact and discrimination, and it is often found where we have not sufficient knowledge of the circumstances to discriminate.

It may seem strange that the forms of friendship, and sometimes much more, should have survived the most profound political divisions. In the Verrines Cicero asks Hortensius: *an tu maiores ullas inimicitias putas esse quam contrarias hominum*

[1] *Att.* X, 8 B, written after the interview from which Cicero concluded *hunc me non amare* (IX, 18, 1).

[2] Cf. *Att.* VIII, 9, 4.

[3] *Fam.* XI, 3, esp. at 4: *nos in hac sententia sumus, ut te cupiamus in libera re p. magnum atque honestum esse, vocemus te ad nullas inimicitias, sed tamen pluris nostram libertatem quam tuam amicitiam aestimemus.*

*sententias ac dissimilitudines studiorum ac voluntatum?* (II, 3, 6). The context indeed shows that he is thinking not of all political disagreements but of those which involved moral principles; an honourable man could not but be hostile to one who repudiated good faith, religion and law. Just as the good of the state might require patriots to be reconciled with personal enemies who had deserved well of Rome—of such reconciliations Cicero could cite many famous examples[1]—so the fatherland took precedence of all ties of amity or kinship (*Phil.* V, 6), and made P. Clodius the enemy of all good men, because he was the enemy of his country (*Prov. Cons.* 24; *Fam.* I, 9, 10); C. Aurelius Cotta (*cos.* 75) could boast of incurring *maximas inimicitias pro republica* (Sall. *Or. Cottae* 6) and Cicero of engaging the enmity of the *perditi* (*Cat.* II, 11). Thus, it was right for Q. Aelius Tubero and other friends of Tiberius Gracchus to abandon him when they saw him *rem publicam vexantem* (*Amic.* 37), and the young Lentulus Spinther took pride in deserting his crony, Dolabella, and his kinsman, Antony, in 43 πατρίδα ἐμὴν μᾶλλον φιλῶν (*Fam.* XII, 14, 7). Yet the evidence previously given shows how reluctant men often were to display overt hostility towards political opponents with whom they had lived on terms of agreeable familiarity, or with whom they had merely maintained the formalities of politeness, even when the issues that divided them were of the most fundamental kind, at times resulting in armed conflict.

It is true that in many instances friendships had been dissolved by less grave dissensions, such as contests for office; but in principle this was regrettable (*Amic.* 33; 63 f.; 77), and I suspect that it was far from being the rule, for despite the frequency of contests we do not find the leading men at Rome in Cicero's time (of which we know most) persistently involved in mutual hostilities. It was disgraceful if on such occasions former friends became open enemies and resorted to *iurgia, maledicta, contumeliae.* Here Scipio Aemilianus was the model; he gave up his amity with Q. Pompeius when the latter cheated C. Laelius of the consulship, and that with Q. Metellus Macedonicus because of some political difference, but *utrumque egit graviter ac moderate et offensione animi non acerba.* Elsewhere Cicero speaks of the *sine acerbitate dissensio* between Scipio and Metellus, though he classes Metellus among Scipio's *obtrectatores et invidi* (*Offic.* I, 87; *Rep.* I, 31). Now *invidi* are often distinguished from *inimici*; thus Cicero often describes the *boni*, with whom he sought to co-operate, as his *invidi.*[2] Such people who harbour *occulta odia* (*Fam.* I, 9, 5) may be *insidiosi amici*, but they are not *aperte inimici.*[3] Despite the contrary statements of some late writers,[4] I do not doubt that Scipio and Metellus continued to speak of each other with outward courtesy, even when their intimacy had been broken; otherwise it is hardly conceivable that Scipio's kin and friends should have let Metellus' sons act as his pall-bearers

[1] *Prov. Cons.* 18 ff.; cf. *Flacc.* 2; *Post Red. Quir.* 23; and see *Fam.* V, 4, 2 and *Post Red. Sen.* 25 for Metellus Nepos' quarrel and reconciliation with Cicero.

[2] E.g. *Att.* I, 19, 6; 20, 3; II, 1, 7; 16, 2; III, 7, 2; IV, 1, 8; 5, 1; *Fam.* I, 9, 5. *Prov. Cons.* 19 distinguishes *alieni* from *inimici*, *Fam.* I, 9, 17 from *amici.*

[3] *Dom.* 29; *Verr.* II, 5, 182; *Mur.* 45; *Fam.* III, 10, 6. In 56 Pompey spoke to Cicero of Curio, Bibulus and *ceteris suis obtrectatoribus* and of *nobilitate inimica* (*Qu. fr.* II, 3, 4); but their hostility was covert, cf. *Qu. fr.* II, 1, 1; 5, 3. Note Caelius in *Fam.* VIII, 14, 2: *sic illi amores et invidiosa coniunctio* (of Caesar and Pompey) *non ad* occultam *recidit obtrectationem* (as might have been expected), *sed ad bellum se erupit.*

[4] Val. Max. IV, 1, 12; Plin. *NH* VII, 144; Plut. *Mor.* 202 A.

(Val. Max. IV, 1, 12). However this may be, their differences did not extend to every political issue; Metellus, like Pompeius whom he was suspected of hating,[1] were united with the friends of Scipio in opposing Tiberius Gracchus.[2]

*Inimicitiae*, open and avowed, were imprudent and surely rare—most common, if we may believe Cicero (*Verr.* II, 5, 180 ff.), with *novi homines*. In 54 Cicero could actually assert that Pompey, who had given as much offence as most men of his day, had not an enemy in the state except P. Clodius (*Fam.* I, 9, 11)! Formally denounced and formally composed, *inimicitiae* arose in the first place (though they might also be inherited) in various ways.[3] Men were well justified in declaring their hatred of an *inimicus patriae* (*supra*).[4] There might be private quarrels, such as partly explained the animosity of Bibulus and Caesar (Caes. *BC* III, 16). Political contentions did not suffice in themselves, unless there was personal abuse or unless a man's status and dignity were injured, as was that of Metellus Nepos in his conflict with Cicero in 62 (*Fam.* V, 2, 6 ff.). Again, just as a man might become the enemy of one who in his view had given an *unjust* legal decision against him,[5] so he might declare hostility against a candidate who had *unfairly* got the better of him, for instance by bribes. Thus the Manlii Torquati became enemies of P. Sulla, not when he stood against L. Torquatus for the consulship of 65 but when he was corruptly returned; they then sought, and obtained, his conviction (*pro Sulla* 90). The hatred Catulus conceived for Caesar, after being defeated by one so young in his candidature for the supreme pontificate (Sall. *Cat.* 49, 2), is a very special case.

To prosecute or testify against a man on charges involving his *caput* or *existimatio* was necessarily a hostile act.[6] It might initiate a feud, or betoken that a feud already existed. It was perhaps the most common cause of enmity, or its most flagrant manifestation. All the more striking therefore is the reluctance and infrequency with which such prosecutions were undertaken. It was legitimate to avenge one's kin in the courts, or to prosecute in the interests of the Republic or of injured subjects. But it was in Cicero's day young men who normally sought or established an oratorical reputation in this way; it was no longer in vogue for men of rank and influence to appear as accusers, and indeed there had been cases, it was held, in which defendants had been acquitted out of prejudice against powerful enemies who assailed them in the courts.[7]

[1] *Font.* 23 (*inimicitiarum suspicio*); 27 (*obtrectatorem*); Val. Max. VIII, 5, 1.

[2] *Rep.* I, 31; *Brut.* 81; cf. Plut. *Ti. Gr.* 14, 2; Cic. *Phil.* VIII, 14.

[3] On *inimicitiae* (hostile acts or declarations) cf. Hellegouar'ch, 186 ff. R. S. Rogers, *TAPA* XC (1959), 224 ff., discusses the formalities, mostly from imperial evidence; *Fam.* V, 2, 5 shows that there might be doubt in Cicero's time whether hostilities existed, requiring formal reconciliation. Hereditary: e.g. Ascon. 62–3 C; *Offic.* II, 50; *Ac.* II, 1. But there were no such secular feuds as in Medieval or Renaissance Florence.

[4] *Offic.* II, 50; *Sull.* 6–7; *Prov. Cons.* 24; *Fam.* I, 9, 10.

[5] *Div. in Caec.* 55–8 (but cf. *Verr.* II, 1, 15); *Verr.* II, 3, 7.

[6] *Font.* 23 ff.; Sall. *Cat.* 49, 2 (Piso); Ascon. 60 C. For what follows cf. generally *Offic.* II, 49 ff. Pliny, *ep.* IX, 13, 2 (*materiam insectandi nocentes, miseros vindicandi, se proferendi*) corresponds to Republican practice.

[7] *Principes* once appeared *pro sociis*, now only *imperiti adulescentes*, *Div. in Caec.* 63 ff.; cf. *Verr.* II, 3, 6; *Cael.* 73 ff.; *Offic. loc. cit.* (last note); Quint. *Inst.* XII, 6, 1; 7, 1 ff.

There was said to be more honour, and there was certainly more *gratia*, to be won from acting for the defence.[1] To prosecute once might be enough, or too much; in old age L. Crassus repented of ruining C. Carbo (*Verr.* II, 3, 3). Cicero won his primacy at the bar by accusing Verres; it was his first prosecution, and, he hoped, his last; in fact, he appeared only once more for the prosecution, against T. Plancus in 52. In his opinion, it was inhumane to accuse a personal enemy on a charge of which he was innocent, but you might properly defend the guilty.[2] At most it was permissible to indulge in frequent accusations of *inimici rei publicae*. No doubt others took a sterner view than Cicero, and were more intent on seeing the laws observed. The accusers of Murena included the upright Cato, who had no private or public quarrel with him (*Mur.* 64), and one, C. Postumus, who had previously been connected with him by neighbourly goodwill and was his father's friend (*ibid.* 56). Cicero speaks of numerous persons who were the common enemies of all accused of *ambitus*; but their readiness to testify for the prosecution did not make them popular (*Planc.* 55). M. Iunius Brutus, a second-century prototype of imperial delators, set out to be a Roman Lycurgus: he was accounted a disgrace to his family (*Brut.* 130). So far as we know, Hortensius, who was counsel for the defence seventeen times, appeared for the prosecution twice,[3] M. Crassus, an assiduous pleader, never.

Cicero counted both Murena and Ser. Sulpicius as friends, but his ties were closer with Sulpicius; he had favoured his candidature (*Mur.* 7–8), but opposed his attempt to unseat Murena. Sulpicius resented what he construed as a breach of friendship. Without reason, according to Cicero, since he himself was ready to advise even *alieni* in their suits with his own friends.[4] Between clients and patron in the courts there need have been no antecedent ties: *etiam cum alienissimos defendimus, tamen eos alienos, si ipsi viri boni volumus haberi, existimare non possumus* (*de orat.* II, 192). Moreover one's friends might be on both sides. In 54 Cicero was prepared to defend as his friends any of the four consular candidates who might be accused of bribery, of which each was equally guilty.[5]

Professor L. R. Taylor writes of 'the unending prosecutions brought from political motives by [a man's] personal enemies'.[6] Yet most of the *principes* in Cicero's time had never been arraigned in the courts. Cicero says that a good man would not even wish to ruin a citizen by making him bankrupt (*Quinct.* 51). *Omnes enim ad pericula propulsanda concurrimus et qui non aperte inimici sumus etiam alienissimis in capitis periculis amicissimorum officia et studia praestamus* (*Mur.* 45). The trial of Scaurus in 54 illustrates this; his advocates, witnesses and suppliants included nearly all the most noted men at Rome, Cicero himself with eight other consulars, his bitter enemies, L.

[1] *Div. in Caec.* 1–4; *Verr.* II, 1, 98; 2, 10 and 179; 5, 189; *Rab. perd.* 1; *Vat.* 5 (*cum in hac civitate oppugnatio soleat,. . .defensio numquam vituperari*); *Mur.* 45; *de orat.* II, 200.

[2] *Reg. Deiot.* 30; *Sull.* 81.

[3] *RE* VIII, 2470 ff. (v. der Mühll).

[4] *Mur.* 9. *De orat.* I, 184, depicts the jurisconsult *praesidium clientibus atque opem amicis* et prope cunctis *civibus lucem ingeni et consili porrigentem*. Cf. Cicero on his own practice: *tantum enitor, ut neque amicis neque etiam alienioribus opera, consilio, labore desim* (*Fam.* I, 9, 17).

[5] *Att.* IV, 15, 9; for his relations to the candidates, *Qu. fr.* III, 1, 16; he preferred Messala, III, 6 (8), 3.

[6] *Party Politics*, 7.

Piso and P. Clodius (though Clodius' brother, Appius, had instigated the charge), and not only Clodius but Milo too; there was even the young son of C. Memmius, one of Scaurus' rivals for the consulship.[1] Plainly this heterogeneous assortment did not constitute a political faction; the scene shows the general unwillingness of the aristocracy to encompass or see the ruin of one of their own class.

It is also characteristic of Cicero that at this trial he spoke with great respect of Appius, with whom he was newly reconciled. I have noted eleven instances in which he professes friendship with the prosecutors of his clients,[2] not to speak of adverse witnesses,[3] and even when he does not go so far, he prefers to apply to them kind or laudatory terms, to avoid the hostility that might arise from contumely.[4] Similarly when Favonius prosecuted Nasica, and Cicero defended him, Favonius was content to express slight censure (*Att.* II, 1, 9).

In these circumstances political affiliations cannot be simply deduced from trials. An accuser might act out of private hostility,[5] the desire to make a name or even care for the public weal; and the most curious medley of people might rally to the defence. I cannot for instance agree with Professor Badian[6] in thinking it politically significant that Marcus Antonius appeared for Manius Aquillius, Gaius Norbanus and Marius Gratidianus or that he excused Norbanus' riotous conduct; this was no more than a *tour de force* of sophistic rhetoric which commanded the admiration of connoisseurs (*de orat.* II, 124). To explain Antonius' action, we need not go behind the reason Cicero gives (*ibid.* 200), that he had obligations to Norbanus as his former quaestor,[7] and if we suppose that he spoke with sincere passion, we may recall that Cicero ascribes to him the view that the orator must be like the actor, 'his whole function suiting with forms to his conceit, and all for nothing' (cf. *ibid.* 193). Cicero actually says that Antonius was careful not to publish his forensic speeches lest they be quoted against him; he did not wish them to be used as evidence of his real opinions; less prudent in publication himself, Cicero denies that his utterances as an advocate indicated his true sentiments (*Cluent.* 138–42). In general his task was to state his client's case, though like other orators he used *auctoritas* as well as eloquence on his behalf.[8] Exceptions might occur. We know that the *pro Sestio* is a political manifesto, because it affirms the same principles as his philosophical works and private letters. But we should recall that Sestius' counsel also included Crassus, who can hardly have shared or relished the proclamation of his political faith that Cicero chose to make on this occasion.

[1] Ascon. 18–20C. Cf. perhaps the trial of Catilina in 65, *ibid.* 87 with *Sull.* 49; 81.

[2] See (i) *Font.* 36; (ii) Ascon. 60 f.; *Brut.* 271 (*pro Cornelio*); (iii) *Cluent.* 10; 118; *Brut.* 271; (iv) *Mur.* 3; 7; 10; (v) *Sull.* 2; 47; (vi) *Flacc.* 2; (vii) *Cael.* 7; 25; (viii) *Planc.* 2 ff.; 58; (ix) *Scaur.* 31; (x) *Rab. Post.* 32; (xi) *Lig.* 21. The bitter attacks on Hortensius in the Verrines are exceptional and did not preclude a hollow friendship later. L. Torquatus' taunts did indeed make him threaten to renounce friendship, *Sull.* 21 f.; 47, but his moderation on this occasion was not unique, *ibid.* 49.

[3] *Planc.* 56; Ascon. 60 f.

[4] *Tull.* 3; *Rab. perd.* 25.

[5] Hortensius could even profess to assume that this was the one legitimate reason, *Verr.* II, 3, 6.

[6] *St. in Greek and Rom. Hist.* 46 f.

[7] Cf. *Div. in Caec.* 61; *Planc.* 28.

[8] *Cluent.* 57; *Mur.* 2; 59; 86; *Sull.* 2; 4, etc. Of course prosecutors were vexed by the success of defending counsel, and it could be said that in getting off C. Cornelius *tr. pl.* 67 Cicero had displeased the *boni*, *Vat.* 5; but cf. *Sull.* 49.

Although *amici* might form a political faction, we must beware of assuming that it was necessarily long lasting; that would be incompatible with the admittedly transient character of many political *amicitiae* (*Amic.* 64). Two men may be attested as *amici* or shown to have acted together on some particular occasion, but that is no proof that they were consistently political allies. Gelzer remarked that 'it would be contradictory of the character of the Roman senator that he should be tied to a group'.[1] It is surely mistaken to treat any senator of high nobility or distinguished talent as a mere follower or henchman of another; such men enjoyed influence of their own and valued their independence. Plutarch rightly says of Marcus Crassus that he made the most frequent changes in his political conduct; he was not a firm friend nor an implacable enemy, but readily gave up his favour or resentment at the bidding of self-interest (*Cr.* 7). No doubt Crassus was peculiarly unscrupulous, but others who were somewhat more influenced by principles or a sense of obligation found themselves compelled to subordinate the interests of their friends to the common good (as they saw it), or to prefer the interests of one friend to those of another, when the rivalries of their friends forced them to make a choice in a conflict of obligations. Cicero, for instance, could not simultaneously back the claims of both Pompey and Lentulus Spinther to restore Ptolemy Auletes. The little we know of Gracchan and Marian times suggests that there was nothing very novel in the kaleidoscopic combinations which bewilder us in the late Republic.

The discussions on the Egyptian question in 56[2] should give pause to those who think of Rome as then divided between the triumvirs and the *boni*, or who believe in a powerful and lasting Pompeian faction. Pompey's veiled ambitions were openly promoted only by two consulars, who ranked as his *familiares*, Afranius and Volcacius Tullus, of whom the latter was to be neutral in 49. Crassus was typically ambiguous and did not exclude Pompey from the task of restoring Auletes, which he probably coveted for himself. Syme suggests that the Lentuli were Pompey's adherents,[3] but Lentulus Spinther was his rival, and the consul, Lentulus Marcellinus, obstructed the ambitions of Pompey and Spinther alike. Spinther counted as a friend of both Pompey and Caesar,[4] yet he clearly regarded himself as one of the *boni*;[5] he could be expected to approve of an encomium on Bibulus (who was adverse to his own ambitions) and of an attack on the lex Campana; and he was critical of Cicero's reconciliation with Crassus and Vatinius. Marcellinus, an old legate of Pompey, and

[1] *Kl. Schr.* I, 208.

[2] *Fam.* I, 1 ff., esp. I, 3.

[3] *Rom. Rev.* ch. 3. He admits that they were not 'all, or consistently, allies of Pompeius' (44, n. 2). There is surely little reason to expect that they would act together. Lentulus Clodianus, censor 70, expelled Lentulus Sura, *cos.* 71, from the senate. Syme does not mention L. Lentulus Niger, accused with his son by Vettius of plotting Pompey's death (*Att.* II, 24, 2; *Vat.* 25). Several Lentuli served under Pompey in his wars, but it seems to me dubious if a general's officers were necessarily his close associates. In 88 Sulla was deserted by his chief officers (App. *BC* I, 57); L. Piso's legates are said to have become hostile to him (*Pis.* 53–4); Cicero's, apart from his brother, had no close connexions with him earlier. L. Furius Philus, *cos.* 136, took out with him to Spain two legates, Q. Metellus and Q. Pompeius, who were on bad terms with him and each other (Val. Max. III, 7, 5; Dio, fr. 82).

[4] E.g. *Att.* III, 22, 2; *Fam.* I, 9, 4; Caes. *BC* I, 22.

[5] *Fam.* I, 9 (everywhere implied).

respectful towards him on the eve of his consulship, was soon involved in ever more strenuous opposition to the triumvirs.[1] As for the *boni*, they were deeply divided, Servilius Isauricus opposing the restoration of Auletes altogether, Cicero, Hortensius and Lucullus backing Spinther, and the rest proposing to entrust the duty to *privati*. At the same time many of them were encouraging Clodius merely because he was on bad terms with Pompey (*Fam*. I, 9, 10).

The relations of the triumvirs themselves are instructive. Crassus is said to have been envious of Pompey from Sulla's time, and though elected consul for 70 with his support, soon began to bicker with him.[2] A formal but hollow reconciliation did not end their hostility; in 65 he secured the appointment of Pompey's open enemy, Cn. Piso, to command in Hither Spain (Sall. *Cat*. 17, 7; 19, 1) and in various ways sought to build up his influence to counterbalance Pompey's. But we need not think their enmity was overt; though Plutarch alleges that in 62 Crassus left Italy out of fear of Pompey or to create that impression, in fact he went to Asia, where Pompey was in control, probably to try (without success) to do a deal with him.[3] In his intrigues of the mid-sixties he had enjoyed the collaboration of the young Caesar. But Caesar was not himself on bad terms with Pompey (cf. *BC* I, 7, 1); unlike Crassus, he supported both the Gabinian and Manilian laws; in 63 he endorsed Labienus' proposal that special honours be accorded to Pompey, and he was associated with Metellus Nepos in 62 in the demand that the command against Catilina should be entrusted to him.[4] He was therefore able to act as an intermediary between Crassus and Pompey in the formation of the triumvirate.[5] By 57 the coalition was breaking down; Pompey even thought that Crassus was plotting against his life, though he was careful not to name him publicly (*Qu. fr*. II, 3, 3–4), and it was again Caesar who healed the breach at Luca.[6] Reaching back to 67, the alliance of Pompey and Caesar was one of the most durable known in Roman political history, and it ended in civil war.

The existence of powerful, cohesive factions may also be questioned, because at Rome friends and kinsmen did not necessarily have the same enemies, and common enmities did not cement common friendships.[7] Cicero and Clodius backed the same candidate in 59 (*Att*. II, 1, 5) and appeared for the same defendant in 54 (*supra*). In 59 Pompey was a friend to both (*Att*. II, 22, 2), and Atticus himself had 'marvellous

[1] Contrast *Qu. fr*. II, 1, with *Fam*. I, 2, 2; *Qu. fr*. II, 5, 3; Dio, XXXIX, 28 and 30.

[2] Plut. *Cr*. 6, 4; 7; 12; *Pomp*. 22–3. Pompey expected *collegam minorem et sui cultorem* but Crassus was *obtrectans potius collegae quam boni aut mali publici gnavus aestimator* (Sall. *Hist*. IV, 48; 51).

[3] Plut. *Pomp*. 43; Cic. *Flacc*. 32.

[4] Gelzer, *Caesar*[6], ch. II. Dio, XXXVI, 43; XXXVII, 22 has, as in his interpretation of some later events (XXXVII, 54–5; XXXIX, 24–6), allowed his knowledge of the civil war to colour and falsify the earlier relations of Caesar and Pompey.

[5] Rice Holmes, *Rom. Rep*. I, 475.

[6] Gelzer, *Caesar*[6], 110.

[7] *Fam*. V, 2, 8 for common friends of enemies; V, 17, 2: *inimici non solum tui verum etiam amicorum tuorum*; *Att*. XIV, 13B, 3: *semper ita statui, non esse insectandos inimicorum amicos, praesertim humiliores*; Caes. *BC* I, 3: *necessarii Pompei atque eorum qui veteres inimicitias cum Caesare gerebant*. In 62 the enmity between Cicero and Metellus Nepos produced only a marked coolness in his relations with Nepos' brother, Celer (*Fam*. V, 1–2, esp. 2, 9–10). Reconciled with Cicero (*Sest*. 130; *Fam*. V, 3), Nepos still backed his brother-in-law, P. Clodius (*Sest*. 89). It was (I think) exceptional if Antony's hatred for Cicero extended to all his friends (Nepos, *Att*. 10, 4); cf., however, Caes. *BC* I, 4, 4, and texts cited on p. 18, n. 6.

conversations' with Clodius which he reported to Cicero (II, 9, 1; 22, 1 and 4). Atticus' life-long practice of being all things to all men is notorious, but perhaps it was not altogether unusual. Appius Claudius was a friend and *affinis* of Pompey (*Fam.* III, 4, 2; Dio, XXXIX, 60, 3); he had also been brother-in-law to Lucullus and gave his daughter in marriage to M. Brutus, who until 49 would not even speak to Pompey as his father's assassin (Plut. *Brut.* 4). Appius could also display hostility to Pompey's friends. In 57 he refused assent to the return of Cicero,[1] which Pompey was promoting, and in 54 he attacked Gabinius (*Qu. fr.* III, 2, 3) and Scaurus,[2] the friends of Pompey, and in conjunction with his optimate colleague, L. Domitius Ahenobarbus, opposed the interests of Crassus with whom Pompey was once more allied; he also engaged in controversy with Cicero (*Qu. fr.* II, 11, 2–3), with whom he had been reconciled, despite the continuing feud between Cicero and his brother, P. Clodius. Again, Cicero himself, restored with Pompey's help in 57, not only felt free to take a fairly independent line in politics until Luca,[3] but even thereafter quarrelled with Crassus and for some time persisted in enmity against Gabinius and Caesar's father-in-law, L. Piso, both of whom he treated and expected public opinion to regard not as mere tools of the triumvirs but as agents responsible for their own acts as consuls in 58. This imbroglio cannot have seemed odd to Lentulus Spinther, who approved of Cicero's reconciliation with Caesar (his own friend) and Appius, but expected him to explain his having made up his quarrel with Vatinius and Crassus (*Fam.* I, 9, 4 and 19–20). It is plain that Roman politicians at this time normally behaved, and expected others to behave, as if they were independent, not members of a group to whose common will or leader they were bound to conform their own actions; and strong proof must be adduced before we can admit that in earlier epochs they had conducted themselves differently.

It is true that in defending his conduct to Spinther, Cicero says that Pompey's friendship counted so much with him *ut quae illi utilia sunt et quae ille vult, ea mihi omnia et recta et vera videantur.*[4] But this was something abnormal; in the very same letter he complains that his *libertas* and *dignitas* were lost, and in the years after Luca he often lamented that the Republic was no more.[5] He was not even free to hate; he had to defend his own enemies, or at least, as with Piso, to abstain from prosecuting them.[6] It was a later remission of his enslavement that Pompey 'humanely' let him criticize some of his own actions when he was defending Milo (*Fam.* III, 10, 10). Cicero was more vulnerable than other consulars of the time, and among them perhaps only Afranius was so completely dependent. And even Cicero could cover his

[1] *Pis.* 35, but cf. *Fam.* III, 10, 8.

[2] *Scaur.* 31 ff. Pompey was openly backing, though he later abandoned, Scaurus as consular candidate (*Att.* IV, 15, 7; *Qu. fr.* III, 6, 3); he had a secret grudge against him (cf. Ascon. 19–20C), of which Appius might perhaps have known.

[3] *Sest. passim*, cf. *Fam.* I, 9, 6 ff. (Against J. P. V. D. Balsdon, *JRS* XLVII, 18 ff. see D. L. Stockton, *TAPA* XCIII, 471 ff.)

[4] *Fam.* I, 8, 2–4.

[5] *Att.* IV, 18, 2; *Qu. fr.* III, 4, 1; 5, 4; *Fam.* II, 4, 1.

[6] *Fam.* I, 9, 19–20 on Vatinius and Crassus; on his quarrel with Crassus the 'boni' *gaudere se dicebant mihi et illum inimicum et eos, qui in eadem causa essent, numquam amicos futuros*; cf. I, 9, 10. Gabinius: *Qu. fr.* III, 1, 15; 2, 2; 4, 2–3 show the insincerity of *Rab. Post.* 32 ff. Piso: Cicero alleged that friendship with Caesar restrained him from prosecuting, *Pis.* 81 ff.

submission by quoting the proverbial apophthegm that friendships should be everlasting and enmities mortal (*Rab. Post.* 32; cf. Livy, XL, 46, 12). In his case, as in others', the second part of the proverb was more apt to be proved true than the first.

In 49 friendships and enmities undoubtedly helped many to decide for one side or the other. The unscrupulous Caelius said that in peaceful controversies one should take the more honourable part, and in civil wars the stronger and safer, but his own choice of Caesar's side was partly determined by his friendship for Curio and hatred of Appius.[1] Pollio acted in a rather similar way, avoiding the camp where his personal enemies were too strong.[2] (It was only later that he came to love Caesar 'summa cum pietate et fide'.) Cicero once said that the only men who joined Pompey in flight were those who had cause to fear Caesar's hostility, a transparent exaggeration at best (*Att.* IX, 19, 2), and Plutarch alleges that Pompey had more followers from personal allegiance than from public principle (*Pomp.* 61, 4). If Syme is right,[3] Labienus himself may serve as an instance, deserting Caesar for an older friend and patron, though it is curious that Cicero did not think of this interpretation of his action, but assumed that everyone would regard it as an implicit condemnation of Caesar's cause. Caesar, of course, would have his readers believe that the war was provoked by the factious hatred of his personal enemies, a partial view we must be wary of accepting.

The difficulty of accounting for men's behaviour at this time mainly by their feuds and friendships is that many had friends and enemies on both sides. Labienus, Lentulus Spinther, Varro and doubtless a host of others were friends of both Caesar and Pompey, and many must have had close connexions in the opposing camp; even Balbus, Caesar's confidant, was permitted not to appear in arms against his old benefactors, Pompey and the consul, Lentulus Crus, and actually to manage the affairs of the latter at Rome.[4] Again, both the leaders made play in their propaganda with appeals to public interest and constitutional principle and affected in their private negotiations to be ready to subordinate their own advantage to the common good (Caesar, *BC* I, 8–9). M. Brutus at least was now reconciled to Pompey, his hereditary enemy, 'rei publicae causa'. It is not likely that he stood alone. Though professions of patriotism may be 'the last refuge of a scoundrel', it would be unwise to assume that they were always insincere. Men do not appeal to standards that no one observes, and hypocrisy serves no purpose where virtue is not to be found.

Cicero's own hesitations are significant. He speaks of the *causa bonorum* and the *turpitudo coniungendi cum tyranno*, yet he often questioned whether resistance to Caesar could succeed, or whether Pompey's victory would not be marred by cruelty and lead, no less than Caesar's, to *regnum*; he would have preferred a compromise peace. His mind endlessly revolved not only the public good, but his own self-interest and his duty to Pompey as a friend, continually emphasizing and consciously over-

[1] *Fam.* VIII, 14, 3; cf. 16 and 17, 1.

[2] *Fam.* X, 31, 2: *cum vero non liceret mihi nullius partis esse, quia utrubique magnos inimicos habebam, ea castra fugi in quibus plane tutum me ab insidiis sciebam non futurum.*

[3] *JRS* XXVIII, 113 ff. But Cicero thought that Labienus seemed *damnasse sceleris hominem amicum rei publicae causa* (*Att.* VII, 12, 5; cf. *Fam.* XIV, 14, 2; XVI, 12, 4).

[4] *Att.* VIII, 15 A, 2; IX, 7 B, 2.

stating the benefits he owed him.[1] Later he could say: *erat obscuritas quaedam, erat certamen inter clarissimos duces; multi dubitabant quid optimum esset, multi quid sibi expediret, multi quid deceret, nonnulli etiam quid liceret*;[2] he himself doubted all these things at once. A man without scruple would surely in these circumstances have chosen his own advantage against all ties, public or private; but a man of honour might resolve his problem by the claims of friendship, because he could fairly plead that he could not see clearly what his public duty was.

Such a man perhaps was Matius, *temperatus et prudens...semper auctor oti*, as Cicero wrote at the time (*Att.* IX, 11, 2). He disapproved of the war and of Caesar's case, and he gained nothing from Caesar's victory, rather suffered financial loss; he followed Caesar as a friend, not as his political leader. He mourned his death, and his critics said that he was putting friendship before the Republic by grieving for a tyrant; his reply was in effect that Caesar had been no tyrant and that there was no proof that his killing had been of public benefit; he still claimed to be as good a patriot as anyone.[3] One might indeed think that the man who wished everyone to feel the bitterness of Caesar's death let private affection weigh too much with him, and that Cicero was right in suspecting him of rejoicing at the general confusion which ensued (*Att.* XIV, 1, 1). But it remains my impression that his loyalty to Caesar and his memory betokens a friendship which cannot be analysed into 'mutual interest and mutual services' and takes us back from the world of political faction towards that realm of ideal friendship with which I started.

The range of *amicitia* is vast. From the constant intimacy and goodwill of virtuous or at least of like-minded men to the courtesy that etiquette normally enjoined on gentlemen, it covers every degree of genuinely or overtly amicable relation. Within this spectrum purely political connexions have their place, but one whose all-importance must not be assumed. They were often fragile, and ties of private friendship could transcend their bounds. The clash of social and economic interests between classes, the constitutional principles in which such interests might be embedded but which men had often come to value for their own sake, the fears, ambitions, greed and even principles of individuals deserve no less consideration than the struggles of factions whose stability can easily be exaggerated,[4] when their existence is not simply imagined. To the historian of ancient Rome, however, if he is not concerned only with the power-struggle but with every aspect of the people's life and thought, the moral ideal which informed the concept of *amicitia* and the polite civilities which social conventions required from all but the few who were declared enemies merit attention for their own sake.

P. A. BRUNT

ORIEL COLLEGE, OXFORD

[1] E.g. *Att.* VII, 12, 3 (*nec solum civis sed etiam amici officio revocor*); VIII, 1, 4; 3, 2, etc.; IX, 13, 3 on exaggeration of Pompey's services.

[2] *pro Marcello* 30; cf. *Lig.* 19.

[3] *Fam.* XI, 27–8, on which see A. Heuss, *Historia* V, 53 ff. and B. Kytzler, *ibid.* IX, 96 ff.; I do not wholly agree with either, but any interpretation of Matius' views must probably remain subjective.

[4] Attempts were often made to strengthen them by marriages, but they might actually introduce new sources of discord (see for one instance E. Badian, *Studies in Gk. and Rom. Hist.* 39 ff.), or at least fail in effect, cf. *Cluent.* 190: *novis inter propinquos susceptis inimicitiis* saepe *fieri divortia atque adfinitatum discidia videmus...ceteri novis adfinitatibus adducti veteres inimicitias* saepe *deponunt*.